Education in a Competitive and Globalizing World

Education in a Competitive and Globalizing World

Effective Pedagogical Skills for a 21st Century Teacher: Reflections, Theories and Practices
Lawrence Meda (Editor)
2023. ISBN: 979-8-88697-919-0 (Softcover)
2023. ISBN: 979-8-89113-146-0 (eBook)

Life Skills in Contemporary Education Systems: Exploring Dimensions
Pooja Gupta, PhD (Editor)
2023. ISBN: 979-8-88697-833-9 (Softcover)
2023. ISBN: 979-8-88697-902-2 (eBook)

Lifelong Learning: Perspectives, Opportunities and Challenges
Isaac Kofi Biney, PhD (Editor)
Paul G. Nixon (Editor)
Rebecca Kleiweg de Zwaan (Editor)
2023. ISBN: 979-8-88697-551-2 (Hardcover)
2023. ISBN: 979-8-88697-579-6 (eBook)

Bilingualism and its Benefits
Genevoix Nana, PhD (Editor)
2023. ISBN: 979-8-88697-500-0 (Hardcover)
2023. ISBN: 979-8-88697-536-9 (eBook)

Undergraduate Research Perceptions and Experiences: A New Zealand Study
Doreen Vikashni Chandra, PhD (Editor)
2023. ISBN: 979-8-88697-506-2 (Hardcover)
2023. ISBN: 979-8-88697-540-6 (eBook)

More information about this series can be found at
https://novapublishers.com/product-category/series/education-in-a-competitive-and-globalizing-world/

Joseph Chacko Chennattuserry
Elangovan N.
and Victor Paul
Editors

Models for Social Responsibility Action by Higher Education Institutions

Copyright © 2024 by Nova Science Publishers, Inc.

All rights reserved. No part of this book may be reproduced, stored in a retrieval system or transmitted in any form or by any means: electronic, electrostatic, magnetic, tape, mechanical photocopying, recording or otherwise without the written permission of the Publisher.

We have partnered with Copyright Clearance Center to make it easy for you to obtain permissions to reuse content from this publication. Please visit copyright.com and search by Title, ISBN, or ISSN.

For further questions about using the service on copyright.com, please contact:

Copyright Clearance Center
Phone: +1-(978) 750-8400   Fax: +1-(978) 750-4470   E-mail: info@copyright.com

NOTICE TO THE READER

The Publisher has taken reasonable care in the preparation of this book but makes no expressed or implied warranty of any kind and assumes no responsibility for any errors or omissions. No liability is assumed for incidental or consequential damages in connection with or arising out of information contained in this book. The Publisher shall not be liable for any special, consequential, or exemplary damages resulting, in whole or in part, from the readers' use of, or reliance upon, this material. Any parts of this book based on government reports are so indicated and copyright is claimed for those parts to the extent applicable to compilations of such works.

Independent verification should be sought for any data, advice or recommendations contained in this book. In addition, no responsibility is assumed by the Publisher for any injury and/or damage to persons or property arising from any methods, products, instructions, ideas or otherwise contained in this publication.

This publication is designed to provide accurate and authoritative information with regards to the subject matter covered herein. It is sold with the clear understanding that the Publisher is not engaged in rendering legal or any other professional services. If legal or any other expert assistance is required, the services of a competent person should be sought. FROM A DECLARATION OF PARTICIPANTS JOINTLY ADOPTED BY A COMMITTEE OF THE AMERICAN BAR ASSOCIATION AND A COMMITTEE OF PUBLISHERS.

Library of Congress Cataloging-in-Publication Data

Names: Chennattuserry, Joseph Chacko, editor.
Title: Models for social responsibility action by higher education
　　institutions / Joseph Chacko Chennattuserry, PhD (Editor), Elangovan N,
　　PhD (Editor), Victor Paul (Editor).
Description: New York : Nova Science Publishers, [2023] | Series: Education
　　in a competitive and globalizing world | Includes bibliographical
　　references and index. |
Identifiers: LCCN 2023043459 (print) | LCCN 2023043460 (ebook) | ISBN
　　9798891130975 (hardcover) | ISBN 9798891132511 (adobe pdf)
Subjects: LCSH: Social learning--India. | Universities and colleges--India.
Classification: LCC LC192.4 .M62 2023 (print) | LCC LC192.4 (ebook) | DDC
　　378.54--dc23/eng/20231004
LC record available at https://lccn.loc.gov/2023043459
LC ebook record available at https://lccn.loc.gov/2023043460

Published by Nova Science Publishers, Inc. † New York

The compilation of research studies provided in this book is informative on many levels. Perhaps its most compelling feature is the in-depth research regarding programs that involve the seemingly intangible, yet possible, advantages of higher education - social responsibility, spiritual generosity, resilience, social- emotional learning, woman empowerment, self-regulation, the justice ecosystem, thought leadership, et al. It could serve as an international guide to developing and/or replicating programs that empower students to help others while strengthening their own abilities. I recommend it highly.

Peter L. Schneller, Ph. D.
Emeritus Professor University of Mount Union Alliance,
OH 44601 USA
schnelpl@mountunion.edu

Contents

Preface xi

Acknowledgements xiii

Chapter 1   Sustainable Environment Protection and Waste Management in Higher Education Institutions: A Case Study 1
Sheeja Karalam and Anupa Raichel Mathew

Chapter 2   Educate, Enable and Empower Future Leaders: A Model for Community Development Through the Child Sponsorship Program 21
Victor Paul and Reena Merin Cherian

Chapter 3   Empowering Women Through Livelihood Interventions: Case Studies from an Impoverished Community 49
Hemalatha, K.

Chapter 4   Context Matters: A Case Study of Community Development Approaches in Tribal Areas 71
M. Maya

Chapter 5   Rendering Support for the Empowerment of Rural Women to Overcome Life Impediments 87
Om Prakash L.T. and Ambrose Shaji

Chapter 6   Socially Responsible Universities and Student Satisfaction: Case Analysis 99
B. Valarmathi, B. Lakshmi and N. Elangovan

Chapter 7   Value Addition to International Students' Exchange Programs Through Engagement in Services 117
Jino Joy and Shrutkirti Singh

Chapter 8	Women Empowerment Through Community-Based Organisations in Rural Karnataka Cyril John	149
Chapter 9	Community-Based Educational Intervention on Emotion Regulation, Self-Esteem, and Behavioural Problems Among School Children Anekal C. Amaresha	165
Chapter 10	Modelling the Role of Institutional Support in Shaping the Social Behaviour of Business Administration Students Jogi Mathew and Tijo Thomas	181
Chapter 11	The Role of Legal Aid Clinics in Enhancing the Employability, Entrepreneurship and Foundation Skills for Law Students: A Qualitative Analysis S. Sapna, S. Nair Jayadevan and M. R. Mallaiah	205
Chapter 12	Sensitization of University Students in Supporting Underprivileged Children Budha Anuradha and Arumugam Senthil Kumar	225
Chapter 13	Student Engagement in Community Development: A Strategy for Whole-Person Development Suparna Majumdar Kar, Jince George and Jiby Jose E.	247
Chapter 14	Volunteering-Based Student Engagement: A Model for Student Well-Being in Higher Education Institutions Joseph Chacko Chennattuserry, Shinto Thomas and Phinu Mary Jose	265
Chapter 15	Developing Authentic Thought Leaders Through the DREAMS Model of Social Action Lijo Thomas, Anuradha Sathiyaseelan and B. Sathiyaseelan	289

Chapter 16	Service-Learning: **A Pathway to Social Responsibility**..............................313 Rory L. Bedford, Ellen D. Smiley and Prentiss C. Smiley	
Chapter 17	**Self-Reflective Learning: A Didactic Model for the Development of the Professional Identity of Social Work Students During the Practical Phase in the Context of the COVID Pandemic**............323 Grit Höppner, Sabine Ader and Swantje Notzon	
Chapter 18	**Institutional Forces of the Social Responsibility Programs of an Indonesian University Beyond Complying with the Law:** **A Case Study of the Unpad Model**...............................345 Ersa Tri Wahyuni	
Index	363	

Preface

The rapidly growing higher education sector world-wide in the 21st century has witnessed proliferation of post-secondary educational institutions (HEIs) as well as mass enrolment of students. In parallel, the global challenges and 'wicked' problems have also posed enormous questions about futures of humanity on the planet. As inter-governmental commitments to Sustainable Development Goals (SDGs) were launched in 2015, the recognition of climate crisis pushed for Paris Agreements later the same year. The Covid -19 pandemic and global manifestations of fires, storms, cyclones, draughts, and the likes have made leaders around the world look for solutions hitherto unknown.

It is in this context that expectations from Higher Education sector to provide knowledge solutions for addressing these challenges have grown. However, the HEIs over past 2-3 decades have been largely focused on providing 'talent recruitment' for individual careers and well-being. Hence, the need to bring back in the public purposes of HEIs into focus. The discourse on public relevance of HEIs links the concept of social responsibility of HEIs to the larger societal response.

Over the past decade, social responsibility of higher education has been defined in myriad ways. Most such approaches tend to 'de-link' the core business of teaching & research from social responsibility. It is the third service mission of HEIs that is expected to deliver University Social Responsibility (USR), much like Corporate Social Responsibility (CSR) in private business.

However, emerging global policy consensus now maintains mainstreaming of social responsibility of all three core functions of HEIs....teaching, research & service. The Third World Higher Education Conference of UNESCO in 2022 clearly concluded that greater engagement of HEIs with diverse societal actors in each context will be essential for higher education to remain relevant to societal needs.

It is in this sense that this new book brings practical models and exemplars of engagement with diverse societal actors to co-produce knowledge solutions that are contextually appropriate and actionable. Co-construction entails respecting and valuing community knowledge, experiential and indigenous, that of women, farmers, workers....who are not academically trained or certified. This book tells stories of HEIs such engagement with excluded communities and their own knowledge and aspirations to transform their lives.

We are delighted that this compendium is edited by Dr Joseph Chacko Chennattuserry, Vice Chancellor, Christ University, who has championed sustainability and social responsibility at the University and has envisioned this book; Dr Elangovan N, Professor, School of Business & Management at Christ University and Former Director of National Institute of Fashion Technology (NIFT), a prolific researcher; and Dr Victor Paul, Director, CSA and Coordinator of Knowledge-for-Change (K4C) Hub, at Christ University, Bengaluru, and pulls together several impactful cases of social responsibility. The book is an important addition to the new insights emerging from the world of practices in the global south.

Dr Budd Hall, Emeritus Professor, University of Victoria, Canada
Dr Rajesh Tandon, Founder-President, PRIA, India
UNESCO Chair in Community-based Research and Social Responsibility in Higher Education

Acknowledgements

We want to express our deepest gratitude to all those who have contributed to developing and publishing this book on Models for Social Responsibility Action by Higher Education Institutions.

First and foremost, we extend our heartfelt appreciation to all the contributors who have extended their expertise and shared their insights on various models for implementing social responsibility in higher education institutions which have been instrumental in shaping this comprehensive work. Their commitment to exploring the multifaceted aspects of social responsibility in higher education institutions has been inspiring.

We are also grateful to Peter L. Schneller, Ph. D., for thoroughly reviewing each chapter and providing constructive comments to tie together the chapters into a book. Your support and endorsement of this project are truly appreciated.

We thank Rajesh Tandon, PhD and Bud Hall, PhD, for providing a thought-provoking preface that sets the stage for understanding social responsibility's significance in higher education. Your insightful perspectives have added great value to this book.

Our gratitude goes to the CSA staff at Christ University for the enormous backend work that kept the process moving. Special thanks go to Nova Science Publisher and the publisher staff for their support throughout the publishing process. Your professionalism and commitment to quality have ensured the successful realization of this project.

Lastly, we would like to express our deepest appreciation to the readers of this book. Your interest and engagement in social responsibility in higher education institutions motivate us to continue exploring and advocating for responsible actions in academia.

Editors

Chapter 1

Sustainable Environment Protection and Waste Management in Higher Education Institutions: A Case Study

Sheeja Karalam[1,*]
and Anupa Raichel Mathew[2]

[1]Department of Sociology and Social Work, Christ University, Bengaluru, India
[2]Social Axiom Foundation, Bengaluru, India

Abstract

Sustainable environment protection and waste management are global concerns that major cities are grappling with, and it is the most important environmental factor that higher educational institutions in India are considering right now. "Parivarthana," – the recycling unit of the Centre for Social Action at Christ University, Bengaluru, is evolved as a paradigm for all higher education institutions in terms of long-term environmental protection through waste management and the efforts of student volunteers. The student volunteers have been successful in sensitizing all members of the University to the importance of environmental conservation, and there is rising evidence of accountability among all members regarding waste management. The basic sense of social responsibility of student volunteers toward environmental sustainability is the primary focus of this chapter.

Student volunteers who have a higher sense of social responsibility have a better attitude toward their studies, which leads to higher academic accomplishment and a desire to take action to address environmental challenges. Their environmental awareness, climate change, the need to

---

* Corresponding Author's Email: sheeja.karalam@christuniversity.in.

In: Models for Social Responsibility Action by Higher Education Institutions
Editors: Joseph Chacko Chennattuserry, Elangovan N. et al.
ISBN: 979-8-89113-097-5
© 2024 Nova Science Publishers, Inc.

reduce greenhouse gas emissions, efficient use of natural resources, waste management, and sustainable consumerism have served as an example for students of other higher educational institutions.

A qualitative method with a case study approach was applied for this research with In-depth interviews with all stakeholders of the unit. The objectives include the participants' understanding of the prevailing process of waste management in the unit, the relation between waste management and Climate change, and the role of the student volunteers and other stakeholders of the Higher Educational Institutions in bringing a model to Sustainable Development and Global Climate Change.

Keywords: higher educational institutions, social responsibility, student volunteers, waste management, sustainable environment protection

1. Introduction

The Earth has undergone various changes due to man-made activities. There is a need to comprehend the importance of how the natural phenomenon of the Earth is changing due to the immense increase in the generation of waste due to the consumption of various resources of the planet. Solid Waste Management is a challenge, especially in India, attributing to the vast expanse of the country. The rapid urbanization in the country, with its diverse physical, climatic, geographical, ecological, social, cultural and linguistic diversity, has made it even more challenging to manage the waste generated (Bhalla et al., 2013). Waste management is an important aspect of sustainability. Wastes are potential resources, and effective waste management with resource extraction is fundamental to effective waste management strategies. Value extraction from waste can be materials, energy or nutrients, which can provide many people with a livelihood (ISWA, 2012). The transition from waste to resources can only be achieved through investment in SWM as this depends on a coordinated set of actions to develop markets and maximize the recovery of reusable/recyclable materials (Sridevi et al., 2012). It involves a complex biological and chemical process that requires efforts in the initiation steps by Subject Matter Experts.

The improper utilization and overconsumption of natural resources have led to significant climate changes (Figure 1). Though waste can be recycled, excessive waste generation's impact on the environment and health is significant. The waste that is generated can be classified into solid waste, liquid waste and demolition waste, and each type of waste has different processes for its management (O'Leary et al., 1988). Solid waste is both biodegradable and non-biodegradable. Effective methods for the recycling of biodegradable waste have been devised. However, the challenging aspect of solid waste management is that non-biodegradable wastes like plastic add to the pollutants in soil and water and affect the yield of the soil.

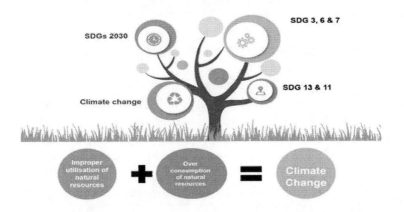

Figure 1. Resources-based SDG Goals.

Further, improper waste management, excessive energy production, and product consumption contribute to climate change by adding carbon-based particles into the air, which are produced while burning petroleum products. The result of this is warmer air, creating a disastrous greenhouse effect. Thus, using recycled materials for our daily consumption reduces the need and dependence on raw materials or natural resources, thus reducing the impact on the environment (Armstrong et al., 2018).

2. Review of Literature

Climate has significantly changed over the years. The planet has become warmer, and the ozone layer is depleting at an alarming rate. The increase in greenhouse gases has led to global warming, which has invariantly melted the glaciers and caused rising sea levels. The excessive consumption of resources like trees and fuel has added to the menace of climate change (Fenger et al., 1993). Climate change has also affected natural flora and fauna, causing endangering of some vital species. Climate change has become a global issue requiring all nations' combined efforts to resolve this issue. The improper disposal of waste has led to the pollution of water bodies, soil and even air. This led to the formulation of the Sustainable Development Goals (SDG) by the United Nations General Assembly in 2015 (Miyazawa, 2012). The Sustainable development goals or global goals are a collection of 17 interlinked global goals designed to achieve a better and more sustainable future for all. Sustainable development intends to be a method of development that meets the needs of the present generation without compromising the ability of future generations to meet their needs. Sustainable development aims to cover different aspects of social development, environmental protection and economic growth.

SDG 7 aims to ensure all access to affordable, reliable, sustainable, and modern energy. This invite recycling the available resources and producing clean and affordable energy. Biogas is a clean energy source that can be produced from biodegradable wastes. SDG 13 urges every nation to take urgent action to combat climate change and its impact. India, as a country with diverse ecological and geographical areas, there are many aspects to be undertaken to ensure that climate change is combated through the combined efforts of the people in the country.

The waste produced can be recycled through various processes. The efforts of many educational institutions, voluntary organizations and environmental activists. The role of educational institutions in taking up projects for the conservation of the environment gives them grounds to initiate evidence-based practices for protecting the environment. As educational Institutions are large organizations, their recycling activities can yield evidence-based practices for other institutions. Small waste management projects will reduce some impact on the environment, and when these initiatives are scaled up, they will contribute significantly to protecting the environment.

The involvement of the aspect of women empowerment in such projects is vital. This is because it will help women who are unable to take up other work to engage in activities that yield financial benefits to their families and empowerment to women (Ortiz Rodríguez et al., 2016). Women empowerment is also a significant aspect of the SDG, wherein SDG 5 focuses on gender equality. SDG 5 aims to eliminate all forms of discrimination and violence against women in public and private spheres and to undertake reforms to give women equal rights to economic resources and access and ownership of property. The initiation of projects wherein women contribute to environment conservation is rapidly rising. Specifically, in the Indian context, women in rural areas migrate to cities to take work that empowers them and sustains their families. Also, various environmental conservation projects and recycling projects taken up in rural areas have positively impacted the environment. Especially, simple process like the production of biogas from degradable wastes by rural women in India has conserved energy.

Waste management poses a challenge in a vast country like India (Bower et al., 1968). It is also widely dependent on small individual efforts to protect the environment. The SDGs are interlinked; hence, while focusing on climate change and producing clean and sustainable energy, people's health will also be improvised. The reduced energy consumption and clean fuel production will reduce respiratory diseases among rural women due to using other non-renewable energy sources. Also, the generation of lesser waste will reduce the pollution of water bodies, soil and air.

Recycling wastes into useful solid products or energy sources has been a practice that is undertaken by many corporates, educational institutions and non-governmental organizations due to the rising climatic issues (Skinner, 1993). The Government is mandating and promoting many such initiatives that ensure waste management. The Government has taken measures to ensure proper segregation of waste in households. Similarly, rainwater harvesting is mandated to be part of every new house being built. Also, the utilization of solar energy has been encouraged (Figure 2).

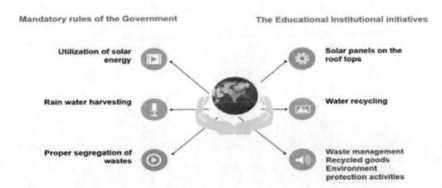

Figure 2. Alignment of Government Regulations and the Universities Initiatives.

Educational Universities are repositories of knowledge. They undertake various research and development activities that ensure innovative measures for protecting the environment. The various departments collaboratively work towards implementing these projects with the maximum utilization of the available resources to study the project's impact. Many educational institutions have set up solar panels on the rooftops to generate surplus electricity that can be provided for the electricity grid. Water recycling in universities reduces excessive water consumption and conserves water. Also, some Institutions manage their solid waste and produce recycled goods. The students of the institution volunteer to perform these activities. Hence these projects instill insight into the protection of the environment and also spread awareness and motivate the youth of the institution to partake in such activities and ensure the conservation of the environment and hence achieve sustainable outcomes.

"Parivarthana" - Recycling Unit of the Centre for Social Action at Christ University, Bengaluru, is evolved as a model for all higher education institutions for sustainable environment protection over waste management (Figure 3). This CSA project has raised awareness of waste management and inculcated best practices of waste management among students, faculty members, and all other members of the University. The Team Parivarthana - the student volunteers, recycling unit staff, CSA Administers, and University Management members have created an environmentally friendly campus with long-term objectives to achieve sustainability and combat climate change (Figure 4).

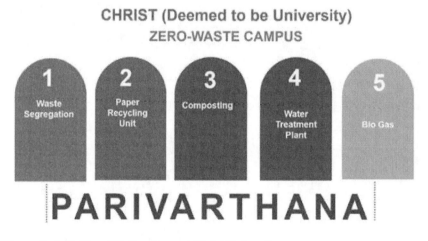

Figure 3. Activities of Parivarthana at Christ University.

Through the review of the literature, it was clear that there is less number of studies conducted in the area of student volunteers in sustainable environmental protection and waste management, their understanding of the process of waste management of the unit in the educational institutions, the relationship between waste management and Climate change, the role of other stakeholders of the Higher Educational Institutions in bringing a model to Sustainable Development and Global Climate Change, even though there is a high prevalence of sustainable environmental protection and importance of waste management system in educational institutions exist in India.

The authors aimed to study sustainable environment protection and waste management in higher education institutions, with the following objectives:

- To understand the overall process of waste management for Sustainable Environment protection
- To comprehend the relationship between waste management and Sustainable Environment protection
- To examine the role of the Officials in maintaining Sustainable Environment protection and Global Climate Change.

Figure 4. Snapshots of activities of Parivarthana.

3. Methodology

The current study focuses on the aspect of studying the recycling of waste and the production of sustainable energy at an Educational Institution. The project utilizes women for the implementation of the project. Through this project, the interlink wherein the recycling project empowers women is studied, and how water recycling is a valuable aspect is studied. The generation of useful products from the solid and paper waste from the institution and the impact it has had on the environment is studied in depth.

The data was obtained from student volunteers, key personnel in Parivarthana, CSA staff, and the faculty members on their perspectives in:

- the overall process of waste management for Sustainable Environment protection
- comprehending the relationship between waste management and Sustainable Environment protection
- the role of maintaining Sustainable Environment protection and Global Climate Change
- Bringing a Model to Sustainable Community Development and Global Climate Change in the Context of Empowerment, social responsibility, and Sensitization.

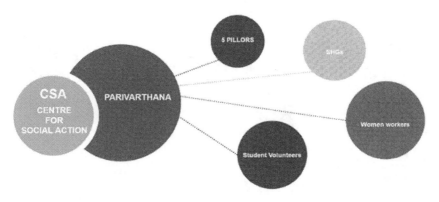

Figure 5. Participants of Parivartana.

A qualitative method with an exploratory case study approach was applied for this research with In-depth interviews with all four data sources of the PARIVARTHANA Unit - student volunteers, key personnel in Parivarthana, CSA staff, and Faculty members. The primary data was analyzed to categorize themes, and the secondary data will be examined through documents from Parivarthana, the CSA website, and observations. A purposive sampling technique was applied for this study to collect 20 Qualitative data from - student volunteers, key personnel in Parivarthana, CSA staff, and Faculty members. A semi-structured interview guide was applied for collecting data from student volunteers, key personnel in Parivarthana, CSA staff, and the faculty members on their perspectives in:

- Prevalent process of waste management for Sustainable Environment protection

- Comprehending the relationship between waste management and Sustainable Environment protection
- The role of maintaining Sustainable Environment protection and Global Climate Change
- Bringing a Model to Sustainable Community Development and Global Climate Change in the Context of Empowerment, social responsibility, and Sensitization.

The data were analyzed for themes using thematic analysis. Informed consent was obtained from the participants before starting the data collection. Confidentiality was maintained. All the study participants have thoroughly explained the study and procedures.

4. Results and Discussion

Thematic analysis is used to analyze the interviews. Here there were two sets of participants involved in the study: the students' volunteers who are part of the initiatives of the Parivartana and the Women staff who are involved in the Parivarthana project responsible for the waste collection and segregation and recycling of wastes into useful products (Figure 5).

4.1. Results of Student's Interview

The participants in the study were three boys and seven girls pursuing their Under-graduation studies. The majority of the students were from the Science course, followed by Commerce and the Arts. Student volunteers' understanding of the prevalent process of waste management for Sustainable Environment protection, comprehending the relationship between waste management and Sustainable Environment protection, the role of maintaining Sustainable Environment protection and Global Climate Change, bringing a model to Sustainable Community Development and Global Climate Change in the context of empowerment, social responsibility, and Sensitization is analyzed here. The data of the student volunteers resulted in the themes as presented in Table 1.

4.1.1. Waste Management Process

Waste Management Process involves a series of intricate steps. The process is carried out by many staff, officials and volunteers. The process involves the segregation of the waste dumped in various bins in the colleges. The paper waste is then processed by mixing with cotton, and then recycled sheets are produced (Figure 6).

Table 1. Themes emerging from the students' interviews

Waste Management Process	Amalgamation, Dehydrating, Segregation, Anaerobic respiration, Biogas-Collection, Food Collection, Recycling
Recycling	Paper production, Products produced, Reduced greenhouse gases, UV filtration, Waste reduction, Water for gardening
Sustainability	Better recycled products, Documentation, Awareness creation, Campus awareness, Increased volunteer ship, Individualistic changes, Waste reduction, In-house selling, Rural Outreach, Scaling up
Impact	Self-learning, Supportive faculty, Experiential learning, Individualistic changes, Insight, Lifestyle changes

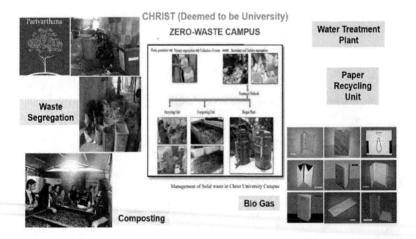

Figure 6. Waste Management Process at Christ University.

Participant 1 said, "So once the waste is segregated, the paper waste is soaked in a huge container and mixed with cotton for several hours, and then it undergoes a process then by these sheets are produced which are then dried and folded and made into a final product. Later on, the strings are added to it at the end."

Paper waste and wet waste are segregated and separated, producing two different by-products that benefit society. The anaerobic respiration of the waste's microbes generates the biogas used as fuel.

Participant 1 said, "On a daily basis, approximately 500 kilograms of food waste is collected on campus. They are then placed into the Biogas plant, which has a sewage collector consisting of an upper and lower chamber. The collector is a floating dome structure, where the domes have a floating gas holder. The food waste flows from the lower chamber to the two domes, which can hold about 150 kilograms of waste, and from the upper chamber to another dome, which can hold about 300 kg. Biogas is formed through anaerobic respiration that takes place inside the domes and is collected in the gas holder. This biogas then flows through the pipes to the kitchens in the Dharmaram campus, where it is used for everyday cooking. The biogas plant, on a daily basis, produces around 25 kilograms of LPG."

4.1.2. Recycling

Recycling is an integral part of waste management, and hence various processes are involved. Through the recycled waste at the Parivartana Centre, two by-products are majorly produced, which are paper bags and biogas. The process of recycling, which is effectively carried out, is the recycling of water. The process involves filtration and ultraviolet to remove the microbes from the water. Later the water undergoes sand filtration to get purified water. The recycled water is used for watering the gardens.

Participant 1 said, "The water treatment plant at Parivarthana uses a long scientific process to ensure that the water is safe for consumption. This process begins with the contaminated water from the entire campus accumulated in the bar screen chamber, where large particles such as plastics and stones are separated. The water then flows up to 2 tanks. In the first tank, this water is treated with potable water. In the second tank, the water undergoes a process of aeration. This water then passes down the settling tank, where the impurities settle at the bottom. Once this is completed, the water goes to the Sand filter tank for filtration. The next step of the water treatment process involves the water going through the Dual Media filter tank, which consists of anthracite coal filters to enable the process. The final filtration process happens when this water passes through the UV filter tank, where the UV rays are used to kill any more impurities that are present. The process of water treatment is now complete, and the clean water is passed to the collecting tank, from where it goes to the storage tank. Every day, around 3 to 4 lakh liters of clean water is produced in this process, which is then used for the gardening of the Dharmaram Ground."

4.1.3. Sustainability

Sustainability is the aspect of ensuring that eco-friendly practices are implemented. It brings about a long-term impact on society and the environment. Scaling up the existing projects to various other regions was suggested as one of the measures to ensure sustainability. Reaching out to rural areas will increase the sustainability of the projects.

> Participant 1 said, "After working in the unit, I realized the importance of waste management and importance of segregation of waste and have reached out to people and informed as many people as possible I could reach in rural areas about the same."

Another aspect of increasing sustainability involves creating more awareness, especially in-campus awareness and getting more in-campus sales as the buyers know the purpose of the products produced.

> Participant 1 said, "I was in charge of Parivarthana stalls several times. My duty was to ensure that the buyers were well-informed about the unit and the women who worked there. After the sales, I had to report back to the respective heads about the same. In my free time, I used to visit the unit wherein I used to help the women in making the product. Once, I was given a special task to approach the HODs of different departments and inform them about the new products launched at the unit."

Increasing the number of volunteers will also provide better opportunities and awareness among a larger group and hence help attain sustainability.

> Participant 2 said, "It should be made compulsory that each one of them on campus has to visit the PARIVARTHANA unit at least once before they exit/graduate. A proper record is to be maintained so that we can keep track of it - making unit exposure compulsory - affirming to other rules of waste management."

4.1.4. Impact On Mind

The students being volunteers of Parivarthana have had a significant impact on their minds. Being part of the initiative, they have gained insight into the conservation of natural resources and how to recycle waste to protect and develop a sustainable environment. They have an opportunity to self-learn and bring out individualistic changes that have helped the students gain more insight into creating a sustainable environment.

> Participant 2 said, "I learnt about the nuances and the science behind the pillars of the Parivarthana unit (i.e., biogas plant, water treatment plant, paper recycling unit, compost pit and waste segregation unit). I started becoming more aware of my imprint in society with respect to waste generation. I started making small lifestyle changes to reduce the amount of waste I generate and switched to more sustainable products."

4.2. Results of Staff and Faculty Interviews

The analysis of interviews of the Women staff at Parivarthana is presented in Table 2. The participants involved in the study were five women who were part of the waste management project. All the women belong to the Weaker Section of Society and live in the nuclear family. They lived in rented houses and were married women between the age of 18 and 20 years. The faculty members involved in the study were three Women Professors who have obtained a Doctor of Philosophy and have observed the Parivarthana Unit.

> Participant 3 said, "My experience at the unit gave me exposure to that aspect of social responsibility. Little things like throwing the right trash in the right bin, reducing the waste I produce, and consuming less water are certain lifestyle changes I adapted to."

Table 2. Themes emerged from staff and faculty interviews

Environmental Protection	Composting
	Paper recycling
	Biogas production
	Paper production
	Water conservation
	Waste segregation

	Rainwater harvesting
	Reduced fossil utilization
Women Empowerment	Financial stability
	Workplace security
	Independence
	Psychological well-being
	Social security
	Employment
Social Value	Awareness creation
	Community mobilization
	Insight
	Social impact assessment
	Consideration
	Recognition
	Effective volunteer ship
	Acceptance
	Safety and hygiene
	Peaceful work atmosphere

4.2.1. Environnemental Protection

The participants mentioned how the projects of the Parivarthana are environmentally friendly and how it ensures the protection of the environment. The process carried out at the Parivartnana also follows the aspect of the Sustainable Development goals wherein renewable energy is produced, and recycled products are manufactured. The major aspect is paper production. The participants segregate the waste into wet and dry and then utilize the wet waste for composting and biogas production.

> Participant 1 said, "Waste disposal only we do at CHRIST (laughs), so we are 13 of us, we segregate it, bundle it in sacks, we send it in a vehicle that comes to collect all these. Food waste all we put it in gas, after cleaning the food waste we clean it. Then we put it in the gas. We also segregate the bottles, tetra pack, and plastics, separate them and tie them up in bundles. Then a van comes, collects it, and it goes. The paper was and all we put it in the machine, and we make paper, files and all those."

The participants mentioned that wet waste was used for composting and biogas production, which is a sustainable practice for energy production.

> Participant 3 said, "So we make many things, no waste in the college. Leaves, we make it manure. So, all the vegetable and fruit peels and waste we clean put it in the machine, then we make it manure."

The teachers mentioned that they ensure the optimum use of energy resources and recycle the paper used by children for assignments and various projects. They ensure water conservation by judicial utilization of water.

The teachers mentioned that they segregate waste on an individualistic basis in order to contribute toward waste segregation. Composting is also practiced for wet waste. In an individualistic manner, they ensured that they utilized menstrual cups instead of sanitary napkins to protect the environment. Also, ensure that the utilization of fossil fuels reduces carbon footprints. As a measure of water conservation, rainwater harvesting is also practiced.

4.2.2. Women Empowerment

The significant aspect that most women who were part of the Parivartana project mentioned were the empowerment that they obtained as part of the project. They mentioned that the work provided them with financial stability, contributing to the family's well-being through their hard work.

> Participant 1 said, "While I was a child, I faced so many difficulties. I was married at the age of 13 then, and initially, it was very difficult as I had to look after four children. My husband met with an accident and lost his leg, due to which I started going to 3 to 4 houses for work and looking after my husband and children. Then I joined college, and I was able to pay off my debts, and I faced many difficulties. Now I have no difficulties in life."

They emphasized that they were independent and lived happy lives working on the project. The workplace security they obtained encouraged them to work efficiently, their interactions with their peers were more engaging, and they enjoyed their work.

> Participant 1 said, "At home, I need to look after my kids, prepare food for them, look into all their needs, actually. That is my responsibility at home. At the workplace, we all come together; we work in unity in a happy manner. We don't fight and all; we interact well with each other."

The workers have good psychosocial well-being as they are independent and because their work environment is safe and secure. The women mentioned that their higher authorities also ensured that their workplace environment was safe for them and gave them a sense of security wherein they could go back and seek help anytime.

> Participant 2 said, "I tell them that college helps me; Simon Sir is there, Father, Sister is always helping me. Nobody from my family supports me; my children only look after their family, but for me, college always is of good help."

The teachers also mentioned that the Parivarthana project empowered women by providing them with employment and financial stability.

4.2.3. Social Value
The aspect of being part of the Parivarthana project has helped the volunteers develops their social values. Some of the participants mentioned that involvement in such projects helped develop better awareness among the community of the hazards of the existing practices and create knowledge about eco-friendly practices to save the environment. They also mentioned that community mobilisation was ensured through this awareness creation.

> Participant 3 said, "For the longest time, as a member of society as a socially "woke" person, I was intellectually unaware of the things that institutions can do to help the world become more sustainable."

The participant clarified how they got more insight about the ways to conserve and protect the environment, wherein it was self-realization to protect the environment as they were witnessing the social impact that the projects brought about in the life of people.

The aspect of the social value that the women get while working in the Parivarthana. They mentioned that they are given consideration and recognition wherein their work is appreciated, and they are motivated to work for society and the University staff and students treat them as family.

> Participant 1 said, "Then, without any difficulty, we could work. They even looked after me well. Simon Sir was very good. He came at the right time, like Jesus, like God and kept all of us happy. Simon Sir should live for 100 years in good health. Earlier, whoever came for work would not stay but leave the job as there was a lot of waste to collect a lot, I can say. All the food waste and everything would come mixed, but then Simon Sir went to the canteen, fought with the people there and convinced them that waste would be collected only if it was segregated. Now everything is going well."

The participants expressed that the acceptance they received from the employers, staff and students at the University increased their morale.

> Participant 3 said life and work are very good. The fathers, madams, sister, Simon, Sir and students treated us very well. They look after us well. We considered them as a family, and they also considered as a family member, and I did not have any difficulty working with Parivarthana."

The participants mentioned that though they worked in waste segregation, they ensured that their safety and hygiene were maintained because they were provided with all safety and hygiene necessities making them feel that they were taken care of from the risks of the work. The employers also ensured a peaceful work environment for the participants wherein they were not demotivated but affirmed for their work.

> Participant 2 said, "Yes, I was the happy, very peaceful atmosphere for work, no difficulties or problems and all, we can work in a clean manner. (laughs). We are 10 of us; right, we work well together."

Awareness through minuscule initiatives in and around the campus has created a significant social impact among the students and staff.

5. Discussion

The current study assessed the Waste Management Process and its sustainability from a Global Perspective. The study involved a holistic perspective wherein the students involved as Volunteers and staff involved in the Waste management project work from the grassroots levels. The student volunteers emphasized their involvement in the project, and the awareness creation about Sustainable practices of waste management impending towards a goal to achieve the Sustainable Development Goals created insight in them to consciously work towards creating a better environment.

They were aware of the grassroots level of the Waste management process, and the study indicated the scientific process followed for biogas and paper production. The sustainable aspect of the in-house selling of the products produced at the campus gives a better boost to carry the project forward and scale up the project of producing recycled products. The outcomes of the project attracted more volunteer ships, ensuring that the youth are more aware of the conservation of the planet, and the impact drives them to put more effort into the project. The study also revealed the impact that engagement in such projects had on the minds of the student volunteers, which was instilled in their minds to ensure they conserve water, segregate waste consciously and also develop eco-friendly habits as a part of their lifestyle. The water recycling project in the current study also revealed the immense importance given to conserving water as part of the Sustainable Development Goals, which emphasizes the significance of conserving every drop of water for the sustainable consumption of future generations. SDG 3 is being implemented through the Parivarthana project as the women are being provided safety equipment and garments to ensure that they work in the segregation of waste. Their health and well-being are ensured, which is evident from the responses of the staff. The water conservation and recycling at the Parivarthana Unit adheres to and ensures the implementation of SDG 6 of clean water and sanitation. SDG 7 is implemented wherein biogas is being produced through composting at the Parivathana Unit, thereby utilizing clean and affordable energy. All the projects at the Parivathana Unit intend to support the SDG 13 of climate action, wherein the protection of the environment is taken care of through water recycling, waste segregation and recycling and composting. The projects of Parivarthana have helped attain the SDG 11 of Sustainable Cities and Communities, wherein it has helped the sustainable development of cities, especially in Bengaluru.

Further, the study with the staff of the waste management project who are part of the project from the grassroots level of segregation to amalgamation to the final production of the paper reveals the empowerment that they have obtained through their involvement in the project. The women obtained financial stability and also experienced psychosocial well-being as part of the work. They mentioned how being part of the work helped them become consciously involved in waste segregation and management and contribute towards creating a better environment for future generations. They mentioned that the social security that they experienced as part of the work was very high. They are active participants in conserving the environment as they segregate waste thoroughly and then ensure the proper recycling of waste to produce effective products.

Conclusion

The renewable energy biogas being produced is very good for the environment and a sustainable method of protecting the environment. They mentioned that they are given recognition for the work they are doing and the staff and employers, and students of the University. The limitations of the study were that the telephonic data collection could not help the researcher get the visual cues. Also, an equal number of male and female participants could not be engaged in the study. The future research prospects can be wherein the experts engaged in the monitoring and implementation of the project can be studied. Also, a quantitative estimation of the students who have been encouraged by the student volunteers to imbibe eco-friendly practices in their life can be taken up.

References

Armstrong, A., Krasny, M., & Schuldt, J. (2018). Climate Change Science : The Facts. In *Communicating Climate Change : A Guide for Educators* (pp. 7-20). Cornell University Press.

Bhalla, B., Saini, M. S., & Jha, M. K. (2013). Effect of age and seasonal variations on leachate characteristics of municipal solid waste landfill. *International Journal of Research in Engineering and Technology*, 2(8), 223-232. https://doi.org/10.15623/ijret.2013.0208037.

Bower, B., Larson, G., Michaels, A., & Phillips, W. (1968). Waste Management. *Ekistics*, 26(156), 438-450.

Fenger, J., Jørgensen, A. M. K., Mikkelsen, H. E., & Philipp, M. (1993). Greenhouse Effect and Climate Change: Implications for Denmark. *Ambio*, 22(6), 378-385.

ISWA (2012). Globalisation and waste management final report from the ISWA task force. *International Solid Waste Association*. http://www.iswa.org/knowledgebase/tfgfinal.

Ikuho, M. (2012). What are Sustainable Development Goals ? *Institute for Global Environmental Strategies*. Retrieved May 19, 2021, from http://www.jstor.org/stable/resrep00768.

O'Leary, P. R., Walsh, P. W., & Ham, R. K. (1988). Managing Solid Waste. *Scientific American*, 259(6), 36-45. https://www.jstor.org/stable/e24989282.

Ortiz Rodríguez, J., Pillai, V. K., & Ribeiro Ferreira, M. (2016). The impact of women's agency and autonomy on their decision-making capacity in Nuevo Leon, Mexico. *Acta Universitaria*, 26(5), 70–78. https://doi.org/10.15174/au.2016.976.

Skinner, J. (1993). *Integrated solid waste management : Recycling in perspective. Ekistics*, 60(358/359), 4-7.

Chapter 2

Educate, Enable and Empower Future Leaders: A Model for Community Development Through the Child Sponsorship Program

Victor Paul[*]
and Reena Merin Cherian[†]

Department of Sociology and Social Work, Christ University, Bengaluru, India

Abstract

The Child Sponsorship Program is an attempt by development organizations to reinstate the rights of a child to education, focusing on the overall well-being of a child and the community. The Sustainable Development Goals view Child Sponsorship Program as a tool for contributing towards development goals and targets. While the conventional models of the Child Sponsorship Program focused on the scholastic performance of children up to the elementary level, several progressive sponsorship programs aim at the whole personal development of the children and their community by ensuring community participation and a development-based approach targeting education, livelihood, empowerment, etc. This program channelized by the Centre for Social Action (CSA), CHRIST (Deemed to be) University), Bengaluru, is a child development program that engages with the goals of holistic development of the child and community development through the Child Sponsorship Program in two urban slum

---

[*] Corresponding Author's Email: victor.paul@christuniversity.in.
[†] Corresponding Author's Email: reenamerin.cherian@christuniversity.in.

In: Models for Social Responsibility Action by Higher Education Institutions
Editors: Joseph Chacko Chennattuserry, Elangovan N. et al.
ISBN: 979-8-89113-097-5
© 2024 Nova Science Publishers, Inc.

communities in Bengaluru. The research aims to study the change brought in the indicators, such as education, behaviour and attitude change, leadership and their holistic development, by the program. It also intends to assess the impact of the program on the development of the family, community and participation of the community members in the academic development of children. The study follows a qualitative study employing in-depth interviewing and Focused Group Discussions with parents and child participants of the communities where the Child Sponsorship Program is implemented. The data is analyzed through qualitative and quantitative software.

Keywords: child sponsorship, education, community participation, community development, holistic development, child development program.

1. Introduction

The ASER Report - 2020 by Pratham claims that almost 90 per cent of children are in schools (ASER Centre, 2020). However, there are reports of high dropout rates with regard to gender and gender parity was flagged as a gap. Even in the school-going population of standard III, almost 20 percent of students could not accomplish cognitive tasks properly. In such cases, the assertion is on quality education and providing scaffolding for students in the community, which is asserted by the Sustainable Development Goals (SDGs) 4. SDG 4 reads, *"Ensure inclusive and equitable quality education and promote life-long learning opportunities for all"* and includes a comprehensive set of targets related to inclusive education and sustainability. One of the targets focuses on building and upgrading child, disability, and gender-sensitive educational facilities that provide safe, non-violent, inclusive, and effective learning environments for all.

For the implementation of Goal-4 and associated targets, the United Nations Development Program (UNDP) has listed a set of agendas called the Mainstreaming, Acceleration and Policy Support (MAPS), intending to generate a coalition and mutual aid of relevant actors through intellectual contribution as a knowledge society for developing strategies for implementation of inclusive and sustainable education.

The United Nations Educational, Scientific, and Cultural Organization's (UNESCO) Framework for Action (FFA)- 2030 calls for progress regarding existing international agreements in favour of higher education and establishes that the tertiary education system can improve access, equity, and quality for not only educational system but also community development. The FFA mentions the convergence of Goal 4 with other SDGs, whilst Goal 17 stresses partnerships for the achievement of other goals. In this scenario, the direction of the erstwhile Planning Commission in 2011 is to ensure engagement and partnership with HEIs in India. In addition, the Higher Education Sustainability Initiative (HESI) directs the HEI to develop sustainability plans with a broader community and assist universities in sustainability in policy, research and practice. This narrative also emanates out of the transformation experienced by the HEIs in India over the last decades, from being academic units to knowledge societies (Tremblay, 2014). Tandon (2019) records several such initiatives in the past decades by HEIs, which are the active engagement of the institutions with the marginalized communities and have proven to have brought social change.

The University of Pune's Samarth Bharat Abhiyan (SBA) program is one such citation wherein a total of 573 villages were adopted for integrated multi-pronged development, including awareness on substance abuse, social of the village, ensuring bio-diversity of the landscape of the villages and developing a 12-point agenda including GIS mapping of villages; socio-economic and health issues. Vishwa Bharati University, West Bengal, under the inspiration of Rabindranath Tagore, initiated a village reconstruction program as early as the beginning of the 20th Century. The recent National Service Scheme (NSS) also provided a distinct uniform space and objective by bringing together service with curriculum and motivated several such initiatives on community engagement by the HEIs.

1.1. Linking Academia to Community and Enhancing Community Development

Ylikoski and Kivela (2017) discuss the Triple Helix Model in the context of the Universities in Norway. Caniels and Van den Bosch (2011) list cases of HEIs working towards community development in India, Japan and the Philippines. Further, Tandon and Pandey's (2019) engagement through Times Higher Education (THE) and UGC highlights the call for Indian HEI to contribute to:

'Promoting deeper interactions between higher educational institutions and local communities for identification and solution of real-life problems faced by the communities in a spirit of mutual benefit.' (2019:46)

The University's initiative for community development through engagement with diverse SDGs represents the two important arms of the Triple Helix Model connecting academia to community development by engaging with the industry and policy actors. It emanates from the concept of knowledge societies where HEIs exchange knowledge, skills, space, and resources with the wider community. Further narrowing in the Indian context, the Ranking lists some of the Indian HEIs, such as the Indian Institute of Technology, in contribution towards Goal 4.

Christ University is also ranked 401 on 600 HEIs globally by THE. This indicates the efforts towards community development and linkage with the knowledge community. The objectives of such extensions include both community development and enhancing the social responsibility and accountability of learners in HEIs.

1.2. The Child Sponsorship Program (Child Sponsorship Program) of the Centre for Social Action (CSA), Christ University: Objective, Origin, Coverage, Stakeholders

The Centre for Social Action (CSA) is Christ University's development action and community engagement wing. The CSA engages in student volunteerism. The Child Sponsorship Program is an initiative taken up by the students at Christ University to support the education of children from lower socio-economic backgrounds. The initiative was started in 1999 by initially sponsoring 52 children from the slums of Rajendra Nagar, Bengaluru, Karnataka, India. Currently, the Child Sponsorship Program extends to over 850 underprivileged children annually. The Sponsorship covers both girls and boys, which entails annual tuition fees, educational material, and stationery for at least one child in a family. The students at the University mobilize the resources. The program connects and scaffolds the sponsored child to the activity centre, facilitating academic and skill development. Unlike the conventional program, the program focuses on long-term engagement and envisages community development through structural support enabling an empowering environment for child development. The child's immediate context of family, school, peers, and community are both a target of the intended change.

In this chapter, we examine the role of Higher Education Institutions (HEI) emerging as knowledge societies through intellectual and social responsibility by supporting holistic child development and community development. The aim is to study the case of the Child Sponsorship Program (Child Sponsorship Program) model facilitated by Christ University in Bengaluru, India, and its impact on child, family, and community development.

2. Review of Literature

Literature relating to major key themes such as 'Child Sponsorship,' 'Whole Person Development, 'Child Sponsorship Program and scholastic improvement,' 'leadership,' "Community development and Child Sponsorship Program,' 'Leadership and Child Sponsorship Program' through the internet and other databases were reviewed using the Boolean logic. Over 200 research articles were identified and reviewed to study the factors affecting sponsorship programs. Organizations such as Save The Children, Plan International, CRY, Child Fund, World Vision, and Compassion International practice Child Sponsorship Programs and have studied the effectiveness of the Child Sponsorship Program practices they follow. Their impact studies and related literature were also referred to.

The recent studies critique the aid and philanthropy-based approach of the Child Sponsorship Programs followed by several organizations and calls for focus on the rights-based and empowerment models forging self-sustenance (Bell & Carens, 2004; Noh, 2019; Wydick et al., 2017). There is also a lack of literature on the family and community development aspect of child sponsorship. The impact measured focuses on the quantitative aspect of academic improvement and school attendance and often ignores the community development and sustainability factor.

2.1. Situating Child Sponsorship Program in Development Practice

The Child Sponsorship Program was one of the foremost interventions in child protection and child survival. It developed as an effective practice with the formation of the Foster Parent's Plan for Children in Spain (now known as Plan International) during the Spanish Civil War in 1937 by British Journalist John Langdon-Davies. This was initiated as a development program for children of the refugees. However, an account Child Sponsorship Program exists during the post-World War-I through interventions such as The British Save the Children Fund and The Society of Friends (Watson & Clarke, 2014). The focus of the earliest forms of Child Sponsorship Programs was education, child protection, adoption, fostering, and child welfare.

CS was termed as the *bedrock of several organizations and one of the most successful stories of private aid agency fund-raising* (Sogge et al., 1996). The CS, in practice, has retained its primordial relevance, strategy and purpose despite the shift that development discourse has taken globally from charity to rights. Glewwe et al., (2014) raise concerns about the lack of literature in the area despite the annual turnover of US$3 billion on the practice for international CS, especially in the domain of the impact on the beneficiaries and the wider community of recipients. Authors like Glewwe et al., (2014) view CS as being delivered through the charity model through the Civil Society Organizations (CSOs) with minimal attempts to reinstate the rights of a child to education with a long-term focus on the overall well-being of a child and community, however, the modes of *giving* still remain conventional. The conventional models of *giving* promulgated by CSOs such as World Vision, Compassion International, Plan International, and Child Fund stress the scholastic performance of children and are myopic in nature. The existing literature has a considerable contribution from the reports generated by the CSOs, hence lacks evidence for the development of the children and their community. It also lacks engagement with the forms of giving and its implications on the recipients. In the context of the Global South, Neilson and Mittelman (2012) have referred to the CS as a practice reinforcing the hegemonic structures as evident in the donor's narratives. Rabbitts (2013) has added the spatiality or geographies of giving and receiving with regard to CS and attempts to study the performative outcome of the CS. Rabbitts (2013) critically connect giving in the context of CS toward religion, neo-liberalism and family. Whilst there is a dearth of literature on CS aiming at community development through Whole Person Development (WPD) targeting education, livelihood, empowerment etc. The existing literature also suggests that the social impact is designed and envisaged by the donors, whilst the nature of forms and degree of the impact is yet to be captured through evidence.

Watson and Clarke (2014) refer to Child Sponsorship Program as a humanitarian approach. Several other references acknowledged Child sponsorship as a foundation for privately funded aid. Later, Child sponsorship is viewed as a tool by corporate entities of the Global North to showcase their social commitment. Watson and Clarke (2014) claim that the Child Sponsorship Program, during its active phase of two decades, mobilized considerable financial resources. Fowler (1992) studied the evolution of the Child Sponsorship Program from mere fund exchange to a more holistic and long-term goal of community development. Jensen, Cobbs & Turner (2016) critiqued the western capitalist model of Sponsorship, terming it consumption-oriented philanthropy, which is far divorced from the empowerment of the beneficiaries and community. However, successful models of Child Sponsorship Programs target the holistic development of the child, including child welfare, child participation, and community development.

2.2. Theorizing Child Sponsorship Program

2.2.1. Ecological Theory
Uri Bronfenbrenner's ecological systems theory focuses on the child within a complex system of relationships. It moves from the child to her macro and chronosystem, which impacts the child, and the relationship and interdependence between the microsystems are referred to as the mesosystem. Several theorists have applied the systems theory to understanding Child sponsorship. However, the objective of the chapter is also to understand if the CSA's model is akin to Bronfenbrenner's theory or suggests a more complex and active model for describing the child's habitat.

2.2.2. Jack Rothmans Locality Développent Model
The model by Rothman (1996) explains the process of interventions in the community through group discussions, full participation, self-help and mutual aid. There is a focus on community organizing in Rothman's model, and the study examines the factors of democratic procedures, indigenous factors, and voluntary cooperation to initiate interventions in the community and collectively review its impact.

2.3. Empowerment and Child Sponsorship Program

Noh (2019) critiqued the aid-based approach of several Child Sponsorship Program programs and called to focus on the Rights-Based Approach (RBA).

The right-used approach to the Child Sponsorship Program applies the framework of norms, principles, standards and goals of human rights. Organizations such as Caritas, Australia, and Oxfam called Child Sponsorship Program contradictory to the RBA approach as poverty and community development targeting contextual changes is not viable through the child focused intervention as that of Child Sponsorship Program. However, CSA's model focuses on the empowerment of the community and the holistic development of the child. The Child Sponsorship Program here is understood as a community development program rather than a linear child-oriented program. It focuses on creating systems within the community to strengthen the child, her family, and the community; hence, it aligns with the RBA. Community ownership is a crucial determinant and theme emerging in the objectives of all CSA community development programs, including the Child Sponsorship Program.

3. Methodology

The study employs a qualitative method emanating from interpretivism's epistemology stance and pragmatism's ontological reality. The methods employed were triangulation of in-depth-interviewing and Focused Group Discussion (FGD) for studying the Child Sponsorship Program on personal, familial, and community development. Empowerment being a conscious social reality, we employed Husserl's phenomenological methodology as it aligns with the objectives of researching the Child Sponsorship Program and lived experiences and transformation of the children and community.

The instruments used were:

- Rating Scale for Children accessing Child Sponsorship Program: Includes 12 items measuring the extent to which change was brought at the personal, familial and community levels.
- Semi-Structured Questionnaire for Children accessing Child Sponsorship Program: It includes 13 items categorized into a. Demographic details and, b. Impact of Child Sponsorship Program on children, families, and community.
- FGD Guide for Children accessing Child Sponsorship Program
- FGD Guide for parents of children accessing Child Sponsorship Program.

Primary respondents were 200 children from two urban slum settlements in Bengaluru-Urban who received Sponsorship with a focus on 100 female and 100 male children, secondary respondents and 40 parents of the children who received the Child Sponsorship Program.

Following the thematic analysis, the narratives were processed thematically, and open codes, theoretical codes and later themes were developed. The codes are later developed into a theoretical model of HEI engagement in child and community development and the practice model of the Child Sponsorship Program and children in the community. Table 1 presents the details of method and tools used for the different categories of the respondents.

Table 1. Methods and tools employed for measurement

Respondents	Method	Tool
1. Students accessing CS-200 (Locations: L.R Nagar, Ambedkar Nagar, Janakiram Layout, Urban Bengaluru, India)	Semi-structured interviewing Structured Interviewing FGD with 20 girls in 2 slum communities FGD with 20 boys in 2 slum communities	Semi-structured questionnaire Rating Scale FGD guide
Parents of Students accessing CS-40 (Locations: L.R Nagar, Ambedkar Nagar, Janakiram Layout, Urban Bengaluru, India).	FGD	FGD Guide

4. Results

The demographic and related details are represented and analyzed through descriptive statistics. The respondents are in the given age group, and it is evident that the maximum is middle school-going students from late childhood up to the elementary education level, followed by junior school-going children from early childhood and last are adolescents who are spread across the senior school level. The age group accessing CS is critical in terms of development trajectory (Table 2). Wydick et al., (2017) share that child accessing Child sponsorship carries forward the benefits to even higher education and adulthood. Age is crucial to cognitive development, and ample scaffolding at this stage can strengthen their cognitive development. As per the ASER Report - 2020, there are serious learning gaps in terms of numerical and reading capacity reported with students from Grades Ist to IVth owing to lack of exposure (ASER Centre, 2020). According to the UNICEF report (2005), it is important to reach children at a very young age as issues related to marginalization and exclusion become difficult at a later stage.

Table 2. Age-wise distribution of children

Age group in Years	Frequency
7-9	37
10-12	46
13-15	54
16-18	63
Total	200

The findings in Table 3 show that a greater number of participants enrolment is more in government schools than in private schools, whilst the Child Sponsorship Program is accessible for both students from government and private schools.

Table 3. Category of school accessed by the children covered under the Child Sponsorship Program

Category of school	Percentage (%)
Government school (State/central government) State (Under the government of Karnataka)	54
Private school (aided as well as unaided)	46

Table 4. Caste Group-wise distribution of respondents

Caste groups	Percentage (%)
ST	2
SC	56
General	14
OBCs	28

Table 5. Religion-wise distribution of respondents

Religious groups	Frequency
Hindus	94
Muslims	35
Christians	71

The findings in Table 4 suggest that more than half of the student population is from the Scheduled Caste (SC) category, while 2 percent are from the Scheduled Tribes and 28 percent are from Other Backward Castes. As per the Census of India (2011), the SC population in the 0-6 category is 13 percent. It is also to be noted that there was a silence with regard to caste identity when probed initially. The silence could be attributed to the discrimination associated with caste identity and the inability to express the same. Within the marginalized groups, there were three respondents who were from nomadic communities. Specifically, the children and families belonging to the Lamani sub-group within the larger realm of the Banjara community, the beneficiaries saw a progressive change in themselves. Table 5 presents the religion-wise distribution of the respondents.

The maximum number of children interviewed have been availing of Sponsorship for 0-2 years, followed by children availing of Sponsorship from 2 years to 4 years. The other largest category is of children availing scholarships from 8-10 years and 10-12 years. The number of years of accessing Child sponsorship is found to be directly proportional to the level of aspirations and (Need for Achievement) n-Ach (Watson & Clarke, 2013; Wydick et al., 2017). Therefore, it could be inferred from the above-mentioned findings more Child sponsorship access, and exposure to child activity centers would contribute to qualitative holistic development.

It is found that the average family size of the respondents is 4.8, and the average family monthly income is Rs. 6775 of all the respondents. Out of 200 children, 156 reported that their father is a Porter *(Coolie)* at the local railway station, while several others are street vendors, daily wage labourers etc. Almost half the children shared that their mothers are domestic workers and work in at least two houses on a daily basis. This indicates a substantial number of parents employed in the unorganized sector. More than half of the students interviewed are first-generation learners, which points to the lack of academic support and scaffolding for the children. A 12-year-old boy shared,

> "My parents are daily wage labourers from Gulbarga, they came here in search of work many, many years ago, and before that, they were farmers, and therefore they did not know how to read and write. Because of this, they were unable to help me with completing my homework. Initially, I used to get scolded by the teacher. It was only after the Akka and Anna, and Mekhala Ma'am at the activity centre started to help that I could complete my home task, else I was planning to drop out of school."

:Dreze and Sen (2002) stated that a significant number of students who dropped out of school are first-generation learners. Their assertion positions the above narrative of the 12-year-old boy.

4.1. Impact of the Child Sponsorship Program and the Activity Centre: Emergent Themes

The narratives were subjected to thematic analysis through codes, and the grouped codes were reduced to themes (Table 6). These emergent themes capturing the experiences of the children and parents are discussed.

5. Discussion

5.1. Activity Centre

The activity centre became a microcosm of positive change in the community by creating a change in the children and cultivating a critical mass through Child sponsorship and daily academic support and support for holistic development. The process is that only students enrolled in the activity centre were eligible to access Child Sponsorship Program. This was initiated to create a space and time for students to interact, reflect, question, and learn together. All children accessing the Child Sponsorship Program were to attend the activity centre on all afternoons (Figure 1).

The facilitator at the centre shared that this was to motivate students regularly and provide remediation through scaffolding and support at the centre. The children were engaged by trained staff along with student volunteers from Christ University who volunteered at the child activity centre and shared knowledge and skills with the children. In the FGDs held with the children, on being asked about the specific skills, it was found that all children referred to the skills being taught by '*Akkas*' (Older sister) and '*Annas*' (Older brother).

Table 6. Themes and sub-themes emerging from the study

S.No	Themes	Sub-themes	Description	N
1	Activity centre	1.1. Classroom learning 1.2. Skills and outcomes 1.3. Learning 1.4. Remediation	The activity centre is seen as a space for bridging the gap in terms of classroom learning and the actual acquisition of skills and tasks. The students see their participation in school and community-related activities as their measured outcome with regard to participation. The activity centre is associated with the learning and acquisition of skills related to communication. Remediation facilitated by the student volunteers in the activity centre for the students is seen as a bridge between classroom learning and student ability or capacity. The children in the community are able to view the activity centre as a value-free space free from fear and anxiety.	134
2	Communication skills	2.1 English 2.2 Language development 2.3. Articulation 2.4. Interaction	The respondents often referred to communication as their key skill. This is a skill they developed during their period of time in the activity centre. The space to interact, share and discuss various aspects of their life is enabled through the activity centre. The students with ample space and opportunity for interaction are able to grasp words and sentences in a multilingual capacity. The children reported the acquisition of English learning through regular interaction with the students from Christ University and also through a project facilitated by the Centre for Social Action. The personality-honing exposures and experiences shared with the students are also seen as a space for them to work on their ability for critical thinking. The students from Tamil, Kannada and Telugu speaking backgrounds also shared to have grasped other languages with ample social interaction facilitated through the space of the activity centre.	194
3	Co-curricular activities	3.1. Art and craft 3.2 Music 3.3. Dance 3.4. Street Play and theatre 3.5 Indoor Games	The activity centre and the volunteers from the University have engaged students in numerous opportunities or co-curricular activities that have helped students hone their skills in art, craft, music, theatre and sports. The students shared to have received the opportunity for competitions and representations at the district and state levels.	113

Table 6. (Continued)

S.No	Themes	Sub-themes	Description	N
4	Confidence	4.1. Speaking 4.2 Participation 4.3 Reaching out 4.4. Participation	Confidence is the most recurrent theme in the narratives by the students, the students define and articulate the space as a value-free space, and it enables them to perform and participate without fear of judgment or being mocked, as I the case of the school or similar spaces. The students also shared their confidence with regard to reaching out to strangers and students of the same age group without any reluctance. The program in the community ensures demographic familiarity is maintained, and this ensures a bias-free space facilitating confidence among the children.	156
5	Better marks and academic performance	5.1. Marks 5.2. Academic performance 5.3 Home tasks	Glewwe et al. (2021) is of the view that Child sponsorship directly impacts the increase of self-esteem, self-efficacy, optimism and aspirations of the children. They claimed a positive relationship between Child sponsorship programs and academic improvement in Kenya, Indonesia and Mexico. The connection was made to increase aspirations, hope and self-esteem. The remediation facilitated by the activity centre and constant follow-up by the community coordinators, and improved interactions with the schools and teachers are found to be effective strategies in ensuring the academic well-being of the students. The completion of the assignment and follow-up initiated by the team of volunteers and community coordinators has led to improved academic performance.	161
6	Student volunteers	6.1. Facilitators 6.2. role-modelling 6.3. Vicarious learning	The student volunteers from the University are perceived as facilities which lead, among	

S.No	Themes	Sub-themes	Description	N
7	Self-respect and self-management	7.1 Self-management 7.2. Leadership 7.3 Resilience	The self-management component of SEL was very evident in the narratives of the children and their parents. One of the parents shared that besides the financial support, the children have become more responsible towards the household affairs, such as saving money, using resources judiciously, asking me to arrange the house and doing the same. This reflects the improvement in the socio-emotional learning of the children across all the competencies, especially the aspect of self-management. Leadership, which is a combination of self-management competency as well as decision-making skills, were found to be a recurrent theme in the narrative, as well as the behaviour of the children in the activity centre. The sense of responsibility and accountability ensured through participation and forged this competency in the children. With the development of SEL competencies, especially accountability, the students are reported to have forged leadership skills that are crucial to self-development as well as community participation.	56
8	Over-all well being	8.1. Overall personality growth 8.2. Whole person development	Whole Person Development refers to the comprehensive and holistic development of an individual's actions and behaviours. It is not only the attainment of definite subject matter knowledge. The whole-person development approach focuses on improving the individual's emotional, social, physical, psychological, spiritual and professional development. Through continuous engagement through the activity centre, there is support for the child with co-scholastic and life-skill orientations such as creative skill, personality and leadership development. Child participation in community development and acquisition of skills facilitates whole-person development and leadership of the sponsored child.	72
9	Family health and well-being	9.1 Family atmosphere 9.2. Shared well-being 9.3. Parental aspirations	The student's higher education motivation is dependent on parental aspiration, income and educational qualification. Chiapa, Garrido & Prina (2012) suggest that parents exposed to highly educated professionals are found to have higher aspirations for their daughters. This was evident in the case of children in the community accessing Child Sponsorship Programs. The facilitation of tuitions fee, learning tools and resources was helpful in improving family well-being, as shared by several children and their parents.	124

Table 6. (Continued)

S.No	Themes	Sub-themes	Description	N
10	Vocational development	10.1 Aspirations 10.2 Professional development	Glewwe et al. (2014) closely examined the link between Child Sponsorship Programs in developing countries and enhanced hope and aspiration for economic empowerment and stability by seeking professional and livelihood development. The authors associated hope and aspiration with an economic model of hope where hope is seen as a driving factor to bridge the aspirational gap. Aspirational gaps were reported in the children interviewed, but the interventions through Child Sponsorship Program and activity centre were appropriate to bridge this gap. This intervention instilled in the children a goal for higher education and seeking a profession of their choice.	97
11	Child parliament	11.1 Community development 11.2 Citizenry 11.3 Accountability	Methods undertaken by the child parliament include involving children in community mobilization through street play and door-to-door campaigns for addressing issues such as dropout, sanitation and drinking water. This is to ensure that the children vicariously through Child Sponsorship Program become 'active citizens ' of the country. The child parliament can be a space for providing students with the scope to develop an active citizenry.	104
12	Support system	12.1. Support system 12.2. Part of the community	The perception of the institution and the coordinators, and the students are of a critical mass or support group within the community. The children look forward to studying in the institution and is a part of the daily narrative in term of help, support, reinforcement etc. The shared feeling of gratitude is also evident among the community members towards the institution in the context of the role played in the empowerment of the community members.	117
13	Community Development	13.1 Child participation in the community 13.2 Development of the community	The model of Child Sponsorship followed by the University is focused on developing the community by strengthening child participation and leadership. It was evident in this case that the children were motivated to understand the issues of the community they were a part of and to work towards the same. For e.g., the street plays based on waste segregation, water wastage and developing awareness tools on COVID-19 protocols could be understood in the context of community development. The students are able to deliberate and develop ideas and strategies on the basis of these aspects.	

Figure 1. The image of participants documenting changes after coming to the Activity Centre at Centre for Social Action (CSA).

Skill learning is at the core of the activity centre and provides an opportunity for students to grow. The students reported having learned visual and performing arts, public speaking, games and sports, and using innovative community media like street play, slogan writing, etc. This extension of the activity centre is named the Child Parliament.

Parliament is a body of students created to ensure child participation in community development. The students who participate in the child parliament are trained and motivated to participate in community development. Some of the activities undertaken by the children's parliament include street play on alcoholism and substance abuse, waste disposal, and safeguarding drinking water.

The children also mobilized the parents of children who dropped out of school to encourage them to re-enroll the children the school. A student shared,

> "We were facing the issues of waste disposal everywhere in the community. We decided to address the issues through a door-to-door

campaign and educate the community about waste segregation and proper disposal. I could see a significant change in the community after that, including my mother. We now segregate the solid and liquid waste and dispose of the same in the BBMP vehicle rather than accumulating the same in the community."

The narrative indicates an example of the issues of hygiene being addressed by the students through the channel of parliament. The children emphasized that they were trained in techniques of community mobilization, such as campaigns, street plays, etc., by the students at Christ University, Bengaluru.

5.2. Academic and Scholastic Improvement

The current study indicates that a significantly high 97 per cent of students felt that the Child Sponsorship Program has *'improved'* their scores and has facilitated overall academic improvement in academics. Unlike other Child Sponsorship Program models, the CSA model aims to study and provide long-term support and earning scaffolding to students. The practice of remediation facilitated through the child activity centre helps to bridge the learning gaps created by lack of accessibility, exclusion and other factors. Boone et al., (2015) assert clear evidence suggesting a marked improvement in the academic performance of students through remedial learning through cluster randomized trials.

5.3. School Performance and Motivation

A parent of a child accessing the Child Sponsorship Program shared, *'my son's teacher praises him a lot, and she always says that the child became more active and confident after going to the activity centre and accessing Sponsorship.* All respondents interviewed, including the parents, shared that there is a heightened motivation to go to school and complete the home and class tasks. The Child activity centre has also made efforts to include the schools of the children also as a key stakeholder in the community development by inviting the schoolteachers and heads to a community program and using school space to nurture child activity centers.

5.4. Language Development

Language development is a key goal of development. 194 out of 200 participants shared that their speaking skills improved over some time after accessing Child Sponsorship Program. All the participants shared about improvement in the English language, and 174 respondents reported to have improvised their writing skills. A child shared, *"Improved in spoken English and took the initiative to participate in activities."* A female 8th grader shared that her reading skills also improved after joining the activity centre.

Another respondent shared,

"When I was studying in 8th 'English Access Micro-Scholarship Program' was started by US Embassy, where its main aim was to teach proper English to the students. Through CSA, I got this opportunity, and this program was for two years. This was the platform where I came to know myself, like my talents and responsibilities. I never thought of going to places like Calicut in Kerala, Visthar camp and HAL, but I went there through access. The Access program has changed my lifestyle from a spool to leather. I think that after access only, I can write or speak in English better. This Access and CSA has been a blessed opportunity that I have got in my lifetime."

The narrative can be synthesized into two points: language development is also positively correlated to the development of self-confidence and self-awareness, as evident in the above narrative.

5.5. Whole Person Development (WPD)

The results show that 77 percent of the respondents shared their confidence *'improved'*, and 3 percent shared the confidence *'highly improved'* after accessing Child Sponsorship Program and visiting the activity centre.

The learning activities conducted at the Activity Centre ensure improved learning and cognition, social-emotional well-being and life skills development of the child. One of the students shared, *"I have gathered multiple skills through my engagement with the activity centre. Dancing, singing, and sports all were taught at the activity centre, and I got the opportunity to participate in the school and win awards also because of the same.'*

Another student shared, *"... we learn life skills, something which parents also miss out on, such as saying namaskaram, sorry, wearing proper clothes, saying thank you etc.'* A synthesis shows positive behavioral changes in which children were trained at the activity centre.

The psychological facet of whole-person development relates to knowing one's inner self. It enhances the individual's self-esteem and self-acceptance. The respondents of the study have also shared that they feel much more confident after coming to the activity centre and assessing the Child Sponsorship Program.

5.6. Social and Emotional Learning (SEL)

A student recipient of the CSP who is now pursuing an under-graduation shared,

'I became good at studying and found myself at CSA.'

Another 14-year-old girl shared that making friends was the aspect that attracted her towards the activity centre. An increase in confidence, increased peer relationships, enhanced self-awareness, self-management, and relationship management are found to be areas where children have reported significant improvement and enhancement, their parents and facilitators at the activity centre. The self-management component of SEL was very evident in the narratives of the children and their parents. One of the parents shared that besides the financial support, the children have become more responsible towards household affairs, such as saving money, using resources judiciously, asking to arrange the house, and doing the same. This reflects the improvement in the socio-emotional learning of the children across all the competencies.

5.7. Leadership Skills

A teacher reported, "my students can mobilize the community for any issues. They know the issues very well and can convince community members to bring change." This indicates the transformative change that has occurred in the lives of the children accessing the Child Sponsorship Program. Adams et al. (2020) are of the view that developing and cultivating a Whole Child requires multidimensional curriculum change and holistic education. As mentioned earlier, schools are unable to alter all the dimensions Froebel mentioned. The focus here is on continued growth in self-management, decision making and relationship management, which is being forged in the activity centre.

5.8. Resilience

A 13-year-old girl shared that her father often would not return home, and she should spend time at a neighbor's home the entire day or on the streets while her mother would be away for the whole day to work as domestic help. She shared that there would not be anyone to help or even feed her during the day. The child shared that she spent almost three years in that situation, which only improved after the Child Sponsorship Program was accessible and she could use the child activity centre. The child emerged as one of the leaders in the activity centre and joined with the child parliament also to mobilize community members. The Child Sponsorship Program ensures that the child not only receives support for education but psycho-social support and a safe and secure space. It garnered her capacities and instilled a growth mentality.

5.9. Family Well-Being

Thirteen-year-old Venkat shared:

> "I have experienced a lot of problems at home due to my father's alcoholism. He would come home drunk every night and would throw away my books sometimes. That is when Akka and Anna from the University came to teach us Street Play. I suggested that we do a street play on alcoholism as I could relate to it. It made a lot of impact on my family and me. My father changed a lot after we performed that play and after he saw me performing in that street play."

As mentioned earlier, in the parental demographics, it was clear that the children belong to lower socio-economic status, and the parents are mostly employed in the unorganized sector. In the FGD held with the women of the SHGs, parents of the children who were accessing the Child Sponsorship Program shared that the major familial benefits are in the context of enhanced saving and family expenditure. Forty-seven percent of students shared that the

Child Sponsorship Program has increased their savings and expenditure on stationery and educational materials. A mother shared that this is a significant help towards the financial security of the family.

5.10. Physical and Mental Health

The parents, activity centre facilitators and volunteers also shared that access to anemia, malnutrition and a holistic diet is an issue. The problem related to diet and deficiency diseases, especially Vitamin C and A, is due to intermittent diet. The respondents did not share the prevalence of general health issues, whilst skin diseases owing to Vitamin C deficiency and safe drinking water are reported by the community. Resilience and other aspects of mental health were also around to be scaffolded with the development of SEL competencies. The coordinators and the students at Christ University were perceived as support systems, and they shared being able to reach out to them.

5.11. Parental Perception towards Children's Education

The findings of the study suggest that nearly 75 percent of the participant's parents were *'motivated'*, and 5 percent were *'highly motivated'* to send their children to higher education. The FGDs with parents revealed the high motivation of the parents to access the Child Sponsorship Program and child activity centre for the career-building of the children.

5.12. Vocational Development

In the FGD with children, they shared to be wanting to become 'doctors,' 'engineers,' 'teachers,' 'cricketers,' 'actors,' 'police,' 'artists' etc.

A 12-year-old boy who loved painting shared that the Child Sponsorship Program hones his skills, and the facilitators never judged him while drawing and allowed his creativity to flow. *"Once an Anna from the college taught me some techniques and this became motivating for me. He also told me to go to a very renowned college in India to study painting, and now I am aiming towards the same."*

This indicates support for the child's career growth. Another 13-year-old girl shared her dreams of becoming an astronaut after *'hearing the story of Kalpana Chawla.'* Figure 2 shows the depiction of her aspiration to 'ride a spaceship one day.'

The activity centre aligns its pedagogy with these aspirations of the children and aims to build skills of the children towards this aspect. One of the participants who work in a call centre now shared that the language, especially English Listening, Speaking, Writing and Reading (LSWR) skills, helped her in seeking employment and supporting her family.

Figure 2. A 13-year-old girl's representation of her dream to be an astronaut.

5.13. Community Development

The child parliament constituted with the children accessing Child Sponsorship Program has initiated several development programs ranging from sensitization and campaigns. There are two elements to the community development aspect of the Child Sponsorship Program. Firstly, the recent trends in Child Sponsorship Programs focus on community development and ensuring the sustainability of the projects through community ownership. Secondly, creating a critical mass of children accessing the Child Sponsorship Program to mobilize their community towards change. The data shows that 77 percent of the children shared they are *'motivated'* to take initiates for the betterment of the country, five are *'highly motivated'* while 17 percent were 'least motivated' or not motivated enough to envisage themselves as community organizers. Development of the community or work towards the same.

However, 78 percent of students reported that there is an overall improved perception towards education.

5.14. Child Participation, Active Citizenry and Leadership in Community Development

The idea of citizenship has been a dynamic one since the times of Plato, wherein citizenship was understood as active participation in the democratic procedure, to the current times, wherein the idea of citizenship has lost its active nature of participation with the representative form of democracy coming on the scene. Benjamin Constant, in his article *"The liberty of the Ancients and the liberty of the Moderns"*, examines the idea of Athenian citizenship and how it is different from our current form of citizenship and cannot be implemented in contemporary times.

With this understanding of citizenship, the Child Sponsorship Program studied children in the activity centre and child parliament, where an attempt was made to unravel the idea of active citizenship for the children. The findings show the importance and operation of the child activity centre and activities of the child parliament in citizen making process of active citizenry such as training in street play, slogan writing, using effective posters etc.

A parent shared:

> 'My child, along with her friends, visited some twenty houses in the neighborhood where children had dropped out of studies. They convinced the parents to send the children to at least a nearby government school and even linked the children to a Child Sponsorship Program. They even brought schoolteachers to talk to their parents."

The findings suggest an active effort to explore the link between schools, activity centers and the idea of active citizenry. They enhance or supplement each other in the process of making students informed and responsible citizens of the state. The main objective of the activity centre, as shared, is to explore various activities and programs that the school has undertaken with the lens of an active citizenry.

6. Implications

The HEI's role in community development emanates from the various SDGs and its role as a knowledge society to aim for community development and empowerment of vulnerable groups.

The findings of the study with Christ University, Bengaluru, show that HEIs as knowledge societies can cultivate and nurture interventions through intellection and social responsibility with student participation, knowledge sharing and effective empirical evidence through intellectual involvement. The Child Sponsorship Program by the CSA of Christ University, Bengaluru, reaches out to the most marginalized and vulnerable sections of the community. The focus on children through the Child Sponsorship Program targets academic aspirations, leadership qualities, linguistic growth, skill-building, and professional development of the child through the activity centre. The children have reported positive growth in all the dimensions, which aligns with Bronfenbrenner's ecological model of child development, where interventions in the primary and secondary systems in the microsystem interact with the child. However, a more comprehensive model adapted from the ecological model is suggested, which reflects closer interaction of the child and her/his microsystem enabled through HEI's direct intervention.

The RBA is to be further strengthened and facilitated as it targets the overall rights-based intervention with the children separated from the charitable model. Additionally, it places the development of the community as a key objective, as the focus is not just on the child but also on the context of the child and continued engagement with the family and community within the framework of RBA. There is a positive change in the familial and parental perception towards education, children's higher education and professional growth and reported reduced dropout rates.

The Child Sponsorship Program has also impacted the children's family economy by enhancing family income and saving. The children accessing Child Sponsorship Program have shared the experience of transforming being a leader and part of the critical mass. Students have received a response through the child activity centre by visiting the Christ University campus, frequently planning educational trips, and participating in university-facilitated sports and cultural activities have enhanced social skills and increased growth mentality. This critical mass can steer changes in the community, such as addressing issues of dropouts, sanitation, alcohol abuse and safe drinking water in the community through street play, theatre, slogans and posters through the democratic process as depicted in Rothman's model of locality development.

Here, the multiple foci of the Child Sponsorship Program are represented, i.e., Child development and community development. Whole Child development is the core objective of the Child Sponsorship Program, and it is manifested through determinants such as academic performance, language development, economic well-being, child leadership and participation and health and nutrition. The secondary focus is on community development which is impacted through livelihood, preventing dropout, sanitation, waste management and safe drinking water through Child Parliament (Figure 3).

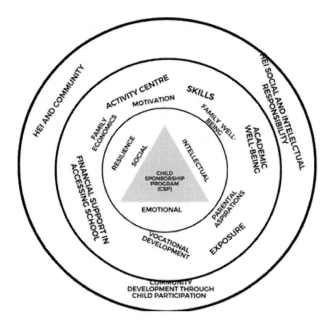

Figure 3. A model of HEI engagement in Child and community development.

Conclusion

The chapter aimed to capture and describe the transformation brought by the Child Sponsorship Program in the child and the community. It is found that through the emerging role of HEIs as knowledge societies, there is the transformation of individuals and communities. The study, following the mixed methodology of in-depth interviews, helped understand the experiences of the children accessing the Child Sponsorship Program and the demographic and other determinants relating to Whole Child Development. It was found that there is a positive change in the children's agency, leadership, participation and personal and behavioural changes. By creating systems such as child activity centers and child parliament, community development is also impacted through the Child Sponsorship Program. It has also led to changes in the attitude of the parents and wider community towards education, schooling, and other development indicators. The students' exposure to sports competitions, activities on the Christ University campus, educational trips and the like have enhanced their growth mentality and aspiration levels. This model of the Child Sponsorship Program is right-based and focuses on ownership and engagement with the community rather than the simple exchange of financial resources. The model of community engagement by HEIs is generated from the codes and themes developed to represent the direction of change developed by the HEIs.

References

Adams, K., Lumb, A., Tapp, J., & Paige, R. (2020). Whole child, whole teacher: Leadership for flourishing primary schools. *Education* 3-13, 48(7), 861-874.

ASER Centre (2020). *Annual Status of Education Report* (Rural) 2020 Wave 1. https://img.asercentre.org/docs/ASER2021/ASER2020wave1-v2/aser2020 wave1report_feb1.pdf.

Bell, D., & Carens, J. H. (2004). The ethical dilemmas of international human rights and humanitarian NGOs: Reflections on a dialogue between practitioners and theorists. Human Rights Quarterly, 26(2), 300–329.

Boone, P., Camara, A., Eble, A., Elbourne, D., Fernandes, S., Frost, C., Jayanty, C., Lenin, M., & Silva, A. F. (2015). Remedial after-school support classes offered in rural Gambia (The SCORE trial) : study protocol for a cluster randomised controlled trial. *Trials*, 16(1), 1-9.

Constant, B. (1988). *Constant : political writings*. Cambridge University Press.

Caniëls, M. C., & Van den Bosch, H. (2011). The role of higher education institutions in building regional innovation systems. *Papers in Regional Science*, 90(2), 271-286.

Chiapa, C., Garrido, J. L., & Prina, S. (2012). The effect of social programs and exposure to professionals on the educational aspirations of the poor. *Economics of Education Review*, 31(5), 778-798.

Cobbs, J. B., & Turner, B. A. (2016). Evaluating Sponsorship through the lens of the resource-based view: The potential for sustained competitive advantage. *Business Horizons*, 59(2), 163-173.

Drèze, J., & Sen, A. (2002). Democratic practice and social inequality in India. *Journal of Asian and African Studies*, 37(2), 6-37.

Fowler, A. (1992). Distant obligations : Speculations on NGO funding and the global market. *Review of African political economy*, 55, 9–29.

Glewwe, P., Ross, P. H., & Wydick, B. (2014). Developing hope: The impact of international child sponsorship on self-esteem and aspirations. *Economics,* Paper 9. The University of San Francisco. http://repository.usfca.edu/econ/9.

Neilson, L. C., & Mittelman, R. (2012). Ideological outcomes of marketing practices : A critical historical analysis of child sponsorship programs. In research in consumer behaviour. Emerald Group Publishing Limited.

Noh, J. E. (2019). Human rights-based child sponsorship: A case study of ActionAid. VOLUNTAS : *International Journal of Voluntary and Nonprofit Organizations*, 30(6), 1420-1432.

Rabbitts, F. (2013). " Nothing is whiter than white in this world" : Child sponsorship and the geographies of charity. PhD Thesis, University of Exeter.

Rothman, J. (1996). The interweaving of community intervention approaches. *Journal of Community Practice*, 3(3-4), 69-99.

Sogge, D., Biekart, K., & Saxby, J. (Eds.). (1996). Compassion and calculation: *The business of private foreign aid.* Pluto Press.

Tandon, R., & Pandey, P. (2019). Disciplines, Professions and the Sustainable Development Goals (SDGs) : Challenges in Higher Education in India. Implementing the 2030 Agenda at Higher Education Institutions : *Challenges and Responses*, 47.

Tremblay, C., Hall, B., & Tandon, R. (2014). Global trends in support structures for community-university research partnerships. UNESCO Chair in Community-based Research and Social Responsibility in Higher Education. UNESCO.

Watson, B., & Clarke, M. (Eds.). (2014). *Child sponsorship: Exploring pathways to a brighter future.* Springer.

Wydick, B., Glewwe, P., & Rutledge, L. (2017). Does child sponsorship pay off in adulthood? An international study of impacts on income and wealth. *The World Bank Economic Review,* 31(2), 434-458.

Ylikoski, T, & Kivelä, S. (2017). Spatiality in higher education: A Case Study in integrating pedagogy, community engagement, and regional development. *International Journal of Innovation and Learning*, 21(3), 348-363.

Chapter 3

Empowering Women Through Livelihood Interventions: Case Studies from an Impoverished Community

Hemalatha, K.[*]
Department of Sociology and Social Work, Christ University, Bengaluru, India

Abstract

This chapter looks at the influence of a livelihood project in empowering women belonging to an impoverished community from one of the most backward regions of the state of Karnataka in Southern India. Jamkhandi taluq of Bagalkote district is one of the poorer taluqs in the state, with a sex ratio of 938 and a female literacy rate of 50.75%. The Centre for Social Action began working in the area around a decade ago. The livelihood project was an offshoot of a project on Population displacement that was undertaken in the region. CSA adopted the Self-Help Approach (SHA) to meet the needs of this community. This gave the necessary impetus for the creation of a livelihood project for disadvantaged women.

The central theme of the chapter is to study the extent of empowerment that is evident among the project's women beneficiaries. This chapter presents the evidence of empowerment using the qualitative case study methodology using ten cases. The theoretical framework provided by the 'Three Dimensional Model of Women Empowerment' is used to present the analysis.

Document review and in-depth interviews are the prominent data sets used to present the study's major findings. The hybrid approach to

---

[*] Corresponding Author's Email: hemalata.k@christuniversity.in.

In: Models for Social Responsibility Action by Higher Education Institutions
Editors: Joseph Chacko Chennattuserry, Elangovan N. et al.
ISBN: 979-8-89113-097-5
© 2024 Nova Science Publishers, Inc.

coding and thematic analysis is used to integrate the insights from the theory used as well as observations from the study. Both within-case analysis and cross-case analysis are used for analysis. The personal, relational, and societal dimensions of empowerment are presented through themes emerging from the data.

The implication of the chapter is the reiteration of the efficacy of the model in empowering women. This model can be replicated in other project areas, and livelihood strategies can be adopted extensively.

Keywords: women empowerment, livelihood intervention, dimensions of empowerment

1. Introduction

Empirical evidence for the past decade shows a positive correlation between women's earnings, productivity, and empowerment (World Bank, 2012). The 2009 World Survey on the Role of Women in Development (United Nations, 2009). showcases the positive multiplier effect for overall social and economic development when women become empowered and can access economic and financial resources. Robust evidence shows that women's access to resources has a stronger impact on their empowerment as well as the well-being of their families and communities at large compared to the situation when men have access to similar resources. Sen (2000) states that when women participate in activities such as initiating micro businesses, society as a whole benefits. There are visible social benefits seen in their enhanced status and independence. Empowerment is manifested in different dimensions as envisaged by scholars. It impacts vital household decisions and has the potential to generate income which changes the nature of their existence.

As part of its social responsibility, Christ University is working with disadvantaged populations. The Centre for Social Action has undertaken projects to meet this objective. The university started working with rural women belonging to the most vulnerable sections of society. One such project at Jamkhandi was envisaged keeping in mind the Self-help approach (SHA). This approach was operationalized through the livelihood opportunities created to empower disadvantaged women.

The present chapter showcases this phenomenon in a disadvantaged community in the northern district of Bagalkote, Karnataka. This is one of the most backward parts of the state, presenting a bleak picture in terms of most parameters on the human development index. The Economic Survey of

Karnataka shows that the incidence of poverty (2011-12) in urban areas is 45 percent whereas, in rural areas, it is 32.1 percent in the district of Bagalkote (IBEF, 2012). The overall incidence of poverty (2011-12) in the district is 37 percent which remains significantly higher than the state average (21 percent). The Gender Inequality Index (GII), which measures the loss in achievements due to gender disparities as measured by three dimensions—Reproductive Health, Empowerment and Labour Force Participation shows that Bagalkot is ranked 27th among all districts of Karnataka, with an index value of 0.130.

The present chapter is based on a study carried out in jamkhandi taluq, where during 2011, the Child Sex Ratio was 938. The total literacy rate is 67.86%, and the female literacy rate is as low as 50.75%. The dropout rate of girls in Jamakhandi at the higher secondary level is 91.6 percent. The occupational profile of this region shows among both genders, 87% of workers carry out main work (employment or earning more than six months) while 13% were involved in marginal activity providing a livelihood for less than six months. This group largely includes women. The livelihood opportunities in the region are abysmally low, and women have remained on the fringes of the development process. (Karnataka.gov.in, 2016).

2. Background

About a decade ago, a group of researchers from Christ University were given a research grant by the International Federation of Catholic Universities to study population displacement in the region, especially after building a large dam called the Almatti Dam. The dam impacted more than one lakh families, pushing the region into a spiral of impoverishment. The researchers wanted to study this dam-building project's economic and psychosocial impact. Their aim was to study the risks to which the population was exposed. They also listed the risks which needed attention and suggested mitigation methods. (Chully & Hemalatha, 2017)

The researchers used one of the most popular and globally accepted models to study relief and reconstruction efforts to address population displacement was propounded by Michael Cernea of the world bank (Cernea, 2008). The model is particularly suited to study the population risks when development processes lead to displacement (development-induced displacement). The model looks at eight risks of displacement, such as landlessness, homelessness, loss of livelihood, etc.

The researchers found from the data collected from 1000 households in the taluks of Bagalkot, Bilgi, and Jamkhandi that significant among all the risks that this population was exposed to be the risk of losing livelihoods. Efforts to mitigate this risk have to involve creating livelihood opportunities for this population (Chully & Hemalatha, 2017).

3. Theoretical Framework

This chapter was based on the theoretical framework provided by Huis et al. (2017). These authors present this model to be used especially in the context of microfinance. The model is titled 'Three-dimensional Model of Women's Empowerment. It proposes that women's empowerment takes place within three distinct dimensions: (1) the micro-level, referring to the individual's personal beliefs as well as actions, where personal empowerment can be observed (2) the meso-level, referring to the individual's beliefs as well as actions in relation to relevant others, which results in relational empowerment (3) the macro-level, where empowerment is seen in the context of outcomes in the broader, societal context where societal empowerment results.

In many ways, the view of Kabeer (1999) also explains this process of empowerment. She sees it as a process through which women acquire the ability to make strategic life choices in a context where this ability was previously denied to them. In the context of the impoverished backgrounds of the women in Jamkhandi and their inability to access basic developmental needs like education, this situation envisaged by Kabeer fits perfectly. The scholar also stresses that the ability to exercise individual choice is dependent on three interrelated elements – resources, agency, and achievements. Resources refer to material, human and social expectations and allocations. The agency is the ability or sense of ability that helps women to define their goals, work on them, and decide their own strategic life outcomes. Achievements include several outcomes, from improved well-being to achieving equal representation of women. Women's empowerment is thus the process of accessing and using resources in an agentic manner to record certain achievements resulting in the empowerment of women.

3.1. Field interventions at Jamkhandi by CSA

Following this study, the Center for Social Action (CSA) decided to work with the impoverished community at Jamkhandi. CSA adopted the SHA approach in this region and worked with women to help them through the self-help process. The SHA is known to be an ideal solution for communities that are devastated by manmade calamities like development-induced displacement. The SHG approach is seen as a methodology that uses interventions to provide women with tools and techniques for making changes in their lives. The focus is on very poor communities, women in particular. This approach is known across communities, where it has been implemented to bring an attitude change among poor women and towards believing in their potential. This is the process that triggers the empowerment of women. The approach goes beyond merely learning and understanding but is achieved through unleashing the suppressed potential of these women. (Eiden et al., 2014).

SHGs are the intentional relationship of 20- 30 individuals (mostly women) who meet regularly to take care of their issues based on shared help and self-improvement. Self-improvement gatherings have risen as one of the real techniques for women's empowerment (Kar & Pradhan, 2018). The CSA Centre in Jamkhandi used the SHG groups to identify the neediest women who could be helped with loans to create livelihoods. With this motive, all the SHGs were purposed to select and recommend women candidates who could receive the loans and who also possess the potential to develop a microenterprise and benefit from it for empowering themselves. Using the Microfinance methodology, the CSA gave loans of 10,000 Rs to selected disadvantaged women. They provided them with extensive training in livelihoods, as well as in money transactions and operating bank accounts. All these were to be applied in the micro-enterprises chosen by the women. The field staff of CSA extended intensive handholding and support. The process model is shown in Figure 1 below.

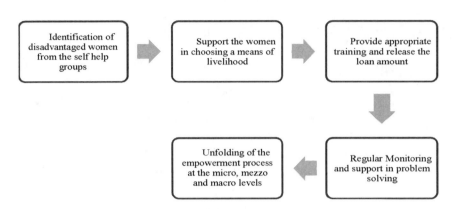

Figure 1. Process Model of the Livelihood Intervention Undertaken at Jamkhandi.

4. Methodology

This chapter is based on the case study research design where ten women who have benefitted from the livelihood initiative of CSA participated. The chapter intends to address two objectives (1) Review the strategies made by CSA to Design and Implement the livelihood program at Jamkhandi Centre. (2) Study the process of empowerment and present the outcomes. The case study design provides a perfect methodology to look at the strategies of the CSA and the practices it undertook to work with disadvantaged women and the changes which unfolded in the lives of impoverished women. According to the requirement of the design, the chapter initially presents a *Within-case analysis*, where the aspects that address the research objectives within each case are presented. This is followed by *Cross-case analysis,* where the ten cases are brought together to draw common themes. For qualitative research, we must distinguish between information relevant to all participants and those aspects of the experience that are exclusive to particular research participants. Such distinctions are necessary because those aspects of an experience that are unique to one individual have limited usefulness outside the interpretation of that individual's experience, although such unique features may be critical to understanding that particular person's story. Both these processes will help in establishing the empowerment that occurs when disadvantaged women are supported to undertake and run small businesses.

Insights from one each case sensitized this author to identify similar information from other cases. As an idea repeatedly occurred in multiple contexts, the author was able to instantiate the idea as a theme. Those themes which had the explanatory force both in individual accounts and across the sample were identified. Analysis of individual cases enabled the author to understand those aspects of explanations that occur not only as individual "units of meaning" but also as part of larger patterns formed by the confluence of meanings within individual cases. A systematic immersion enabled the author to sense the lived experience of each of the women. Significant statements were identified by the author to comprehend the lived experience of the ten participants. Comparison of the significant statements led to identifying categories of statements common to all participants; thus, subthemes and themes were formed (Ayres et al., 2003).

The author constructed a semi-structured interview guide to cover the different areas of empowerment, and the data was collected through trained field animators who have worked with all the SHG groups in the area. The data were transcribed, coded, and recorded by the researcher. The themes which emerged were used to address the objectives of the study.

5. Results

The collected data was analyzed, and themes were identified. The results of this process are presented in this section.

Table 1 presents some of the features of the participants, such as their marital/social status, educational attainment, number of family members, and the livelihood enterprise undertaken by them.

Table 1. Participant's characteristics

	Marital status	Education	Size of family	livelihood/business chosen
Participant 1	Married	Lower Primary	5	Tailoring
Participant 2	Married	Seventh standard	4	Goat rearing
Participant 3	Unmarried/ Disabled	Tenth standard	8	Tailoring
Participant 4	Married	Seventh standard	4	Buffalo rearing
Participant 5	Devadasi	Seventh standard	8	Tailoring and buffalo rearing
Participant 6	Married	Pre-university	7	Collaborates with her husband's Welding business
Participant 7	Devadasi	Illiterate	9	Goat rearing
Participant 8	Widow	Illiterate	4	Mobile Kirana store
Participant 9	Widow	Illiterate	8	Goat rearing
Participant 10	Married	Pre-University	5	Buffalo rearing

The three-Dimensional Model of Women's Empowerment provides support to gain a deeper understanding of women's empowerment in the field of microfinance services. The process suggests that women's empowerment from a community development perspective is observed in three dimensions of a woman's life, namely the personal, the relational, and the societal. This can be understood as the changes seen in the woman, and her changed relational dynamics, placing her on an equal footing with others. The data from the present study reveals this in the changed perspectives of the spouse, brothers, and other members of the immediate family. This is also reflected in her interactions and standing with other members of the community. The perception of community members and the resulting changes indicate the respect that the women receive and greater acceptance into the economic and social spheres of communities.

The within-case analysis reveals that one needs to delineate the three dimensions of empowerment as suggested in the model. The analysis reinforces the importance of microloans and their ability to stimulate and usher in strong changes in the lives of these women. At the individual level, person-based changes are evident. The changes in her capacities and her ability to make thoughtful choices are clear.

The microfinance services in the present study are structured around offering small loans, training in livelihoods, and connecting individuals to financial institutions. These processes initiate a liberating and strengthening effect on women. An intense process of self-discovery and growth is evident in each of the women in the present study (Table 2). Empowerment begins with a process of prioritising life's major concerns and addressing them using one's own capacities. When this happens in families who are poverty-stricken, an immediate impact on the quality of life of all members of the family is seen. This impacts the personal standing of women within families and places them in a better position to bargain for great acceptance in decision-making and running the family.

Since the entire exercise began with an impetus to start and maintain a livelihood, the impact on the woman's interaction with the larger community and her business dealings with the various stakeholders cover the third dimension suggested in the model. An enhancement in her knowledge about the relevant markets, customers, and other business partners enlarges her circle of mutual influence, and her capacity to influence many of these element's results in empowering her. The process showing changes from before the intervention, during the intervention phase, and post-intervention is shown in Table 2 above. The narratives highlight the dimensions of empowerment.

Table 2. Narratives extracted from the within-case analysis

	Verbatims expressing the situation before the initiation of livelihood activities	Verbatims expressing the changes during the beginning of the livelihood activities	Verbatims expressing the changes after the adoption and engagement in the livelihood activities
PARTICIPANT 1	"To tell you the truth, the family was in a critical state with only one person working as a coolie.	"I had an old machine. With the loan, I decided to buy a new machine with different settings to stitch fall and PICO for the sarees."	"Decision-making related to the schooling of children is left to me. If I have to go somewhere, I go alone and tell him later.….. from a tailor, I have become the chairman of the cluster-level sangha. People look at me with respect…"
PARTICIPANT 2	"Both of us had no education; we barely know about reading a passbook."	"We felt goats would be easier. Having buffaloes would have been difficult. As both of us were going out for coolie work, the goats would graze and look after themselves."	"Today, my relationship with my husband has changed; if I forget something related to the sangha, he reminds me. He listens to our sangha discussions, and I believe he is happy that I am learning about these issues."
PARTICIPANT 3	"My disability was a curse."	"Slowly, word-by-mouth information spread so that I could stitch well. They started giving me their clothes. They have confidence in me that I can stitch anything they want. I can design dresses the way they want. They trust me to do a good job".	"Earlier, my parents and brother would take all the decisions. Now, if I tell them that something may be the right thing to do, they listen to me. I am part of the family's decision-making processes."
PARTICIPANT 4	"Family faced terrible poverty and want. Our time was very bad."	"My daughter is six years old now, and my husband discussed her schooling with me. He wanted my opinion about her education."	"…. now I have a few buffaloes. I want to buy more and partner with my Sangha members to build a large shed. They have great confidence in my skills in dealing with the buffaloes as well as the customers.
PARTICIPANT 5	."Earlier, it was difficult to save 50 Rs. There were many businessmen doing the same business, and they knew the business well. I was quite frightened of failure."	"Training sessions were very useful. They inspired me to"	"I plan to open a shop. My son has to start a business, and I will help him…. I am an inspiration to many women who have started rearing buffaloes, and their lifestyle has improved."

Table 2. (Continued)

	Verbatims expressing the situation before the initiation of livelihood activities	Verbatims expressing the changes during the beginning of the livelihood activities	Verbatims expressing the changes after the adoption and engagement in the livelihood activities
PARTICIPANT 6	"Money also was not sufficient; we had to borrow from others. Space for keeping the machine was a problem."	"The changes in the attitude I was seeing earlier were slow, and there was change."	"Schooling decisions are completely left to me. I independently handle them. I am also able to help my husband in the business. When people come to meet him, I can join in the discussions. Even when he is absent, I can talk to the customers independently".
PARTICIPANT 7	"Thinking of the early day is very disturbing."	"I became more aware of doing this business. A lot of information was shared with us, and I began networking with people.	"I did not know how to talk to people. I started meeting different people. I have no hesitation now in talking to people. In the SHG meetings, even if there are conflicts, I am able to discuss the details and help in the decision-making process.
PARTICIPANT 8	"Earlier, I had no idea how to come out of the situation."	"The training in marketing was very useful, and I am able to move from Jamkhandi to Mudhol and Alaguru as well".	"I go alone and buy legumes. For selling, I go to the santhe alone. I know the price of the legumes and am able to buy from the wholesale market. I go alone to buy from the wholesale market."
PARTICIPANT 9	"Many problems were there. Money was the problem. Space was a problem, and people in the neighborhood also gave trouble."	"Initially, several problems were solved during my discussions with CSA members. We were trained well in goat rearing."	"......even now, I am facing several problems; I am able to think through these problems. I am able to talk to others about these issues related to this business."
PARTICIPANT 10	"The troubles we had in the family were so serious."	"My mother-in-law is a coolie. While coming back from work, she brings fodder for the animals. She supports me in this business. I never used to have money for myself."	"Earlier, I could not speak in the sangha. I was frightened. I feel so much more courage. I could not manage basic accounts. I go to the bank and deposit everyone's money. I manage household expenses".

5.1. Cross-Case Analysis

This analysis was carried out by combining the individual cases and deriving the subthemes and themes from the codes. Hybrid coding and thematic analysis were carried out based on the theoretical framework and the inductive process of analysing the transcripts.

Themes and Sub-Themes

Theme 1: Disadvantaged status	*Sub-themes* Social status Education status Financial status

The strategic approach to working with disadvantaged women was to adopt the SHA approach, which was primarily designed to identify the marginalized and poor people in the communities and build their capacities to participate equally in society. The poverty reduction strategies were designed to target individuals who are socially excluded, marginalized, vulnerable, and disadvantaged.

The process of empowering people through livelihood promotion activities is based on the philosophy of human rights and is a very important tool in the development sector. The impoverished women are given clear pathways to emancipate themselves. The first theme that was distilled was to showcase the dire circumstances from where these women began this journey.

The sample consists of five married women living with their husbands and who have found support from their spouses. They speak of the dire circumstances they were living in ……*earlier it was a tough situation. To tell you the truth, the family was in a critical state with only one person working as a coolie....* (P-1 mother of three). All of them recollected the poverty they faced in the early days and the critical condition that the families faced. "*...earlier, it was difficult to save 50 Rs (P-5 from the Devdasi tradition).* The process of empowering these women is essential for developmental changes to occur. Unless these women were taught to contribute and discover their strengths and potential, there was no way out for impoverished families. CSA, therefore, decided to use its vast network of SHG groups to identify and support these women who were in dire need. A process was initiated in the SHG groups to recommend one of the women who had to transition through a tough life situation and needed the support of a well-designed livelihood promotion intervention.

Adding to their poor financial status was the poor educational status of these women. None of them was educated beyond basic schooling, which could have made them employable. The social and economic situation of the families forced these women to give up education and remain unemployed or rely on unskilled low, paying jobs. *"..... Neither of us had an education. We barely knew about reading a passbook.* (P2, coolie woman who started rearing goats). The vicious nature of the circumstances in which they lived and existed with multiple oppressive factors is evident in the words of the disabled participant.

"..... My brother took me out of school and made me sit at home. I could not attend college because of the distance, and my brother was not willing to let me use the bus. Even though ICICI bank was willing to give me training, my family refused to send me. Then I wanted to get training in ITI. My brother had to fill out the form. I was not sure about getting trained till my brother filled out the form. (P3, disabled)

Two of them were widowed and were taking care of the children and working in unskilled jobs. They speak of the untold miseries in bringing up children and sending them to school. "There *was a huge problem. Nobody would help us with a single rupee. We had to earn and eat (survive). Things were very critical at home. Only my mother was working. My father would not earn enough, just enough to manage himself. We were four daughters, and my mother had to manage alone. (P3. 26-year disabled person).*

Two of the participants come from the Devadasi tradition. This is one of the most heinous practices where young girls are dedicated to gods. This practice has degenerated into prostitution, and the victims suffer many forms of humiliation. These two participants had come out of this tradition but were looking for support to strengthen their resolve. The loan given by CSA and active participation in the SHG group has played a significant role in the empowerment of these women.

Theme 2 Transition	Sub-themes
	1. SHG participation
	2. Loan scheme
	3. Meetings with CSA members
	4. Training
	5. Livelihood choice

This theme has significance in understanding the strategy of CSA in undertaking empowerment activities and working with disadvantaged women as part of the philosophy of CSA and Christ University.

The second theme that emerged from the data was the transitioning process and the events and processes that it involved. The key sub-theme seems to be their membership of the SHG and their active participation in them. All of them tell the transforming effects the SHG meetings had in their lives. *"........The sangha meetings were important. They (CSA staff) would come and talk to us, and they also trained us in rearing goats. When we had problems with keeping the goats, the CSA members helped us in finding space to keep them"* (P2, coolie). There is a reiteration from all the participants about the services provided by CSA staff in training them and supporting them. All of them have undergone training provided by the staff of CSA. These sessions were pitched on the technical aspects of the business undertaken. Besides, they were trained in financial matters, and everyone knew the financial transaction their business would entail. *".... participation in the SHG meetings was very helpful. I go to the bank and carry out all the transactions. I know about earning and saving. I received training about all this. I learnt to manage bank transactions through my participation in the SHG meetings'* (P3, disabled person). *".... CSA gave a lot of training. SHG members gave a lot of support"* (P8, widowed, worked as coolie).

The intervention that CSA designed was to provide a loan of 10.000 Rs and support the women in choosing the business. They were continuously followed up, and support was lent throughout the initial stages. During the meetings, the strategies for choosing a particular business were discussed, and each individual was supported in choosing an appropriate business. *"We felt goats would be easier. Having buffaloes would have been difficult. As both of us were going out for coolie work, the goats would graze and look after themselves"* (P2, coolie). The SHG groups, CSA staff, and the families were supportive in visualising the needs of the business with the potential that individuals already have. The strategy was to utilize their strengths *"Many of our people make this trade...our land also has water and fodder. I was comfortable with the idea of doing this business"* (P4, unemployed earlier). The circumstances that the women came from were studied thoroughly, discussions were held, and decisions were made. *"........we never knew any other trade. We had no land, we decided to buy goats"* (P7, Devadasi background).

The services provided by CSA in designing the project based on the need analysis and the monitoring and follow-up services reinforced the will that the women had shown in starting a business to support the family and benefit from it at the individual and family levels.

Theme 3 Initial problems	Subthemes
	Fears
	Barriers
	Poor community support

Despite all the efforts to start their businesses and come out of precarious situations, the women report several initial problems. These problems caused doubts and fears in them. The field staff of CSA and the SHG groups was supportive in overcoming these and helping the woman in continuing their endeavour. These problems were different for different participants. *"Many problems were there. Money was the problem. Space was a problem, and people in the neighbourhood also gave trouble.* (P 9, widowed with five children). Several of them recall the hostile attitude of the community and the condescending attitude that was displayed in the earlier days. After the initial successes, the women were accepted by the communities, and their efforts were acknowledged. "*.......Others did not believe in this endeavour. There was a negative attitude. Earlier, we had a problem with money, a place for the buffaloes and support from others in the family and the community*" (P4, mother of two). The business required goodwill in the community, and the participants found it difficult to build this initially. The ill will and the discriminatory approach are evident from the words of the disabled participant "(People said) *With one leg how will she work the sewing machine? People gave me a lot of trouble. They were unwilling to give their clothes." (P 3, disabled).* "*Getting customers was a problem. Took me time to understand all the issues related to this business*" (P8, widowed, coolie).

The earlier fears of handling the business were many. These women had never ventured into the world or met people. They had to find the strength to overcome these issues. In the empowerment process, the stage of self-discovery and the belief in the self is an important milestone. Women overcome their fears and develop courage as part of this process. Their thirst to prove others wrong and to reassure themselves of their self-worth is clear from the data.

Specifically, the fear of handling money for the first time in their lives and the fear of failure used to haunt the participants. *"I would shiver to handle 500 Rs. I was asked to keep accounts in the SHG, and I was very frightened that I would make mistakes. They asked me to maintain the record book. I have made mistakes, but I received support and corrections from the SHG members and the CSA staff." (P3, disabled)*

One of the main themes in feminist political ecology highlights that these barriers are caused by gendered knowledge, where there is differential access for women to knowledge, training, and a supportive environment to learn. It becomes critical to raise awareness in matters of money and to deal with customers. This has to be done before and during the capacity-building activities undertaken (Deere & León (2001). The process of having access to and ownership of resources and learning to utilize them is what leads to 'iterative change' (Agarwal, 1994; Goldman et al., 2016). It has been found that empowerment is the result of going through the process of obtaining natural resources, training, and support that lead to women realizing their rights. NGOs, such as the CSA, use various approaches for empowerment and helping women claim access to tangible and intangible resources.

Theme 4 Change at the individual level	*Sub-themes* Confidence Self-esteem Mobility Ability to Meet with various people/organizations

Several scholars have highlighted changes that occur at the individual level could constitute an important element of the entire empowerment process. At the level of the personal, several sub-themes emerged, such as confidence, self-esteem, the capacity to move outside the house independently, and the ability to meet people and visit organizations alone and speak for oneself. From the cultural context where these women come from, these attributes are quite unheard of. Women are usually homebound, and their interaction with the outside world and meeting strangers, especially those who do not belong to the family circle and conducting business with them is not a common occurrence. The process of starting micro-enterprises and running the business opened several vistas to these women. "B*esides milk, I am now selling curd, butter, and ghee, and I learned to produce these products and sell them to my customers. I decided to prepare all these at home. I am not dependent on anyone. People recognize me as a person who is doing business. My skill at doing this business had enhanced." (P4, mother of two children).* The management of enterprises and the process of conducting the business have triggered several changes, and the women recount how the processes undertaken as part of the business have helped in the transition process. *"I go alone and buy legumes. For selling, I go to the santhe (village fair) alone. I know the price of the legumes and am able to buy them from the wholesale* *market. Even here I go alone to buy at the wholesale market" (P8 widow who worked as a collie).*

One of the sub-themes that emerged and was noticed repeatedly was mobility. They report with pride that they can move out of the house independently and travel to different places such as banks, gram sabha meetings, and schools. The ability to travel alone and face the related challenges of answering questions from strangers and connecting effectively was imbibed by these women, along with their ability to run the business effectively. *"I attend panchayat meetings. I got a machine from the panchayat. I know all about the government facilities, and I can use them. I am also a member of the SDMC, I attend all the meetings."* (P3, disabled women). The ability to talk at different meetings and get the business done is reflected in the words of a participant. *"I became more aware of doing this business. A lot of information was shared with us, and I began networking with people. I did not know how to talk to people. I started meeting different people. I have no hesitation now in talking to people. In the SHG meetings, even if there are conflicts, I am able to discuss the details and help in the decision-making process.* (P7, participant who belonged to the devadasi tradition). Women who belonged to depressed communities, like those who belong to the tradition of devadasi, seem to have been greatly impacted by the livelihood intervention. They are now able to survive without their traditional occupation. In spite of having come out of the traditional occupation, they were pushed to extreme poverty because of their illiteracy and lack of fruitful occupations. In the words of another woman from a similar background,

> *"I realize that only when we have confidence, we can grow. I used to take a lot of loans and struggle. I have no fear now, and I give money to others. I feel I will not go wrong. I discussed this with my sons and asked them to be brave and surge ahead. Even when they hesitate, I push them to do more. I have learned to talk business with different shopkeepers; I can converse with different people about business. I have got one son and a daughter married. Another son, I have got educated."*
>
> *(P5, women from the tradition of devadasi)*

The impact on socially distressed women in dire financial need was higher. The ability to run a socially approved business and to bring up children and get them married is something unheard of within this community. It takes a lot of courage and grit to transition from the traditional vicious web and settle the lives of children in a normal fashion. The changes at the level of the individual have changed the outlook of women and helped them challenge society's norms.

A sense of equality and personal growth is also evident. *"These days I go ahead with my ideas and inform my family later. Today I don't need my family's permission to receive an order from customers. From someone who stayed at home and managed cooking for the family, I am managing money that I have earned and the money from the SHG (P3, disabled and unmarried).*

Similar observations are also made by married women who share the burden of running the family with the husband," schooling *decisions are completely left to me. I independently handle them. I am also able to help my husband in the business. When people come to meet him, I can join in the discussions. Even when he is absent, I can talk to the customers independently.* (P6, partner in her husband's business). All of them speak of the courage they feel now to face life's challenges and the confidence they have gained to handle new situations." *Because of the insights I have gained, I want to try tailoring or have a bangle shop. I am confident that I can do this. I want to learn and do. Earlier I could not speak in the sangha. I was frightened. I feel so much more courage" (P10, young mother who was unemployed).*

Developing a sense of self, a sort of personal empowerment which is not dependent on others, is something internal that poor women can develop and strengthen. This rests within the individual herself. All participants of this study credit self-awareness as a turning point in their life, the first time that they thought, or had the license to think, about themselves and their potential. (Paterson, 2008).

Theme 5 Relational empowerment	*Sub-themes* Position within the family Decision-making within families Participation in household matters

Empowerment also included the position of the woman in relation to other significant members of her life. In this chapter, it would mean husbands, in-laws and children, and sometimes the entire family. In the context of patriarchy, the limits to women's empowerment are frequently hinted at. Her participation in decision-making, the concern shown by others for her growth, and the perceived enhancement in her position in the family form part of relational empowerment. These were the sub-themes that emerged in this study. Previous studies have spoken about the decision-making in relation to the schooling of children, and the responsibility related to this is completely transferred to the women. *"My daughter is six years now, and my husband discussed her schooling with me. He wanted my opinion about her education"* (P4, mother of two). The additional money has helped the family to choose better schooling options for the children, and this is completely dependent on the women to bring in extra money into the family. *"Children were going to a government school. We decided to send them to private schools as we had money to pay their fees"* (P6, woman who invested in her husband's business).

The participants speak of the respect they receive from significant others within the family. They perceive this as an enhancement of their position within the family from a marginalized position. Women participants representing different stages of the life cycle have reported this. *"Today, my relationship with my husband has changed. If I forget something related to the sangha, he reminds me, He listens to our sangha discussions, and I believe he is happy that I am learning about these issues"* (P2, illiterate, who used to work as a coolie*)*. Another elderly woman with grandchildren also expresses similar sentiments" *respect at home has increased both my sons and daughters-in-law are showing respect and support me in my decisions. When I discuss with them, they listen to my views."*

The economic independence these women have shown has changed the perception of others within the family. From dependence to a position of contributing to the family's well-being has changed the attitude of others, especially those placed in a traditional position of opposition, like daughters-in-law and male members of the family.

The change in decision-making processes that some women were able to facilitate within their families is evident in the accounts presented. Kabeer and Subrahmanian (1996) write that poor and marginalized women are often dependent on relationships of patronage of the male members of the family rather than a sense of equality within the family to ensure their survival. Scholars have observed that claiming autonomy and independence for themselves has led to defining their own priorities. This has often resulted in 'sacrificing the protection of hierarchical familial relationships. Surmounting this and claiming respect from within the family and interactions on an equal footing becomes very important in the empowerment process.

Women have to work on developing support within their own families. There are examples of people's families becoming their strongest supporters - even in the face of intense community opposition. This is evident in the case of both the Devadasi participants. Though the site of women's empowerment is within themselves, they have also developed increasing channels of support from within their families. In several cases, these involve the male members of the family, such as sons, husbands, and brothers.

Theme 6 Societal empowerment	Sub-themes
	Repayment
	Role model
	Willingness to support others
	Collaborate with SHG members
	Business expansion
	Change in society's attitude

The third relevant dimension has been the empowerment of women from the point of view of society. Their position and contribution to the larger community. All the participants have repaid their loans. The result of the livelihood enterprise has been the enhancement of their family's income and the upward mobility of the family. Several of them very poignantly say that now they can give loans to others, and the neighbours no longer avoid them. They have become an inspiration to others and are playing an active role in empowering others and showing them ways to transform their lives. They acknowledge the role of the SHGs in their lives and wish to support other members of the SHGs." *My own sangha members have asked questions about this business. They have several queries about the business. Many sangha members have now started rearing goats. In fact, people from the other sanghas have also contacted me and started this business".* (P2, mother of two) In a few cases, it is seen that they have taken part in social action movements and fought society's attitudes and managed to change a few practices. *I was part of the social action movement when I participated in the movement to get the liquor shop closed. It was near the school; we fought and got it closed."* During the process, the participant learned to network with officials *"I know the social welfare officer, child development probationary officer, and the panchayat development officer." I think I can talk to MLA and MP if the need arises."* (P7, Belongs to the tradition of Devadasis)

This participant goes on to talk about how she inspired a group of devadasis to come out of this tradition and her continued efforts in this area.

"*Earlier, we had no respect. We formed a group and prayed to God. We made a pledge to stop the devadasi practice, and we have eradicated it. It was a stigma, and we were disgusted. Today we are living a life outside this practice, and people, including the police, respect us. I have grown beyond that; both the children are educated.*"

(P7, woman from the Devadasi tradition)

The most telling subtheme has been the confidence they show to expand their business, partner with others and offer employment to other disadvantaged families. One participant speaks of a family of an alcoholic, which she wants to support and teach the women of that family to start a microenterprise. The deep empathy for the situation of other families and their sense of responsibility to support them and train others is also evident in several instances. *"Now I have a few buffaloes, and I want to buy more and partner with my sangha members to build a large shed. They have great confidence in my skills in dealing with the buffaloes as well as the customers' (P 4, mother of two)*. It is put more succinctly by another participant *"I think partnerships are good for business. A lot of learning is possible when we are together. I would like to train other young girls and school dropouts on business processes. I can give employment and train girls to become self-employed.* (P3, disabled women).

The need to expand their horizons and build their businesses further will be another important expression of societal empowerment. Besides the confidence required, this reflects their wish to grow as entrepreneurs. Enhancing a woman's ability to contribute to a community is to be seen as an important sign of the development of the community. Equal participation in the processes of a community is also a significant sign of empowerment.

To summarize the various accounts presented above, it can be said that **nothing feeds and frees like money.** To the research participants, microfinance seems to have provided a ground for transformation to economic and social independence. For microfinance to effectively contribute to women's empowerment, it has to also facilitate a deep sense of awareness and discovery of their own potential. This will lead to greater relational empowerment. From being a dependent member to an active contributor to the family's resources, along with consistently showing growth and evolution, will earn women appreciation from the significant players in her life. The changes in the family's finances and the contribution of the woman to this have projected her as a role model. It is to be also remembered in culturally backward communities when women join women dominated SHGs and participate enthusiastically, social acceptance is higher. Business, which runs within the home and with the support of family, is also culturally more acceptable.

6. Conclusion

Drawing out the main findings of the study, we find that women in these small businesses believe that microfinance helped them tide over the everyday shortage of money to meet needs without having to ask their husbands/fathers/brothers for money. All these women have found this very liberating. They find this exhilarating, and it gives them a sense of independence. Compared to the earlier days, this has enhanced the self-confidence and esteem of women. Considering the success seen in this project site, CSA can use the model of empowerment in other centres.

The semi-literate status never allowed these women an opportunity to venture out of the confines of their homes earlier. This is changed, and women report their ability to move outside their homes freely and confidently. The increasing income indicates economic independence, which is most certainly a precursor for development and empowerment. The indicators of empowerment: (i) economic independence (ii) making decisions (iii) mobility outside the house(iv) ownership of assets (v) making purchases; (vi) freedom from domination and making own choices (v) being self-reliant are all clearly evident in the account presented in this chapter. Mayoux (2011) felt the process of microfinance has the potential to trigger positive outcomes in the lives of women. This chapter speaks of these outcomes related to resource accessibility, agency, and achievement and the choice that women made to usher great changes in their lives.

References

Agarwal, B. (1994). Gender and command over property: A critical gap in economic analysis and policy in South Asia. *World Development*, 22(10), 1455-1478. https://doi.org/10.1016/0305-750x(94)90031-0.

Ayres, L., Kavanaugh, K., and Knafl, K. A. (2003). Within-case and across-case approaches to qualitative data analysis. *Qualitative Health Research*, 13(6), 871- 883. https://doi.org/10.1177/1049732303013006008.

Cernea, M. M. (2008). Compensation and benefit-sharing : Why resettlement policies and practices must be reformed. *Water Science and Engineering*, 1(1), 89-120. https://doi.org/10.1016/s1674-2370(15)30021-1.

Chully and Hemalatha, K. (2017). Preventing Risks to population displacement: Defining Models of Educational Action. Centre for publications, Christ University.

Deere, C. D., and Leon, M. (2001). Who owns the land ? Gender and land-titling programmes in Latin America. *Journal of Agrarian Change*, 1(3), 440-467. https://doi.org/10.1111/1471-0366.00013.

Eiden, A., Kowertz, D., Steiner, G., Frey, I., Grothe, L., Beyer, S., and Janissen, S. (2014). *The self-help group approach manual*. Kindernothilfe e.V.

Goldman, M. J., Davis, A., and Little, J. (2016). Controlling land they call their own: Access and women's empowerment in northern Tanzania. *The Journal of Peasant Studies*, 43(4), 777-797. https://doi.org/10.1080/03066150.2015.1130701.

Huis, M. A., Hansen, N., Otten, S., and Lensink, R. (2017). A three-dimensional model of women's empowerment: Implications in the Field of Microfinance and futures directions. *Frontiers in Psychology*, 8, https://doi.org/10.3389/fpsyg.2017.01678.

IBEF (2012). Economic survey of Karnataka 2011-2012. India brand equity foundation, https://www.ibef.org/download/Karnataka-260912.pdf.

Kabeer, N., and Subrahmanian, R. (1996). *Institutions, relations and outcomes: Framework and tools for gender-aware planning* (Vol. 357). Brighton : Institute of Development Studies.

Kabeer, N. (1999). Resources, agency, achievements: Reflections on the measurement of women's empowerment. *Development and Change*, 30(3), 435-464. https://doi.org/10.1111/1467-7660.00125.

Kar, S., and Pradhan, A. (2018). Women empowerment in India. *Globus An International Journal of Management & IT*, 9(2), 1-11.

Karnataka.gov.in (2016) District profile Bagalkote. http://apfstatic.s3.ap-south-1.amazonaws.com/s3fs- public/Karnataka_ Bagalkot. pdf? n_bB53i5buDsuka2uabTUQGDo1dc_C.P.

Mayoux, L. (2011). Taking gender seriously: Towards a gender justice protocol for financial services. *The Handbook of Microfinance*, 613-641. https://doi.org/10.1142/9789814295666_0028.

Paterson, R. (2008). Women's empowerment in challenging environments: A case study from Balochistan. *Development in Practice*, 18(3), 333-344. https://doi.org/10.1080/09614520802030383.

Sen, A. (2000) Population and Gender Equity. *The Nation*. 2000.

United Nations (2009). 2009 World Survey on the Role of Women in Development: Women's Control over economic resources and Access to financial resources, including Microfinance. United Nations Publications.

World Bank (2012). World Development Report 2012 : Gender Equality and Development. World Bank. https://openknowledge.worldbank.org/ handle/10986/4391.

Chapter 4

Context Matters: A Case Study of Community Development Approaches in Tribal Areas

M. Maya[*]
Department of Sociology and Social Work, Christ University, Bengaluru, India

Abstract

Tribal development initiatives aim to address aspects of marginality covering educational, occupational, social and political dimensions. A review of literature on the challenges in effective tribal development discusses narrow vision, implementation strategy, the attitude of people involved in the implementation and lack of community participation as hindrances in realising the desired goals. This chapter explores the need to have a context-specific approach to realise the community development goals in tribal areas considering the cultural and economic diversity of Scheduled Tribes in India. A single embedded case study has been used to understand tribal development initiatives in the three project sites, namely Manikgarh, Maharashtra; Bastar, Chhatisgarh and Niravilpuzha, Kerala. All these projects aim at the overall development of the community either through a child-centred approach or through a self-help approach. A constructive outcome-based evaluation model has been used in analysing the developmental approach, and in-depth interviews and FGDs were conducted with the project staff. An attempt has been made to study the impact on direct beneficiaries at micro, meso and macro levels. It explores the ways in which universities could become change agents through socially responsible engagements in tribal areas. This chapter would contribute towards developing a social responsibility model for other universities to emulate.

---

[*] Corresponding Author's Email: maya.m@christuniversity.in.

In: Models for Social Responsibility Action by Higher Education Institutions
Editors: Joseph Chacko Chennattuserry, Elangovan N. et al.
ISBN: 979-8-89113-097-5
© 2024 Nova Science Publishers, Inc.

Keywords: scheduled tribes, child-centered development, self-help approach, community development, constructive outcome evaluation, social responsibility model, SDG-1

1. Introduction

Scheduled Tribes (STs) are considered to be one of the marginalised sections of the population, and welfare measures for them are a constitutional obligation in India. In spite of the interventions since independence, both by the government as well as by non-government organisations, the conditions of marginality still remain the same for most of the tribal communities in India. A significant amount of research studies is also emerging in the domain of tribal studies and development studies. However, the question is about the gap between the texts of development and acts of development. It is often the lack of disconnect between theory and praxis that affects the attitude of academicians, policymakers and practitioners. This chapter explores a model of social responsibility at Christ, Deemed to be University, India, which has a critical engagement with issues of marginalised, especially the scheduled tribes, in its curricula and also provisions for students to have experiential learning through the community tribal development initiatives implemented by its wing, centre for social action (CSA).

2. Review of Literature

It is recognised that STs remain one of the poorest populations in India. According to the fourth round of the National Family Health Survey (NFHS-4), 45.9 percent of the scheduled tribe population in India suffer from poverty. It also highlights the extreme levels of malnutrition and higher rates of Maternal Mortality Rate (MMR), Infant Mortality Rate (IMR) and stunted growth of children in this category (IIPS, 2017). All these indicators are very crucial to a developmental plan for the nation. In order to realise the Sustainable Development Goal (SDG-1) of eradicating all forms of extreme poverty, we need to have a concrete strategy for addressing aspects of poverty and malnutrition among STs by helping them to have a stable economic base which is sustainable.

Special emphasis has been given to tribal development since independence. Article 275 of the Indian Constitution ensures special budgetary provisions for tribal development through special assistance to the state and union territories and also for better administration in the scheduled areas. Although the budgetary allocation for tribal development in the first three five-year plans was minimal, special emphasis on this was initiated from the fifth five-year plan onwards. Along with the efforts by government agencies, there are quite a large number of Non-Governmental Organisations (NGOs) working in the tribal areas and contributing significantly to the welfare of tribals. The idea of a partnership between a government organisation and a non-governmental organisation (GO-NGO) is also considered to be an effective strategy for development initiatives, especially in the post-1990 period (Thamminaina, 2018).

However, the efforts over seven decades since independence are yet to showcase a visible outcome in terms of reducing poverty and enhancing the overall welfare of STs across India. The tribal communities are still at varying levels of economic development and marginalisation. Based on the notified list of STs in the states and union territories, there are around 745 different tribal communities (GoI, 2021) spread across the country, and together, they constitute 8.6 percent of the national population (MTA, 2017). These communities vary widely in terms of socio-cultural practices, occupation, economic conditions, political representation and other aspects of marginalisation. Among these 745 communities, there are 75 tribal communities which are categorised as Particularly Vulnerable Tribal Groups (PVTG) as they experience a much deeper level of marginalisation owing to their subsistence level of the economy, pre-agricultural level of technology, extremely low literacy and a stagnant or declining population. There are tribal communities converted to other religions and having a high level of interaction with the non-tribal population. Many a time, they would have a more advantageous position to reap the benefits of the affirmative policies of the government for STs.

Studies that look into the problems and issues involved in tribal development initiatives have sighted various reasons like the neglect of tribal areas in spite of constitutional provisions, inadequate administrative machinery (Mahapatra, 1994), inadequate fund allocation and excessive politicisation (Srivatsava,1998), unequal distribution of infrastructural facilities, especially for agriculture and depletion of resource base (Goel & Vasisht, 1992), lack of proper communication (Kulkarni,1980), benefits being cornered by tribal elites (Vaid, 2003) and, lack of coordination between government and local community (Mahapatra, 1994).

So, while planning for an effective tribal development initiative, one needs to keep in mind the diversity within as well as the issue of the benefits being cornered among the 'tribal elites.' This chapter explores how an understanding of the 'context', or the specific social background is essential to have a sustainable community development programme in tribal areas to realise the SDG goal of eradicating poverty.

3. Methodology

This chapter is a qualitative study using a single embedded case study design and explores the tribal development experiences of three project sites of CSA, the community development wing of Christ University, namely Manikgarh, Maharashtra; Bastar, Chhattisgarh and Niravilpuzha, Kerala. All these projects aim at the overall development of the community either through a child-centred approach or through a self-help approach. A constructive outcome-based evaluation model has been used in analysing the developmental approach. In-depth interviews were conducted with key informants from each of these sites to understand how the project is being implemented. At the second level, interviews were conducted with the field staff, and three FGDs were conducted with beneficiaries to understand the impact of these interventions at the micro, meso and macro levels. Based on the data collected from the field and an analysis of project reports, context specificity has been explored. Data collected were analysed thematically. University ethical clearance was taken prior to the study and followed all ethical guidelines. In order to understand the social responsibility of the university towards the marginalised tribal communities, interviews were conducted with CSA staff as well as faculty facilitating field exposure to students. A model was thus formulated which could be emulated by any other university.

4. Results

A child-centred approach keeps the child as the foci while taking decisions about their lives and works in partnership with them and their families. Along with equipping children with adequate skills and capabilities for effective participation, it creates awareness and sensitivity among adults about the needs, priorities and potentials of children (Auriat et al., 2001). For long-term sustainable community development, empowerment of children is very crucial, and therefore, the entry-level activity would be educational support to the needy children in terms of supply of learning materials, constant guidance and motivation through community-level learning centres as well as through additional skill-building sessions. At the next level, the needs of the family of these children are addressed. The focus could be on collective efforts to address social problems like alcoholism or domestic violence and on efforts to enhance the economic condition of the family. Initiatives could be employment generation activities, skilling and training on savings.

This approach was employed in the Manikgarh region, which is a completed project and is currently followed in Niravilpuzha, which is a project in its initial phase. Manikgarh hills in the Chandrapur district of Maharashtra was one of the poorest pockets inhabited by the tribal communities of Kolam, Gond, the nomadic group of Banjaras and a few members of Mang and Mahar who belong to the Scheduled Casts (SCs). Community development was introduced by the Center for Social Action (CSA) in the 24 hamlets in the year 2009. Among these, ten hamlets were exclusively Gond regions; five hamlets belonged to the Kolam tribes, and two were Banjara hamlets. Among the rest, except in five hamlets which were exclusively for SCs, others had mixed populations. However, extreme poverty was something common to all the hamlets.

The indigenous tribes in this region were Kolam, who are regarded as one of the PVTGs, and they were into cultivation. They account for 11 percent of the population in Manikgarh Hills. Gonds are a significant tribal community in central India, and they constitute 40 percent of the population in this region. Gonds are into agriculture and are more enterprising than the Kolams. Banjaras were a nomadic group who migrated from the Marathwada region and settled here. They constitute 16 percent of the population and have a relatively improved socio-economic and political status. Mangs and Mahar are deprived communities who used to engage in scavenging, repairing shoes and preparing leather products. Because of the nature of the occupation, they were considered untouchables, and many of them were moving away from their traditional occupation. Because of the unique cultural practices and identity, all these five groups have settled at a distance from one another in and around the same hamlets.

In order to initiate the community development programme in this region, CSA used the child-centric approach (Figure 1). The focus was on the educational and nutritional well-being of children. Activities were introduced at the schools and anganwadis, and had sought active support from the primary health centres. The provision of learning materials and learning support through tuition/ activity centres motivated the students, and it had an impact on the educational advancement of children. The second phase was to reach out to the families of children and then at the community level.

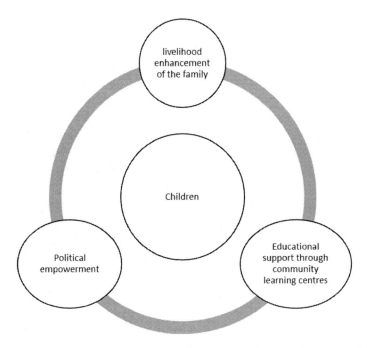

Figure 1. Child-centric model of community development.

During the five years of the project, the important issues which were addressed with the help of the community included lack of employment opportunities, lack of irrigation facilities, poor agricultural productivity, higher rate of seasonal migration, lack of infrastructure at schools, poor quality of education, drop- out rate, especially for girl children, functioning of the anganwadis, lack of health facilities, malnutrition, poor infrastructure and ineffective Panchayati raj institutions.

The high level of chronic poverty in this region was mainly due to small land holdings, infertile land, poor agricultural productivity and lack of livelihood opportunities. People also were not aware of government schemes and the modalities to get them. Severe malnutrition and other health issues were affecting both women as well as children. Lack of adequate staffing at schools, along with the medium of interaction, resulted in a lack of motivation for children to be at school. For instance, children of *Kolam* tribes were unable to follow either Marathi or Hindi.

Although the health awareness programmes had some positive changes in the health-seeking behaviour of people in this region, their impact is not similar among all categories of people (Figure 2). For instance, members of *the Kolam* community still prefer to keep themselves away from institutional delivery and vaccinations. It was also difficult to make a behavioural modification among all these communities to completely stop the practice of open defecation. Inter-tribal differences were a major problem which affected people's participation in public health issues. Due to the continued efforts, child malnutrition was reduced to 4.7 percent (from 8 percent prior to the project launch) by the end of the project period.

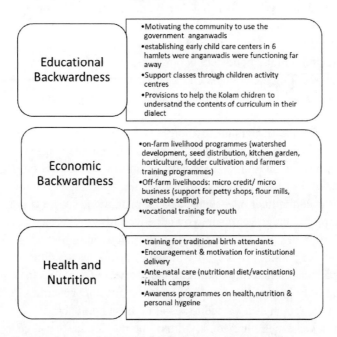

Figure 2. Community Development Initiatives at Manikgarh region.

In order to strengthen the economic base of the community, a range of on-farm and off-farm livelihood programmes were introduced. On-farm programmes like watershed development programmes in 12 hamlets, distribution of seeds, fertilisers and pesticides, promotion of kitchen gardens in all the 24 hamlets, distribution of fruit trees and farmers training in 21 hamlets helped to have an increase in crop yield and income of the farmers. Knowledge of improved techniques not just helped the farmers to have more yield but also reduced the migration of marginal farmers for work. However, there was no effort to identify and promote traditional crops, and many farmers preferred to cultivate cash crops like soybean and cotton. Exploitation by money lenders is another challenge. Around ten different kinds of income generational activities were promoted as non-farm livelihood initiatives. Financial support was given to buy goats, to start grocery shops, garment shops, vegetable selling, bangle selling and flour mills. Such initiatives were primarily beneficial to the landless people and the differently abled people.

Vocational training was given to the youth in nursing (ANM and GNM), and all of them are working in different hospitals. Mobile repairing and computer courses helped a very small percentage of a youngster to gain employment, but most of them have entered other jobs like operating JCBs (earth movers), which provide them with more income. Among adolescent girls who received tailoring training, around 35 percent use that skill for earning. Training in the honey collection appears to be more benefitting, and the tribals are selling the collected honey to a nearby NGO.

Formation of Community-Based Organisations (CBOs), which took almost three years to be fully functional in all the settlements, helped the community to take ownership of their welfare and the gradual exit of the external agency from the project site. One of the major challenges is the large-scale illiteracy among the community members. A federation has been established with the representatives of self-help groups and village development committees. Capacity-building programmes were conducted for CBO members to empower them to own the welfare activities in the area after the withdrawal of CSA from the project site. Networking with a number of agencies in the public, private, ad voluntary sectors was another strategy to help ensure the sustainability of development-oriented activities in the region. The community is motivated to continue the income generation activities initiated in the region as it helped to sustain the economic base.

Similarly, the CSA project in Niravilpuzha, Kerala, is a recent project initiated a year ago. This region has members of two PVTGs, namely *Kurichias* and *Kattunaikars,* as well as another tribal community *Paniya*. Each of these tribal groups has its own unique cultural identity. As an entry-level activity, the project team focused on the school to provide additional learning support. However, the ongoing COVID-19 pandemic affected the project as schools were closed. So currently, the project is limited to a *paniya* settlement where they have started a learning centre to help the children.

On the other hand, the self-help approach is employed in the Bastar region. There are 34 villages in the Pakhanjore tehsil of Kanker district in the Chhattisgarh state of India. This Bastar region is inhabited predominantly by tribal communities *Gonds, Oraons* and *Halbi*. Three are also a few families belonging to SC and OBC communities. *Gonds* are the original primitive tribal communities in this region, and *Oraons* are the migrated tribals from the eastern part of Chhatisgarh. Due to the long period of missionary activities in the region, most of the *Oraons* are converted to Christianity, and the *Halbi* consider Christians as lower caste. Due to the cultural differences, the relationship between *Gonds* and *Oraons* is not very positive, and many a time, the inter-tribal conflict between them impedes welfare activities.

A community development project was introduced in this region in 2017, initially for a period of three years which was further extended to another two years. The 34 villages are divided into four clusters, and there are 71 self-help groups with the participation of around 910 women. The self-help approach as a strategy ensures the holistic development of women and children. The interventions could be broadly categorised into three aspects, namely economic, social and political (Figure 3).

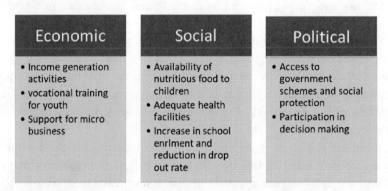

Figure 3. Community Development Activities in the Bastar Region.

The formation of women's self-help groups was the first phase in this area. However, out of the 81 SHGs, only 71 are functional, as the community members in some hamlets feel that they should be part of the government-run

SHGs to gain benefits. A culture of savings and microfinance is promoted through the SHGs, and the SHG fund is a great support for the group members in times of need. The SHG loan is distributed for the purpose of land development, goat rearing, fishery, grocery shop, vegetable business, flour mills and such small businesses. It is also benefitting agricultural farmers because instead of taking a loan from landlords or money lenders, they started taking loans through SHG members, which they could repay after harvest.

Training on agricultural techniques and other on-farm support services have improved crop yield, and farmers are slowly moving towards the cultivation of cash crops. At the cluster level, there are efforts to initiate collective cash crop farming, which may be more profitable. However, such initiatives are from the *Gonds*.

The economic independence of women, along with capacity-building sessions on goal setting, children's education, health, nutrition etc., have led to their social and political empowerment too. The impact is visible through the collective actions of women to fight against social evils like alcoholism and domestic violence. According to the beneficiaries, it is the stable income as well as the possibility to raise their voice against the hitherto personal or family issues that motivate them to be part of the SHGs.

Awareness about the welfare support mechanisms available and the modalities to achieve them is considered to be one of the major achievements of women. Being part of SHGs and the support from the project staff helped them to have good networking with various governmental agencies to negotiate for their legitimate rights. For instance, the ma Jagriti group in Junawar could reach out to the district administration to add left-out households of their village to the ration card/ card for public distribution system (PDS) issuance list. The same group has also filed an application at the District Collector's office to take action on their claims for individual forest rights under the Forest Rights Act (FRA), 2006. Similarly, the cluster-level association of Bethiya could evacuate the alcohol shop in Bethiya with the support of the police.

SHGs are also monitoring the educational support that their children receive, and according to one beneficiary, having the opportunity to visit government offices and see people there, she is motivated to provide a better education to her children.

SGs have also taken the initiative for the village development work. So far, accessible road connection was established in seven villages, four villages were electrified, and tube wells were installed in five villages to ensure drinking water. The political empowerment of women could be measured not just in terms of collective negotiations and actions. Eight women members have become members of village institutions, and this is a remarkable change in the area.

Although the ongoing pandemic, the inter-tribal rivalry and the presence of insurgent groups in a few villages have slowed down the pace of activities in this region, the self-help approach that considers women as the entry-level actors are having a lasting impact not just on their families but also to the community at large.

5. Discussion

In order to achieve the SDG goal of eradicating all forms of poverty from everywhere by 2030, the country needs to have concrete policies, especially for SCs and STs. It requires coordinated efforts to enhance access to basic services, social protection and building resilience against natural disasters that affect the resource base of these communities. Poverty is related to multiple levels of deprivation. It is often manifested in terms of diminished opportunities for education, inability to participate in decision-making at the political level as well as social discrimination. These become more acute in the case of STs, who form the poorest sections of the population in the country. The diversity of these categories of population in terms of social and economic conditions makes the interventions more challenging. Unless we have an empowerment strategy which helps them manage their own deprivations in a sustainable manner, the country cannot achieve its goal in a meaningful manner.

There are three ways of empowerment and social change, according to Ife (2013). It includes policy and planning, social and political action, education and consciousness-raising. This is very significant for a sustainable community development initiative. Empowerment through policy and planning could be achieved by developing structures and institutions to bring more equitable access to resources or services and opportunities to participate in the life of the community. Participation can also enable people to increase their power through some form of action that equips them to be more effective in the political arena. We also need empowerment through education and consciousness-raising because the broad-based education process equips people with the necessary knowledge and information. Such a process could enable the community to take ownership of the development in their region. The case study presented here highlights the manner in which the implementing agency, CSA, is trying to focus on these three dimensions so that they can exit from the projects once the empowerment of the beneficiaries attains in a meaningful manner.

Figure 4 narrates the understanding of poverty among scheduled tribes and shows how extreme poverty at the individual, familial or community level draws a community open to a development programme envisaged by an outside agency, and the possibilities of a stable economic base draw people together. The local community knew the rhythms of the community better, and having local members as project staff helped in mediating the inter-tribal differences in an amicable way so that the larger developmental goals were not compromised. In order to effectively address the issue of poverty and to ensure community development, four parameters are crucial, viz., livelihood or economic aspects, educational backwardness, political marginalisation and most importantly, the socio-cultural factors.

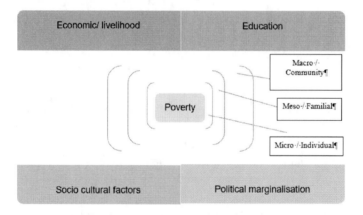

Figure 4. Understanding Poverty among Scheduled Tribes.

While discussing participatory development, Chambers (1997) considers participation as something that empowers the marginalised to challenge the power directly. According to Ghai (1990), participatory development should aim to empower the deprived and the excluded by enabling them through monopolistic political and economic structures. If we use the lens of Arnstein (1969), participation unlashes the power to achieve individual and collective social development and to influence structural reforms. This is clearly evident in the community development initiatives of CSA, especially in the Bastar region.

Martinussen (1997) views development as a culturally grounded process where the community becomes the primary agent of development 'from below.' Outsiders, including donors, researchers, or technocrats, can neither formulate objectives nor define what development is outside their own cultural sphere. In the three regions discussed in this chapter, there were multiple tribal groups residing in the same geographical area but maintaining their own identity, which is completely different from others. On a closer reading of their internal dynamics, one could observe a sense of social gradation amongst these different groups. A homogeneous action plan that is more general in nature will have differential acceptance and implications among diverse groups.

A higher education institution that has a strong commitment to enhancing its responsibility towards the marginalised sections of society would be following a two-pronged strategy. On one side, student social responsibility can be nurtured through critical reflections inbuilt into classroom transactions. Direct community engagement focusing on the sustainable development of marginalised groups, including tribal communities, is another strategy. In the model followed by Christ University (Figure 5), there is a possible synergy between these two. Exposure to the tribal development initiatives of the Center for Social Action (CSA), the community engagement wing of the university, through field visits and service-learning opportunities, helps the students to connect the theoretical discussions in class with empirical realities. Meaningful reflective learning in class facilitated by the teacher can help the students to understand the significance of 'context' while dealing with tribal issues. This knowledge and awareness can make the students informed about the uniqueness of each tribal community and their culture. The cultural competence thus gained will be an asset for them in their future engagement with these communities, and they also need to keep ethical values in mind.

The informed students then can either take up micro-level research projects for their dissertations or choose tribal areas for their internships or service-learning. We need to produce a more evidence-based understanding of how tribal communities perceive their developmental concerns and how they respond to community development initiatives. This would be beneficial for policy-making and effective NGO interventions. Culturally sensitive students and teachers can bridge this gap, and the orientation they get through the proposed model help in gaining better clarity. Thus, the socially responsible activities of the university in tribal areas will have a larger impact on universities becoming change agents, providing a vision and direction for tribal development.

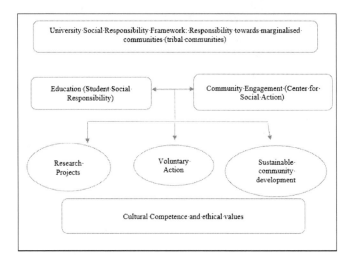

Figure 5. Model of Social Responsibility and Community Engagement for Universities.

Conclusion

If India needs to achieve the SDG goal of eradicating poverty, it needs to have specific strategies for different categories, including the tribal population. The case study clearly depicts certain challenges and also possibilities to achieve the national target in tribal areas. Each geographical area is unique in terms of the resource base and climate, and each tribal community is unique in its own way. Only an approach that takes into account the ground realities through people's active participation can resolve the issues. Often it is the lack of awareness and improper communication channels that make these categories more vulnerable to any economic or climatic shocks. Capacity-building initiatives need to be given priority at the community level so that community development initiatives would result in qualitative changes on a sustainable level. At the same time, knowledge of this should be included in the curricula with the larger goal of building a generation who are sensitive to the people in the margins. India is a country with over 700 tribal communities spread across the nation. Similar socially responsible models could be emulated by other universities too.

References

Arnstein, S. R. (1969). A ladder of citizen participation. *Journal of the American Institute of Planners,* 35(4), 216-224.

Auriat, N., Miljeteig, P., & Chawla, L..(2001). Overview - identifying best practices in children's participation. PLA Notes. Issue 42. The International Institute for Environment and Development (IIED). https://www.iied.org/sites/default/files/pdfs/migrate/G01958.pdf?

Chambers, R. (1997). Responsible well-being—A personal agenda for development. World Development, 25(11), 1743-1754.

Ghai, D. (1990). Participatory development: Some perspectives from grassroots experience. In *Trade, Planning and Rural* Development (pp. 79-115). Palgrave Macmillan.

Goel, S. K., & Vasisht, A. K. (1992). Discriminant Analysis of Agro-Economic. Development Indicators. for Tribal Areas In Hills and Plains. *Indian Journal of Agricultural Economics*, 27(3), 404-409.

GoI, (2021).State/Union Territory-wise list of Scheduled Tribes in India. The Ministry of Tribal Affairs, Government of India. https://tribal.nic.in/ST/LatestListofScheduledtribes.pdf

Ife, J. (2013). Community development in an uncertain world. Cambridge University Press.

IIPS (2017). National Family Health Survey (NFHS-4), 2015-16. International Institute for Population Sciences (IIPS). https://dhsprogram.com/pubs/pdf/fr339/fr339.pdf.

Kulkarni, S. D. (1980). Problems of tribal development in Maharashtra. Economic and Political Weekly, 1598-1600.

Mahapatra, L. K. (1994). Tribal development in India. Vikas Publishing House.

Martinussen, J. D. (1997). Introduction to the concept of human development. *In Integrated farming in human development: proceedings of a workshop*: March 25-29, 1996, Tune Landboskole, Denmark (p. 9). DSR Forlag.

MTA (2017) State / UT wise overall population, ST population, percentage of STs in India / State to total population of India / State and percentage of STs in the State to total ST population. The Ministry of Tribal Affairs. https://tribal.nic.in/ST/Statistics8518.pdf.

Srivastava, S. P. (Ed.). (1998). The development debate: Critical perspectives. Rawat Publications.

Thamminaina, A. (2018). Catalysts but Not Magicians: Role of NGOs in the Tribal Development. SAGE Open, 8(2), 2158244018785714.

Vaid, N. K. (2003). Tribals, anthropologists and social activists in India. *The Eastern Anthropologist*, 56(2-4), 449-456.

Chapter 5

Rendering Support for the Empowerment of Rural Women to Overcome Life Impediments

Om Prakash L.T.[1,*] and Ambrose Shaji[2,†]

[1]Department of Sociology and Social Work, Christ University, Bengaluru, India
[2]Centre for Social Action, Christ University, Bengaluru, India

Abstract

The socio-cultural and economic landscape of rural India is not totally conducive for women. Surveys and reports in this regard would suggest the continuous existence of gender-based discrimination and its negative effects on the status and livelihood of rural women. Recognizing this situation, the Centre for Social Action (CSA) has pioneered its efforts to sensitize and involve youth (especially students) in the mitigation of rural issues and has been supporting women in select villages by promoting Self Help Groups (SHGs). These SHGs, in turn, organize capacity-building and empowerment programmes for the women to enhance their livelihood and socio-economic well-being. The present study is designed to understand the impact of CSA's intervention on the status and livelihood of women in the select project sites. Towards this end, we collected data from a sample of 150 women beneficiaries of CSA's initiative using a structured interview schedule. The study used a mixed-method design. The study's outcome indicates a positive correlation between women's participation in CSA initiatives and their status and

---

[*] Corresponding Author's Email: om.prakash@christuniversity.in.
[†] Corresponding Author's Email: shaji.a@christuniversity.in.

In: Models for Social Responsibility Action by Higher Education Institutions
Editors: Joseph Chacko Chennattuserry, Elangovan N. et al.
ISBN: 979-8-89113-097-5
© 2024 Nova Science Publishers, Inc.

livelihood improvements. The results are encouraging that they would help one formulate effective models similar to this one for the empowerment of women.

Keywords: women, empowerment, self-help group, status, rural, livelihood

1. Introduction

Although global economic development has resulted in important benefits to women across societies, gender gaps and persisting feminisation of poverty are a reality, especially in the developing and underdeveloped worlds. Moreover, the benefits are not evenly distributed. According to United Nations (UN), there are areas which showcased a positive picture of the development of women in terms of four key indicators, viz. increased life expectancy; girls' enrolment for primary education; decline in total fertility rate, and increase in women's access to family planning practices. At the same time, it is noted that compared to men, women do not fare well in education and health (United Nations, 1995).

Women constitute a majority of the poor, both in urban and rural areas. But women have to play a major role in overall poverty alleviation and national development. According to a World Bank Report on Gender Equality (2010), a positive correlation exists between overall poverty alleviation, women's men's earnings and their productivity. Also, another survey (UN DESA, 2009) indicated that overall social and economic development would be phased when women have equal access to economic and financial resources as men. Evidence points out that women's development, in addition to poverty reduction, would also lead to the welfare of children and better household management. Noted economist Amartya Sen noted the importance of women's economic participation and societal empowerment (Sen, 2000). For him, society as a whole would benefit only when women participate in economic activities. Beyond doubt, it is proven time and again that women's empowerment has been essential for a society's sustainable development and economic growth.

In this chapter, the effectiveness of the model used by CSA to empower women in rural areas and the role of students as agents of positive change in the lives of the beneficiaries are investigated. The women beneficiaries of the project are interviewed using a structured interview schedule to assess their participation and benefits accrued, especially in terms of economic independence, networking and autonomy in decision-making. Participation of the women in the CSA programmes through the SHGs is an intervening variable for the study. Age, education, community, occupation, and marital status of the participant women are some of the independent variables. Income, participation in decision-making, differential ability to avail government services, social networking, social skills acquired etc., are considered dependent variables. From the study, it is expected that the effectiveness of the model used by CSA can be assessed. The results would help policymakers and researchers frame models similar to this for the empowerment of rural women.

2. Review of Literature

'Empowerment' has become a buzzword of policy making in today's society, accompanied by an unprecedented focus on economic development. A peek into the concept of empowerment would help us to locate the role of CSA in helping rural women in the project sites to empower themselves, both socially and economically. Though most of the approaches to empowerment are tweaked to see the economy as playing the most significant role, the importance of 'social' is not completely ruled out. One of the agreed-upon ways in academia and policymaking is to see empowerment as a process which enables an individual to redefine his/her possibilities and options to have the ability to act upon them (Eyben et al., 2008). Thus, freedom (social and economic) as a defining feature is built into the process of empowerment, as without freedom, one cannot redefine his/her possibilities. In a similar line, Kabeer (2002) saw empowerment as the expansion of people's ability to make strategic life choices in a context where this ability was previously denied to them. Both views emphasised the importance of freedom from the shackles of traditionally held social, political and economic impediments.

The World Bank, in its definition of empowerment for economic growth and poverty reduction, considers empowerment as the expansion of assets and capabilities of poor people to participate, negotiate, influence, control, and hold accountable institutions that affect their lives (World Bank, 2002). Fundamentally, empowerment is the enhancement of one's capabilities to make a difference in their surroundings and, thereby, one's own life. Through one's empowerment, socio-cultural norms and institutions of a society, which were restrictive, can also be influenced for a positive change. Thus, empowerment, at times, becomes cyclic, making the empowered help the rest empower themselves by altering the social structure. In a patriarchal society like ours, social, economic and political empowerment of women has to be structurally rooted on the one hand and the activation of their agency on the other hand. In the process, making women themselves active participants is of paramount importance. At the same time, understanding empowerment depends on the context and characteristics of the concerned group and society. Therefore, empowerment for one person or group cannot be assumed to have a similar effect on other individuals or groups.

The clutches of patriarchy are deep-rooted and binding on rural women. Regressive familial and social ties coupled with traditionally held notions of morality and economic dependency hinder rural women. A study by Malhotra et al., (2002) found that household and family relations play a central part in controlling women's agency and resulting in disempowerment. Therefore, it is important that women's empowerment programmes aim at dispensing the shackles, in the form of family and immediate community, which prevent women from exercising their agency. Jejeebhoy and Sathar (2001), in their study, found that freedom to take economic decisions and mobility, absence of threat from husband, and access to and control over resources are the key indicators of women's autonomy. In a similar study, Mason et al., (2003) found that women's power in household economic decisions, their role in family-size decisions, their freedom of movement, and their ability to resist coercive controls by the husband are the determining factors of autonomy and empowerment. However, they also established that the empowerment of women could not be all-encompassing as it is multi-dimensional. Thus, it is possible that women can be empowered in some respects and not in others.

Subjective (self)-interpretations of what one feels are an important criterion for the understanding of empowerment, the reason that empowerment is not directly observable. Therefore, perceptions of the women beneficiaries of CSA's interventions were recorded in their own contexts and analyzed to measure their empowerment. For instance, to understand if women's participation in CSA's programmes enhanced their say in household decision-making, a researcher has to depend upon the subject's own interpretation and experiences. Elements of empowerment embedded in the CSA's approach and the targeted community-driven approaches of the CSA to help women take control or at least to become stakeholders of the decision-making process which involves their lives were also analyzed.

3. Methodology

Data for this chapter has been collected from the beneficiaries of three rural Community Development Projects (CDP) of CSA from three different sites, viz. Chethana Project at Hoskote, Pragathi Project at Yeldur, Kolar and Unnathi SHA Project at Jamkhandi. Of these three projects, Unnathi SHA Project has been comparatively more aimed at directly influencing the lives of women, whereas the Chethana and Pragathi projects are aimed at the welfare of children. The latter two projects were also considered for the present study for the reason that many aspects of them deal with the empowerment of women - mothers of those child beneficiaries of the project - as the empowerment and welfare of women is a precursor to the education and welfare of children. For instance, although Pragathi was originally a child-focused community development project, it has begun to educate and help women with finance generation, management and development of entrepreneurial skills. CSA's intervention in the lives of women across the project sites has been through Community-Based Organisations (CBOs), including Self Help Groups (SHGs), Village Development Committees (VDCs) and Farmers' Groups.

Towards this end, we use a variant of the mixed methods called embedded design. In this design, the researcher would depend upon any one data set (either quantitative or qualitative), whereas the other data set can be used as supportive/supplementary evidence. For instance, if the researcher considers quantitative data as primary, qualitative data can be used for supportive/supplementary evidence and vice versa (Creswell, Plano Clark, et al., 2003). It involves the collection of both quantitative and qualitative data. For the present study, the researchers have used quantitative data as primary and qualitative data to support and supplement findings. The survey, in-depth interviews, focus group discussions, and non-participant observation are used as tools to collect data. Data collected using an interview schedule has been analyzed using SPSS. Qualitative information collected using interviews, observation and focus group discussions were used to supplement the findings wherever necessary.

A sample of 150 respondents, 50 each from three project sites, were selected using Simple Random Sampling. The sample is from the members of SHGs who are also the women beneficiaries of the CSA programmes. Only those who are part of the CSA-sponsored programmes are considered for the study. In order to find the connection between the level of participation and empowerment, special attention is put in place to include respondents without regard to their participation/involvement level in the programmes. In addition to this, FGDs were conducted with the participants, and the points that emerged were recorded. Observation as the tool was used in noting the discussions in the regular meetings of the SHGs.

4. Results

As mentioned earlier, all the respondents are women beneficiaries of the CSA projects in the select areas, viz. Hoskote, Yeldur and Jamkhandi. A brief understanding of the profile of these respondents would help us in the better analysis and interpretation of results. Of the 150 respondents interviewed, over 93 per cent are from nuclear families. This is quite shocking but indicative of the transformations in the family structure in rural India. Although we assume that joint families mark the essence of rural life, finding here quite contradicts it. One reason for it is that the sample villages have seen development beginning with the fourth quarter of the last century, accompanied by rural-to-rural migration. A lot of our respondents are first-generation migrants from nearby villages. However, many other characteristics of migrants are absent from them as they are from close-by villages and have relatives in the present ones. Agriculture and casual work are considered the main family occupations by over a majority (63.4 per cent) of the respondents, followed by daily wage earners from nearby companies and construction work (21 per cent). It is observed that the women respondents of the study mostly consider their husbands as the potential earners of the family, with only a few exceptions. Although it is the case, the later part of this chapter demonstrates the role of CSA in the upliftment of women participants.

Of the total respondents interviewed, 38.7 per cent of them do not own any land for agriculture, whereas 51.3 per cent do have their own land, although in small amounts, between 5-50 cents for agricultural purposes. Also noted that around 3 per cent of the respondents own over 2 acres of land each. An overwhelming proportion of the respondents are Hindus (85.3 per cent), followed by Muslims (5.3 per cent), Christians (2 per cent) and others (7.3 per cent). Another important aspect of the profile of the participants of this study to be noted is that over a majority (68 per cent) of the respondents are from scheduled castes (51.3 per cent) and scheduled tribes (16.7 per cent). As we are aware, women from these social backgrounds are usually regarded as doubly oppressed, one in terms of their belongingness to an oppressed caste group in the social structure and another in terms of their status as women in the clutches of the patriarchal system, especially a rampant one in the rural areas.

There are interesting, relevant data to be noted with respect to the connection between family, education and community life of the respondents of the study. Ninety percent of the respondents selected for the study are married, and there are 12 (8 per cent) widows. Interestingly three unmarried women are also part of the study. However, it is noted from group discussions that these women feel that only marriage brings with it many responsibilities and therefore, though they are free to join before marriage, the social, financial and familial demands after marriage would make it possible for them to join SHGs and programmes of CSA. Some of them quipped that they were aware that marriage would bring with it these responsibilities and hardships, so why do they jump into taking these responsibilities in advance than waiting for the time to come to fruition? There exists a link between education and their outlook towards life. For instance, of the total of 150 respondents selected for the study, one-fourth (25.3 per cent) are illiterate, over one-third (36 per cent) of them have completed high school, and 30.7 per cent of the respondents have completed their primary education. During group discussions, those with relatively more education expressed the importance of family planning. Data collected also show a slight decrease in the number of children with higher educational qualifications than women. However, on many occasions, the participant women have expressed their helplessness with regard to this, as most of the decisions are made within the family by their male counterparts. A later part of this article explores the role of their participation in the CSA-sponsored programmes in empowering them in this regard. The role of CSA in the empowerment of these participant women can be grouped under three headings viz Gender Relations, Economic Upliftment and Social Networking.

5. Discussion

5.1. Empowerment and Gender Relations

One's empowerment can be operationally defined in terms of feeling powerful and competent in the social context of their living, feeling self-worthy and increased self-esteem. Empowerment, in most cases, is defined in terms of one's ability to cope with the socio-cultural environment within which they live than learning to ignore them (Itzhaky & York, 2000). The ability of women to overcome or remove the structural and institutional blocks to achieve their goals has also been a recurring theme in the understanding of women's empowerment. It is worth here of mentioning some of the defining variables identified by Zimmerman and Rappaport (1988) in the understanding of empowerment, which is relevant to the present study in understanding the empowerment of the women participants. They are the locus of control, change control, belief in powerful others, control ideology, self-efficacy, sense of mastery, perceived competence, desire for control, civic duty, leadership, community activities, and level of involvement. The following passages will explain the observations from the field with regard to the variables mentioned above and related ones.

Beyond any reasonable doubt, participant women have opined and exhibited much better control of their family and life chances. In a patriarchal society like the one they are part of, this cannot happen without sustained efforts from their end. Their participation in the programmes and activities of CSA has led to their increased awareness and sense of self-worthiness. True that there are close links between their increased ability to control their life chances and their economic betterment. They have become better decision-makers with their ability to pre-empt actions and their ramifications with increased confidence. They have also developed a sense of mastery over what they do with the mutual support and encouragement that they receive from peers. Peer support groups formed by the CSA have come in handy in this regard. Associated with their sense of mastery is their sense of competence. It is noticeable from the FGDs conducted that their perceived competence level to accomplish tasks and accomplishment proportion have increased manifold with the CSA intervention in the area.

Another important change noticed is with regard to their desire to hold power and control the socio-economic ambience of their society to their advantage. As is common to any society rooted in the patriarchal ideology and organization of life, the mental constructs and lifestyle of the participants of our study from the select three project sites are deeply rooted in patriarchy. It is surprising and mentionable the changes that they experienced in this regard with their participation in the CSA programmes. An overwhelming proportion of the participants opined that they are now willing to take responsibilities beyond the issues of their immediate family. They have developed a desire to hold power and participate in decision-making. It is a notable change as many have expressed their earlier status as dominated by shyness and avoidance. Today, many of them hold small leadership positions in the village/organisation/group and do feel as important and have self-worth. Their awareness of civic responsibilities, thirst for leadership and participation in community activities have also recorded a notable increase. Thus, their participation in the CSA-sponsored schemes and programmes has enriched them in terms of overcoming some of the traditionally and structurally rooted barriers of gender inequality.

5.2. Economic Empowerment

Approaches toward the bidirectional relationship between women's empowerment and economic development can largely be put under two different but related registers. On the one hand, many development economists and policy analysts are of the opinion that only development can drive down gender inequality. They put forth the opinion that the trickling down of the economic benefits to the women and poor sections of the population would lead to better gender relations and equity. On the other hand, a stream of scholars is of the opinion that gender inequality is a hindrance to economic development. They are of the opinion that unless women participate in mainstream economic activities, development is a distant dream (Duflo, 2012). Given the data we have, we are of the opinion that this relationship is truly bidirectional, at least at the micro level. It is observed that the participation and empowerment of women in social and political life have led to their economic empowerment and well-being on the one hand. Whereas on the other, economic empowerment, in general, and economic self-reliance, in particular, have served as a pre-condition for the social and political upliftment of women.

The data collected from the select project sites of CSA are also indicative of this bidirectional relationship between economic development and gender equality. CSA's initiatives have either initiated or facilitated the participation of women in mainstream economic activities. For instance, CSA's intervention has led to a considerable number of women opening their Saving Bank Accounts and related documents like PAN. Their participation in the microfinance activities of the CSA-facilitated/sponsored SHGs has made it mandatory for them to open Saving Bank Accounts for small financial transactions. This, in turn, helped them develop confidence and economic self-reliance. Some of them have opined that their economic participation and involvement in the SHG activities have attracted more respect from family members. An overwhelming (97 per cent) proportion of the participants of the study opined that their involvement in the CSA-sponsored SHGs has gained them more power in economic decision-making and reduced their dependency on the earning male members of the family. Interestingly, it is found that their participation in decision-making, both within the family and SHG, is more based on their economic activity than their educational level.

It is also understood that the decrease in their economic dependency on their male counterparts in the family due to their participation in the microfinance activities of the SHGs has also provided them with the confidence and will to take independent economic decisions. For instance, earlier in the case of financial burden or indebtedness, usually, the female children were pulled out of school to earn for the family. Nowadays, the female members of the family can mostly manage such eventualities and help their female children continue their education. It is also noted that usually, male children are not pulled into work as their parents believe that their education is a must as they will take care of the family in the future. Thus, gender disparity prevails in this regard. Many assumed that early work is meant for females and is infra dig to male children. With the growing participation of women in economic activities through the CSA-sponsored SHGs, many such prejudices and structural discriminations faced by women are withering away to the blossoming of a new enabling situation for women empowerment in the select project sites.

5.3. Social Networking and Empowerment

The term Social Network is used here in its limited meaning that refers to the participants' contacts and friends. The present section of this chapter seeks to understand the role of the CSA initiatives in helping the women beneficiaries in the project sites to develop a network and rapport with members of the society, leadership and other fellow beneficiaries. It also seeks to trace the advantages of this networking in the lives of the participant women. It is observed that networking has helped these women in alleviating their capability poverty. Their networking with fellow women has provided them with the confidence and support to initiate and sustain new efforts. Overall, the intervention of CSA in this regard can be understood at two levels viz the ability of women to network with others and helping these women tap the positive impact of networking back into their lives.

As far as the networking ability of these women is concerned, the role of CSA is one of 'coercive' aiming at a positive result. Women beneficiaries of the CSA programmes are given training on interpersonal skills and are mandated to interact and network with fellow beneficiaries for smoother functioning of the SHGs. The role of CSA in providing them with a conducive environment for the development of mutually supportive and positive relationships among the participant women is notable. With more networking comes their ability to negotiate for the better. Nevertheless, CSA has also helped them taping the benefits of their networking back into their lives. For instance, many women participants opined that they came to know more about their fellow participants, although neighbours, after becoming members of SHGs. Also, their participation in SHGs has made them contact officials outside the village. For instance, it is their participation in SHGs that made their first visit to the bank. Some in the leadership positions quipped that although they were initially hesitant to interact with bank and government officials, their awareness of the cause and purpose of their actions, aimed at the benefit of the members of their SHG, has often motivated and provided them with the necessary 'courage' to create the necessary network and contacts. Their exposure to the world outside their village and networking have also provided them with the necessary skills and moral strength to speak up against gender injustice and domestic violence.

Conclusion

The term women empowerment is a cliché in the academic world. Its different dimensions are mostly explored from different disciplinary frameworks. Although the interdisciplinary understanding of women's empowerment is relatively new, many of the avenues of interdisciplinarity in this regard have also been saturated with data and research. Even though the theoretical bases and frameworks for the understanding of women's empowerment are strong, they lack data related to practice to generate models of empowerment. Here is an attempt aimed at praxis. We collected data about the intervention of CSA through SHGs on the lives of women in select project sites. This chapter indicated that the role of CSA in empowering women in the select project sites is manifold and established a strong connection between the socio-economic empowerment of women and their participation in the CSA-sponsored programmes. The present study thus established the importance of an external agency in propelling positive growth through empowerment. This can be considered a model for women's empowerment in the rest of the country and has the scope of developing as a model framework of women's empowerment.

References

Duflo, E. (2012). Women Empowerment and Economic Development. *Journal of Economic Literature*, 50(4), 1051–1079. https://doi.org/10.1257/jel.50.4.1051.

Eyben, R., Kabeer, N., & Cornwall, A. (2008). *Conceptualising empowerment and the implications for pro-poor growth.* DAC Poverty Network by the Institute of Development Studies, Brighton.

Itzhaky, H., & York, A. S. (2000). Empowerment and community participation : Does gender make a difference? *Social Work Research*, 24(4), 225–234. https://doi.org/10.1093/swr/24.4.225.

Jejeebhoy, S. J., & Sathar, Z. A. (2001). Women's Autonomy in India and Pakistan : The Influence of Religion and Region. *Population and Development Review*, 27(4), 687–712. https://doi.org/10.1111/j.1728-4457.2001.00687.x.

Kabeer, N. (2002). Resources, Agency, Achievements: Reflections on the Measurement of Women's Empowerment. *Development and Change*, 30(3), 435–464. https://doi.org/10.1111/1467-7660.00125.

Malhotra, A., Schuler, S. R., & Boender, C. (2012) *Measuring Women's Empowerment as a Variable in International Development,* The World Bank, Washington DC.

Mason, K. O., & Smith, H. L. (2003). Women's empowerment and social context: Results from five Asian countries. *Gender and Development Group,* World Bank, Washington, DC, 53(9).

Sen, A. (2000). *Development as Freedom,* New Delhi : Oxford University Press.

UN DESA, (2009). *World Survey on the Role of Women in Development,* United Nations Publication.

United Nations (1995). *Human Development Report- UNDP* (1995). United Nations.

World Bank (2002). *Empowerment and Poverty Reduction : A Sourcebook.* Washington DC : World Bank.

Zimmerman, M. A., & Rappaport, J. (1988). Citizen participation, perceived control, and psychological empowerment. *American Journal of Community Psychology*, 16(5), 725–750. https://doi.org/10.1007/bf00930023.

Chapter 6

Socially Responsible Universities and Student Satisfaction: Case Analysis

B. Valarmathi[1,*],
B. Lakshmi[1,†]
and N. Elangovan[2,‡]

[1]Department of Commerce, Christ University, Bengaluru, India
[2]School of Business and Management, Christ University, Bengaluru, India

Abstract

Universities play the dual role of providing new knowledge and inculcating a sense of social responsibility in student citizens to contribute to community development. Higher Education Institutions (HEIs) are often expected to be socially responsible. The principal focus of this chapter is to determine the dimensions of University Social Responsibility (USR) and examine its impact on student satisfaction. A case study research was conducted with 299 students from a private university in India. Exploratory and Confirmatory Factor Analysis were used to identify the dimensions of USR. A structural equation model was used to analyze the impact of USR on student satisfaction, with gender and volunteerism in USR activities as moderators. The results show that student satisfaction is influenced by their perception of USR activities undertaken by the university. Findings indicate that the degree of influence of USR on satisfaction is more among female than male students. Contrastingly, the degree of influence of USR on satisfaction remained the same for volunteers and non-volunteers, indicating that the

---

[*] Corresponding Author's Email: valarmathi.b@christuniversity.in.
[†] Corresponding Author's Email: lakshmi.b@christuniversity.in.
[‡] Corresponding Author's Email: elangovan.n@christuniversity.in.

In: Models for Social Responsibility Action by Higher Education Institutions
Editors: Joseph Chacko Chennattuserry, Elangovan N. et al.
ISBN: 979-8-89113-097-5
© 2024 Nova Science Publishers, Inc.

university is transparent in its USR activities. The findings highlight the importance of USR actions and how these activities lead to increased student satisfaction. The study also discusses the model adopted by the university to achieve higher standards of USR that other HEIs can adapt.

Keywords: university social responsibility, student satisfaction, structural equation model, moderation, India, USR model, dimensions of USR

1. Introduction

Society entrusts universities to shape students and enable them to become responsible citizens in their workplaces or society (Latif, 2018). The purpose of universities is to provide knowledge and learning, keeping in mind the expectations of their primary stakeholders. However, globalization has compelled universities to innovate, compete and survive in the commercial landscape. Understanding the needs of the student community has become vital to provide them with better services and ensuring that they are content. Providing quality education is no longer the sole objective of HEIs. The higher education sector is undergoing a significant transformation and is looking for new opportunities to enhance students' overall university experience. The stakeholders expect academic institutions to focus on societal needs and concerns (Vázquez et al., 2016; DeShields et al., 2005). The current chapter proposes USR as an opportunity for universities to reimage and sustain themselves in this challenging environment and ensure continued engagement and satisfaction of its students (Burcea & Marinescu, 2011).

USR, simply put, is a holistic approach towards ethical and sustainable management, assuming responsibility for the effects and consequences of its strategies, structures and policies on stakeholders, society and the environment. Universities should be resilient to transit through challenging times through responsible activities. Students' satisfaction and the quality of services are the strategic plans to remain sustainable in this dynamic environment. Universities have a leading role in creating responsible citizens. They should provide opportunities for the overall development of students.

2. Review of Literature

2.1. Students Satisfaction

USR implementation has proven to be highly effective in HEIs. There has been considerable change in the curriculum, greening campuses through responsible consumption and policies to promote healthy relationships with students (Ramos et al., 2020). For educational institutions, ensuring students' satisfaction is crucial for growth. Studies reveal that student satisfaction leads to higher academic engagement and retention for higher education in the same institution (Elliott and Shin, 2002; Vázquez et al., 2016). In their study, Mwiya et al. (2017) reveal a positive relationship between crucial service quality indicators, namely assurance, tangibility, reliability, empathy and responsiveness, with overall student satisfaction. Students' behaviour largely depends on their perception of the quality of services received from the institution. HEIs should seek feedback and information from students, seeking their level of satisfaction. Feedback would help institutions make necessary changes in the infrastructure, curriculum and policies governing students' interests. There should be a mechanism for continuous change and improvement in the existing service for students.

Institutions can plan expansion programmes and attract new students when the existing ones are satisfied (Negricea, Edu, & Avram, 2014). Many universities conduct student satisfaction surveys as part of their routine practices, opening the institutions to new avenues they can explore. The analysis of such surveys could reveal factors leading to students' satisfaction or dissatisfaction. The dissatisfying indicators should be carefully examined and addressed. If not dealt with, these grievances could lead to students discontinuing the course or making them give negative reviews of the institution (Popli, 2005; Richardson, 2005). From time to time, a review of services will enable institutions to provide better facilities. They can leverage these services for various activities, from planning the curriculum to engaging them in community development activities. The current study focuses on how social responsibility activities lead to satisfied learners. Although there has been very little literature to examine them, the present study will urge universities to engage students in meaningful activities to ensure satisfaction.

2.2. Antecedents of University Social Responsibility

2.2.1. Responsible Management and Teaching

HEIs are responsible for the change in education and society and should promote it through inclusive education and a sound management policy. Having a structured approach and procedures will ensure the smooth conduct of activities. Responsible initiatives and plans implemented through curriculum and pedagogical design measure the institution's success. Social responsibility, ethics and sustainability courses should be covered to enable students to contribute effectively to community development. There should be expert talks frequently to understand gaps in the theory learnt in classrooms. Practical exposure through projects and active involvement in societal programmes should be encouraged.

The United Nations propagates the idea of sustainable education through its principles and sustainable development goals. The field has received immense attention from scholars and academics since Holman's framework for management education. In his study, Holman (2000) questions the purpose, nature and value of the university and the role of higher education in society influenced by the sustainability agenda of the United Nations. However, universities have addressed the issues through teaching rather than strategic action at the institutional level (Cicmil et al., 2017).

Therefore, universities must go beyond teaching courses on social responsibility, ethics, and sustainability to foster diversity and equal opportunities for students and develop a campus culture that encourages human and social values and promotes civic solidarity. The management should consider students' opinions to provide fair and equal opportunities to all and recognize their participation in the decision-making process. They must have a system to provide awareness and encourage social and ethical solidarity. Holman (2000) propagates the change in pedagogy required to develop students' critical thinking and managerial skills in the workplace.

2.2.2. Responsible Research

HEIs are not merely knowledge acquirers but also creators and disseminators. Knowledge creation and application are possible through systematic and scientific research. Educational institutions' core philosophy is generating new knowledge to enhance the quality of life. Building research competencies of the staff will improve student learning and the development of skills and expertise (Sánchez-Hernández & Mainardes, 2016). Universities must provide sufficient research training to equip staff and students to contribute to human development. The prevailing education system should foster change from teaching to research-based institutions (Altbach, 2009). The MHRD has also specified quality standards to acquire research qualifications. It also encourages universities to strive to contribute to developing theories and knowledge. The HEIs must achieve research excellence and continuously apply environmentally friendly technology and processes (MHRD 2020).

2.2.3. Responsible Environmental Activities

Education should make us responsible for our environment and community. Education for the Environment (EE) should foster critical thinking and change students' behaviour (Short, 2009). Young people look for opportunities and participate when they are encouraged to give their contributions. Change in their behaviour will be evident when they are involved in solving societal issues and concerns. If environmental activities are part of the curriculum, it is easy for students to explore the environmental impact. HEIs should organise environmental awareness programmes to sensitize students about their responsibility to conserve natural resources and prevent environmental degradation. They should be allowed to develop campaigns as part of educational activities to spread knowledge to nearby communities. Institutions should have mechanisms to manage waste generated through recycling units. The EE programme at the institution should make students develop and execute independent projects concerning environmental protection. The institution is responsible for creating environmental ambassadors who advocate sustainable consumption and energy-efficient behaviour in public and private places (Tidball & Krasny, 2007).

2.2.4. Responsible Collaboration for Volunteering Activities

Volunteering activities make students cultivate certain traits, which make them involved with society beyond self-gain. Volunteering activities among students in India began with the National Cadet Corps (NCC) inception in 1948 and the National Service Scheme (NSS) in 1969. These two national voluntary organisations instilled a passion for serving the nation and society through various activities. Active participation in social reforms promotes ethical and moral ethos in students. There is a high correlation between student volunteering and self-esteem (Holdsworth, 2014). HEIs must collaborate with NGOs and other social organisations to provide students ample exposure to community service. Collaboration is essential to drive community engagement and participation (Marschalek, 2017).

3. Research Methodology

Drawing upon Hinkin's (1995) and Schwab's (1980) research, we followed a deductive approach in developing questionnaires for this study. We identified six dimensions of USR from a thorough review of existing literature. A self-administered online questionnaire measured the items on a five-point Likert scale ranging from Strongly Disagree (1) to Strong Agree (5). The items for the constructs were adapted from prior studies (Vázquez & Hernández, 2013; Vázquez et al., 2014; Vázquez, 2016; Matten & Moon, 2004; Christensen et al., 2007). This questionnaire development method is popularly used (Kim & Kim, 2016), specifically in USR (Vázquez et al., 2014).

The required data were collected from Christ University. The sampling technique used was judgemental and convenient sampling, based on the willingness of students to participate in the study. Only final-year undergraduate and postgraduate students were included. To have fair representation from both genders, we sent questionnaires to an equal number of male and female students. We also ensured equal representation of volunteers and non-volunteers in USR activities. Out of 299 students who responded, 127 were males (42.5%), and 169 were females (56.5%). Also, 138 (46.2%) were volunteers in USR activities, and 161 (53.8%) were non-volunteers.

4. Results

We ran an exploratory factor analysis using the SPSS 22 statistical package to determine the dimensions of USR based on the students' perceptions. The Kaiser-Meyer-Olkin (KMO) statistics (p = 0.956) confirmed the adequacy of sample size for factor analysis. A KMO statistic greater than 0.6 is ideal (Kaiser & Rice, 1974). Bartlett's test of sphericity is significant (p < 0.01), further confirming the suitability of data to run an exploratory factor analysis. We ran a principal component analysis with varimax rotation. The study extracted four factors explaining 69 per cent of the total variance. About 17 items out of 33 did not load or loaded into more than one factor and therefore had to be dropped. The Cronbach alpha and the cumulative variance for the factors extracted are reported in Table 1.

Table 1. Results of Exploratory Factor Analysis

Factors	Items	Factor Loading	Cronbach's Alpha	Cumulative Variance
Responsible Environment Activities (REA)	Takes the initiative in reducing Environmental degradation (REA3)	0.846	0.923	20.464
	Proper recycling and waste management methods adopted (REA5)	0.816		
	Sensitizing educational campaigns on environmental protection in areas of influence which are close to the university (REA4)	0.737		
	Conduct environmental awareness programmes on Campus and Community (REA1)	0.703		
	Provide education and skill development to local communities (REA6)	0.688		
	Activities are aligned with environmental conservation (REA2)	0.674		
Responsible Teaching and Management (RT & RM)	Encourages recognition of students and opinions and participation (RTM2)	0.663	0.860	38.167
	Management encourages human and social values and promotes civic solidarity (RTM3)	0.625		
	Fosters respect for diversity and provides equal opportunities among students (RTM1)	0.618		
Responsible Collaboration for Volunteering Activities (RCV)	Collaborates with public services and NGOs in sustainable initiatives (RCV2)	0.813	0.895	54.119
	Organisation and sponsoring of performances are committed to both local and regional social and environmental development (RCV3)	0.746		
	The organisation of volunteering programmes for students in collaboration with partnering universities (RCV4)	0.723		
	Collaboration with companies, public services or NGOs in social projects to help the disadvantaged (RCV1)	0.685		
Responsible Research (RR)	University provides discussion-based sessions to explore research opportunities for solving social problems and knowledge generation (RR2)	0.732	0.890	69.024
	University provides ample resources and support for research in solving social and environmental problems (RR3)	0.717		
	University provides research education and training (RR1)	0.705		

Table 2. Convergent and Discriminant Validity of Constructs

Constructs	Construct Validity (CR)	Average Variance Explained (AVE)	Maximum Shared Variance (MSV)	Average Shared Variance (ASV)	Convergent Validity	Discriminant Validity
REA	0.924	0.971	0.530	0.508	Yes	Yes
RTM	0.831	0.621	0.607	0.529	Yes	Yes
RCV	0.896	0.684	0.551	0.530	Yes	Yes
RR	0.877	0.704	0.607	0.562	Yes	Yes

4.1. Confirmatory Factor Analysis - Measurement Model

To analyze the construct validity, we conducted a CFA. We can establish the construct validity by confirming convergent and discriminant validity (Hair et al., 2006). Construct validity is the extent to which the items measure the construct they are proposed to be measuring. Convergent validity is ensured when CR > 0.70, CR > AVE (Average Variance Explained), and AVE > 0.50 (Hair et al., 2006). Discriminant validity is ensured when the AVE of each construct is greater than its shared variance with other constructs, i.e., MSV < AVE and ASV < AVE (Fornell & Larcker, 1981). Discriminant validity refers to the degree to which the constructs are different from each other. It refers to the degree to which the items measure only one construct without cross-loadings. As shown in Table 2, the standardized factor loadings are greater than 0.5, and AVE is greater than 0.5, ensuring the convergent validity of the constructs.

Further, the CR value is greater than 0.70; this ensures that convergent validity for all the latent constructs is statistically satisfied. AVE values should be larger than their respective squared inter-construct correlations for discriminant validity.

4.2. Second-Order Measurement Model

This chapter employed a second-order factor as the first-order factor model showed high correlations (>0.70) between the constructs, indicating that USR is a multi-dimensional construct with sub-constructs (Bowen & Guo, 2011; Byrne, 1994). A casual flow from USR to its sub-constructs was drawn to assess the relationship between the primary construct and its sub-constructs

(Hair et al., 2006). The second-order measurement model was a good fit with the indices above the required threshold (See Table 3). The R^2 of all sub-constructs are around 0.7, with one sub-construct at 0.68, confirming that USR is a second-order factor (Figure 1).

4.3. Structural Equation Model

We ran a structural equation model to examine the influence of students' perception of USR on their overall satisfaction with the university. The results indicated that students' perception of USR positively affected overall student satisfaction ($\beta = .79$, $p < .001$) (Figure 2). The model fit values are reported in Table 3, R^2 was 0.63, indicating that the student's perception regarding the sub-constructs of USR together explains about 63 per cent of the variance in students' satisfaction. The results of the moderation analysis confirm that gender and volunteering activities moderate the relationship between the student's perception of USR and their overall satisfaction with the university.

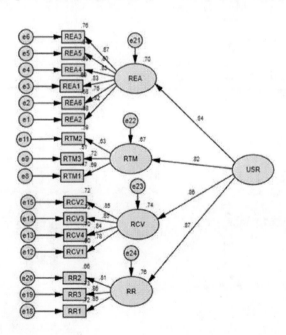

Figure 1. Second-Order Model.

Table 3. Model Fit indices of Measurement Model and SEM

Indices	Thumb rule	Measurement Model (First Order)	Measurement Model (Second Order)	Structural Model
Chi-square/df	<5	2.756	2.732	2.632
P value for the model	>0.05	0.000	0.000	0.000
CFI	>0.95	0.951	0.951	0.946
GFI	>0.95	0.906	0.905	0.890
AGFI	>0.80	0.869	0.871	0.858
RMSEA	<0.05	0.077	0.076	0.074
P Close	>0.05	0.000	0.000	0.000
PCFI	>0.50	0.777	0.792	0.813
PNFI	>0.50	0.756	0.770	0.787

Table 4. Hypothesis Testing

Hypothesis	Standardized Regression weights	Remarks
H1: Students' perception of USR positively influences their overall satisfaction with the university	0.774***	Supported
H2: Gender moderates the relationship between students' perception of USR and their overall satisfaction with the university	0.742*** (Male) 0.807*** (Female)	Supported
H3: Volunteering in university responsibility activities moderates the relationship between students' perception of USR and their overall satisfaction with the university	0.778*** (Volunteers) 0.777*** (non-Volunteers)	Supported

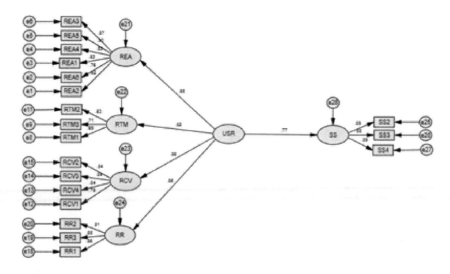

Figure 2. Structural Equation Model.

5. Discussion

This chapter extracts four dimensions of USR: Responsible Environment Activities, Responsible Teaching and Management, Responsible Collaborations for Volunteering Activities and Responsible Research employing Principal Component Analysis and validating the same by applying Confirmatory Factor Analysis. Similar dimensions of USR are brought out in the case study of ASEAN universities with USR initiatives in the study by Symaco and Tee (2019). Another survey by Aleixo et al., (2018) also shows that the stakeholders have identified similar dimensions of USR. Contrary to our findings, Vázquez et al., (2014) extracted six dimensions of USR – external projection, research, education in environmental values, internal management, university-firm relationships and education in social values. However, a thematic analysis of available academic literature also revealed education, research, management, and community engagement to be popularly discussed activities as part of USR (Larrán Jorge & Andrades Peña, 2017). Our analysis proposes USR as a second-order multi-dimensional construct drawing from the study by Sánchez-Hernández and Mainardes (2016).

A legion of literature has proven that social responsibility activities would enhance the competitive advantage of organizations. By extending this concept to universities, the current study proposes that the competitive advantage for universities is higher student satisfaction. The study's findings provide empirical evidence that a positive perception of students about the USR activities of the university would increase their satisfaction. The conclusion is consistent with the study conducted by Vázquez et al., (2016) in Spain and also previous studies such as Christensen et al., (2007), Setó-Pamiés et al., (2011), and Vazquez (2014). Universities must implement strategies to address students' problems by focusing on the dimensions of USR extracted in the current study to improve students' satisfaction and achieve competitive advantage (Jain et al., 2017; Saeidi et al., 2015; Yu et al., 2017). Our second finding is that the satisfaction of female students is more positively influenced by their perception of USR than their male counterparts. This indicates gender equity, providing all necessary facilities to promote higher education among female students (Deshmukh, 2017). Interestingly, volunteering in USR activities shows negligible moderation between student perception of USR and their overall satisfaction, indicating that even the students not actively participating in USR activities share a positive perception regarding USR activities of the university. This is positive news to the institutions indicating that even non-volunteers are aware of the USR initiatives and share the same perception as volunteers.

It is now established through empirical evidence the significance of USR activities for an educational institution. In the next section, the USR model of Christ University is explained, which universities can adopt.

5.1. USR Model of the University

The university carries on the USR activities primarily through a dedicated unit – Centre for Social Action (CSA). CSA strives to sensitize the student community to work for the betterment of weaker sections. The focus of the centre is the empowerment of the marginalized and the creation of inclusive societies. The centre has seven broad focus areas, which allow students to showcase their social responsibility towards the community's needs. CSA is a voluntary student organisation where students from any course can join to work towards a humane and just society. Issues such as child rights, socio-economic development of women, youth and farmers, livelihood, community mobilization, and environment/climate change issues are addressed.

The activities carried on by CSA under the four USR dimensions extracted in the chapter are explained in this section (Figure 3).

5.1.1. Dimension 1 - Responsible Environment Activities

Parivarthana - Waste Management Unit on the campus empowers women workers in the university who earn their livelihood by converting trash to treasure to create sustainable waste management models. The unit's motto is to "Reduce, Reuse, Recycle." Paper waste is converted into various products such as envelopes, folders, and diaries. Wet waste is collected from the canteen and food courts inside the campus, converted into manure to be sold to outsiders and used for gardens. There is also a wastewater treatment plant on campus. The wastewater on campus is treated and reused at the Parivarthana unit, making the campus a zero-waste campus. Food waste is also converted into biogas, which is used on campus. The biogas plant produces about 25 kilograms of LPG per day.

Community Development Programme – This programme focuses on rural development, urban slum development, and tribal development. The rural development initiatives focus on health, education, social/community development, empowering community-based organizations (CBOs), land development, agricultural development, and empowering the community through women - socially, politically, and economically in Karnataka, Maharashtra, Kerala, Telangana, and Chhattisgarh. About 134 villages are covered through this intervention, focusing on livelihood, child development and women empowerment. The urban slum programme is operational in ten slum communities, i.e., seven in Bengaluru and three in Ghaziabad. The Child Sponsorship programme, supports the slum children through the education activity centre. The programme has established a computer system, and a day-care centre. Finally, the tribal community development set-up helps in the school enrolment of tribal children, assisting in the functioning of Anganwadi and income generation livelihood models based on farming. The other activities include providing employment opportunities to children after the 10th grade through the BOSCH bridge growth and Employability programme.

5.1.2. Dimension 2 - Responsible Teaching and Management
Child Sponsorship Programme (CSP)– 'Educate a Child Sponsorship' is the annual flagship event of CSA. The programme allows every student to contribute towards the educational needs of school children in adopted communities. Every year, 800 children are supported through the child sponsorship programme. The current year focused on community development programmes, in which funds were collected to support the health and nutritional benefits of slum children and their family members. The programme also focuses on sustainable improvement in quality life through quality education, training in life skills, and imparting skills for future employment and income. The projects are spread across three different slum areas in Bengaluru: the 3D Project at Janakiram near Kammanahalli, Vriddhi Project at L R Nagar and Ambedkar Nagar Koramangala.

Students Volunteer Programme -The students' voluntary body has four wings and two projects. The wings are Activity Centre, Drishti, Prayatna and Media & Communication. Each wing has its own motto and set of activities to focus on all aspects of social responsibility. The Activity Centre focuses on the overall development of children in the project areas. The volunteers of the wing conduct after-school fun-filled activities and classes to engage students in interactive learning. The wing also has a committee to review the syllabus in the project areas. The Drishti wing of CSA aims to sensitize people through visual and audio art-Drishti acts. Drishti spreads awareness through forms of theatre, primarily street theatre, in campus and project communities. They also organise workshops and release concept videos to educate marginalized and student communities. The Prayatna wing works towards a sustainable environment where volunteers engage in nature walks, clean-up drives, animal shelter visits, and other environmental campaigns. They also closely work with the Parivarthana - Waste Management Unit of Christ University. The Media and Communication wing of CSA is mainly responsible for documenting and developing content and design through writing, photography, and videography. They write content for magazines, make videos, posters, and newsletters to be published in various forums. Project Matram works for the holistic development of children, making them self-sufficient and confident and increasing their communication skills. They also offer training workshops for the skill development of children. Finally, Project Yuva works towards educating women in the project areas and the students on sustainable menstruation (inclusive of economic sustainability). They organize workshops and training to inform women about health and hygiene related to sustainable menstruation.

Responsible Environmental Activities	Responsible Teaching and Management
Responsible Collaboration for volunteering Activities	Responsible Research

Figure 3. University Social Responsibility Model.

Partnership with Government and UNAI - The university collaborates with government and international Bodies. Social Entrepreneurship, Swachhta and Rural Engagement Cell (SES REC), set up by the Mahatma Gandhi National Council of Rural Education, Department of Higher Education, Ministry of Education, Government of India, has given guidelines to universities in five areas. They include sanitation, hygiene, waste management, water management, energy conservation, and greenery. The cell conducts workshops to orient the university to carry out innovative and sustainable activities on campus and community. The university must submit a yearly audit report to the cell. The university was successfully able to complete the energy and water audit. The university is also a member of the

United Nations Academic Impact body, which drives all educational institutions to achieve the 17 sustainable development goals. The university was able to organise multiple orientation sessions for these goals. The CSA has successfully conducted a pan-university conference on selected goals, in which students were asked to present their research findings. The centre also organised panel discussions and poster competitions to portray its vision of these goals.

5.1.4. Dimension 4 - Responsible Research
Project Disha – This project invites proposals on social and economic development from faculty members and students. 'Precision Method for Pest Detection in Plants using the Clustering Algorithm in Image' is a project that aims to reduce loss from agriculture due to plant disease. It helps identify plant diseases before any loss, increases productivity, and monitors the health of plants, which will help in farming. The development of AI machines for sex identification of pupa and cocoon-cutting is a DSC-funded project of Disha. The university also encourages faculty members to publish their research work in reputed journals and encourages students to participate in socially beneficial initiatives.

Conclusion

The findings show that students' perception of USR is significant for their overall satisfaction with the university. Therefore, we suggest that universities focus on socially responsible activities and not limit themselves to just imparting knowledge. Current students would be future managers and citizens. Universities that are socially active and foster sustainability would also imbibe such culture in their students. The findings recommend that universities undertake socially responsible activities, achieve sustainable goals and high-quality standards and provide a rich campus experience. The chapter uses an exploratory, followed by a confirmatory analysis to identify the sub-constructs of USR, using the sample of a single university. The chapter also discusses the USR model followed by Christ University. Further research is required to confirm the model with data from different universities. Researchers can also explore new constructs of USR through structured interviews to build a comprehensive USR model.

References

Altbach, P. G. (2009). *Trends in Global Higher Education: Tracking an Academic Revolution: A Report Prepared for the UNESCO 2009 World Conference on Higher Education.*

Bowen, N. K. & Guo, S. (2011), *Structural equation modelling – pocket guides to social work research methods.* Oxford University Press.

Burcea, M., & Marinescu, P. (2011). Students' perceptions on corporate social responsibility at the academic level. Case study: the Faculty of Administration and Business, University of Bucharest. *Amfiteatru Economic*, 13(29), 207–220.

Byrne, B. M. (1994), *Structural Equation Modeling with EQS and EQS/Windows: Basic Concepts, Applications, and Programming,* Sage Publications, University of Ottawa.

Christensen, L. J., Peirce, E., Hartman, L. P., Hoffman, W. M., & Carrier, J. (2007). Ethics, CSR, and sustainability education in the Financial Times top 50 global business schools: Baseline data and future research directions. *Journal of Business Ethics*, 73(4), 347–368.

Cicmil, S., Gough, G., & Hills, S. (2017). Insights into responsible education for sustainable development: The case of UWE, Bristol. *The International Journal of Management Education*, 15(2), 293-305.

DeShields, O. W., Kara, A., & Kaynak, E. (2005). Determinants of business student satisfaction and retention in higher education: applying Herzberg's two-factor theory. *International Journal of Educational Management*, 19(2), 128-139. https://doi.org/10.1108/09513540510582426.

Elliott, K. M., & Shin, D. (2002). Student satisfaction: an alternative approach to assessing this important concept. *Journal of Higher Education Policy and Management*, 24(2), 197–209.

Fornell C, & Larcker. D. F. (1981) Evaluating structural equation models with unobservable variables and measurement error. *Journal of Market Research*, 18, 39–50.

Gallardo-Vázquez, D., & Sánchez-Hernández, M. I. (2013). Corporate social responsibility in higher education: Best practices at the University of Extremadura. *Edulearn Proceedings*, pp. 1332–1340.

Hair, J. F., Jr, Black, W. C., Babin, B. J., Anderson, R. E., & Tatham, R. L. (2006). *Multivariate data analysis* (6ª ed.). Pearson Prentice Hall.

Hinkin, T. R. (1995). A review of scale development practices in the study of organisations. *Journal of Management*, 21, 967–988.

Holdsworth, C. (2010). Why Volunteer? Understanding Motivations for Student Volunteering, *British Journal of Educational Studies*, 58(4), 421-437. https://dx.doi.org/10.1080/00071005.2010.527666.

Holman, D. (2000). Contemporary models of management education in the UK. *Management Learning*, 31(2), 197e217.

Kaiser, H. F., & Rice, J. (1974). Little Jiffy, mark IV. *Educational and psychological measurement*, 34(1), 111-117.

Kim, S. B., & Kim, D. Y. (2016). The impacts of corporate social responsibility, service quality, and transparency on relationship quality and customer loyalty in the hotel industry. *Asian Journal of Sustainability and Social Responsibility,* 1(1), 39-55.

Latif, K. F. (2018). The Development and Validation of Stakeholder-Based Scale for Measuring University Social Responsibility (USR). *Social Indicators Research,* 140(2), 511–547.

Marin Burcea & Paul Marinescu, (2011). Students' Perceptions on Corporate Social Responsibility at the Academic Level. Case Study: The Faculty of Administration and Business, University of Bucharest," *The Amfiteatru Economic Journal,* Academy of Economic Studies, 13(29), 207-220.

Marschalek, I. (2017). Public Engagement in Responsible Research and Innovation. A Critical Reflection from the Practitioner's Point of View. *PhD diss.,* University of Vienna. https://www.zsi.at/object/publication/4498/attach/Marschalek_Public_ Engagement_in_RRI.pdf.

Matten, D., & Moon, J. (2004). Corporate social responsibility education in Europe. *Journal of Business Ethics,* 54(4), 323–337.

MHRD (2020), *National education policy 2020,* available at: https://static.pib.gov.in/ WriteReadData/userfiles/NEP_Final_English_0.pdf.

Mwiya, B., Bwalya, J., Siachinji, B., Sikombe, S., Chanda, H. and Chawala, M. (2017) Higher Education Quality and Student Satisfaction Nexus: Evidence from Zambia. *Creative Education,* 8, 1044-1068. https://doi.org/10.4236/ce.2017.87076.

Negricea, C., Edu, T., & Avram, M. (2014). Establishing Influence of Specific Academic Quality on Student Satisfaction. *Social and Behavioral Sciences,* 116, 4430-4435.

Philip C. Short (2009) Responsible Environmental Action: Its Role and Status In Environmental Education and Environmental Quality, *The Journal of Environmental Education,* 41(1), 7-21, https://doi.org/10.1080/00958960903206781.

Popli, S., (2005). Ensuring customer delight: a quality approach to excellence in management education, *Quality in Higher Education,* 11 (1), 17-24.

Ramos, P., Cisneros, H., Bencomo, M. and López, J. (2020) University Social Responsibility Advancement in Mexico's Higher Education Institutions: A Comparative Study. *Open Journal of Business and Management,* 8, 2029-2047. https://doi.org/10.4236/ojbm.2020.85124.

Richardson, J. T. E., (2005). Instruments for obtaining student feedback: a review of the literature, *Assessment and Evaluation in Higher Education,* 30 (4), 387-415.

Sánchez-Hernández, M. I., & Mainardes, E. W. (2016). University social responsibility: a student base analysis in Brazil. *International Review on Public and Nonprofit Marketing,* 13(2), 151–169.

Schwab, D. P. (1980). Construct validity in organisation capital perspective. In B. M. Staw & L. L. Cummings (Eds.), *Research in organisational behavior,* (2) (pp. 3–43). JAI Press.

Setó-Pamiés, D., Domingo-Vernis, M., & Rabassa-Figueras, N. (2011). Corporate social responsibility in management education: current status in Spanish universities. *Journal of Management and Organization,* 17(5), 604–620.

Tidball, K., & Krasny, M. (2007). From risk to resilience: What role for community greening and civic ecology in cities? In A. Wals (Ed.), *Social learning towards a more sustainable world* (pp. 149–164). Wagengingen Academic Press.

Vázquez, J. L., Aza, C. L., & Lanero, A. (2014). Are students aware of university social responsibility? Some insights from a survey in a Spanish university. In *International Review on Public and Nonprofit Marketing*, 11(3), 195–208. https://doi.org/10.1007/s12208-014-0114-3.

Vázquez, J. L., Aza, C. L., & Lanero, A. (2016). University social responsibility as antecedent of students' satisfaction. *International Review on Public and Nonprofit Marketing*, 13(2), 137–149.

Chapter 7

Value Addition to International Students' Exchange Programs Through Engagement in Services

Jino Joy[1],*
and Shrutkirti Singh[2]
[1]Department of Social Work, Christ University, Bengaluru, India
[2]Department of Psychology, Christ University, Bengaluru, India

Abstract

Social responsibility has been an emerging concept in Higher Educational Institutions in India. Promoting social responsibility through international students' exchange programs helps students' capacity to improve their cultural, social and service knowledge to bring about sustainable and meaningful development. This chapter looks at the impact of the interventions of international students in slum communities, especially working with children and women for their academic, health and economic empowerment. This was a qualitative study using a self-structured interview schedule. Data were collected from twenty international students from universities of Norway and the Netherlands who were placed in urban slums for five years and thirty children and women from urban slums of Bangalore who benefitted from this program. A purposive sampling method was used, and the data were analyzed using thematic analysis. This chapter reveals the development of children and women through international students' programs and helps showcase further planning for innovative programs for vulnerable populations. Attitudes of both groups towards cultural differences and

---

* Corresponding Author's Email: jino.joy@res.christuniversity.in.

In: Models for Social Responsibility Action by Higher Education Institutions
Editors: Joseph Chacko Chennattuserry, Elangovan N. et al.
ISBN: 979-8-89113-097-5
© 2024 Nova Science Publishers, Inc.

the expectation and effectiveness of the exchange program may also be described in this chapter. This chapter intends to help plan international exchange programs from different dimensions benefiting the slum communities for their development and sensitizing cultural differences from different perspectives.

Keywords: social responsibility, exchange students, urban slums, education, health, economic empowerment

1. Introduction

Higher education institutions have a role in connecting with the community and bridging the gap between education and community welfare. According to Singh (2017), societal challenges can be addressed through the involvement of the student community. The development of the country by addressing social concerns and eradicating inequalities and discrepancies in society is possible with the help of such programs. In fact, Community university engagement has now become prominent through producing relevant knowledge that has the potential to bring sustainable solutions to various problems of the communities. The universities involved in such practices are referred to as socially engaged institutions.

There are many ways in which this engagement benefits the students as well. First, the students become sensitized about the struggles of the people. Second, this motivates them to become agents of change and take up the responsibility to change society. Third, it gives an opportunity for experiential learning and for the community for empowerment and sustainability.

There are several areas that can be benefited from these programs. For example, these socially engaged institutions can especially help people living in marginalized communities having the need for guidance and support to address problems of basic needs of life. Aggarwal and Chugh (2003) explain that urban areas are considered to be well-off places with the latest technologies, proper facilities and infrastructure, high income, modern lifestyle, educational facilities, etc. But the marginal group, like the people in the slums, continue to suffer from a lack of proper health facilities, education, and sustainable income. If these people are not understood properly, or understanding differs on different levels, then the policies drafted never be achieved by the marginalized group.

Similarly, certain vulnerable populations need attention as well. Though some of the problems are mentioned in general, different groups of people like children, youths, adults and the elderly face specific challenges in the slums. Their needs are different and different kinds of intervention are also required to find solutions to them. The involvement of higher education institutions has a major role in the development of the community, as the students of these institutions are future policymakers and bureaucrats. Students involved in community development have a positive impression of diversity, and they prepare themselves to work with people of diverse cultures. They are aware of the cultural differences, social identities, difficulties and challenges, which has a scope for them to learn new skills and knowledge (Fozdar & Volet, 2012).

Gutiérrez et al. (2005) explain that the focus of social work education was given on oppression, diversity, and social justice due to civil rights struggle and community organization. This is relevant even now that the shift is growing towards multiracial, multicultural and multiethnic contexts due to growing economic inequalities. Putting together theoretical knowledge in practical settings can help in the development process, which can help achieve the desired outcome. This can help in empowering low-income communities and promote more multicultural interaction within and among diverse groups.

Acknowledging this phenomenon, many international universities are looking for platforms for their students to receive experience on-field and create a difference in the disadvantaged community. Diversity of culture and socio-economic problems also interest international students as it provides opportunities to study those problems and find solutions. Some international universities also ensure that students learn the dynamics of different cultures and their difficulties and equip them to manage those problems. As a result, the students who are interested in working with diverse cultures generally have a positive orientation and adapt themselves to change. This contributes significantly to their professional growth.

Broadly, most of the international movement of students focuses on helping disadvantaged communities. The exchange of students focuses on improving and enhancing the living conditions and situations of local people by enhancing their skills. The major focus of the students is poverty, inequality, financial management, human rights, ecology and environment, health-related problems, chronic illness, gender equality, education, etc. This interdisciplinary approach helps to use theoretical knowledge in practical settings. Students are encouraged to develop their global awareness through the exchange program. This gives an opportunity for the students to create a structure for the local people with their knowledge, empowering the people and building their capacity to obtain resources required for their improvement. (Fozdar & Volet, 2012). This chapter aims at investigating the impact of the interventions of international students in the slum communities in terms of academic, health and economic empowerment.

2. Review of Literature

2.1. Education

Education is one of the top priorities for the children of urban slums. It is commonly accepted that education helps in finding solutions to different problems that prevail in society. According to Desai (1989), education is the base of development. Education leads to the development of human-based resources and potential and, in turn, supports further progress. For example, it automatically leads to economic development. Hence, education and socio-economic development are linked to each other and help accomplish the goals of the nation.

However, it is also true that children in the slum have limited access to education. It is very often found that many children drop out of school due to various reasons. For example, there may be issues related to the accessibility of the schools. The government schools may not be very close to the children, and they may have to go too far to get educated. Most of the time, primary schools are found in the slums, and for upper primary and secondary, they may have to go to another neighbourhood. Transportation could be another challenge for them to reach these schools. Issues can also be related to resources within the school. Sometimes the school may not be in a position to accommodate the students as the capacity is less. The quality of the education provided may not be up to the mark, and the teacher-student ratio is imbalanced. A limited number of teachers may have to deal with all the subjects, and the efforts put in by the teachers may not be sufficient as per the need. Teachers, sometimes, are not trained enough to handle the students, which can affect the learning outcome of the students.

Affordability of education also becomes an issue at times. There are private schools in the slum localities where the students need to pay fees and get educated. The financial background of the slum population may not be in a situation to pay huge amounts of tuition fees and get the children educated. Sometimes the parents enroll them in private schools and will not pay the fees, which will end up denying the child the chance to take exams and get a transfer certificate to another school. Even if some parents can afford to pay the fees, the infrastructure and other facilities may not be sufficient. These all can lead to children dropping out of school and becoming illiterate. To be considered literate, the child should have completed at least four years of schooling. Early dropout from school encompasses a larger number of adult illiterates at their later stage. Considering the dropouts from the schools, this is a drain of wealth and resources as there is a lot of investment made in the education of the children. If the education for the disadvantaged, like the children in the slums, is not designed properly, there could be more drain of money and resources (Desai, 1989).

In addition to this, reporting inflated education statistics is also prevalent in India. According to Desai (1989), it is over-reported that 90% of children are enrolled in schools for their education. This takes place due to the fact that grants provided by the government are based on the number of children enrolled in schools. Official statistics say that out of 100 children enrolled in grade 1, only 40 children complete grade 4, and only 20-25 children reach up to class 8. Though this study was conducted in 1989, some of the information is relevant even today in the context of the slum populations.

There are also other disadvantages for the slum children which hinder their education. Peer group influence is one among them, as children are prone to be influenced by their counterparts. The students who drop out of school can attract other students to follow their path, which leads others to drop out of school. Household work is another factor that affects the education of children. Kumar and Shukla (2016) pointed out that the time spent by children on household work can make them physically tired, making use of their energy which affects cognitive skills like grasping or paying attention and concentration. If this time is spent on their homework, tuition, and reading, it can produce better results in their learning outcome. Studies proved that any kind of child labour has an adverse result on school performance at elementary and secondary levels in terms of test scores, failing or repeating grades, and there are chances of dropping out. Work can affect learning, enthusiasm and interest in performing school tasks. More time spent on work can affect the cognitive development of children. Mothers' engagement in the labour force pushes their children to engage in domestic child labour. In the context of a slum, it is the elder female child who takes care of the maid's work when the mother works as a maid in other houses for wages. Factors like age, gender, family size, number of siblings, and order of birth decide the amount of work or responsibilities laid on a child. As the child grows older, the expectations from the child are also more in low-income families.

There are rules and norms in place to provide education for children, but the expected result has not been achieved so far. Though the schools are showing a hundred percent enrollment, the outcome is not monitored properly. To get grants and other benefits from the government and other resources, the schools are showing maximum enrollment. After enrolment, the students are not guided properly or monitored, and they get dropped out of school. In India, the state government is responsible for ensuring the quality of education in schools, proper implementation and bringing educational reforms. They are given the freedom to make use of finance and other resources based on their needs. The disparities in educational growth are an ongoing concern, and policymakers could not succeed in finding a solution to it. A future-oriented approach is required to ensure the learning needs of the disadvantaged group of children and not merely follow the costumed practices which are meant for others. Most of the policymakers are from the middle or upper middle class, and they need to understand the marginalized and include them as well while drafting the policies (Aggarwal & Chugh, 2003).

These gaps can be bridged through university student engagement with disadvantaged children. As they are the leaders of tomorrow, it is important for them to know the realities and struggles of the children living in the slum environment. According to Singh (2017), higher educational institutions have introduced the concept of social responsibility or community engagement, which is very popular in Western universities. The theoretical knowledge learned in the classroom is converted to experiential learning in the community. There are lots of international students who come to developing countries to understand the problems of the people and learn from them. They practice their skills and talents to find solutions for the problems of the disadvantaged community, which is a mutual benefit. International students come as exchange students for a longer or shorter duration, depending on the type of service they want to engage in.

Singh (2017) brings out that community engagement can take place in different forms, such as linking learning with community service, linking research with community knowledge, sharing knowledge with the community, devising new curricula and courses, including practitioners as teachers and social innovation by students.

The international students, during their engagement with the children from slums, reported that they need to be provided with quality education, and currently, it does not achieve the goals expected. Their intervention with the children of slum communities has helped them to streamline their education a bit. Through their support in the supplementary education centers, they have helped them to learn the concepts better, introduced easy ways of learning, learning through different activities, educated them that learning is not mugging up the lessons rather it is knowledge production, developed a curriculum for them, introduced schedule for learning, introduced physical activities as part of learning. Kumar and Shukla (2016) narrate that education is a process, and learning outcomes give a better understanding of the status of a person. The intervention of the international students has helped the children of slums to learn the concepts differently, kindled the fire of learning, understand the concepts from multicultural dimensions and understand that education can change their life.

2.2. Health

The slum atmosphere has an impact on the health of the people apart from external factors like food and shelter. The realization of health needs arises only when they are ill, and by then, it is too expensive for them to get treatment. Various reasons for ill health are crime, drug abuse, lack of knowledge on health prevention, malnutrition, difficulty in tracing people with ill health, etc. (George et al., 2019).

According to Ezeh et al. (2017), children are the most vulnerable group of people among the slum population. It is even more severe when they come across different health problems like diarrhoea and malnutrition, which can affect the physical development and cognitive development of children. Deficiency in nutrition causes various developmental problems and even ends up in mortality. One of the major reasons for child mortality is malnutrition in slums, and in Northern India, 77 per cent of the population lacks sufficient food facilities. They are deprived of nutritious food, and they depend on street vendors and pre-cooked food, which consists of one-fifth of the required calories. Breastfeeding can reduce child mortality, but due to the labour market, children are not provided with adequate breast milk.

Though a few illnesses like malaria can have a major impact on the children of rural areas, child mortality is more in urban slums. Surveys conducted in some of the urban and rural areas of different countries indicated that slum children are more prone to child mortality. Inappropriate sanitation facilities in the slums contribute to Gastrointestinal infections and Cholera. Poor housing and inappropriate waste management lead to Leptospirosis.

Slums are adaptable places for Aedes Mosquitoes to spread dengue fever. Social factors like overcrowding and mobility of the people in the slum can cause diseases like tuberculosis, HIV and the recent outbreak of Ebola, etc. The health of the slum population is affected because of the physical and social environment they reside in, which is beyond poverty alone. Most of the time, the health of the people living in slums is covered under urban health, which needs special attention as the neighborhood can create severe health problems when compared to the other urban developed areas. (Ezeh et al., 2017)

Though there are many health problems in the slums, all these need to be addressed and solutions to them are found. The involvement of local self-government can prevent the majority of the problems. But it does not happen all the time due to various reasons. The involvement of higher education institutions and students can help in understanding the problems and finding solutions to them to a certain extent. International students are attracted towards finding solutions to such problems. Gutiérrez et al. (2005) bring out that multicultural community works are based on consciousness-raising, and they need to develop a complex understanding of the situation and skills to gain power. Consciousness-raising can be done orally by telling the history of the relevant social issues prevailing in the community and social conditions existing and interacting with people who have the power to change problems. This will help the students to design tools, create awareness, educate people on the issue through different means and identify resources to solve the problem. The application of knowledge from an established country to the real-life problems of the urban slum population can find solutions.

According to Singh (2017), it is important to evaluate and measure community engagement by higher educational institutions as it benefits the community, students and the educational institutions and socio-economic and cultural contribution at different levels. Community involvement helps the students in their career preparation, understanding the problems of the community and connecting theoretical knowledge to practical settings. Communities, in turn, benefit by addressing the problems the students are focusing on. Fozdar and Volet (2012) describe that international students enhance their knowledge of ethnic diversity, understand different problems of people in the other corner of the world, become part of a growth process, become involved in community planning and development, and cultural identity in the post-colonial world, Social Justice, Human Rights, advocacy, empowerment, capacity building, understating and responding to differences, etc.

2.3. Economic Empowerment

Economic security is another challenge for the people living in slums, especially for women. Men are engaged in different kinds of labour like coolie, construction works, painting works, driving and other works. Women are engaged in housekeeping work and take up the role of maid to support their family income. According to Rambarran (2014), women in India are considered marginalized traditionally and being in slums adds to the adverse effects. The two different ways of empowering them are through education and income generation programs. As most of the women in the slums are aged and busy supporting their families for income, the possibility of educating them is over-ambitious. There are many challenges associated with the income generation program for the women in the slums. The majority of the women in the slums are uneducated, and they engage in the jobs of an unskilled workforce like child rearing, domestic work, housekeeping, etc.

It is important to ensure the development and empowerment of women living in slums. The empowerment of women leads to gender equality and social inclusion. Bhatia and Singh (2019) explain that financial inclusion is one of the mandatory elements for development. It has become a priority for many countries, including India, to provide affordable financial services. Financial empowerment can drive gender equality. Women empowerment is a process of including women in power and strengthening them in the areas of economic, political and social dimensions, which is essential for global progress. If the women are financially stable, other developments can accompany them. To promote this, one of the United Nations Sustainable Development Goals (SDG) focuses on financial inclusion. This will help the women to make decisions for themselves, at home, in financial matters and security, use of resources, mobility, and legal awareness, which promotes their development and well-being.

Poverty is the major factor that hinders economic security and empowerment. Poverty is not merely the absence of income, but it is also the deprivation of basic capabilities. Parsuraman and Somaiya (2016) point out that addressing women's economic development can help in bridging the gap between poverty, food security, inclusive and sustainable economic growth and gender equality. This is met through skill enhancement, availability of resources, improved decision making, etc., which adds social acceptance and values to the person. Gender equality can be addressed only through women's participation. Hence their skills have to be enhanced for active participation. Skill training is a pathway for the improvement in the quality of employment, which caters to economic empowerment. Skill development training enhances women's empowerment by increasing the confidence level of women, decision-making, capability and well-being. Vocation-based skill training can enforce economic empowerment by which they also become partners of development and visible in the workforce. Skill development training helps in enhancing skills and increases productivity and family income.

Parsuraman and Somaiya (2016) narrate that though there was a demand for tailoring and beauty care earlier among the slum women, now there is a shift in it into computer training, fashion designing, and entrepreneurship skills, which leads to self-employment. Such training has helped to inspire other women in the slum also to get skill enhancement training and get engaged in some activities which they were not doing earlier. This has motivated them to form microfinance institutions and self-help groups where the women form a group with 12-20 members and initiate small kinds of entrepreneurship. This has helped them to have access to credit, which they depended on the money lenders earlier for a huge rate of interest. Self Help-Groups have instilled a habit of saving among the slum women, collectively working for an economic growth process, and it opened a way for access to credits. The production-based training has helped the women to explore the market and penetrate these markets for the business. This has promoted the self-esteem and self-confidence of slum women, and they found that they are recognized in their community.

The international students have helped the women living in the slums to develop and enhance their skills in the areas of business promotion among the women group. They have helped them in forming the self-help group and taught them business skills, helping them to think of business and income generation programs, production, packing, branding and labelling, quality control, marketing, etc. to a certain extent, this has helped the women to earn additional income for the family and support their family at the time of emergency.

Some of the sustainable development goals focus on the education, health and economic empowerment of the people. Considering the situation of the people living in the slums, it is important to make cities and human settlements inclusive, safe, resilient and sustainable. These demands address socio-economic, environmental and political problems by the concerned authorities. Addressing inequalities is the first and format task of urban development and transformation in urban injustice. Urban planning is an essential requirement for the development of marginalized communities. This helps the residents to overcome their basic challenges. One of the important aspects of development is providing the necessary education for the inhabitants. Along with this, socio-economic problems and health problems of the people need to be addressed to have a better living. Urban inequalities need to be washed off, and they need to be given an environment for better living. To achieve the task, planners need to have skills, capacities, and values and keep the urban area on their priority list. (Wesely & Allen, 2019). International students, local students, higher education institutions, non-government organizations and other well-wishers are doing their best to eradicate the inequalities in slums. It is the need of the hour for the bureaucrats and the governing body to put this in place.

3. Methodology

This chapter focuses on the intervention of international students from the Netherlands and Norway in the urban slum communities of Bangalore, namely Lakshman Rao Nagar in Koramangala and Janakiram Layout in Kammanahalli. The samples were nineteen international students who were part of the community connect and thirty-three children and women with whom they engaged for a minimum of three months. This chapter is qualitative in nature, and descriptive data were used and collected through an online form with long-answer type questions. The purposive sampling method was used to select the sample. The analysis was conducted using thematic analysis. This attempt has helped in tracing the learning, development and challenges of international students and the help and support received by the children and women from urban slum communities, which mutually benefited their growth and development.

4. Results

The international students participating in the exchange programme were placed in different supplementary education centers and urban slum communities. They participated in projects where they conducted interventions and research to help the community in areas of education, health and livelihood. This section is divided into four parts. The first part describes the demographic information of the children and adults of the community. The second part involves the living conditions and the changes in the same by the interventions of the students. The next two parts discuss the overall challenges and recommendations and students' learnings, respectively.

4.1. Sample Characteristics

The participants from the community consisted of 14 children (Mean age = 13.21, range = 12-15 years, SD = 0.97) and 19 adults (Mean age = 39, range = 23-49, SD = 6.7). All the children were enrolled in schools and were studying in 6th-9th grades. The family income ranged from 8,000-20,000 INR (Mean income = 12,5000 INR) per month for a family of 5-6 individuals. On average, the adults had eight years of education ranging from 0-15 years.

In this research, 19 international students participated. Fifteen students were residents of the Netherlands, three belonged to Norway, and one was from Germany. The majority of the students studied social work in college.

The following sections describe the results of the thematic data analysis.

4.2. Living Conditions and Interventions

Overall responses about the living conditions highlighted issues due to poverty and the perseverance in the community sample. To understand the experiences, some questions asked to the community were "Explain how healthy you are and the kind of health problems you come across in your life", "explains the education assistance you have been receiving", "Explain why the children from the slum are getting dropped out from the school", etc. The questions asked to the international students included "Explain your observations about the income generation/livelihood/education/health status of people living in the urban slums of Bangalore", "explain the actual health situation of the people in the urban slums when you saw them in the initial days", and so on.

Based on the responses to these questions, the themes found for this section are

(a) positive experiences- an acknowledgement of the satisfactory factors,
(b) the poverty loop - poverty reinforcing itself, and finally
(c) resilience despite these conditions.

4.2.1. Positive Experiences

This theme encompasses the existing developments and adequate living conditions that the participants acknowledge. Regarding education, the children in the community have English medium schools at easily accessible distances. They receive adequate support in their education, for example, from the teachers, family, school and other organizations. Apart from teaching, teachers assist them through doubt clarification and teaching computers. The school and other organizations aid them by providing midday meals and school supplies. Many children's families help them in their education. This involves adequate financial, motivational and tutoring support. Either the parents tutor them themselves (e.g., in Kannada) or enrol them in tuition classes outside of school.

A child's verbatim expressing the same is as follows:

> *"My teachers clear the doubts and conduct a class test which is very useful for my exams. They give class work for references, like giving some key points and revision. My parents support me by paying the fees. And in tuition, they clear the doubts. By going to tuition, I have improved a lot in my studies."*

Apart from these sources, the children also feel supported by the neighbourhood. Children reported that they like the helpful activities and programmes running in their locality. Along with that, six children mentioned that being with their friends and family encourages them to be kind, respectful, helpful and obedient. These factors, in turn, support their education and personality development.

> *"[I learn] to be respectful, help others, obey, be kind to others. It improves our knowledge, learning new things, and being grateful to the family members."*

With respect to health and livelihood, most of the adult members of the community reported having food at least three times a day, and even though money was scarce, they were managing their food and shelter.

4.2.2. The Poverty Loop

This emerged as a significant theme across the areas of education, health and livelihood. In education, the loop appeared from the responses by the international students and the community children.

> "Money seems to be the most common negative factor in children's education. The urban slums are very poverty-stricken, and as we understand it, not all children within a single family can enrol in school due to lack of funding. Many children had to take care of their younger siblings, which makes doing schoolwork at home less of a priority."

Similar responses indicated how circumstances are not supportive for many of the children. For example, due to financial constraints at home, parents could not afford the school fee, and children were pushed to work and earn to support the family or look after younger siblings as the parents and older siblings left for work. Many children did not receive support for their education beyond 12-13 years of age. Moreover, due to these hardships, parents did not see the value in educating their children. Apart from issues in the family, other factors due to scarcity of funds, low quality of education, lack of resources and sanitation, and unsafe environment for girls further contribute to maintaining insufficient levels of education in the slum children. It is visible that factors emerging due to insufficient financial resources result in reinforcing poverty. In other words, it is "the poverty loop" that stops children from receiving a good education.

Neighbourhood factors like alcoholism and the absence of role models further increase the burden of the environment on education. Other factors like getting involved with bad company in the slums, early marriages, lack of interest in education and more interest in working also result in dropping out of school. On top of that, there were many limitations in the infrastructure and quality of resources in the school. For example, the classrooms were overcrowded, there was a lack of furniture, the classrooms were distracted, and chaotic, and different ages and levels of children were present in the same classroom. All these factors result from a shortage of money and result in the same.

> "Alcoholism was a very widespread problem within the slums, which also pressured children to do more work at home. Home life is important to school performance, and a troubled home life makes it difficult for the children to perform well in school."

This loop of poverty was evident in health and livelihood as well. Poverty, malnutrition, infections, and other health issues were present in the community. As a result of financial constraints, people did not have enough time to look after their diet and their children's dietary requirements. There was insufficient hygiene, inaccessible healthcare, low treatment adherence, and overall lesser resources. They took increased health risks, and there was a decreased priority on their health. On top of this, low awareness about health and nutrition (due to inadequate information) is added to the factors resulting in the low health status of the community. Prominent health issues in the community were headaches, body pain, seasonal colds, fatigue, and chronic conditions like diabetes and blood pressure problems.

> *"I have observed that poverty comes accompanied by a lack of knowledge concerning health. The overall awareness and understanding of their own health situation and risks seem low."*

Professionally, many of them were manual labours and house helpers. They could afford only essentials, somehow afford school fees for their children, could not manage to save and were not in a position to bear any unexpected costs. The financial crunch, limited resources like electricity, and substandard working conditions further impact education and skill building and keep them in low-paying jobs, continuing poverty. Livelihood factors also influence the health factors discussed above. There is a lack of opportunities and proper education for this stratum of the population, further prolonging "the poverty loop".

> *"Since children from young ages are expected to perform heavy tasks in the households such as…. This, in turn, leads to lower performance in education of the children and thus a better chance at a well-paid job later on in life."*

The following verbatim by one student aptly expresses the poverty loop interlinking education, health and livelihood.

> *"A low income per family causes a less healthy situation because families often cannot afford healthier alternatives. Parents did not receive an education that provided them with the skills to improve their living situation. There is little knowledge of proper nutrition, and little information is available for the people in the slums."*

4.2.3. Resilience
International students' observations about the children, the school and the community gave rise to this theme. They mentioned how despite being in the middle of their circumstances (mentioned earlier), children in the schools were very eager to learn, interested, attentive, motivated, and hopeful about the

future. They knew the value of education and worked hard. There were also families that supported the education of their children. With respect to schooling, even with challenges, the teachers were making every effort to provide the best education they could.

Other than that, the cost of education was reduced, midday meals were provided, the school was supporting mothers, spreading awareness about education, and at some places, there was psychologist's support for the children as well. The international students also found various abilities in the children. For example, despite academic challenges in subjects and teaching, almost all of them were multilingual in Indian languages.

> *"They [teachers] did the best they could to teach the children. Many of the kids were tired, and we felt like they had a hard living situation. The room/classroom was very small, but we understand it's much better than not having a place at all. The 'aunties', as they called them, were great. They cared for the children, and they helped us translate if needed."*

Outside of the school, there were other organizations that were providing funding to schools and financial support to families. Awareness programmes and some other initiatives were also conducted by volunteers. These efforts were supported and encouraged by the community members. They readily made use of their learnings.

> *"The biggest contribution to the income generation did not come from me. It came from the passionate people in the slum who were enthusiastic about the ideas we shared and decided to pick it up with the other women."*

Overall, it is visible that despite the harsh conditions the community was enduring, there was a presence of resilience and support within and outside the community.

4.3. Themes Related to Interventions by International Students

As a part of the programs, the international students conducted various interventions to bring specific changes in areas like education for children, malnutrition in the community, business development, establishing self-help groups to promote livelihood, etc. The following themes emerged from the analysis of the impact of the interventions based on the participant's responses.

Some questions asked to the community were "Explain how the international students have helped to increase your income or promote your livelihood", "explain how international students' intervention was beneficial for you for your better health", and "What are the different kinds of techniques/strategies the international students used for your academic development", etc. International students were asked questions like "Explain your contribution to the income generation of the people living in the urban slums of Bangalore", "explain the changes you have observed in the children after your service for these children", and so on.

4.3.1. Structured Fun and Learning

This was the major theme that resonated in the responses of both international students and children in the supplementary education centres. The international students used many movements and audio-visual-based activities to teach children. For example, games, storytelling, debates, sports, videos, music, etc. The international students also built long-term academic resources for the school and students. For example, systematic timetable, easy and practical methods of learning and teaching, workbooks, exercises, posters, and bringing already existing resources like state- syllabus books into the curriculum. They also gave individual attention and tutoring wherever needed.

A child expressed himself in the following manner:

"They conducted activities in different ways which were related to topics. It was an easy method. I have implemented it in school, and it helped me remember the sentences easily. I learnt new words, new activities and games."

"They conduct games/activities that involve us both physically and mentally. Sometimes there were moving activities, and craft making helped"

During the process, the children were supportive as well. They helped the international students translate and explain to other (younger) children when required. They were disciplined and participative in the activities. This support developed over time with international students.

"The students were very helpful to us when it came to the language barrier. They would help translate certain words and phrases which were difficult for the younger children to understand."

4.4. Development of Self

The intervention overall kindled more kindness, confidence, discipline, happiness, and concentration in the school children. They were delighted with this new way of learning and embraced it quickly. Changes in self-concept, self-esteem and self-grooming were also reported. The theme that emerged was the "development of self". There was an influence on the characteristics of children, an increase in knowledge (about the world and language) and resulted in learning for teachers as well.

> *"[I] Understood how to manage and express emotions by building self-awareness and handling impulses."*

4.4.1. Awareness is Key

This theme emerged from the responses of the participants involved in interventions towards improving the health status of the community. The recipients of the intervention reported gaining very important and useful learnings like increased knowledge about healthy diet, water quality, water intake requirements, sleep, stress, the importance of exercise and medical treatment. The techniques used by the international students to achieve this included giving information using visually appealing charts and pamphlets and teaching easy methods to follow a healthy diet through practical lessons. This increase in knowledge resulted in better eating practices and curbing malnutrition (as measured by the UNICEF malnutrition monitoring tool), changes in diet, and lower glucose levels in Type-2 Diabetes Mellitus patients. They also ensured the establishment of long-term programmes together with welfare organisations and local community people to maintain the change.

The effort is visible in the following sentences by an international student while talking about curbing malnutrition:

> *"This was obtained by creating healthy, affordable recipes and by informing mothers of children in the daycare Centre about these healthy alternatives. Also, a program was created to make sure new parents that joined the daycare were provided with the necessary information about healthy nutrition."*

4.4.2. Business Development and Marketing

The international students were placed in organisations that worked to improve livelihoods in urban slum communities. They used three ways to improve income generation - making a business development plan (promoting the business locally and online by identifying places for stalls, identifying markets, and selling through Facebook), increasing the variety of products by introducing more crafts and training the people in sales and marketing. For example, they trained them to communicate effectively with customers. One way this was achieved was by specifying the information to be provided to the customers, like the procedure of making the product, beneficiaries and individuals involved in the initiative, hygiene practices, and so on. They also guided the establishment of other strategies of business development, like proper accounting. As a result of these efforts, the community members experienced an indirect increase in their income, improved skills, and more efficient use of their time.

One community member mentioned:

"I have learned from them how to communicate. Their communication has helped in more sales which were difficult for us. They helped in identifying the places where stalls can be set up."

The students also helped build a self-help group for women to increase financial security, support from banks, and overall opportunities. The students used solution-oriented working techniques and research about other developing countries to inform their interventions better. They expressed that the ideas they communicated were grasped by the community readily.

"The intervention of setting up a self-help group helped the women to become aware of the opportunities in their neighbourhood and how they could use their connections to achieve their goals. Getting aware of the opportunities may have helped them a bit in a way to a better income."

4.5. Challenges and Recommendations

Both the community and international students faced many challenges and offered suggestions. They were asked questions like "Explain the challenges you were facing during their intervention and now", "explain how international students' programs can be made more effective for better results", "Explain how cultural differences have influenced your engagement with the people", etc. Four main themes emerged from their responses - cultural differences, other challenges (work challenges, academic and personal difficulties), and recommendations.

4.6. Cultural Differences

There are four categories in the theme of cultural differences:

4.6.1. The Challenge of Verbal and Non-Verbal Language
Almost all the participants mentioned language difficulties. This was due to differences in first languages and the English accent of international students and resulted in miscommunications or hindrances in the interventions they planned. Apart from spoken language, there was difficulty in interpreting non-verbal communication as well. The gestures and mannerisms were different between the cultures.

4.6.2. Attitudes to Time
The international students experienced a disregard for time agreements and a lack of punctuality from the community members and co-workers. They had difficulty adjusting to these and the pace of work, which seemed to be slower. Cultures differ in their chronemics (the role of time in communication). On the one hand, Europe predominantly has monochronic nations, and India, on the other hand, is a polychronic country. This means that programs are planned with an overall vision and entail many changes in plans, many tasks are done at once, and documentation is generally disliked (Van Everdingen & Waarts, 2003). This created a source of adjustment problems for international students.

4.6.3. Gender Norms
Many international students observed the differences in gender roles in the community. Adjustment to those social norms was very difficult due to the inequality among the genders.

> *"Cultural exchange was, for me, a wild ride. For me, I travelled thru a phase where I loved all the Indian adventures, colours, people and food. But after a few months, a phase started where I hated all men in India (oops) due to inequality. Of course, I exaggerate a little now. All the stories I read and heard made me realize how cruel the world can be. This duality of love and hate towards the country is what makes India unforgettable for me."*

4.6.4. Discipline Methods

While interacting with school children, the international students experienced a disregard for their authority. One major reason described by them was the difference in discipline methods. On the one hand, the teachers at the school employed an authoritarian way of teaching and discipline, involving punishments, minor threats, and more power distance than the international students were familiar with. In contrast, international students employed an authoritative way. They found that the students were used to a stricter pattern and did not accept their authority. The students adjusted to this in different ways. Some students adopted the authoritarian style, while others increased interaction and built rapport. As a result, the students became interested and started respecting the international students' authority.

> *"Let me explain. If a child is "used" to being slapped or something along the line. That is the ultimate punishment for misbehavior. That child will then know that everything before the physical punishment or the threat of it is sort of fine. Not that bad of a behaviour. So, when there are instances where my authority is put on the line, a simple "stop that!" would do little."*

4.7. Other Challenges

4.7.1. Challenges at Work

There were various field challenges for the students. For example, they experienced a lack of structure at internships. They adjusted by resolving issues themselves and seeking help from the programme coordinator and staff. In the supplementary education setups, exchange students faced difficulty in teaching due to differences in teaching styles. In addition, while developing businesses, they found a lack of documentation and inconsistency in product information. While communicating with the community members during interventions for health, they experienced that individual in the community refrained from asking for clarification while having doubts. However, they managed it with the help of the local community.

4.7.2. Academic and Personal Challenges

As exchange students in India, students faced a few academic challenges. For example, they trained in Europe and were required to apply the knowledge in a very different country. This posed both a challenge and a learning opportunity for the students. Besides this, simultaneously completing the academic tasks of both the source and host universities was taxing. Finally, many of them experienced a lack of time available to them to do the intervention and see the impact of those interventions.

Regarding personal challenges, they faced housing difficulties, cleanliness issues and some initial prejudices in themselves.

4.8. Recommendations

The international students gave many responses to questions like "What are recommendations you have for the exchange program" and "Explain how the income/health/education of the people/children can even be improved better according to you with the help of international students", and the community gave their ideas for questions like "share your thoughts and suggestions for the improvement for the income generation program."

Exchange students shared ideas about additional support to the supplementary education centres through their engagement. For example, by increasing reciprocal learning between the exchange students and children to improve cultural exposure, being role models and mentors for the children, using their strength in English for the language development of the children, and structuring their own classes with more flexibility to be able to achieve this, and so on.

Some recommendations requested were for teachers, the course, classes and other infrastructure. They experienced an absence of teachers and felt the teaching was repetition based, under stimulating, and not good enough and suggested teachers learn other teaching styles and provide a consistent presence to the children in order to improve the quality of education. An increase in teachers' salaries and better resources will aid the same. They believed that the students should be differentiated based on levels for studying separate courses rather than being put in the same class together; this will help reduce chaos and disruption. Lastly, w.r.t. the infrastructure, they posed that a bigger classroom size and better furniture will aid education. However, at the same time, they acknowledged the challenges of working in low-resource settings.

One common recommendation made by the community children and adults alike was regarding the speed of speech of the exchange students. They wanted them to speak slowly to resolve the difficulty of understanding their accent. Along with that, they suggested that international students should be given information about the community and its challenges in advance. For example, challenges and techniques of working with children who dropped out of school. In supplementary education centres, students, in unison, requested even more practical lessons with games and activities. Participants from the health interventions stated the need for improving the interventions by increasing the duration, reducing the pace, and increasing the number of programmes. Lastly, participants from livelihood interventions proposed introducing more kinds of products (e.g., product series for men), receiving support in international export of the products, and more ideas for business expansion will help improve the program further.

Overall, for the program, the exchange students felt that more information in the initial stages and better structure and planning is required. They want to make projects more sustainable. According to them, this can be achieved by a transition phase of old and new international students working together and handing over the projects or by staying longer and doing follow-ups. One student also felt that having another coordinator for business studies along with social work would be even better for their and the community's development.

4.9. Themes in the Process, Experience and Learning of the International Students from the Exchange Program

4.9.1. Process
For most of the students, the selection process for the program consisted of writing an application letter. Some were selected based on additional interviews, motivation letters, research proposals or the level of their grades. Financial eligibility was also checked. Visits to the embassy and visa processing were additional tasks.

After selection, the students interacted with experienced students and received cultural training and tips from teachers.

There was a lot of documentation involved during the exchange program. For example, providing a plan, writing reports and assignments, making logbooks of their work, paperwork relating to the University, and external paperwork like residency permits and police registration in the country.

During the program, they received the help and guidance they wanted from the host university and worked with people who were passionate about their work. They were also supported by the staff in the initiatives run by CSA.

4.9.2. India!

The main motivation for the students to choose India in their exchange programmes was their interest and curiosity about India. Almost all of them wanted to explore India. Some also wanted to see education and social work in India. Connections between the educational institutions and good reviews of the programme enhanced that motivation further. They believed that with this exploration, they would benefit in their personal growth, and they would gain more knowledge about the world.

4.10. Learnings

This theme has three categories - personal growth, academic and professional growth, and cultural/social growth.

4.10.1. Personal Growth

The students had to learn to be very adaptable when they arrived in India and worked here. The social norms and other challenges discussed in the previous section were very different from their home countries. These challenges helped them to learn to be flexible, adjust, and improvise when needed. Their ability to communicate and connect with different kinds of individuals is also enhanced. They learnt different ways of communication and how to work through language difficulties. Many planning skills were also sharpened further during the course of the programme. Students reported an increase in their confidence as well. Other personal learnings were about their goals, personality, and creating more openness in themselves.

4.10.2. Academic and Professional Growth

The students learnt about social work in India. They mentioned having a "broadened view of social work". They could see the impact of social work towards the betterment of the community. The practical experiences helped them understand the subject better. They saw the impact of hunger and poverty face-to-face and learnt to work in low-resource settings. They also realized how bringing a change takes time and that small steps are important towards bringing bigger changes. They developed characteristics in themselves that are needed to implement projects on the ground. Lastly, some also involved themselves in Participatory Action Research and found it beneficial for their academic growth. Overall, participating in the exchange program was useful academically and professionally because of what they experienced in India.

4.10.3. Cultural Growth

All the participants reported that huge learning was about the culture of India. Their knowledge about this part of the world has increased tremendously. They came across different social norms, and their view of 'poor' people had also expanded by their experiences working in the slums.

5. Discussion

5.1. Cycle of Poverty

The cycle of poverty is a "self-reinforcing mechanism that causes poverty, once it exists, to persist unless there is an outside intervention" (Aghion & Durlauf, 2005). These self-reinforcing mechanisms are established because factors that can help elevate poverty, in turn, require money. For example, factors such as education, starting a business, taking help/training for a business, obtaining land/other resources, etc. all require money. The same was observed in the results of this study. Financial resources to improve education, health, and business were unavailable. The poverty trap was impacting education, health and livelihood, and vice versa.

The poverty trap in education means that individuals remain uneducated and, as a result, poor because of a lack of resources to invest in education. This can happen because of a variety of factors. As seen in our results, families did tend to remove financial support after a certain age and expect children to get married, take care of younger children or have a full-time job to support the family. Barham et al. (1995) emphasized a similar point of the role of family income in the poverty trap and education. The family may not be able to afford education for the children or lose an individual's valuable earnings upon pursuing education instead of a job. These discourage poor families from investing in education.

Beliefs about poverty also have a huge influence on the academic progress of children and are important factors in maintaining the cycle of poverty. As identified in the results, when education is not found valuable, parents are hesitant to support their children. Further, in an implicit manner, beliefs about education and academic success may influence children indirectly. For example, if a child is believed to not succeed or is 'destined to be a manual labour', any possibility of failure, even after putting effort into learning, may be shameful for the kid. This results in a lack of interest or a reduction in the capacity of the children.

Further, a poor neighbourhood has additional inhibitory factors like safety issues, hygiene issues, and lack of 'social closure' (Coleman, 1998) between parents and teachers, which add to low-quality education and ultimately support the poverty trap (Noguera, 2011). This was also evident in the findings of this research - some reasons for dropping out were lack of sanitation and safety for girls. A lack of involvement of families was also observed. These issues impact the experience of education coupled with other beliefs, quality of education and financial resources, as discussed above.

Along with education, health and socio-economic status have been linked widely as well (Pillay-van Wyk & Bradshaw, 2017). As observed in the results of this study, the poverty cycle is present in the health status of communities too. Because of the reduced priority of health, individuals are rendered incapacitated, and poverty is maintained further by developing incapability or less efficiency in pursuing education or profession. Along similar lines, Guerrero et al. (1998) emphasized how "health cannot be dealt with while ignoring poverty". They point out that poverty is the reason many children do not get vaccines, and people do not get clean water, healthcare, medicines, and so on.

Lastly, a similar pattern is played out in their livelihood as well. The cycle of poverty maintains itself by keeping people in low-paying jobs. Due to factors like lack of education, malnutrition, lack of resources, etc., individuals are deficient in the ability to progress in their profession. This alternatively is also called the 'livelihood cycle'.

To tackle the problem of this ongoing loop of poverty, external interventions are needed. There are various examples (see Noguera, 2011; van der Berg et al., 2011; Blandón et al., 2017) where the community, external agencies and governments have come together to break this cycle for many. For example, providing social services along with education in poor neighbourhoods resulted in improved academic outcomes for children (Darling-Hammond, 2010).

The interventions by international students also resulted in improvement for the community. For example, children grow academically by increasing their knowledge, developing personal characteristics, and enhancing the motivation required for academic achievement. The interventions also helped bring health awareness to the community and resulted in curbing malnutrition.

The students ideated, gave guidance, and carried out a business development project to enhance the livelihood options of the people involved. It is evident that the involvement of exchange programs in social work in India has many mutual benefits.

5.2. Resilience

The results found a lot of resilience in the children and adults of the community, which was also an important factor in the success of the exchange programs. It is evident in one student's narrative:

> *"The people were supportive. If I needed help, I was always supported by the people in LR Nagar."*

As reported earlier, the children were enthusiastic and motivated, and the adults readily used the international student's interventions for their benefit, despite the conditions. They wanted to improve their quality of life. Social resilience, as defined by Keck and Sakdapolrak (2013), has three dimensions of capacities - coping capacity, adaptive capacity and transformative capacity. Coping capacity means the ability to cope with and overcome adverse events. In the results of this research, it was visible that children were resilient in education against adverse conditions like lack of support from the family, alcoholism in the family, neighbourhood disturbances, etc. Adaptive capacity in social resilience denotes the ability to "learn from past experiences and adjust themselves to future challenges in everyday lives". This was also observed in the children and adults who were willing to look at their existing conditions and readily made changes with the help of interventions. For example, children learn the language and do new activities to help themselves study better, and adults adapt themselves to new ways of having a healthy diet. Lastly, transformative capacity means the ability to "access assets and assistance from the wider socio-political arena". This capacity in the community was slowly developing as they participated in the interventions and helped in the implementation of the program. There were community stakeholders involved in the programs run by the CSA department. More interventions and help to such communities will result in increasing this resilience and finally breaking the cycle of poverty. This resilience can further be used to enhance the well-being of the slum community.

5.3. Advantages and Disadvantages for Exchange Students

Overall, the engagement of international students was found to be very beneficial. The benefits for the community were increased awareness about health and factors related to health, increased knowledge among students, enhanced self-esteem and motivation, and improvement of business for working individuals. The engagement helped both the community and international students grow culturally. Similar results have been found in other studies, and the phenomenon of mutual cultural growth is often termed as 'building cultural humility'. It is identified as an important takeaway for participants in both the host and source country (Thampi, 2021).

As a result of international collaboration, the students who were part of the program also gained significant learnings. Academically, some students learnt how social work is practised in India. They developed a deeper understanding of poverty. They experienced the steps in bringing a change firsthand. Similar results have been found in many other studies. For example, in "The Exchange Experience in India" (Alphonse, 2008; as cited in George & Delarosa, 2009), the author mentions that international students learn to involve themselves in the local context, contribute to local initiatives, and come with a "heightened awareness of global injustices and inequalities". These experiences also help cultivate enthusiasm for international social work practice.

The students also reported an increased ability in communication and social skills. This development occurred as a result of interacting with the local community, making decisions with co-workers, implementing the intervention, etc. Alphonse (2008) mentions a similar growth in "striking relationships with individuals and organisations" that international students experience by taking part in exchange programs.

5.4. Challenges for Students in Exchange Programs

As specified in the results, there are various challenges like cultural differences in language, social norms about gender and work, norms about time, differences in quality of life, and other issues that interfere and yet provide a growth edge in the exchange programs.

Some authors recommend a few steps to help tackle these issues. Lough (2011) emphasizes the role of the supervisor in the host institution as crucial in enhancing reflection and learning (Lough, 2011). It is essential to receive support from the host institution to overcome the challenges of the host country. This was very evident in the responses of the students:

> *"I was very satisfied with how members of faculties and staff assisted us during the program. They were helpful and understanding of our origins, and we never felt like we were being judged or criticized due to our cultural and professional differences. They answered our questions, and they helped us understand certain things that we may not have been able to understand ourselves. The staff at the urban slums were helpful and made us feel highly welcome."*

Similarly, Thampi (2021) also highlighted the need for institutions to communicate beforehand to reduce challenges for students. A similar need was put across by the participants of the research as well.

Based on the challenges and recommendations found in this research, the authors present some suggestions as preparation for international students.

1. Cultural training - A brief training session to familiarize the students with the culture, traditions, social norms and language of the host country will help in building acceptance and provide opportunities to adjust. For example, it was requested that the international students speak slowly as there was difficulty understanding their English accents. A brief history of the country may also help develop more empathy towards the culture of the host country. Along similar lines, a reflective session on preexisting prejudices and inhibitions in the students about the countries of destination will assist in bringing awareness and resolution of the same.
2. Information about ongoing projects in the host country - preparation about participation and options of projects must be provided well in advance to give an opportunity to the students to gather sufficient information about the context and work requirements for different programs. For example, there was a request to help students gain knowledge about working with school dropout students before their participation in the project. Some students also researched Self-help groups in developing countries to better help the community. More opportunities to do this will be beneficial for both the students in the host country.
3. Work division among the universities - students must be informed about all the documentation required in both universities prior to the

beginning of the programme. The collective requirements of assignments must be decided to keep the well-being of the students in mind, accounting for various factors such as new environments and work challenges. On the same lines, supervisors from both universities must be available to guide students' learning and reflection throughout the exchange program at regular intervals.
4. Work flexibility for exchange students - on the field, when students feel they can contribute much more, they should not be limited due to the structures of the ongoing projects. An option to explore more impactful initiatives must be kept open. For example, options in teaching.
5. Sustaining the work - the international students expressed the need to sustain their work by transferring the project to other students or increasing the duration of their involvement. Any of these steps will be beneficial to both the community and the exchange students.
6. Information on other challenges like housing, formalities, etc. - an information leaflet about the procedures and on-ground challenges of other life aspects in the host country will help the new students. Input from experienced students can be included in the same to help exchange students prepare and problem-solve effectively during their stay.

Overall, the involvement of exchange students in various projects is profitable to both the community and the students. These opportunities can be made even more fruitful by further steps discussed in this section. Challenges are posed with involvement in a new culture. However, a similar magnitude of development opens up as well.

6. Conclusion

This chapter aimed to explain how the involvement of international students in initiatives for community well-being can result in fruitful outcomes for both students and the community. The results found that there were many issues that the community children and adults were dealing with, mainly related to the 'poverty loop', which were improved with the interventions of the exchange students. Changes were seen in the children's development of self and education and adults' awareness of health-related information and livelihood development. The students also benefitted at personal, academic, professional and cultural levels. Major themes in challenges faced were related to cultural differences in time, language, gender norms, and discipline methods for students. Other challenges included other work, academic and personal challenges. Several recommendations provided by the students and community were also summarized under a separate theme. Lastly, these themes were discussed in light of existing research and implications for student exchange programs, and further suggestions were provided. This research shows that effective intercultural exchange can result in value addition to all the parties involved.

References

Aggarwal, Y., and Chugh, S. (2003). *Learning achievement of slum children in Delh*i. Operations Research and Systems Management Unit, National Institute of Educational Planning and Administration.

Aghion, P., and Durlauf, S. (Eds.). (2005). *Handbook of economic growth*. Elsevier.

Alphonse, M. (2008). International Social Work Practice : The Exchange Experience in India. *Canadian Social Work Review/Revue Canadienne De Service Social*, 25(2), 215-221. http://www.jstor.org/stable/41669896.

Barham, V., Boadway, R., Marchand, M., and Pestieau, P. (1995). Education and the poverty trap. *European Economic Review*, 39(7), 1257-1275.

Bhatia, S., and Singh, S. (2019). Empowering Women Through Financial Inclusion : A Study of Urban Slum. *Vikalpa The Journal for Decision Makers*, 44(4) 182–197.

Blandón, E. Z., Källestål, C., Peña, R., Perez, W., Berglund, S., Contreras, M., and Persson, L. Å. (2017). Breaking the cycles of poverty: Strategies, achievements, and lessons learned in Los Cuatro Santos, Nicaragua, 1990–2014. *Global health action*, 10(1), 1272884.

Coleman, J. S. (1998). Foundations of social theory. Harvard University Press.

Darling-Hammond, L. (2010). Teacher education and the American future. *Journal of teacher education*, 61(1-2), 35-47.

Desai, A. S. (1989). Education of the child in urban slums: An overview of factors affecting learning and responsive action through social work. *The Indian Journal of Social Work*, 1(4). 505-523.

Ezeh, A., Oyebode, O., Satterthwaite, D., Chen, F., Ndugwa, R., Sartori, J., Mberu, B., Melendez- Torres, G. J., Haregu, T., Watson, S. I., Caiaff, W., Capon, A., and Lilford, R. J. (2017). The history, geography, and sociology of slums and the health problems of people who live in slums. *Lancet*, 389. 547–558. http://dx.doi.org/10.1016/ S0140-6736(16)31650-6.

Fozdar, F., and Volet, S. (2012). Intercultural learning among community development students: positive attitudes, ambivalent experiences. *Community Development*, 43(3), 361-378. https://doi.org/10.1080/15575330.2011.621085.

George, C. E., Norman, G., Wadugodapitya, A., Rao, S. V., Nalige, S., Radhakrishnan, V., Behar, S., and Witte, L. (2019). Health issues in a Bangalore slum: findings from a household survey using a mobile screening toolkit in Devarajeevanahalli. *BMC Public Health*, 19, 456. https://doi.org/10.1186/s12889-019-6756-7.

George, P., and Delarosa, E. (2009). Nuance and Subjectivity in International Exchange : A Response to "The Exchange Experience in India". *Canadian Social Work Review / Revue Canadienne De Service Social*, 26(1), 115-119. http://www.jstor.org/stable/41669905.

Guerrero, R., Jancloes, M., Martin, J. D., Haines, A., Kaseje, D., and Wasserman, M. P. (1998). How the cycle of poverty and ill health can be broken. *Bmj*, 316(7142), 1456.

Gutiérrez, L., Lewis, E. A., Nagda, B. A., Wernick, L., and Shore, N. (2005). Multicultural community practice strategies and intergroup empowerment. *The handbook of community practice*, 341-359.

Keck, M., and Sakdapolrak, P. (2013). What is social resilience? Lessons learned and ways forward. *Erdkunde*, 67(1), 5-19.

Kumar, K. K., and Shukla, T. (2016). Education Outcomes & Child's Work : A Case Study of Children in Slum. *Educational Quest*, 7(2), 117.

Lough, B. (2011). International volunteers' perceptions of intercultural competence. *International Journal of Intercultural Relations*, 35, 452–464. https://doi.org/10.1016/j.ijintrel.2010.06.002.

Noguera, P. A. (2011). A Broader and Bolder Approach Uses Education to Break the Cycle of Poverty. *Phi Delta Kappan*, 93(3), 8–14. https://doi.org/10.1177/003172171109300303.

Parsuraman, S., and Somaiya, M. (2016) Economic Empowerment of Women Promoting Skills Development in Slum Areas, A report of study sanctioned by the Ministry of Women and Child Development. https://wcd.nic.in/sites/default/files/Final%20Report-TISS-%20Skill%20in%20slums.pdf.

Pillay-van Wyk, V., and Bradshaw, D. (2017). Mortality and socio-economic status: the vicious cycle between poverty and ill health. *The Lancet Global Health*, 5(9), e851-e852.

Rambarran, R. (2014). The Socio-Economic Status of Women in the Urban Slums of India. MPRA Paper No. 62736. https://mpra.ub.uni-muenchen.de/62736/.

Singh, W. (2017). Gauging the Impact of Community University Engagement Initiatives in India. *ASEAN Journal of Community Engagement*, 1(1), 1-16

Thampi, K. (2022). Internationalisation of social work education in India through student exchanges : challenges and prospects. *Social Work Education*, 41(8), 1601-1616.

Van der Berg, S., Burger, C., Burger, R., de Vos, M., du Rand, G., Gustafsson, M., Moses, E., Shepherd, D., Spaull, N., Taylor, S., van Broekhuizen, H., and von Fintel, D. (2011). Low-Quality Education as a Poverty Trap. Stellenbosch Economic Working Papers : 25/11, Universiteit Stellenbosch University.

Van Everdingen, Y. M., and Waarts, E. (2003). The effect of national culture on the adoption of innovations. *Marketing letters*, 14(3), 217-232.

Wesely, J., and Allen, A. (2019). De-colonising planning education? Exploring the geographies of urban planning education networks. *Urban Planning*, 4(4), 139-151.

Chapter 8

Women Empowerment Through Community-Based Organisations in Rural Karnataka

Cyril John[*]
Department of Sociology and Social Work, Christ University, Bengaluru, India

Abstract

Women empowerment is an active multidimensional process to enable women to realize their identity and power in all spheres of life. Self Help Groups (SHGs) have played a significant role in women's empowerment. Through the SHGs, the dreams and desires of women came into reality. The current study examines women's empowerment through community-based organisations in rural Karnataka (Hoskote, Jamkhandi and Kolar). The chapter aims to determine the impact of SHGs on rural women's lives and whether it contributes to women's empowerment. The chapter follows a mixed-method research design. Thirty well-performing SHGs from three Centre for Social Action (CSA) project sites in rural Karnataka, namely Hoskote, Jamkhandi and Kolar, were considered for this chapter. A simple random sampling technique was used. Ten members from each SHG were selected, and three hundred SHG women samples were recruited. Responses from the samples were collected using pre-designed questionnaires.

The results state that there is a well-evident improvement in women's economic, social, familial and political status after joining the SHG. The chapter concludes that SHG has caused significant change and development in women's socio-economic, familial and political life in rural Karnataka.

---

[*] Corresponding Author's Email: cyril.john@christuniversity.in.

In: Models for Social Responsibility Action by Higher Education Institutions
Editors: Joseph Chacko Chennattuserry, Elangovan N. et al.
ISBN: 979-8-89113-097-5
© 2024 Nova Science Publishers, Inc.

Keywords: women, empowerment, SHG, economic status, social status, familial status, political status and SHG

1. Introduction

As a result of the societal and structural barriers, the condition of women is miserable. The famous economist and Nobel laureate Amartya Sen state that women worldwide have less access to "substantive freedoms" such as education, employment, health care, and democratic freedoms (Sen, 2001). Global Education Monitoring Report of 2016 states that 1 in 10 girls compared with 1 in 12 boys were out of primary school in 2014 (UNESCO, 2016). Studies state that pregnancy-related deaths and diseases remain unacceptably high. In 2015, an estimated 303,000 women died from pregnancy-related causes (WHO, 2015). Women missing from all levels of government- local, regional, and national, have less economic freedom and cannot own land are some of the other chief issues women face globally (Dworkin, 2015). All these facts point towards the feminization of poverty, which in turn means women's unequal share of poverty in terms of wealth, choices and opportunities (Sen, 2001).

Various intervention approaches have been developed by governments, development agencies, and women's groups in order to address the needs of women and women empowerment. One among these approaches is women's SHGs. The basic assumptions of this income-generating group programs are to give women access to working capital, increase their ability to generate choices, exercise bargaining power, develop a sense of self-worth, develop a belief in one's ability to secure desired changes and the right to control one's life (Dworkin, 2015). SHGs act as a platform through which women come together for the purpose of solving their common problem through mutual support and aid.

SHGs originated in the year 1975 in Bangladesh by Mohammed Younus. During the eighties, there was a serious attempt by the Government of India to promote an apex bank to take care of the financial needs of the poor, informal sector and rural areas. Later, NABARD (National Bank for Agriculture and Rural Development) took steps and initiated a search for alternative methods to fulfil the financial needs of the rural poor and informal sector. NABARD was initiated in 1986-87, but the real effort was taken after 1991-92 from the linkage of SHGs with the banks (Narang, 2012).

SHG is a small voluntary initiative to form into a group. It is an informal and homogenous group of not more than twenty members because any group having more than 20 members has to be registered under the Indian legal system. That is why it is recommended to be informal to keep them away from bureaucracy, corruption, unnecessary administrative expenditure and profit motive (Narang, 2012). In fact, it is a home-grown model for poverty reduction that simultaneously works to empower and shape the lives of its members better. Groups are expected to be homogenous so that the members do not have conflicting interests and all members can participate freely without any fear. The SHGs movement has triggered a silent revolution in India's rural credit delivery system. SHGs have been proved as an effective medium for delivering credit to the rural poor for their socio-economic empowerment (Kondal, 2014).

The concept of Self-Help Groups has its roots in rural areas, and it has been introduced along rural and semi-urban women to improve their living conditions. Though it is applicable to men in our country, it has been more successful only among women. Economic activities were started by women through the SHG movement. In India, this scheme is implemented with the help of NABARD as a main nodal agency in rural development. It is a self-employment generation scheme for especially rural women who don't have their own assets. The word 'empowerment' means giving power. Power means having the capacity and the means to direct one's life towards desired social, political and economic goals or status (Narang, 2012). Empowerment provides greater access to knowledge and resources, more autonomy in decision-making, greater ability to plan lives, more control over the circumstances which influence lives, and freedom from customs, beliefs and practices. Thus, the empowerment of women is not just a goal in itself but is key to all global development goals. Empowerment is an active multidimensional process to enable women to realize their identity and power in all spheres of life.

SHGs have really changed the lives of women, especially rural women. Through the SHGs, the dreams and desires of women came into reality. This chapter examines women's empowerment through Community-Based Organisations in rural Karnataka (Hoskote, Jamkhandi and Kolar). The chapter aims to find out the impact of SHGs on the life of rural women and whether it is contributing to women's empowerment.

2. Review of Literature

In the 21st Century, too, we could see rapid growth in the problem of Indian rural poverty. According to the National Statistical Office (NSO), Report 2019, 30 million people in rural India fell below India's official poverty line (Bhattacharya & Devulapalli, 2019). Major causes of poverty among India's rural people include high levels of illiteracy, inadequate health care, minimal access to social services, and lack of access to productive assets and financial resources (KHF India, n.d.).

In his study, Manjunatha states that women, in general, are the most disadvantaged people in the rural regions of India, and poverty has many disadvantages for this group. He further states that rural poverty in India can be eradicated mainly by providing economic support to rural people, particularly to rural women. Providing economic support or loans to rural women helps them to empower, not only economically but also socially. This, in turn, will strengthen the whole society in general (Manjunatha, 2013). Here comes the significance and relevance of SHGs.

Women's participation in SHGs has tremendously impacted the life patterns and styles of poor women. They have been empowered at various levels as individuals and as family, community and society members. Women come together to solve their common problems through self-help and mutual help. Self Help Groups are considered one of the most significant tools in the participatory approach to women's economic empowerment. It is a tool to remove poverty and improve women's entrepreneurship and financial support in India (Geethanjali & Prabhakar, 2013).

Kondal states that SHGs play a greater role in increasing women's empowerment by making them financially strong, as well as it helped them to save an amount of money and invest in further development. Additionally, SHGs create confidence for social and economic self-reliance among the members in the two villages. It develops awareness programs and schemes, loan policies etc., (Kondal, 2014).

Experiences of women state that the positive effects of SHGs on economic, social, and political empowerment include familiarity with handling money and independence in financial decision-making; solidarity; improved social networks; and respect from the household and other community members (Dworkin, 2015). The women involved themselves more in making decisions regarding the education of their children, the investment of the family, managing the family's economic assets and bringing up cohesion among the members of the family and others for a better living (Rao,

2013). The spirit for the social and economic upliftment of members is the significant contribution of each and every SHG.

Empowerment signifies 'making somebody ground-breaking, encouraging the feeble to achieve quality', and with regards to ladies' strengthening, the term has come to signify ladies' expanded command over their lives, bodies and condition. Today, the empowerment of women, and poor women specifically, is the pushed region of advancement activity in India. In any case, the idea of women's empowerment is moderately new, particularly in advancement (Senthilkumar et al., 2020). SHGs' role in empowering women in rural areas is significant. The social impact of SHGs on women's empowerment is noticeable. It brings social cohesion among the poor at the grassroots level. Field evidence shows that SHG members can easily get involved in households' decision-making and bring positive changes in their life. SHGs provide a sufficient platform for social participation and encourage the members for better interactions with society. SHGs could change women's social outlook and social status tremendously. Such continuous efforts lead to the societal transformation of women in rural areas (Rajagopal, 2020). Social empowerment means that the woman should get an important place in her family and society and should have a right to enable her to make use of available resources. It has resulted in uplifting the living conditions of poor household women, developing their self-confidence, self-esteem, and self-respect. As women have increased presence in banks, Gram Panchayats, and various Government committees, their social status is somewhat elevated. The social impact of the SHG program increased involvement in Decision-making, awareness about various programs and organisations, increased access to such organisations and increased expenditure on Health and Marriage events. There is a Change in the attitude of male members of the families. Now they are convinced about the concept of SHG and encourage women to participate in the meetings. Women reported that they have savings in their name, and it gives them confidence and increased self-respect (Saravanan, 2016).

According to the National Commission for Women (NCW) - (Status of Women 2011), in India, women work for longer hours than men. The proportion of unpaid activities to the total activities is 51% for females as compared to only 33% for males. Over and above this unpaid work, they have the responsibilities of caring for households which involves cooking, cleaning, fetching water and fuel, collecting fodder for the cattle, protecting the environment and providing voluntary assistance to vulnerable and disadvantaged individuals in the family. This shows that there is still a long journey ahead towards women's empowerment. Women regularly save small amounts of money and mutually agree to contribute a common fund. However, this does not fulfil all their needs. Indebtedness has become the hallmark of rural life (Saravanan, 2016). Economic development and harmonious growth of a country would be possible only when gender bias has triumphed over. Problems faced by women are looked upon as a problem of social welfare rather than development. Women in developing countries live in virtual seclusion, deprived of the rights she holds and unable to access even the most basic services. Microfinance activity is mainly focused on women's empowerment with the notion that women can handle financial matters better than men. Many efforts are made by developing counties like India to make women a part of the development process and to uplift the status of women folk. An empowered woman in a family act as an indicator of the socio-economic growth of the family, which in turn helps the growth and development of the country (Priyakumari & Karthik, 2017).

A community's socio-economic background considerably influences the attitudes, values and perceptions of the individuals composing it. So, for the proper analysis of the role of social factors in political participation, a brief account of the socio-economic profile of sample respondents, in particular, is presented in this section. The institutions do not work in a vacuum; the given socio-economic and political circumstances determine the shape of the institutional process. The socio-economic variables, to a great extent, determine the variations in political participation level. Political behaviour, like any other aspect of human behaviour, takes place in a particular socio-economic and cultural milieu. It is affected by social structure, economic development and historical factors combined together. Background characteristics of an individual play an important role in formulating his/her preference and decisions. The most significant aspect of women's empowerment commences with the involvement in the decision-making process in household activities. Self-help groups have been founded with the motive of creating awareness among women in all areas (Teja, 2016).

Political empowerment, decision-making, and leadership significantly improved self-confidence, followed by self-esteem, self-respect, and leadership role in the family. This is due to the fact that, after joining SHG, the women are more aware of their roles, responsibility, and rights. Their self-confidence, self-esteem, and self-respect have increased as they started financially contributing to the family, and subsequently get respect which improves the confidence level of the women. On the other hand, connecting with the same level of women and working in a group also helps to gain confidence and make them capable of handling any situation as a group. Moreover, women are more empowered economically, followed by social and political empowerment (Hushenkhan, 2008).

The development of a country like India is impossible without developing the rural area and rural population, particularly women. In recent years SHGs have helped immensely in mobilizing rural women and driving them towards economic empowerment. The empowerment of rural women not only helped in uplifting their status but also the upliftment of the whole family and society. The fate of the women is not decided by others anymore, and they can help themselves; this is the basic purpose of SHGs. The principle of SHG revolves around mutual cooperation and self-help for development. The study suggests that after joining SHG, there was a significant improvement in occupation and income status. The study also reveals the positive effects of joining SHG on the decision-making status of the women in the family, increased knowledge about basic banking activities and positive attitude towards entrepreneurship. It was also found that the availability of low-interest credit facilities helped the family to carry out the economic activity for the family's well-being (Sucharita & Bishnoi, 2019).

Evidence has shown that poverty alleviation and empowerment through self-help can expand the capabilities of women in several areas of significance to the quality of life. Empowerment as a comprehensive process, therefore, may require interventions that work on the social environment – shaped as it is by culture and history – as well as individuals. Women from the SHG program confirmed that a primary motivation for participation was the financial benefits though there also cited self-confidence and greater freedom to move out of the house as key motivators. In terms of daily experience, the ability to interact socially with important people like bank officers and political representatives was also mentioned (Anand et al., 2020).

3. Methodology

In this chapter, thirty well-performing SHGs from the Centre for Social Action (CSA) and three project sites in rural Karnataka, namely Hoskote, Jamkhandi, and Kolar, were selected. Ten members from each SHG, thus making it to three hundred SHG women sample from places like Hoskote, Jamkhandi and Kolar in rural Karnataka. Simple random sampling was applied. Primary data was collected directly from the respondents with the aid of a self-made questionnaire.

The chapter employed a mixed method. Responses from the samples were collected using pre-designed questionnaires, focus group discussions (FGD), and collection of case studies. While analyzing the data, triangulation was also conducted to authenticate the data.

The sample universe of the study is CSA Project Sites, and the population is SHG members of the CSA project in the Hoskote, Jamkhandi and Kolar areas of Karnataka. The sample unit of the study is a woman who is an SHG member of the CSA project in the Hoskote, Jamkhandi and Kolar areas of Karnataka.

The measures for Socio-demographic Proforma include questions on the name of the project site, village and name of the SHG; participant's age, religion, caste category, educational qualification, marital status, family composition (members of the family, their age, sex, education, occupation, and income), do the respondent own a house, land, monthly income and expenditure of the respondent's family.

Socio-economic, political and familial empowerment of women was measured using a questionnaire that consisted of a list of statements dealing with the respondents' general feelings about themselves. There are 32 questions in all, with three sections: questions 1 to 8 deal with economic status, 9 to 16 on social status, 17 to 24 regarding familial status and 25 to 32 are all about the political status of the respondents. The data was collected by completing the self-structured questionnaire, conducting FGDs and a case study. Triangulation was conducted to cross-check the quantitative as well as qualitative data obtained.

Responses from the questionnaire were analyzed through Statistical Package for Social Sciences (SPSS) version 21. Item analysis was employed to Analyse the data, and the results were presented in a tabular format. Prior permission from the CSA and SHG women (participants) was obtained for data collection. The purpose of the research was well explained to the participants. Participation was voluntary, and the participants were totally free to discontinue at any point in the study. The utmost level of confidentiality was ensured and avoided any misuse or exaggeration of the data.

4. Results

The data were self-reported by the selected samples on the hard copies of the questionnaire. Altogether, 300 SHG women participated in the study. After the completion of data collection, the data were analyzed using Statistical Package for Social Sciences (version 23, International Business Machines

Corporation, US). Item analysis was employed to analyze the data, and the results were presented in tabular format.

4.1. Socio-Demographic Profile

Socio-demographic details of the respondents were analyzed using item analysis, and the results are presented in Table 1.

Table 1. Socio-demographic profile

Factor		f	Percentage
	20-30	72	24.00
	31-40	125	41.66
Age	41-50	70	23.33
	51-60	31	10.33
	61-70	02	0.66
	Hindu	290	96.07
Religion	Muslim	09	03.00
	Other	01	00.03
	SC	138	46.00
Caste	ST	70	23.03
	OBC	65	21.07
	Other	27	09.00
	Illiterate	143	47.07
	Primary	70	23.03
Education	Secondary	69	23.00
	Intermediate	08	02.07
	Degree and above	10	03.03
	Married	268	89.03
Marital Status	Unmarried	05	01.07
	Widow	27	09.00
Living in own house	Yes	294	98.00
	No	06	02.00
	Concrete	82	27.03
Type of house	Tiled	196	65.03
	Thatched	22	07.03
	Cultivation and Animal husbandry	38	12.07
	Labour	198	66.00
Occupation	Business	5	01.07
	Housewife	45	15.00
	Studying	01	00.03
	Others	13	04.02
Owning land	Yes	180	60.00
	No	120	40.00

4.2. Economic Status

The results state that there is a significant improvement in the economic status of the respondents (Table 2). The study states that three fourths of the respondents are of the opinion that there is a steady increase in monthly income and savings after joining the SHG. In addition to this, the respondents are of the opinion that after joining SHG, employment generation happened, and their standard of living improved. In short, the economic status of the respondent's family improved after joining the SHG.

Table 2. Economic status

Factor		f	Percentage
There has been an increase in my monthly income after joining the SHG	Agree	44	14.07
	Strongly Agree	265	85.03
There is an increase in my monthly saving after joining the SHG	Agree	32	10.07
	Strongly Agree	268	89.03
Credit facilities have increased after joining the SHG	Agree	56	18.07
	Strongly Agree	244	81.03
The economic status of the family has improved after joining the SHG	Agree	110	36.07
	Strongly Agree	190	66.03
The standard of living has improved after joining the SHG	Disagree	01	00.03
	Agree	122	40.07
	Strongly Agree	177	59.00
Through SHG, employment generation happened	Agree	127	42.03
	Strongly Agree	173	57.07

4.3. Social Status

Results depict the fact that there is a significant improvement in the social status of the women after joining the SHG (Table 3). After joining the SHG, changes happened in the words and deeds of the women. Their awareness of government schemes and policies increased. The SHG has positively affected women's participation in social activities and relations and improved the decision-making power of women.

Table 3. Social status

Factor		f	Percentage
Changes occurred in words and deeds after joining SHG	Agree	143	47.07
	Strongly Agree	157	52.03
Improved awareness regarding government schemes, rights and policies after joining the SHG	Disagree	01	00.03
	Agree	113	37.07
	Strongly Agree	186	62.00
Gained better social status and decision-making power after joining the SHG	Disagree	01	00.03
	Agree	147	49.00
	Strongly Agree	152	50.07
Participation in social activities improved after joining the SHG	Disagree	03	01.00
	Agree	119	39.07
	Strongly Agree	178	59.03
Relations with others have improved after joining the SHG	Disagree	02	00,07
	Agree	92	30.07
	Strongly Agree	206	68.07
Improved in leadership qualities after joining the SHG	Disagree	01	00.03
	Agree	78	26.00
	Strongly Agree	221	73.07

Table 4. Familial status

Factor		f	Percentage
Freedom to express your feelings and opinions	Agree	145	48.03
	Strongly Agree	155	51.07
Freedom to decide for which purpose the loan amount be utilized	Disagree	13	04.03
	Agree	119	39.07
	Strongly Agree	168	56.00
Freedom to decide for oneself (pregnancy, job etc.)	Disagree	80	26.07
	Agree	61	20.03
	Strongly Agree	159	53.00
A positive attitude from the husband while you are functioning with the group	Disagree	01	00.03
	Agree	110	36.07
	Strongly Agree	189	63.00
A positive attitude from the children while you are functioning with the group	Agree	56	18.07
	Strongly Agree	244	81.03
A positive attitude from the in-laws while you are functioning with the group	Disagree	01	00.03
	Agree	66	22.00
	Strongly Agree	233	77.07
Able to spend quality time with the family	Disagree	02	00.07
	Agree	100	33.03
	Strongly Agree	198	66.00

4.4. Familial Status

Results showcase the fact that the familial role and status of the individuals significantly changed after being part of SHG (Table 4). After joining SHG, women's freedom to express their feelings and opinions, decide for themselves, and decide for which purpose the loan amount is to be utilized has significantly increased. Women are receiving positive attitudes and encouragement from their husbands, children and in-laws. In addition, women are of the opinion that despite their busy schedules with the functioning of the SHG, they can find quality time for their family members.

4.5. Political Status

The political status of the women also changed a lot after being part of the SHG (Table 5). Since the women joined the SHG, their involvement and contacts with political parties increased; they started to attend Gram Sabha meetings and succeeded in representing the local issues before the political leaders and officials. In short, the political status of the women tremendously changed after being an SHG member.

Table 5. Political status

Factor		f	Percentage
Involved in any political party after joining the SHG	Disagree	09	03.00
	Agree	147	49.00
	Strongly Agree	144	48.00
Attend Gram Sabha meeting after joining the SHG	Strongly Disagree	21	07.00
	Disagree	105	35.00
	Agree	143	47.07
	Strongly Agree	31	10.03
Developed contacts with political leaders after joining the SHG	Disagree	75	25.00
	Agree	183	61.00
	Strongly Agree	42	14.00
Feel that you got some political recognition after joining the SHG	Strongly Disagree	01	00.03
	Disagree	93	31.00
	Agree	153	51.00
	Strongly Agree	53	17.07
Succeeded in securing your rights from the government	Disagree	01	00.03
	Agree	266	88.07
	Strongly Agree	33	11.00

Factor		f	Percentage
Succeeded in representing local issues before political leaders and officials	Disagree	11	03.07
	Agree	239	79.07
	Strongly Agree	50	16.07

5. Discussion

Even though women constitute almost half of the total population of the world, their social, economic and political status is lower than that of men, and they have been subjected to the domination and oppression of a particular order for centuries and even today. They are customarily expected to confine themselves to household environments and play a passive role as daughters, daughters-in-law, wives and mothers. They are typically considered weaker than men. This attitude has constrained their mobility and, consequently, they lack opportunities to develop their personalities.

Women belonging to underprivileged and poorer sections, irrespective of their social strata or region, are in no position to unknot their problems. They have lagged in the fields of education, skill development and employment, and as a result, their work is greatly undervalued in economic terms. Women's lack of empowerment is believed to be an important factor in this situation; hence they require social and economic protection. Therefore, they need familial, economic, social and political empowerment. Women empowerment is a critical determinant of familial as well as economic well-being, social status and political power. Microfinance aims at providing the urban and rural poor, especially women, with savings, credit and insurance and aims to improve household income security and, in turn, endeavours to empower women.

Women, in fact, contribute more than half of the wealth of nations and yet they are denied familial, economic, social and legal rights and privileges that such a contribution often entitles men to. The Beijing meets and subsequent meets emphasized a great hope which will take equity. There has been a perceptible shift from viewing women as targets of welfare policies to treating them as critical agents for development. Now the emphasis has shifted from development to empowerment. Undoubtedly, human development and people's participation go hand in hand. Our planning process has underscored the need for women's empowerment for the country's progress. It augurs well for the country that it has now been recognized that women have the key to substantial development. The efforts at improving the economic conditions of women certainly enhance their status in society. Literacy and education would sharpen women's awareness in manifold spheres, including the political sphere.

Government/semi-government and non-governmental organisations empower women through legislation, policy and special programs for women. The government of India has created effective institutional frameworks to strengthen the movement for women's empowerment after independence. Several programs and remedial measures are taken up to develop and uplift women. Several Acts were framed for the betterment of women, say, the Employees State Insurance Act 1948, the Factories Act 1948, the Mines Act 1952, the Plantation Labour Act 1970 and the Payment of Gratuity Act 1970. A number of provisions were made in the Criminal Procedure Code, the Hindu Marriage Act and the Hindu Adoption and Maintenance Act to provide special protection to women.

SHGs emerge as an important strategy for empowering women and alleviating poverty. SHG is a 'people's scheme', and its organization is a significant step towards empowering women. An SHG is a voluntary group formed to attain some common goals. Most of its members have a similar social identity, heritage, caste or traditional occupations and come together for a common cause and manage resources for the benefit of the group members.

The distinguishing feature of the SHGs is creating social and economic awareness among the members. Social awareness enables the members to lead their lives in a sound hygienic environment and pursue a better life. The woman members involve themselves more in taking decisions regarding the education of their children, the investment of the family, managing the economic assets of the family and bringing up cohesion among the members of the family and others for a better living. Every member of the SHGs has felt the need for more involvement in economic activities. The spirit for the social and economic upliftment of members is the significant contribution of each and every SHG.

Conclusion

It can be concluded that the main motive behind the formation of the group by the sample respondents in the study area is to obtain financial support from the government and, in turn, to support the family. Neighbours and animators are the main motivating persons to encourage the women to form SHGs in the study area. No conflicts are found among the group members. The study finds that there is a shift from borrowing loans for consumption purposes to production purposes after joining SHGs. After joining SHGs, sample respondents know about the importance of economic activities to women. Their role in the family is also increased. They are socially and politically aware after associating with SHGs.

It can be concluded that the impact of SHGs is not uniform in all the sample villages. This could be attributed to several factors like motivating persons, satisfaction over functioning, percentage of increase in monthly income, non-food consumption expenditure, percentage of increase in monthly savings, level of knowledge, the dominance of husband, participation in social service activities, political activeness, political recognition and problems faced.

Improved awareness levels, adequate training, raised self-employment opportunities, increased savings and increased self-confidence to borrow from various sources are the major contributions to the better performance of the sample SHGs. However, there are various drawbacks such as the inadequate amount of loans, negative attitude of banks, delay in sanctioning of loans, lack of knowledge to manage the financial affairs of the group due to lower levels of education and lack of knowledge on the rules and regulations for the functioning of the SHGs.

References

Anand, P., Saxena, S., Gonzales, M. R. & Dang, H. (2020). Can Women's Self-Help Groups Contribute to Sustainable Development? Evidence of Capability Changes from Northern India, IZA Discussion Papers, No. 12940, Institute of Labor Economics (IZA), Bonn.

Bhattacharya, P., & Devulapalli, S. (2019). India's rural poverty has shot up. https://idronline.org/indias-rural-poverty-has-shot-up/.

Dworkin, C. B. (2015). Economic Self-Help Group Programs for Improving Women's Empowerment: A Systematic Review. Campbell Systematic Review, 1-182.

Geethanjali, R., & Prabhakar, K. (2013). Economic development of women through self help groups in YSR district, Andhra Pradesh, India. *Studies on Home and Community Science*, 7(1), 25-34.

Hushenkhan P, G. S. (2008). Political Empowerment of Women through Self Help Groups (SHGs) : A Study in Andra Pradesh. *The Indian Journal of Political Science*, 69, 609-617.

KHF India (n.d.). Rural poverty in India. www.jkhfindia.org: https://www.jkhfindia.org/news/indias-rural-poverty.html.

Kondal, K. (2014). Women Empowerment through Self Help Groups in Andhra Pradesh, India. *International Research Journal of Social Sciences*, 13-16.

Manjunatha, S. (2013). The Role of Women Self–Help Groups in Rural Development of Karnataka State, India. *International Research Journal of Social Sciences*, 23-25.

Narang, U. (2012). Self Help Group : An Effective Approach To Women Empowerment In India. International Journal of Social Science & Interdisciplinary Research, 8-16.

Priyakumari, S. V., & Karthik, D. S. (2017). Impact of Self-help Group in Economic Empowerment of Rural Women-A Study. *Journal of Advanced Research in Dynamical and Control Systems*, 409-414.

Rajagopal, N. (2020). Social impact of women SHGs: A study of NHGs of 'Kudumbashree'in Kerala. *Management and Labour Studies*, 45(3), 317-336.

Rao, M. B. (2013). Self-help groups and empowerment of women: a case study in Guntur District of Andhra Pradesh. PhD Thesis, Acharya Nagarjuna University. https://shodhganga.inflibnet.ac.in/handle/10603/8124.

Saravanan, M. (2016). The impact of self-help groups on the socio-economic development of rural household women in Tamil Nadu - A study. *International Journal of Research*, 4(7), 22-31.

Sen, A. (2001). The many faces of gender inequality. The New Republic, pp. 35-39.

Senthilkumar, C.B., Dharmaraj, A., Indhumathi, C., Selvam, V., & Kandeepan, E. (2020). A study on women empowerment through self-help groups with special reference to Villupuram district in Tamil Nadu. *Journal of Critical Reviews*, 7(6), 355-359.

Sucharita, S. & Bishnoi, I. (2019). Impact of Joining SHG on the Lives of Rural Women and their Families. *International Journal of Science and Research*. 8(1), 914-918. http://dx.doi.org/10.21275/ART20194416.

Teja, D. R. (2016). Political empowerment of women with respect to the self-help groups (A Case study of Visakhapatnam, District. Andhra Pradesh State). *International Journal of Academic Research and Development*, 1(11), 2455-4197.

UNESCO (2016). Global Education Monitoring Report. https://gem-report-2016.unesco.org/en/chapter/parity/.

WHO (2015). Retrieved from https://www.who.int/reproductivehealth/topics/maternal_perinatal/en/.

Chapter 9

Community-Based Educational Intervention on Emotion Regulation, Self-Esteem, and Behavioural Problems Among School Children

Anekal C. Amaresha[*]
Department of Sociology and Social Work, Christ University, Bengaluru, India

Abstract

Recently, there has been a trend where higher education institutions are designing and implementing community-based educational interventions for underprivileged children in the community. It is important to understand whether these interventions are useful to the children in improving their psychosocial development. In this chapter, the author discusses the learnings from an explanatory sequential mixed methods study which aimed at assessing the impact of community educational intervention provided by a higher educational institution on self-esteem, emotional regulation and bbehavioralproblems among adolescents in rural Karnataka. The study included 250 adolescents who were beneficiaries of community educational intervention and another 250 who were non-beneficiaries. Besides this, the chapter also highlights the qualitative results grounded in the focus group discussions to understand the stakeholder's perspective on community educational interventions. Finally, the author demonstrates the processes and mechanisms of change and presents a critical discussion from the quantitative and qualitative data analytic lens. The author anticipates that community educational interventions provided by higher educational institutions are extremely

---

[*] Corresponding Author's Email: amaresha.c@christuniversity.in.

In: Models for Social Responsibility Action by Higher Education Institutions
Editors: Joseph Chacko Chennattuserry, Elangovan N. et al.
ISBN: 979-8-89113-097-5
© 2024 Nova Science Publishers, Inc.

impactful. Several critical factors of stakeholders, institutional, and rural communities might bring change and sustainability in benefits among rural adolescents.

Keywords: children, educational intervention, community, self-esteem, emotion regulation, behavioural problems

1. Introduction

The social, economic, and political changes over the past few decades have impacted Indian higher education and educational institutions. Moreover, globalisation and modernisation have shaped the universities' vision and mission, which are not just restricted to higher education; rather, it has forced them to provide education beyond the university structures (Vasilescu et al., 2010). Hence, several universities in India have expanded their work beyond academics and research. It is important for higher education institutions to have partnerships with the stakeholders of the neighbouring communities for outreach activities (Jongbloed et al., 2008). The higher educational institutions concentrate on the themes such as education of children and youth, women empowerment, and livelihood while working with the communities. Indian constitution provides free and compulsory education for all children between 6 to 14 years of age. Also, the Right of Children to Free and Compulsory Education (RTE) Act 2009 provides legal status to the constitutional provision. Both these advocate for compulsory, satisfactory, and equitable quality education with essential standards for the children in India (GoI, 2021).

Despite these efforts, thousands of children are deprived of free quality education, especially in rural communities. There is a great disparity in terms of psychosocial development or social skills among rural and urban school-going children. Urban school-going children have better opportunities for quality education and other skill development activities. In this regard, it is important to focus on the psychosocial development of children in resource-deprived rural areas. Hence higher educational institutions have wide scope for community-based educational interventions. If we look at the mental health perspective, rural children lack school mental health services in comparison to urban school children. There could be several reasons. First and foremost, the orientation of school teachers on mental health disorders. Next, the absence of mental health professionals and mental health services at the primary health care systems and the local government institutions such as schools and anganwadis in India. The childhood years, especially school-going age, are recognized as an important period for the psychosocial development of cognitive functioning (Anderson, 2002) and literacy skills (Aram, 2005), which are essential not only for academic success but even for academic transition. Children who do not demonstrate academic and learning difficulties at the schools will not have poor academic scores, truancy or dropout (Gubbels et al., 2019). More importantly, they cope well with peer groups (Ullah & Wilson, 2007), and there is a negative relationship between childhood internalizing and externalizing problem behavior (Ansary & Luthar, 2009; Aunola et al., 2000). There are many internalizing factors (emotional problems such as anxiety, distress, or stress, etc.) and externalizing factors (behavioral problems such as attentional or conduct issues) along with intelligence quotient and communication or language abilities (Alloway & Alloway, 2010; Hogan et al., 2010) that predict academic performance. However, one of the most important factors to be researched among school-going children is emotion regulation. Emotional regulation is defined as *"a multifaceted construct, including the awareness, understanding, and acceptance of one's emotions; the ability to control impulsive behaviors when experiencing negative emotions; and the ability to modify strategies for managing emotions according to situational demands and goals"* (Gratz & Roemer, 2004). It is established that emotional regulation is important for school children's academic success (Graziano et al., 2007). Another construct that is crucial for school children to succeed in academics, co-curricular, and extracurricular activities is self-esteem (Fathi-Ashtiani et al., 2007). In a general sense, self-esteem refers to self-worth. Rosenberg (2015), in his book "Society and the Adolescent Self-Image," defined self-esteem as a *"positive or negative attitude of a person toward him/herself."* Hence, this chapter is interested in exploring the impact of community-based educational intervention on emotion regulation, self-esteem, and behavioral problems among school children.

2. Review of Literature

There is a relationship between emotional regulation, self-esteem and behavioral problems among school-going children (Gómez-Ortiz et al., 2018). Systematic reviews on interventions for emotional regulation among school children (Schlesier et al., 2019) reported that there are different models of emotion regulation interventions.

1. Cognitive behavioral model (Daunic et al., 2012; Smith et al., 2014)
2. Positive behavioural interventions (Cook et al., 2015)
3. Child-focused classroom curriculum program based on the social information processing theory (Terzian et al., 2015)
4. Social and emotional learning program (Schonfeld et al., 2015)
5. Mindfulness-Orientated Meditation (Crescentini et al., 2016)
6. Anger Diary (Renati et al., 2011)
7. School dog-Teacher-Team Animal Intervention (Beetz, 2013)

Though these studies have focused on emotional regulation among children in 1st to 4th grade, they have not exclusively assessed emotional regulation as an outcome variable during school hours (Schlesier et al., 2019). Self-esteem is extensively researched among school children, and several systematic reviews have explored the effects of various interventions on different groups of school children (Augestad, 2017; Dale et al., 2019; Kolubinski et al., 2018; Murray et al., 2017). Moreover, there are systematic reviews on teacher, parent, and peer-delivered interventions for internalizing and externalizing behaviors of children (Buchanan-Pascall et al., 2018; Corcoran et al., 2018; Feiss et al., 2019; Werner-Seidler et al., 2017). However, these studies predominantly come from western countries, and there is a lack of research exploring community-based interventions supported by higher educational institutions on emotion regulation, self-esteem, and behavioral outcomes among school-going children. Therefore, it is essential to understand the effects of community-based interventions that are delivered by community members and supported by higher educational institutions, especially in countries like India, where resources are underutilized

Children require a conducive learning environment for their holistic development. However, India, being a resource-poor country, faces challenges in providing such an environment, leading to school dropouts due to the inaccessibility and unaffordability of quality education. This poses a significant challenge for the government in ensuring the right to education for all, including underprivileged children in poor rural communities. In this context, partnerships between corporate entities, higher educational institutions, and government initiatives become impactful in addressing these issues. Recently, higher education institutions have taken the initiative to design and implement community-based educational interventions for underprivileged children in the community. However, there is a lack of studies to understand whether these interventions are beneficial for the children in terms of improving their psychosocial development. Hence, conducting studies to assess the impact of these intervention programs becomes crucial.

CHRIST (Deemed to be University), Bengaluru, is one of the major higher education institutions in Southern India, involved in community-based interventions with its developmental wing, Centre for Social Action (CSA). The CSA works on various developmental projects for children, women, and various marginalized groups in urban slums, rural, and tribal villages across India. This chapter explores how the community-based educational intervention program benefits underprivileged rural children by improving their emotion regulation, self-esteem, and behavioral problems. In this regard, we propose two models in the absence of supporting literature, which could be helpful, and have not been explored by any studies. The first model involves direct engagement of university faculties and students with the children of the community. The second model entails the higher educational institution mapping and utilizing the resources in the community, such as educated youth or community members with potential qualifications and skills, to participate in delivering interventions aimed at improving emotion regulation, self-esteem, and reducing behavioral problems among school-going children. The latter model is thought to be more sustainable and cost-effective than the former model. Hence, the current study aims to explore the usefulness of such a model in two districts of the Indian Southern state of Karnataka. Specifically, the study examines the impact of the university-supported community-based educational intervention on emotion regulation, self-esteem, and behavioral issues among rural children. As part of this process, the current study compares the children who have received CSA-supported community-based intervention with those who are not part of the intervention to understand the program's effectiveness.

3. Methodology

3.1. Study Design

The study has adopted a quasi-experimental design with a post-test comparative group design to assess the impact of the community-based educational intervention (CSA-benefited) group and the non-CSA-benefited group on outcome variables such as emotion regulation, self-esteem, and behavioral problems among school-going children. This design is particularly useful in situations where there are no established baseline scores of the outcome variables.

3.2. Study Groups

The community-based intervention group, also known as the CSA benefited group, comprises school children who actively participate in activities at the community activity centers. The CSA operates these community centers in each of the project villages with the assistance of educated volunteers, most of whom are either studying or working and have educational backgrounds ranging from 12th grade to undergraduate level. Every evening, these dedicated volunteers conduct activities at the community centers for two hours, catering to school children from 1st grade to 10th grade. They receive supervision and training from project coordinators employed by the CSA, who are qualified professional social workers with a Master's in Social Work and several years of community work experience. The volunteers conduct the activities for the school children from 1st grade to 10th grade on the following aspects.

1. Conducting skill-building activities such as life skills activities
2. Engaging in responsible civic activities to take action on locally prevalent issues
3. Conducting sports and cultural activities
4. Enhancing good study habits
5. Giving assistance to students with poor academic grades and connecting them with their peers with good academic grades
6. Career guidance to outgoing students
7. Observance of all nationally important days

The non-CSA benefited group comprises 1st to 10th-grade school-going children who are not attending the community activity centers of CSA but have volunteered to participate in the study assessments. These children predominantly attend private schools in those localities.

3.3. Setting, Sample and Sampling

The data were collected in two districts, Bagalkot and Kolar, in the Karnataka State of Southern India, where CSA has implemented community-based projects. These two districts are considered backward in terms of education and health, with predominantly agrarian communities. Within these project areas, CSA has implemented health and educational projects for underprivileged children and livelihood projects for women.

Participants in the study were selected regardless of their educational level, including those attending primary, high school, or higher secondary schools, as well as those who have completed primary, high school, or higher secondary education. They were all residents of either Bagalkot or Kolar project areas, where CSA's projects have been implemented. As mentioned earlier, the study comprised two groups: CSA-benefited adolescents who actively participated in CSA's community activity centers, and non-CSA-benefited adolescents. A total of 318 adolescents participated in the study, of which 207 were CSA-benefited adolescents and 111 were non-CSA-benefited adolescents. The recruitment and identification of all the participants were conducted by volunteers from the community activity centers and project coordinators.

3.4. Tools for Data Collection

A semi-structured questionnaire was utilized to collect socio-demographic data, including information on gender, age, grade, and family details.

Emotion regulation: It was measured using the Difficulty in Emotional Regulation Scale–Short Form (DERS-SF) (Kaufman et al., 2016). The DERS-SF is an 18-item questionnaire that assesses emotional responses in six domains: non-acceptance, goals, impulse, awareness, strategies, and clarity of emotion. Respondents rate their responses on a 5-point Likert-type scale, ranging from 1 (Almost never) to 5 (Almost always). Higher scores indicate more difficulty in emotion regulation. The scale demonstrates good internal consistency, with Cronbach alpha scores ranging from .75 to .89 (Hallion et al., 2018).

Self-esteem: It was measured using Rosenberg's Self-Esteem Scale (Rosenberg, 1965), consisting of ten items that assess a person's perception of their own worthiness as a human being. The scale employs a 4-point Likert-type scale, ranging from 1 (strongly disagree) to 4 (strongly agree). The scale includes an equal number of positively and negatively worded items, such as feelings of satisfaction with life and feelings of failure. It shows excellent internal consistency, with alphas ranging from .85 to .88.

Behavioral Problems: To evaluate behavioral problems among adolescents, the Strengths and Difficulties Questionnaire (SDQ) teacher version was employed. This tool helps screen for behavioral issues and pro-social behavior in adolescents. The SDQ teacher version comprises 25 items, divided into five subscales: Emotional problems, conduct problems, hyperactivity problems, peer problems, and pro-social behavior. Teachers rate each item on a 3-point scale, from 1 (not true) to 3 (certainly true)..

3.5. Data Collection

The quantitative data were collected by the community center volunteers and CSA field project coordinators using Google Forms. They received training from the principal investigator on data collection procedures. The collected data was securely stored in Google Drive with password protection, and access was restricted to only the principal investigator.

3.6. Data Analysis

The data were edited and coded using the statistical application Jamovi (Version 1.6). The team conducted descriptive statistics such as frequency, percentage, mean and standard deviation for demographic details. The hypotheses testing was conducted using an independent sample t-test to compare the mean differences between CSA benefited group and non-CSA benefited group.

3.7. Ethical Considerations

This study was approved by the Institute Review Board of CHRIST (Deemed to be University). All study participants were provided with a thorough

4. Results

4.1. Description of the Respondents' Characteristics

Table 1 depicts the socio-demographic details of both groups. The total number of participants was higher in the CSA beneficiary group (207) compared to the non-CSA beneficiary group (111). There was an overall higher number of females in the CSA beneficiary group, while a greater number of males were present in the non-CSA beneficiary group. The non-CSA beneficiary group had slightly older participants compared to the CSA beneficiary group. The CSA beneficiary group had an average attendance of 4.15 years at the activity center. Regarding monthly family income, the non-CSA beneficiary group reported higher income compared to the CSA beneficiary group.

Table 1. Socio-demographic details of the participants

Demographic Details	CSA (N = 207) Mean (SD) / N (%)	Non-CSA (N = 111) Mean (SD) / N (%)
Gender: Male	90 (28.30)	57 (17.92)
Gender: Female	117 (36.79)	54 (16.98)
Age in years	13.9 (1.84)	14.4 (1.73)
Current Grade	8 (1.74)	8.41 (1.67)
Years of Attending the CSA activity centre	4.15 (1.60)	NA
Monthly Family Income	13385 (7790)	14383 (4322)
Fathers' Age	42.4 (4.91)	41.9 (4.60)
Mothers' Age	36 (4.36)	36.1 (4.82)
Fathers' Education	3.34 (4.07)	4.31 (4.09)
Mothers' Age	2.76 (3.90)	3.32 (3.89)

4.2. Hypotheses Testing

H1: There will be significantly lower difficulties in emotional regulation among school-going adolescents who benefited from CSA compared to those who are non-beneficiaries.

The results showed that the CSA beneficiary group had significantly lower mean scores on emotion regulation difficulties compared to the non-CSA beneficiary group, especially on the awareness (t = 3.76, p < 0.001) and clarity sub-scales (t = 2.66, p < 0.05). However, there was no significant difference in other subscales and total scores of difficulties in emotion regulation.

H2: There will be significantly higher self-esteem among school-going adolescents who benefited from CSA than those who are non-beneficiaries.

The results showed that mean self-esteem scores were significantly higher among the CSA beneficiaries compared to non-CSA beneficiaries (t = 10.88, p < 0.001).

H3: There will be significantly lower behavioral problems among school-going adolescents who have benefited from CSA than those who are non-beneficiaries.

The CSA beneficiary group had significantly lower mean scores on behavioral problems such as conduct (t = 3.15, p < 0.005) and hyperactivity (t = 2.21, p < 0.05) and showed better pro-social behavior (t = 4.03, p < 0.001). However, there was no statistical difference between the groups on emotional problems and peer problems. Overall, the results showed that the CSA beneficiary group has better gains over the non-CSA beneficiary group.

Table 2. Mean comparison of CSA group and non-CSA group on strengths and difficulties, difficulties in emotion regulation and self-esteem

	CSA (N = 207) Mean (SD)	Non-CSA (N = 111) Mean (SD)	Statistic	df	p	Cohen's D
Difficulties in Emotion Regulation Scale (DERS)						
Awareness	5.73 (2.4)	6.86 (2.6)	-3.76	317	<.001	-0.4411
Clarity	5.53 (2.1)	6.20 (2.1)	-2.66	317	0.008	-0.312
Goals	5.90 (2.03)	5.69 (2.42)	0.828*	317	0.408	0.0971
Impulse	5.92 (2.49)	5.67 (3.06)	0.799*	317	0.425	0.0937
Non-acceptance	4.94 (1.5)	5.28 (2.4)	-1.508*	317	0.133	-0.1769
Strategies	5.32 (1.8)	5.60 (2.5)	-1.097*	317	0.274	-0.1286
DERS Total	33.3 (7.3)	35.3 (11.7)	-1.809*	317	0.071	-0.2122
Self-esteem Scale Total	32.5 (3.03)	28.9 (2.27)	10.887*	317	<.001	1.2771

Table 2. (Continued)

	CSA (N = 207) Mean (SD)	Non-CSA (N = 111) Mean (SD)	Statistic	df	p	Cohen's D
Strengths and Difficulties Questionnaire						
Emotional problems	3.16 (2.7)	2.78 (2.1)	1.277*	317	0.202	0.1498
Conduct problems	1.38 (1.5)	1.99 (1.7)	-3.158	317	0.002	-0.3704
Hyperactivity	1.61 (1.7)	2.01 (1.8)	-2.215	317	0.027	-0.2598
Peer Problems	2.72 (1.3)	3.03 (1.5)	-1.79*	317	0.074	-0.21
Pro-social Behaviour	9.30 (1.3)	8.65 (1.4)	4.033	317	<.001	0.473

* Levene's test is significant (p < .05), suggesting unequal variances.

5. Discussion

The results indicated that the CSA beneficiary group had significantly lower mean scores on emotion regulation difficulties compared to the non-CSA beneficiary group, particularly on the awareness and clarity sub-scales. Additionally, the CSA beneficiary group showed significantly higher self-esteem and lower mean scores on behavioral problems such as conduct and hyperactivity, while also exhibiting better pro-social behavior.

These outcomes result from several years of CSA's presence in the community. Studies show that when a higher educational institution is involved for a longer period, it could get positive outcomes as a result of its commitment (Schudde, 2019). As the results indicated that CSA beneficiaries are having less emotional regulation difficulties, this could be attributed to several factors, such as the role of activity centres and the nature of the activities. The activities suggest that the CSA beneficiaries were involved in a variety of activities such as life skill activities, responsible civic activities, sports and cultural activities. There is evidence that life skill training potentially improves emotion regulation and overall well-being (Mirzei & Hasani, 2015; Mohammadkhani & Hahtami, 2011).

This chapter also reveals that the community educational intervention has significantly improved the self-esteem scores among CSA beneficiaries. Previous studies have found that after-school programs with skill-building activities (Haider & Burfat, 2018), sports (Moeijes et al., 2018), and cultural activities (Mak & Fancourt, 2019) have a positive association with self-esteem among adolescents (Welhenge et al., 2018). The community activity centers have adopted peer-supported learning strategies, which could promote healthy social relationships among the children. One of the longitudinal studies found an association between social relationships and self-esteem. Hence, the current model appears to enhance the quality of social relationships among adolescents. Consequently, the current study's observations corroborate the previous literature.

Some of the important findings of this study are that CSA beneficiary children showed significantly lower scores on conduct and hyperactivity problems and higher pro-social behavior. This could be because the community activity center engages the children in meaningful activities, such as academic, co-curricular, and extracurricular activities. Additionally, it promotes civic responsibilities. All these activities are considered self-regulatory activities. These activities reduce behavioral issues and promote pro-social behavior, which prepares them for real-world challenges (Pandey et al., 2018).

The chapter highlights that CSA's community education model has a significant impact on multiple child outcomes. This model involves utilizing community volunteers and operating community activity centers to improve life skills and civic sense among school-going children. It also engages them in co-curricular and extra-curricular activities and promotes peer learning. However, it is essential to interpret the results with caution as this study is not a true experimental design. Without established baseline assessments, it is challenging to determine cause-and-effect relationships and generalize the findings. Therefore, future studies should be conducted using randomized controlled trials to test this model thoroughly. Nonetheless, this study provides a preliminary assessment of the impact of CSA's community education model on child outcomes. The model has the potential to be replicated with a similar group of participants in other regions and cultural contexts due to its lower costs for implementation and sustainability of the project.

Conclusion

In conclusion, this chapter aimed to explore the impact of community-based education on emotion regulation, self-esteem, and behavioral issues among school-going children. The preliminary results showed promising outcomes, indicating that the model is impactful in reducing difficulties in emotion regulation and improving self-esteem and pro-social behavior among school-going children. However, further systematic studies are warranted to fully understand the effectiveness of the current model.

References

Alloway, T. P., & Alloway, R. G. (2010). Investigating the predictive roles of working memory and IQ in academic attainment. *Journal of experimental child psychology*, 106(1), 20-29.
Anderson, P. (2002). Assessment and development of executive function (EF) during childhood. Child Neuropsychol, 8(2), 71-82. https://doi.org/10.1076/chin.8.2.71.8724
Ansary, N. S., & Luthar, S. S. (2009). Distress and academic achievement among adolescents of affluence: A study of externalising and internalising problem behaviors and school performance. *Development and Psychopathology*, 21(1), 319-341. https://doi.org/10.1017/S0954579409000182
Aram, D. (2005). Continuity in children's literacy achievements: A longitudinal perspective from kindergarten to school. *First Language*, 25(3), 259-289.
Augestad, L. B. (2017). Self-concept and self-esteem among children and young adults with visual impairment: A systematic review. Cogent Psychology, 4(1), 1319652.
Aunola, K., Stattin, H., & Nurmi, J.-E. (2000). Adolescents' Achievement Strategies, School Adjustment, and Externalizing and Internalizing Problem Behaviors. *Journal of Youth and Adolescence*, 29(3), 289-306. https://doi.org/10.1023/A:1005143607919.
Beetz, A. (2013). Socio-emotional correlates of a schooldog-teacher-team in the classroom. *Frontiers in Psychology*, 4, 886.
Buchanan-Pascall, S., Gray, K. M., Gordon, M., & Melvin, G. A. (2018). Systematic review and meta-analysis of parent group interventions for primary school children aged 4–12 years with externalising and/or internalising problems. *Child Psychiatry & Human Development*, 49(2), 244-267.
Cook, C. R., Lyon, A. R., Kubergovic, D., Wright, D. B., & Zhang, Y. (2015). A supportive beliefs intervention to facilitate the implementation of evidence-based practices within a multi-tiered system of supports. *School Mental Health*, 7(1), 49-60.
Corcoran, R. P., Cheung, A. C., Kim, E., & Xie, C. (2018). Effective universal school-based social and emotional learning programs for improving academic achievement: A systematic review and meta-analysis of 50 years of research. *Educational Research Review*, 25, 56-72.
Crescentini, C., Capurso, V., Furlan, S., & Fabbro, F. (2016). Mindfulness-oriented meditation for primary school children: Effects on attention and psychological well-being. Frontiers in Psychology, 7, 805.
Dale, L. P., Vanderloo, L., Moore, S., & Faulkner, G. (2019). Physical activity and depression, anxiety, and self-esteem in children and youth: An umbrella systematic review. *Mental Health and Physical Activity*, 16, 66-79.
Daunic, A. P., Smith, S. W., Garvan, C. W., Barber, B. R., Becker, M. K., Peters, C. D., Taylor, G. G., Van Loan, C. L., Li, W., & Naranjo, A. H. (2012). Reducing

developmental risk for emotional/behavioural problems: A randomised controlled trial examining the Tools for Getting Along curriculum. *Journal of School Psychology*, 50(2), 149-166.

Fathi-Ashtiani, A., Ejei, J., Khodapanahi, M.-K., & Tarkhorani, H. (2007). Relationship between self-concept, self-esteem, anxiety, depression and academic achievement in adolescents. *Journal of Applied Sciences*, 7(7), 955-1000.

Feiss, R., Dolinger, S. B., Merritt, M., Reiche, E., Martin, K., Yanes, J. A., Thomas, C. M., & Pangelinan, M. (2019). A systematic review and meta-analysis of school-based stress, anxiety, and depression prevention programs for adolescents. *Journal of Youth and Adolescence*, 48(9), 1668-1685.

GoI. (2021). Right to Education. GoI. https://dsel.education.gov.in/rte.

Gómez-Ortiz, O., Roldán, R., Ortega-Ruiz, R., & García-López, L.-J. (2018). Social anxiety and psychosocial adjustment in adolescents: Relation with peer victimisation, self-esteem and emotion regulation. *Child indicators research*, 11(6), 1719-1736.

Gratz, K. L., & Roemer, L. (2004). Multidimensional assessment of emotion regulation and dysregulation: Development, factor structure, and initial validation of the difficulties in emotion regulation scale. *Journal of Psychopathology and behavioral assessment*, 26(1), 41-54.

Graziano, P. A., Reavis, R. D., Keane, S. P., & Calkins, S. D. (2007). The role of emotion regulation in children's early academic success. *Journal of School Psychology*, 45(1), 3-19. https://doi.org/https://doi.org/10.1016/j.jsp.2006.09.002

Gubbels, J., van der Put, C. E., & Assink, M. (2019). Risk Factors for School Absenteeism and Dropout: A Meta-Analytic Review. *Journal of Youth and Adolescence*, 48(9), 1637-1667. https://doi.org/10.1007/s10964-019-01072-5

Haider, S. I., & Burfat, F. M. (2018). Improving Self-Esteem, Assertiveness and Communication Skills of Adolescents through Life Skills Based Education. *Journal of Social Sciences & Humanities* (1994-7046), 26(2).

Hallion, L. S., Steinman, S. A., Tolin, D. F., & Diefenbach, G. J. (2018). Psychometric Properties of the Difficulties in Emotion Regulation Scale (DERS) and Its Short Forms in Adults With Emotional Disorders [Original Research]. *Frontiers in Psychology*, 9(539). https://doi.org/10.3389/fpsyg.2018.00539

Hogan, M. J., Parker, J. D., Wiener, J., Watters, C., Wood, L. M., & Oke, A. (2010). Academic success in adolescence: Relationships among verbal IQ, social support and emotional intelligence. *Australian Journal of Psychology*, 62(1), 30-41.

Jongbloed, B., Enders, J., & Salerno, C. (2008). Higher education and its communities: Interconnections, interdependencies and a research agenda. *Higher education*, 56(3), 303-324.

Kaufman, E. A., Xia, M., Fosco, G., Yaptangco, M., Skidmore, C. R., & Crowell, S. E. (2016). The Difficulties in Emotion Regulation Scale Short Form (DERS-SF): Validation and Replication in Adolescent and Adult Samples. *Journal of Psychopathology and behavioral assessment*, 38(3), 443-455. https://doi.org/10.1007/s10862-015-9529-3.

Kolubinski, D. C., Frings, D., Nikčević, A. V., Lawrence, J. A., & Spada, M. M. (2018). A systematic review and meta-analysis of CBT interventions based on the Fennell model of low self-esteem. *Psychiatry Research*, 267, 296-305.

Mak, H. W., & Fancourt, D. (2019). Arts engagement and self-esteem in children: results from a propensity score matching analysis. *Annals of the New York Academy of Sciences*, 1449(1), 36-45. https://doi.org/10.1111/nyas.14056

Mirzei, S., & Hasani, J. (2015). The effectiveness of life skills training in cognitive emotion regulation strategies of adolescents. *Journal of North Khorasan University of Medical Sciences*, 7(2), 405-417.

Moeijs, J., van Busschbach, J. T., Bosscher, R. J., & Twisk, J. W. (2018). Sports participation and psychosocial health: a longitudinal observational study in children. *BMC public health*, 18(1), 1-11.

Mohammadkhani, S., & Hahtami, M. (2011). The effectiveness of life skills training on happiness, quality of life and emotion regulation. *Procedia-Social and Behavioral Sciences*, 30, 407-411.

Murray, M., Dordevic, A. L., & Bonham, M. P. (2017). Systematic review and meta-analysis: the impact of multicomponent weight management interventions on self-esteem in overweight and obese adolescents. *Journal of pediatric psychology*, 42(4), 379-394.

Pandey, A., Hale, D., Das, S., Goddings, A.-L., Blakemore, S.-J., & Viner, R. M. (2018). Effectiveness of universal self-regulation–based interventions in children and adolescents: A systematic review and meta-analysis. *JAMA pediatrics*, 172(6), 566-575.

Renati, R., Cavioni, V., & Zanetti, M. A. (2011). Miss, I got mad today! the anger diary, a tool to promote emotion regulation.

Rosenberg, M. (1965). Rosenberg self-esteem scale (RSE). Acceptance and commitment therapy. Measures package, 61(52), 18.

Rosenberg, M. (2015). *Society and the adolescent self-image*. Princeton university press.

Schlesier, J., Roden, I., & Moschner, B. (2019). Emotion regulation in primary school children: A systematic review. *Children and Youth Services Review*, 100, 239-257. https://doi.org/https://doi.org/10.1016/j.childyouth.2019.02.044.

Schonfeld, D. J., Adams, R. E., Fredstrom, B. K., Weissberg, R. P., Gilman, R., Voyce, C., Tomlin, R., & Speese-Linehan, D. (2015). Cluster-randomised trial demonstrating impact on academic achievement of elementary social-emotional learning. *School Psychology Quarterly*, 30(3), 406.

Schudde, L. (2019). Short-and long-term impacts of engagement experiences with faculty and peers at community colleges. *The Review of Higher Education*, 42(2), 385-426.

Smith, S. W., Daunic, A. P., Barber, B. R., Aydin, B., Van Loan, C. L., & Taylor, G. G. (2014). Preventing risk for significant behavior problems through a cognitive-behavioral intervention: Effects of the Tools for Getting Along curriculum at one-year follow-up. *The Journal of primary prevention*, 35(5), 371-387.

Terzian, M. A., Li, J., Fraser, M. W., Day, S. H., & Rose, R. A. (2015). Social information-processing skills and aggression: A quasi-experimental trial of the Making Choices and Making Choices Plus programs. *Research on Social Work Practice*, 25(3), 358-369.

Ullah, H., & Wilson, M. A. (2007). Students' academic success and its association to student involvement with learning and relationships with faculty and peers. *College Student Journal*, 41(4), 1192-1203.

Vasilescu, R., Barna, C., Epure, M., & Baicu, C. (2010). Developing university social responsibility: A model for the challenges of the new civil society. *Procedia-Social and Behavioral Sciences*, 2(2), 4177-4182.

Welhenge, C., Wickramanayake, D., Wickramasekara, M., Wijayarathne, W., Wijeratne, N., Zangmo, L., & Kasturiratne, A. (2018). Extra-curricular activities and self-esteem of school children in the Colombo District.

Werner-Seidler, A., Perry, Y., Calear, A. L., Newby, J. M., & Christensen, H. (2017). School-based depression and anxiety prevention programs for young people: A systematic review and meta-analysis. Clinical psychology review, 51, 30-47.

Chapter 10

Modelling the Role of Institutional Support in Shaping the Social Behaviour of Business Administration Students

Jogi Mathew[*] and Tijo Thomas

School of Business and Management, Christ University, Bengaluru, India

Abstract

The relevance and scope of teaching social responsibility and ethical behaviour to business students has been widely discussed among academicians worldwide (Giacalone & Thompson, 2006). Presently all business schools emphasize teaching social responsibility to the students. But the effectiveness of this education on the student's social responsibility was not evaluated in the past. This study tries to fill this gap by conducting an empirical study on the effectiveness of social responsibility projects undertaken by undergraduate business students for their overall development. The study hypothesized that the course support and institutional support would influence the student's perception of social responsibility, which in turn affects the student's academic performance. For this purpose, the study was conducted among 450 students who have undergone a social responsibility course. The path analysis method was used to test the hypothesized model.

Further, the study also evaluated the moderation effect of gender on this model. The study's major finding indicated that the social responsibility course and the organizational support positively impacted students' social responsibility perceptions, which, in turn, influenced

---

[*] Corresponding Author's Email: jogi.mathew@christuniversity.in.

In: Models for Social Responsibility Action by Higher Education Institutions
Editors: Joseph Chacko Chennattuserry, Elangovan N. et al.
ISBN: 979-8-89113-097-5
© 2024 Nova Science Publishers, Inc.

students' academic performance. The study suggests that business institutions should emphasize social responsibility initiatives.

Keywords: social responsibility, business students, academic performance, social behavior, institutional support, higher educational institutions

1. Introduction

Social responsibility has become an inclusive term, an inevitable part of any organization. Until the last decade, social responsibility was termed as responsible citizenship or even educated in the civic sense, which has evolved as a discipline to the current status. Social Responsibility (SR) has now reached a priority status as a discipline globally due to its heavy reliance on sustainable business and core competence, which is also very crucial on a global scale of operation (Vasilescu, Barna, Epure, & Baicu, 2010). The initiatives related to social responsibility were started by organizations of large scale that felt the need for this intervention (Jenkins, 2006; Vázquez-Carrasco & López-Pérez, 2013). A lot of organizations embraced social responsibility realizing the significant effect it creates, especially in the area of the most crucial sustainable competitive advantage (Moneva-abadía et al., 2019; Valdez-Juárez et al., 2018). Organizations strongly believe that the application of social responsibility will enable them to achieve a winning combination along with their stakeholders, customers and the society at large, which will certainly contribute to their profits (Rim & Kim, 2016). Yet the evolution of corporate social responsibility (CSR) in educational institutions, government and Non-Governmental Organisations (NGOs) is not up to the mark in comparison to the corporates, mainly in terms of the application of the plans. It is suggested that organizations which strive for people at large and the planet with less focus on profitability could use the concepts of social responsibility or even sustainable growth to articulate their resolve to the society at large (Pompper, 2017).

Carroll (2016) is of the opinion that universities cannot be equated to global corporations and claims that they require a distinct status and need to be treated differently. As explained by Vallaeys et al. (2009), the role and application of university social responsibility (USR) are to be certainly differentiated from CSR, as it deals with a specific set of needs to be accomplished and concerns and has to impact the future generation. There is an overwhelming response vouching for the positive role of universities in promoting social responsibility by imbibing it in teaching, research, and even in their strategic plans (Muijen, 2004; Cotton et al., 2007; Hopkinson et al., 2008). To achieve this, the intervention by the universities has a key role in preparing the new generation for the challenges of globalization and incidental economic growth and even in designing a sustainable society across the world (Setó-Pamies et al., 2011).

Higher educational institutions (HEIs) have a dominant role in shaping not only the social, even the cultural aspects, which mostly leads to a paradigm change through the interpretation of research results as well as through the impact of subject matter experts, leadership roles and visionaries who create the future (Lozano, 2011). There is a current discussion world across vouching for education and training to enhance more skills and build up young leaders who dare to meet challenges through research solutions and get equipped to be an active part of public policymaking. And this social commitment can be honed only by a focused approach to the teaching pedagogy, which certainly should possess a structured program in social sensitization. Another novel illustration that HEIs show the world is the new avenues and trends in campus management, which contribute a lot of positive learning. Also, HEIs can showcase an example to society through their understanding and commitment through careful campus management. Ultimately the HEIs social commitment extends to being a credible employer and contributing talent to both the business and to the social environment (Galang, 2010).

There is a trend among premier business schools to integrate social responsibility into their postgraduate curriculum across the world (Navarro, 2008; Wright & Bennett, 2011; Larrán Jorge et al., 2017). This revelation is due to the paradigm shift in social orientation, which leads to competence in business postgraduates. Yet undergraduate students have not reaped the benefits of this in many parts of the world due to a lack of conviction towards their social bent of mind. Nowadays, the role and impact created by social responsibility and a focused behaviour towards ethics and values in business graduates are heavily discussed by academic experts worldwide (Giacalone & Thompson, 2006). Currently, a majority of business management institutes teach social responsibility to their students. In spite of providing a social awareness program, there is an absence of measuring the value it has added to the students. This study though it has all research inputs and empirical support, also tries to fill the gap by attempting to grade the effectiveness of the social responsibility project created for undergraduate business administration students exclusively for their inclusive growth and their overall development.

The prime objective of this chapter is to explore the role of course support and institutional support in the student's social responsibility perception. An analysis was undertaken to understand the involvement and, thereby, the effectiveness of social responsibility projects undertaken by undergraduate business administration students for their overall development. The study also examined the student's social responsibility perception, which also translates to the academic performance of the students. The research study used the technique of path analysis to test the hypothesized model. The chapter has been structured into the following sections. The next section deals exclusively with literature review and hypothesis development. The subsequent part deals with data collection methods and the tools employed for data analysis. The following section discusses the results of the analysis and their corresponding interpretations, which also lead to the valid conclusions of the study, which is also a certification of the impact of the social responsibility project. The limitations encountered in the study and the scope for further research, which emulates from this study, are also explained in this head.

2. Review of Literature

These are days when social challenges are demanding that universities have strong interventions in society and have a vital role in its development and empowerment (UNESCO, 1998). It is in this background there needs to be a serious introspection on Higher Education Institutions (HEI), their scope and implications (Xavier, Goddard, Hall, Hazelkorn, & Tandon, 2017). Researchers are of the opinion that HEIs need to possess an undiluted approach towards the promotion and universal commitment to seeing to it that higher learning aspects are perfectly positioned. There are also philosophical and global responsibility goals to be achieved as these are the only accepted and effective means of dealing with local and global communities "in order to sustain social, ecological, environmental, technical, and economic development" (Shu-Hsiang, Jaitip, & Ana, 2015). It is at this juncture the importance of merging social responsibility in higher education, which surely can change the world by incorporating compulsory social responsibility courses. This involves exposing a student to real-time training which involves a student's research and getting insight from challenges posed to them. When the social responsibility courses also evaluate checking out understanding and commitment, this is not only a great realization but also an exemplification of responsible campus management (Tilbury, 2011). It is imperative that educators have to make students visualize through multiple modalities that they have to understand and acknowledge the negative effects that business decisions and actions may create on society and the probable collateral damage (Setó-Pamies et al., 2011). HEIs, at the same time, also have been exposed to the recent developments of globalization, technology, innovation, and the need for sustainability. These facts push the transformation process through multiple reforms (Vasilescu et al., 2010). Ultimately, the end objective of any HEI management should be to accomplish the social, environmental and economic responsibilities of their students (Gomez & Girotto, 2015).

The modern-day HEI recognizes the fact that they need to market their programmes not only because of the increasing competition but also to create differentiation (Gibbs & Coffey, 2004). Social responsibility (SR) has emerged as a reason for competition in higher education (Savitz & Weber, 2007; Aber et al., 2009). Incidentally, even Service Marketing is a distinct process in the day-to-day functioning of most HEI, particularly the ones who are society-oriented (Nguyen, 2016). Considering this fact of evolution, one of the most recent trends in HEI marketing is social responsibility. Social responsibility has also been explained as a crucial part of higher education and the management process of the course described by the World Declaration on Higher Education focusing on the Twenty-First Century (Vasilescu et al., 2010). It's interesting to look at HEI management oriented towards fulfilling not only social and environmental but also economic responsibilities (Gomez & Girotto, 2015). Vukasovic (2008) tried to explain this paradigm shift as dramatic, which is also supposed to bring out a lot of change in higher education settings, and this is an opportunity to conduct reforms with the strong edge of integrity. HEIs' community outreach mission is reaching out to multiple communities in the form of civic engagements (Furco, 2014). The civic engagements of the School of Business and Management at Christ University also reach multiple communities, including free mentoring and tutoring for working-class children. These community outreach activities are further escalated to the next level also in close coordination with the teaching and research dimensions (Razak & Afendras, 2014). To be socially responsible is an intrinsic component which cannot be separated from higher learning institutions and their educational mission (Dahan & Senol, 2012). This outcome is in the service of the public interest (Waters & Ott, 2014), which makes it important to recognize the practice of profit-mindedness motive, which still remains dominant and relevant still among nonprofit academic institutions. A huge shift in this scale demands HEIs to endorse the most important values of social responsibility and societal transformation, which will empower students to become future global citizens (Ike, 2017). Social responsibility, looking at another dimension, is the most important contribution that the organization provides to society (Augustiniene et al., 2015; Toremen, 2011).

As reported by Adams (2018), HEIs create value for students, their employers and society through knowledge and critical thinking skills; students and their current and future families (through the incomes that students go on to generate); employers of students, the economy, communities and society (through the skills that universities develop in students). Academic institutions provide students with a platform to encourage critical thinking and path-breaking research endeavour. However, the central or state governments, different industries, various organizations, the market environment, different communities and society at large (through the outcomes of research and research partnerships) have different interventions. Considering these aspects, Adams (2017) accounts that know-how of what value and its creation has been dynamic over time. Here the environmental and social factors which provide risks and opportunities are very critical in the creation of long-term value. It has become a current practice of business schools to implement socially responsible initiatives having the sole idea of grooming future leaders, managers, and workers who are thereby prepared to cope with the environmental, social, and economic systems creating challenging propositions in their careers (Deale et al., 2009; Stubbs & Schapper, 2011). At Christ University, the SRP (social responsibility project) is taking care of this seasoning with the undergraduate management students. Through this, they are exposed to social sensitization and moral and ethical values are instilled in them through the NGO visit they undertake for 30 hours. In most of the leading universities concerned with different education programs, educationalists argue for the compulsory inclusion of a course in ethics, social responsibility and sustainable development, especially in the disciplines of Economics and Business Management (Matten & Moon, 2008). Social engagement by HEI has become one of the trump cards of the leading universities. In these institutions, social service is an indispensable part of the mission statement, which is most of the time equated to teaching and research (Shek et al., 2017).

Students joining colleges and being a part of the curriculum also having high expectations on the development of the traits of self-understanding and self-development. There is undue importance in promoting and teaching social and personal responsibility to the students, which is an integral part of the university's social responsibility (USR). Still, the operating issue of which pedagogy can disseminate and provide a long-lasting effect is still a challenge (Dey & Associates, 2010). There is a realization among the stakeholders that the integration of socially responsible practices and courses involves a laborious process. Effective integration of social responsibility in management education poses a lot of challenges in the form of implementation and the mode of learning (Sammalisto & Lindquist, 2008; Rusinko, 2010). The ongoing deliberation is to find an answer to whether there is a compelling need to merge social responsibility into the existing courses, or else to be taught as independent courses, or whether it is a better policy to introduce new programmes having a strong essence of it (Rusinko, 2010). Looking at social responsibility from the perspective of a programme, it could be incorporated into an all-new structure as a major, minor, or even as a lone program. Social responsibility can be integrated with an existing structure, even as a course incorporating a new topic like social entrepreneurship. There is a good scope for teaching social responsibility using a case study approach or even an experiential mode of delivery (Rusinko, 2010). Whatever approach is used, attaching social responsibility to the business curriculum demands strong handholding from the disciplines like finance, organizational behaviour, entrepreneurship, and strategic management. Even if it's aligned with other papers, students will certainly leverage it for the better operation and management of day-to-day businesses (Jurowski, 2001; Rusinko, 2010). The end results of these are very clear. At the end of the term, as an outcome, they certainly are transformed into socially responsible citizens (Kevany, 2007). Rusinko (2010) came up with a finding that a meaningful curricular engagement with social responsibility helps students to cultivate personal as well as leadership skills.

There is a document which provides a framework, a unified natural curriculum and relevant guidelines for "Fostering Social Responsibility and Community Engagement" with respect to HEIs in India (University Grants Commission, 2020). This document was developed by an expert committee with multiple rounds of deliberations, which finally came up with a new compulsory course in community engagement which was designed for all UG and PG students in HEIs. The intervention expected from the compulsory course is not just community engagement but an attempt to realize and appreciate the rural field realities, which concludes to be holistic, respectful and inspiring. There are also academic institutions which have exhaustive curriculums which train students in the skills which make them efficient in doing non-manual labour jobs, which later lead to bachelor's degrees and also provide students with the preparedness of the understanding of society and the environment (Metzger et al., 2010). The student's perception of the facilities provided by the university is one of the key influences on their decision to join the programme (Briggs & Wilson, 2007), and in days to come, the scope to be a part of social projects and environmental actions will be the features of choice.

This thought about the core concept has been inspired by the thought that "Educating the mind without educating the heart is not education at all"- Aristoteles. Social responsibility also happens to be an ethical philosophy which propounds that an individual or even a business establishment has an obligation to contribute back to society (Brodeur, 2013). It is an accepted philosophy that colleges and universities create not only an attitudinal impact, but even the student's actions are also heavily reliant on their social responsibility initiatives. These social activities have a binding on any student's personal and social responsibility, which mostly translates to future behaviour (Siebel, 2009). Through the professional training imparted to them, they transformed themselves into community service agents and committed to civil society. This provides them with awareness-raising empowerment which makes them capable of dissemination of knowledge (Beltrán-Llevador et al., 2014). The student's university life is much beyond the classroom happenings as the students prepare to be a part of and voice of society which ultimately offers them challenges and forces them to propose solutions. The knowledge imparted by the universities not just provides conceptual and technical skills but also provides them with social skills to transform them into socially responsible citizens. The social initiatives in the universities improve civic knowledge and skills, which meets the demand and attention on civic learning and positive initiatives in community engagement (Musil, 2012).

The focus on social responsibility in varied disciplines like politics, science, business, and the media are increasing and is transformed into a serious topic that students need to appreciate in the right spirit and explore. Being valuable on its own account, a socially responsible approach is a holistic view of education involving a comprehensive conversation that delivers crucial transferable skills and behaviours. These skills include not just analytical and critical thinking but also managing information, arguing and communicating effectively. A socially responsible approach also inculcates respect for the diversity of people, cultures and environments and even standing for social justice. The unparalleled approach to equity and human rights is also important, along with fostering personal responsibility and citizenship. Now it could be concluded that sustainable development practices, to a certain degree, will be certainly influenced by the manner in which future leaders respond and adapt to social responsibility practices which leads to a transformation (Rosnan et al., 2013). Social responsibility harmonizes the efforts of both the business entities and the social sector and makes use of well-grounded professionals as agents of change towards sustainable growth and development (Deswal & Raghav, 2013).

The study results of Gomez et al. (2018) identified the public perceptions and attitudinal attributes of students. The higher education sector is a crucial stakeholder and an important entity inculcating social responsibility as well as sustainable development for the upcoming generations who have to be transformed into ethical professionals. The past few decades have shown a phenomenal thrust in social responsibility, which was emulated by educational, corporate, and government organizations into the new norm of social entrepreneurship. Sustainability drives the application of service learning to multiple initiatives, social-oriented leadership and programmes involving character development (Sosik & Jung, 2018; Ibrahim & Angelidis, 2011; Crocetti et al., 2012; Sooksomchitra et al., 2013). This chapter deals with a modelling framework which involves a student-based analysis to understand whether HEIs deploy a long-term strategic perspective and involve all their stakeholders. This long-term strategy, directed at students, will not only be able to optimize their positive impact on society but also helps in reducing negative influences if applicable. Now such socially transformed adults will certainly possess a strong character embedded with citizenship, essential traits of mutual and social trust and positive perspectives of human nature. These self-motivated individuals create success stories by being an active part of financially successful and profitable organizations (Melo & Galan, 2011). There needs to be a thorough introspection to check out the extent to which individuals and their moral judgments are influenced by social regulations. The expectations from the professionals coming out of HEIs and their group affiliations, according to Passini (2014), look to be very fruitful in examining their social responsibility in the contexts of social norms and expectations.

Benabou and Tirole (2010) tried to examine the attributes possessed by individuals to get motivated for socially responsible and ethical behaviour. Their findings confirmed that institutional social responsibility is initiated by altruism and material benefits as well as driven by self-esteem-related thoughts. Added to this, the researchers also reaffirm that the motives are also mutually interdependent. The policymakers and social activists need to have a good understanding to spearhead the interactions and thereby influence individuals and thereby ultimately deal with meaningful engagements and socially responsible behaviours. Aguilera et al.'s (2006) came out with a model which considered social change, individuals' perceptions of justice and care for the social environment as the important antecedents of social responsibility. Social responsibility is considered as an individual's difference in concerns for justice and care and also refers to one's commitment towards civic duty. It also involves an obligation to endorse public interest beyond self-interest with the intention of helping others without expecting back. (Crocetti et al., 2012) tried to explain social responsibility as a natural human occurrence and a social behaviour which was authenticated by (Witt, 1990) that it can be cultivated. Social bonding creates perceptions of injustice, moral principles, caring, and many positive social behaviours which go along with social responsibility (Hoffman, 2001). These days, which are filled with rapid changes and exhaustive interactions, academic institutions are the most influential pillars of social responsibility (Dima et al., 2013). This support goes on beyond current stakeholders to incorporate future stakeholders also. The central role played by education and awareness to accomplish good social behaviour is crucial to sustainability processes (Tang et al., 2011). Universities educate and train future business leaders to instil prerequisite skills in graduates, essentially considering dynamic requirements concerning social responsibility (Pesonen, 2003). The outcomes of studies by authors (Aguinis & Glavas, 2017; Glavas & Kelley, 2014; Shin et al., 2016; Zafar & Ali, 2016) confirm that organizations' social practices have far-reaching consequences. One of the most important outcomes as a result of this knowledge is enhanced work engagement. Based on this understanding, the following hypothesis is proposed for the current study:

H_1. *Institutional supports have a significant positive impact on Course supports*

H_2. *Institutional supports have a significant positive impact on student's social responsibility*

H_3. *Course supports have a significant positive impact on student's social responsibility*

The conceptual understanding of Personal and Social Responsibility (PSR) was propounded by Knefelkemp and Hersh and was revised subsequently by Dey and Associates (Reason, 2013). PSR has five dimensions striving for excellence, cultivating academic integrity, contributing to a larger community, taking the perspective of others seriously and developing competence in ethical and moral reasoning and action (Boyd & Brackmann,

2012; Glass, 2013; Ryder & Mitchell, 2013). The proposed model for this chapter is developed considering the understanding of relevant theoretical concepts and biased hypotheses. Figure 1 depicts the suggested model explaining the factors leading to social responsibility.

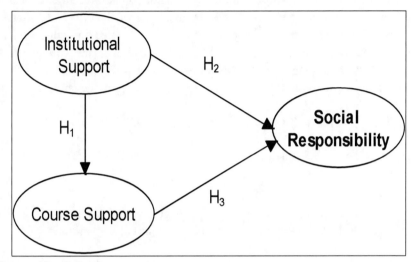

Source: The Author.

Figure 1. The proposed conceptual framework.

3. Methodology

The major aim of the study is to evaluate the role of university support and programme support in developing students' socially responsible behaviour. Specifically, the study aims to understand the effectiveness of institutional support and course support in creating social responsibility among students through the social responsibility project. The social responsibility project is a course in the Bachelor of business administration (BBA) program of Christ University, which is aimed at giving exposure to students to the social problems of society. To evaluate this hypothesis, we conducted a survey among BBA students who have undertaken social responsibility projects in the last two years. A total of 800 questionnaires were distributed among the students, and they received 419 valid responses, as per Table 1.

The questionnaire consisted of twenty questions, in which two questions measured demographic factors like the name and gender of the respondents.

The remaining 18 questions measured institutional support, course support and social responsibility behaviour. These questions were adopted from the Personal and Social Responsibility Inventory (PSRI). PSRI is an institutional Climate Measure which specializes in campus climate surveys, which was developed originally for another initiative named Core Commitments. This initiative involved educating students to instill personal as well as social responsibility in them and was sponsored by one of the leading educational global associations, the Association of American Colleges and Universities (AACU). The following Table 2 Reliability score (Cronbach's alpha) of the variables shows the reliability score of the variables used in the study.

Table 1. Gender-wise distribution of respondents

Gender	Frequency	Percent
Male	229	56.4
Female	177	43.6

Source: - Primary data.

Table 2. Reliability score (Cronbach's alpha) of the variables

Variable	Cronbach's alpha	Number of items
University support	.897	9
Program support	.891	6
Social Responsibility	.590	3

Source: Primary data.

As can be observed from Table 2, the Cronbach's alpha value of university support (0.897) and program support (0.891) lies in the reliable category (0.84–0.90), and the score for social responsibility (.590) is at a satisfactory level (0.58–0.97) (Taber 2018).

4. Results

The major aim of this chapter was to evaluate the role of social responsibility projects undertaken by undergraduate students on their social responsibility behaviour. The data was collected from the second and final-year students who have undertaken the project in their first year. From the literature reviewed, it was hypothesized that university support would lead to the social responsibility behaviour of the student. It indicated that when the students presumed that the university is predominantly giving importance to the social responsibility of the student, then there is a higher chance that the student will show a higher social responsibility. Further, the support of the university for social responsibility is hypothesized to have a positive influence on the programmes which emphasize the development of positive social responsibility behaviour. For evaluating this hypothesis, the study used the Structural equation modelling (SEM) method using the AMOS software. The following Figure 2 and Table 3 indicate SEM model analysis results.

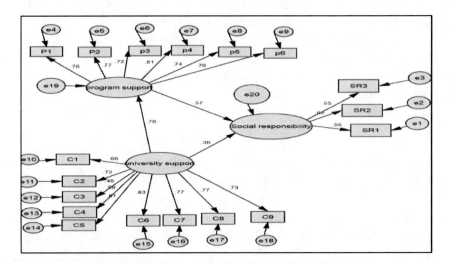

Figure 2. The test models.

Table 3. Model estimates and notes

Hypothesis	Standard estimates	CR.	Significant/ not significant
H1 University support influence program support	.758	11.405	***
H2 University support influences social responsibility behaviour	.359	3.816	***
H3 course support influences social responsibility behaviour	.568	5.641	***
Chi-square			499.422
Degrees of freedom			132
P value			.000
Goodness fit index (GFI)			.866
Adjusted Goodness fit index AGFI			.826
Comparative Fit Index (CFI)			.906
Root Mean Square Error of Approximation (RSMEA)			.083

Source: Survey.

For the analysis of the model, five indicators of model fit were evaluated. Multiple indicators were used to showcase the efficacy of the model used. The Chi-square analysis of the model indicates a value of 499.422(132) that the model is not significant at P> .05% level. It indicates that the model did not fit the data well enough. Further, the Goodness fit index shows a value of 0.866, which is more than 0.85, indicating a good fit for the model. The AGFI value of 0.826 is more than the accepted value of .75, indicating a good fit for the model. Further, the Comparative Fit Index (CFI) value of .906 is also more than the required level of .75, indicating a good fit for the model. Further, the analysis of the Root Mean Square Error of Approximation (RSMEA) showed a value of .083, which is more than the required maximum level of .05, indicating a poor fit of the model. So, after considering all the indexes, we can conclude that the model is found to fit the data well, with three out of five indexes showing a good fit. Further analysis was undertaken to evaluate the hypothesis. In the study, we had three major hypotheses.

Hypothesis H_1 indicated that the student perception of university support in social responsibility would positively influence course support provided to social responsibility. This hypothesis was based on the assumption that when the students assume that the university provides support for social work it will influence the support provided by the course, which aims at supporting social responsibility among the students. From Table 3 Model estimates and notes, the regression weight value for hypothesis 1 is at 0.758 with a CR of 11.405(P<0.05), indicating a significant relationship between university support and course support. This indicates that when the respondents presume a positive University support for social work will positively influence the perception of respondents towards the course support for socially responsible courses. This finding is in line with our hypothesis, which is based on the assumption that the university's social responsibility will influence the course support provided to the socially responsible courses.

Hypothesis H_2 suggests that when University support towards social responsibility will positively influence the student's socially responsible behaviour. This hypothesis is based on the assumption that the university's support towards social responsibility will increase the social responsibility behaviour of the students. From Table 3, it can be seen that the regression weight of the hypothesis is 0.359 with a CR ratio of 3.816 (P<0.05), indicating a significant positive relationship between university support and students' social responsibility behaviour. This finding suggests that when the students presume that the university gives considerable importance to social responsibility, then the students will also show socially responsible behaviour.

Hypothesis H3 suggests that when the students presume that the course supports social responsibility, then it will induce positive social responsibility behaviour among the students. As can be seen from Table 3 Model estimates and notes, the regression weight of the hypothesis is 0.568 with a CR ratio of 5.641 (P<0.05), which indicates a positive relationship between course support and students' social responsibility behaviour. These findings are in line with our hypothesis, which suggests that when the main focus of the course is social behaviour, the course will attain this behaviour.

For further analysis, the direct, indirect, and total effect was evaluated. The following table 4 shows the direct, indirect and total effect of university support and course support on the social responsibility behaviour of the students.

Table 4. Direct, indirect and total effect

variable	Indirect effect	Direct effect	Total effect
University support	0.432	0.359	0.790
Course support		0.569	0.569

Source: Survey.

From Table 4, it can be seen that the total effect value of university support is 0.790, which is more than the course support effect of 0.560. This indicates that the role of the university in imparting social behaviour is more than the course. Further, the indirect and direct effect analysis shows that the influence of university support is partially mediated by course support. This indicates that when the university provides considerable support for social responsibility, then the students from that university tend to provide positive social responsibility behaviour.

5. Discussion

The major aim of this chapter was also to model the effect of university support on the student's social behaviour through the mediation of course support. Christ University in Bengaluru is dedicated towards the holistic development of a student's personality. This all-around development is not possible without a range of social responsibility programmes. There are dedicated programmes from the Centre for Social Action as well as exclusive programs from each department to contribute. The School of Business and

Management is a dynamic arm of Christ University, and its reputed Bachelor of business administration (BBA) program has won a lot of laurels so far. This chapter targeted a specific course offered to BBA students, which also has a mandatory project attached to it called a social responsibility project (SRP). Here a first-year student gets formal permission and spends 30 hours in an NGO to understand their operations and be a part of it. In this process, the student is exposed to a real-time situation where they are acquainted with elderly people, disabled people or underprivileged people. This experience is new to them; even otherwise, it is expected to instil compassion and solidarity and form a positive attitude towards the needy. This trait ought to be developed in the first-year students, which with the later follow-up programmes in the subsequent years, will form a real basis for developing social behaviour. This positive attitude could shape them into daring, broad-minded, compassionate professionals in the future. This could be in tune with the future CSR initiatives of their organizations, for which our students will be well prepared with a better emotional quotient (EQ). This study intends to measure the impact of this programme on students as well as to get suggestions from the students to make it more experiential and livelier.

This chapter reveals that the student's perception regarding the university's support for social responsibility will positively influence their perception regarding social responsibility courses and their social behaviour. When the university provides ample support for social responsibility, the students will have a positive attitude towards the courses aimed at social service. At Christ University, the first two mission statements indicate the concentration of the university towards social responsibility projects. Further, many initiatives from CSA, the no plastic initiative and the Sponsor a Child initiative, indicate greater emphasis the institution gives to social service. This will have a positive impact on the perception of the university as a socially responsible university. Further, this perception will positively influence the course that emphasizes the social behaviour of the students. Courses like the social responsibility project, which encourages the student's social behaviour, will enhance the social responsibility behaviour of the students. The social responsibility project is a flagship project the students have to undertake in their second-semester break. This project aims at giving the student exposure to social problems of society. The students are required to undertake a 4-week project work under any NGO. This project is a two-credit course at the end of which students need to submit a report. The evaluation of this report includes viva and report evaluation. The students are required to provide a weekly work report which will be evaluated by the examiners.

6. Limitations of the Research study

The major limitations of the study were that the study was undertaken post social responsibility project because of which the pre-disposition of the students towards social responsibility behaviour was not considered. This study used quantitative data and analysis exclusively, which curtailed the qualitative implications.

7. Future Research

Future studies can evaluate this aspect by conducting a pre and post-study on the student's perceptions before and after the social responsibility project. A qualitative data collection with appropriate analysis deploying qualitative methodologies will certainly explore a lot more conclusions.

Conclusion

The findings of the study indicate that the university's support for social responsibility activities will enhance the social responsibility behaviour of the students. This indicates that those universities which want their students to have socially responsible behaviour should give emphasis on social responsibility projects. The major limitations of the study were that the study was undertaken post social responsibility project because of which the pre-disposition of the students towards social responsibility behaviour was not considered. Future studies can evaluate this aspect by conducting a pre- and post-study on the student's perceptions before and after the social responsibility project.

References

Aber, J. D., Kelly, T., & Mallory, B. L. (2009). *The sustainable learning community: one university's journey to the future*. University of New Hampshire Press.
Adams, C. A. (2017). Conceptualizing the contemporary corporate value creation process. *Accounting, Auditing & Accountability Journal, 30*(4), 906–931. https://doi.org/10.1108/aaaj-04-2016-2529.

Adams, C. A. (2018). *Let's Talk Value - How universities add value*. Let's Talk Value - How universities add value | Advance HE. https://www.advance-he.ac.uk/knowledge-hub/lets-talk-value-how-universities-add-value.

Aguilera, R. V., Williams, C. A., Conley, J. M., & Rupp, D. E. (2006). Corporate Governance and Social Responsibility: a comparative analysis of the UK and the US*. *Corporate Governance: An International Review*, *14*(3), 147–158. https://doi.org/10.1111/j.1467-8683.2006.00495.x.

Aguinis, H., & Glavas, A. (2017). On Corporate Social Responsibility, Sensemaking, and the Search for Meaningfulness Through Work. *Journal of Management*, *45*(3), 1057–1086. https://doi.org/10.1177/0149206317691575.

Augustiniene, A., Jociene, J., & Minkute-Henrickson, R. (2015). Social Responsibility of Comprehensive Schools: Teachers' Point of View. *Social Sciences*, *87*(1). https://doi.org/10.5755/j01.ss.87.1.12315.

Beltrán-Llevador, J., Íñigo-Bajo, E., & Mata-Segreda, A. (2014). La responsabilidad social universitaria, el reto de su construcción permanente. *Revista Iberoamericana De Educación Superior*, *5*(14), 3–18. https://doi.org/10.1016/s2007-2872(14)70297-5.

Benabou, R., & Tirole, J. (2010). Individual and Corporate Social Responsibility. *Economica*, *77*(305), 1–19. https://doi.org/10.1111/j.1468-0335.2009.00843.x.

Boyd, K. D., & Brackmann, S. (2012). Promoting Civic Engagement to Educate Institutionally for Personal and Social Responsibility. *New Directions for Student Services*, *2012*(139), 39–50. https://doi.org/10.1002/ss.20021.

Briggs, S., & Wilson, A. (2007). Which university? A study of the influence of Costa and information factors on Scottish undergraduate choice. *Journal of Higher Education Policy and Management*, *29*(1), 57–72. https://doi.org/10.1080/13600800601175789.

Brodeur, D. R. (2013). Mentoring young adults in the development of social responsibility. *Australasian Journal of Engineering Education*, *19*(1), 13-25. https://doi.org/10.7158/d12-014.2013.19.1.

Carroll, A. B. (2016). Carroll's pyramid of CSR : taking another look. *International Journal of Corporate Social Responsibility*, *1*(1), 1-8. https://doi.org/10.1186/s40991-016-0004-6.

Cotton, D. R., Warren, M. F., Maiboroda, O., & Bailey, I. (2007). Sustainable development, higher education and pedagogy: a study of lecturers' beliefs and attitudes. *Environmental Education Research*, *13*(5), 579–597. https://doi.org/10.1080/13504620701659061.

Concetti, E., Jahromi, P., & Meeus, W. (2012). Identity and civic engagement in Adolescence. *Journal of Adolescence*, *35*(3), 521–532. https://doi.org/10.1016/j.adolescence.2011.08.003.

Dahan, G. S., & Senol, I. (2012). Corporate social responsibility in higher education institutions : Istanbul Bilgi University case. *American International Journal of Contemporary Research*, *2*(3), 95 – 103.

Deale, C., Nichols, J., & Jacques, P. (2009). A Descriptive Study of Sustainability Education in the Hospitality Curriculum. *Journal of Hospitality & Tourism Education*, *21* (4), 34-42.

Deswal, P., & Raghav, N. (2013). Corporate social responsibility: a relationship between business organizations and the society, *OIDA International Journal of Sustainable Development, 6*(11), 37-44.

Dey, E. L., & Associates. (2010). *Developing a moral compass: What are the campus climate for ethics and academic integrity?* Association of American Colleges & Universities: https://www.aacu.org/sites/default/files/files/core_commitments/moral compassreport.pdf.

Dima, A.M., Vasilache, S., Ghinea, V., & Agoston, S. (2013). A model of academic social responsibility, *Transylvanian Review of Administrative Sciences, 38,* 23-43.

Furco, A. (2014, October 9). *IV.6.3. Strategic Initiatives to Impact the Institutionnalisation of Community Engagement at a public research university.* Report : Higher Education in the World 2014. https://upcommons.upc.edu/handle/2099/15281.

Galang, A. P. (2010). Environmental education for sustainability in higher education institutions in the Philippines. *International Journal of Sustainability in Higher Education, 4*, 138-150.

Giacalone, R. A., & Thompson, K. R. (2006). Business Ethics and Social Responsibility Education : Shifting the Worldview. *Academy of Management Learning & Education, 5*(3), 266–277. https://doi.org/10.5465/amle.2006.22697016.

Gibbs, G., & Coffey, M. (2004). The Impact Of Training Of University Teachers on their Teaching Skills, their Approach to Teaching and the Approach to Learning of Their Students. *Active Learning in Higher Education, 5*(1), 87–100. https://doi.org/10.1177/1469787404040463.

Glass, C. R. (2013). Strengthening and Deepening Education for Personal and Social Responsibility. *New Directions for Higher Education, 2013*(164), 83–94. https://doi.org/10.1002/he.20077.

Glavas, A., & Kelley, K. (2014). The Effects of Perceived Corporate Social Responsibility on Employées Attitudes. *Business Ethics Quarterly, 24*(2), 165–202. https://doi.org/10.5840/beq20143206.

Gomez, C. L., & Girotto, M. (2015). Strategic Management in Universities: A Conceptual Framework Based on Ibero-American Higher Education Systems. In Humberto, C. M. J., Couture, P. L., & Llinàs-Audet Xavier (Eds.), *Strategic Management of Universities in the Ibero-America Region: A Comparative Perspective* (pp.1-43). https://doi.org/10.1007/978-3-319-14684-3_1.

Gomez, L., Pujols, A., Alvarado, Y., & Vargas, L. (2018). Social responsibility in higher educational institutions : An exploratory study. In D. Crowther, S. Seifi, & A. Moyeen (Eds.), *The goals of sustainable development. Approaches to global sustainability, market, and governance* (pp. 215-230). https://doi.org/10.1007/978-981-10-5047-3_13.

Hoffman, M. L. (2001). *Empathy and moral development: implications for caring and justice.* Cambridge University Press.

Hopkinson, P., Hughes, P., & Layer, G. (2008). Sustainable graduates: linking formal, informal and campus curricula to embed education for sustainable development in the student learning experience. *Environmental Education Research, 14*(4), 435–454. https://doi.org/10.1080/13504620802283100.

Ibrahim, N. A., & Angelidis, J. P. (2011). Effect Of Board Members Gender On Corporate Social Responsiveness Orientation. *Journal of Applied Business Research (JABR)*, *10*(1), 35-40. https://doi.org/10.19030/jabr.v10i1.5961.

Ike, O. F. (2017, August 1). *Ethics in Higher Education as Tool for Discovering Our Ultimate Destiny*. Globethics.net Library Homepage. https://repository.globethics.net/handle/20.500.12424/166326.

Jenkins, H. (2006). Small Business Champions for Corporate Social Responsibility. *Journal of Business Ethics*, *67*(3), 241–256. https://doi.org/10.1007/s10551-006-9182-6.

Jurowski, C. (2001). A Multi-cultural and Multi-disciplinary Approach to Integrating the Principles of Sustainable Development into Human Resource Management Curriculums in Hospitality and Tourism. *Journal of Hospitality & Tourism Education*, *13*(5), 36–50. https://doi.org/10.1080/10963758.2001.10696713.

Kevany, K. D. (2007). Building the requisite capacity for stewardship and sustainable development. *International Journal of Sustainability in Higher Education*, *8*(2), 107–122. https://doi.org/10.1108/14676370710726580.

Larrán Jorge, M., Andrades Peña, F. J., & Muriel de los Reyes, M. J. (2017). Analyzing the inclusion of stand-alone courses on ethics and CSR. *Sustainability Accounting, Management and Policy Journal*, *8*(2), 114–137. https://doi.org/10.1108/sampj-05-2015-0033.

Lozano, R. (2011). The state of sustainability reporting in universities. *International Journal of Sustainability in Higher Education*, *12*(1), 67–78. https://doi.org/10.1108/14676371111098311.

Matten, D., & Moon, J. (2008). "Implicit" and "Explicit" CSR : A Conceptual Framework for a Comparative Understanding of Corporate Social Responsibility. *Academy of Management Review*, *33*(2), 404–424. https://doi.org/10.5465/amr.2008.31193458.

Melo, T., & Galan, J. I. (2011). Effects of corporate social responsibility on brand value. *Journal of Brand Management*, *18*(6), 423–437. https://doi.org/10.1057/bm.2010.54.

Metzger, C., Maynard, R., Vultaggio, J., Daizen, T., Promboon, S., Ip, K. Y., & Park, S.-Y. (2010). A Comparative perspective on the secondary and post-secondary education systems in six nations : Hong Kong, Japan, Switzerland, South Korea, Thailand and the United States. *Procedia - Social and Behavioral Sciences*, *2*(2), 1511–1519. https://doi.org/10.1016/j.sbspro.2010.03.227.

Molina, N., Sierra, O., Restrepo, V., & Mondragón, J. (2012). Provision of services for SMEs. Theoretical bases for the university social responsibility model of the Faculty of Administrative and Accounting Sciences of the University of La Salle. *Gestión & Sociedad*, *5*(1), 55–71.

Moneva-abadía, J. M., Gallardo-vázquez, D., & Sánchez-hernández, M. I. (2019). Corporate Social Responsibility as a Strategic Opportunity for Small Firms during Economic Crises. *Journal of Small Business Management*, *57*(sup2), 172–199. https://doi.org/10.1111/jsbm.12450.

Muijen, H. (2004). Corporate social responsibility starts at university. *Journal of Business Ethics, 53*(1), 235-246.

Musil, C.M. (2012). A 'national call to action' from the National Task Force on Civic Learning and Democratic Engagement. In D. Harward (Ed.), *Civic Provocations*. (pp. 69-74). Bringing Theory to Practice.

Navarro, P. (2008). The MBA Core Curricula of Top-Ranked U.S. Business Schools: A Study in Failure? *Academy of Management Learning & Education*, 7(1), 108–123. https://doi.org/10.5465/amle.2008.31413868.

Nguyen, T. M. (2016). Learning approaches, demographic factors to predict academic outcomes. *International Journal of Educational Management*, 30(5), 653–667. https://doi.org/10.1108/ijem-06-2014-0085.

Passini, S. (2014). The effect of personal orientations toward intergroup relations on moral reasoning. *Journal of Moral Education*, 43(1), 89–103. https://doi.org/10.1080/03057240.2014.884489.

Pesonen, H.-L. (2003). Challenges Of Integrating Environmental Sustainability Issues Into Business School Curriculum : A Case Study From The University Of Jyväskylä, Finland. *Journal of Management Education*, 27(2), 158–171. https://doi.org/10.1177/1052562903251412.

Pompper, D. (2017). *Corporate social responsibility, sustainability and public relations : negotiating multiple complex challenges*. Routledge.

Razak, D., & Afendras, E. (2014). *II.5. Engagement beyond the third mission : the experience of Albukhary International University*. Report : Higher Education in the World 2014. https://upcommons.upc.edu/handle/2099/15272.

Reason, R. D. (2013). Infusing Social Responsibility into the Curriculum and Co-curriculum : Campus Examples. In Reason, R. D. (Eds.), *Developing and accessing personal and social responsibility in college* (pp. 73–81). https://doi.org/10.1002/he.20076.

Rim, H., & Kim, S. (2016). Dimensions of corporate social responsibility (CSR) skepticism and their impacts on public evaluations toward CSR. *Journal of Public Relations Research*, 28(5-6), 248–267. https://doi.org/10.1080/1062726x.2016.1261702.

Rosnan, H., Saihani, S. B., & Yusof, N. M. (2013). Attitudes Towards Corporate Social Responsibility among Budding Business Leaders. *Procedia - Social and Behavioral Sciences*, 107, 52–58. https://doi.org/10.1016/j.sbspro.2013.12.398.

Rusinko, C. A. (2010). Integrating sustainability in higher education: A generic matrix. *International Journal of Sustainability in Higher Education*, 11(3), 250-259.

Ryder, A. J., & Mitchell, J. J. (2013). Measuring Campus Climate for Personal and Social Responsibility. In Reason, R. D. (Eds.), *Developing and accessing personal and social responsibility in college* (pp. 31–48). https://doi.org/10.1002/he.20074.

Sammalisto, K., & Lindhqvist, T. (2008). Integration of sustainability in higher education: A study with international perspectives. *Innovative Higher Education*, 32(4), 221–233.

Savitz, A. W., & Weber, K. (2007). The sustainability sweet spot. *Environmental Quality Management*, 17(2), 17–28. https://doi.org/10.1002/tqem.20161.

Setó-Pamies, D., Domingo-Vernis, M., & Rabassa-Figueras, N. (2011). Corporate social responsibility in management education: Current status in Spanish universities. *Journal of Management & Organization*, 17(5), 604–620. https://doi.org/10.1017/s1833367200001280.

Shek, D. T., Yuen-Tsang, A. W., & Ng, E. C. (2017). USR Network : A Platform to Promote University Social Responsibility. In Shek, D. T. L., & Hollister, R. M. (Eds.), *University Social Responsibility and quality of life a global survey of concepts and experiences* (pp. 11–21). https://doi.org/10.1007/978-981-10-3877-8_2.

Shin, I., Hur, W.-M., & Kang, S. (2016). Employees' Perceptions of Corporate Social Responsibility and Job Performance : A Sequential Mediation Model. *Sustainability*, *8*(5), 493. https://doi.org/10.3390/su8050493.

Shu-Hsiang, C., Jaitip, N., & Ana, D. J. (2015). From Vision to Action – A Strategic Planning Process Model for Open Educational Resources. *Procedia - Social and Behavioral Sciences*, *174*(1), 3707–3714. https://doi.org/10.1016/j.sbspro.2015.01.1103.

Sibbel, A. (2009). Pathways towards sustainability through higher education. *International Journal of Sustainability in Higher Education*, *10*(1), 68–82. https://doi.org/10.1108/14676370910925262.

Sooksomchitra, A., Koraneekij, P., & Na-Songkhla, J. (2013). Education for Social Responsibility: The Use of CSCL in Undergraduate Service-Learning Modules. *Creative Education*, *04*(09), 59–62. https://doi.org/10.4236/ce.2013.49b012.

Sosik, J. J., & Jung, D. (2018). The Full Range Leadership Development System. In Sosik, J. J., & Jung, D. (Eds.), *Full range leadership development pathways for people, profit, and Planet* (pp.38-70). https://doi.org/10.4324/9781315167206-2.

Stubbs, W., & Schapper, J. (2011). Two approaches to curriculum development for educating for sustainability and CSR. *International Journal of Sustainability in Higher Education*, *12*(3), 259–268. https://doi.org/10.1108/14676371111148045.

Taber, K.S. (2018). The Use of Cronbach's Alpha When Developing and Reporting Research Instruments in Science Education. *Research in Science Education* 48(6), 1273–1296. https://doi.org/10.1007/s11165-016-9602-2.

Tang, K., Robinson, D. A., & Harvey, M. (2011). Sustainability managers or rogue mid-managers ? *Management Decision*, *49*(8), 1371–1394. https://doi.org/10.1108/00251741111163179.

Tilbury, D. (2011). *Education for sustainable development: an expert review of processes and learning*. Paris, France : UNESCO.

Toremen, F. (2011). The responsibility education of teacher candidates. *Educational Sciences : Theory and Practice*, *11*(1), 273277.

UNESCO. (1998). Autonomía, responsabilidad social y libertad académica. In VII Conferencia Mundial de Educación ED.98/CONF.202/CLD.49. Paris, Francia. https://unesdoc.unesco.org/ark:/48223/pf0000116345_spa.

University Grants Commission. (2020). *Fostering Social Responsibility & Community Engagement in Higher Educational Institutions in India*. https://www.ugc.ac.in/e-book/UBA/mobile/index.html.

Valdez-Juárez, L., Gallardo-Vázquez, D., & Ramos-Escobar, E. (2018). CSR and the Supply Chain : Effects on the Results of SMEs. *Sustainability*, *10*(7), 2356. https://doi.org/10.3390/su10072356.

Vallaeys, F., Cruz, C., & Sasia, P. M. (2009). *Responsabilidad social universitaria: manual de primeros pasos*. McGraw-Hill.

Vasilescu, R., Barna, C., Epure, M., & Baicu, C. (2010). Developing university social responsibility: A model for the challenges of the new civil society. *Procedia - Social and Behavioral Sciences*, *2*(2), 4177–4182. https://doi.org/10.1016/j.sbspro.2010.03.660.

Vázquez-Carrasco, R., & López-Pérez, M. E. (2013). Small& medium-sized enterprises and Corporate Social Responsibility: a systematic review of the literature. *Qual Quant*, *47*(6), 3205–3218. https://doi.org/10.1007/s11135-012-9713-4.

Vukasovic, M. (2008). The integrity of higher education from essence to management. *Proceedings of the Seminar of the Magna Charta Observatory, September 19 2007, The Management of University Integrity* (pp. 23-26). Bononia University Press, Bologna.

Waters, R. D., & Ott, H. K. (2014). Corporate social responsibility and the nonprofit sector: Assessing the thoughts and practices across three nonprofit subsectors. http://repository.usfca.edu/cgi/viewcontent.cgi?article= 1024&context=pna.

Witt, L. A. (1990). Person—Situation Effects and Gender Differences in the Prediction of Social Responsibility. *The Journal of Social Psychology*, *130*(4), 543–553. https://doi.org/10.1080/00224545.1990.9924616.

Wright, N. S., & Bennett, H. (2011). Business ethics, CSR, sustainability and the MBA. *Journal of Management & Organization,17*(5), 641-655. https://doi.org/10.5172/jmo.2011.17.5.641.

Xavier, G. V. F., Goddard, J. B., Hall, B. L., Hazelkorn, E., & Tandon, R. (2017). In *Towards a socially responsible university: balancing the global with the local*. Girona; GUNi, Global University Network for Innovation.

Zafar, M., & Ali, I. (2016). The Influence of Corporate Social Responsibility on Employee Commitment: The Mediating Role of Employee Company Identification. *Asian Social Science*, *12*(12), 262-280. https://doi.org/10.5539/ass.v12n12p262.

Chapter 11

The Role of Legal Aid Clinics in Enhancing the Employability, Entrepreneurship and Foundation Skills for Law Students: A Qualitative Analysis

S. Sapna[*]
S. Nair Jayadevan[†]
and M. R. Mallaiah[‡]
School of Law, Christ University, Bengaluru, India

Abstract

Access to justice is the basic postulate of a legal system. In this endeavour, universities have a unique institutional advantage to make a potential contribution to 100% access to justice by fostering a strong culture of social responsibility through innovative pro bono legal service initiatives and inculcating the professional value of legal service in the students and motivating them to develop a critical consciousness for social justice linked to the holistic development of law students. Consequently, the impact analysis of this training on global opportunities, both in terms of employability and higher education, formed the kernel of this chapter. Through in-depth interviews, focus group discussions and perspectives of researchers as participants in state-level Legal services clinics, data was collected. Several key indicators were identified to analyze the expanded and holistic role of legal aid clinical education to effectively prepare students for their future. The

---
[*] Corresponding Author's Email: sapna.s@christuniversity.in.
[†] Corresponding Author's Email: jayadevan.nair@christuniversity.in.
[‡] Corresponding Author's Email: mallaiah.mr@christuniversity.in.

In: Models for Social Responsibility Action by Higher Education Institutions
Editors: Joseph Chacko Chennattuserry, Elangovan N. et al.
ISBN: 979-8-89113-097-5
© 2024 Nova Science Publishers, Inc.

study crystallizes a model for legal aid clinical courses by which Universities can deliver cutting-edge life and employability skills and enhance the professional competence of law students through direct participation in legal aid services.

Keywords: legal aid service, employability, entrepreneurship, model for legal services clinic

1. Introduction

"Legal education plays an important role in socializing the next generation of lawyers, judges, and public policymakers. As gatekeepers to the profession, law schools have a unique opportunity and obligation to make access to justice a more central social priority" (Green, 2004).

The law school is a spawning ground for advocates, jurists and the judiciary, making their role in the access to justice movement an extremely important social responsibility. At the convergence of new technologies, innovations and interdisciplinary perspectives, law schools need to plug that critical link towards advancing state legal systems to strive for access to justice for all, as there is a huge unmet need for legal representation for the poor. This exercise, where the law students get to be involved in direct participation in legal aid as a clinical legal education, provides the law schools with the opportunity to advance the legal profession by contributing to local and national access to justice collaborations. The Bar Council of India, which is a regulatory body for legal education in India, has enforced the Legal Education Rules, 2008, under which several law schools have launched initiatives to strengthen the relationship between legal education and practice in the service of access to justice.

To the extent that engagement with the justice system already exists, the key reflection observed in law schools in the USA is the training of future lawyers through experiential legal learning and "practice-ready curriculum," as well as developing and promoting a culture of pro bono legal service (Rickard, 2018).

Each of the services that law schools engage in can grow and further embed as part of the surrounding justice ecosystem. Law schools can collaboratively work with the State, for instance, in the guise of the State Legal Services Authority, to improve resources while educating students in the process. The Legal Service Clinic established in the law schools is that formal link to connect students, clients and the State, and basically, it is the connection between theory and practice. A corollary in this regard is drawn to the medical colleges to embed practice opportunities into legal education (Sandefur & Selbin, 2009).

The Report of the Expert Committee on Legal Aid, India -1973 has documented the impact analysis of legal aid for law students in the following area;

Firstly, a growing clientele from the downtrodden and underprivileged will generate innovative demands upon the legal profession, calling for new skill sets to deal with unethical systems and thus leaning towards weaker sections and sensitisation for injustice. The spirit and enthusiasm of the youth in law schools can help meet these demands and transform society.

Under proper supervision law, students can impart excellent legal advice and advocacy to the people. This can extend to remote areas and rural sites where the official agencies may not be able to serve. Professional responsibility and accountability to the public can be best learnt in legal aid clinics. Real-life problems and conflicting value choices instil in the students the necessary perspective, a sense of relevancy and skill to apply professional ethics in concrete situations. Community engagement through legal advocacy and literacy can have a far-reaching impact on society.

The most important by-product of integrating legal aid in law school is it drives legal education towards socially relevant and professionally valuable education. A student experiences real legal problems concerning actual people by involving in interviewing and counselling, negotiation and management of human relations, fact gathering, fact consciousness and a sense of relevancy, legal research and writing, handling crisis situations and intelligent decision making and above all an appreciation that law is the only one method of solving the problem and not always the best method.

Consequently, the impact analysis of this training on global opportunities, both in terms of employability and higher education, will form the kernel of this study. This study argues for the extension, replication and improvement of those pro bono initiatives from the perspective of its outcome to impact employability, entrepreneurship and development of foundational skills for law school to make law students future ready.

A qualitative research analysis of the model adopted by Christ University for its legal aid programme and the legal service clinic forms the core of this study. In-depth interviews were conducted with students, both alumni & current batch, to explore the impact of participation in the legal aid exercise, of having met the clients directly and working with the State Legal Services

Authority in the development of their legal skills. Focus group discussions with High Court Judges, District Judges, Members of the State Legal Services Authority, the Dean of the School of Law, Christ University and the Faculty in charge of the Legal Aid Committee shed light on the 'right to counsel movement', especially in rural areas and highlighted the benefits for law students in this exercise. As this study was undertaken during the covid- 19 pandemic, the observation brought focus to the specific challenges of access to justice during lockdown times, specifically in the case of the economically and socially disadvantaged. The transition to an e-legal services clinic brought in its unique advantages but also new concerns.

The aims of this chapter are:

- To assess the role of clinical legal aid education in impacting employability, entrepreneurship and foundation skills of law students
- To assess the role of law schools in providing legal aid services
- To build a social model of legal service course structure to be replicated by other law schools in the country.

2. Review of Literature

2.1. Social Responsibility in Higher Education Institutions (SRHEI)

Universities play a vital role in building a more equitable society insofar as they train students to act with social responsibility in their personal and professional lives (Dima et al., 2013; Giacalone & Thompson, 2006; Naval & Ruiz-Corbella, 2012). To be attuned to the growing importance of social responsibility in higher education institutions (SRHEI), universities take up diverse activities to ensure students engage in community needs beyond the University's environment (Dima et al., 2013, p. 25).

SRHEI, by definition, is-

The need to strengthen civic commitment and active citizenship; [...] developing a sense of civil citizenship by encouraging the students and the academic staff to provide social services to their local community or to promote ecological and environmental commitment for local and global sustainable development (Vasilescu et al., 2010, p. 4178).

In Spain, it is conceptualized as an imperative to revisit universities, using values and techniques that motivate responsibility towards society and follow a sustainable model, both internally and externally (Comisión Técnica de la Estrategia Universidad 2015, 2011, cited in Naval & Ruiz-Corbella, 2012, p. 110).

In Mexico, SRHEI is understood as principles and values that are responsive to the community and impact the teaching, research and extension programmes (Aldeanueva Fernández & Jiménez Quintero, 2013, p. 18).

In 2014 in Peru, Nueva Ley Universitaria (New University Act) was passed to provide a legal framework to the theoretical framework of SRHEI.

In India, the University Grants Commission (UGC) during 2019 adopted the National Curriculum Framework and Guidelines for Fostering Social Responsibility & Community Engagement in Higher Education Institutions in India. The UNESCO Conference on Higher Education held in Paris in July 2009 expressly enjoins a duty on HEIs to advance social responsibility through its core missions of teaching, research and service to lead in global knowledge transfer to address global challenges like food security, environmental issues, energy, public health etc.

2.2. The Role of University-Based Legal Aid Clinics in Access to Justice

In India, social responsibility through Legal aid was first introduced by Justice PN Bhagwati under the Legal Aid Committee, which was formed in 1971. Legal aid refers to the provision of free legal services to people who are unable to bear the cost of legal representation and access to courts in India. Free legal aid is, therefore, the most important component to provide access to justice to all without discrimination, financial or otherwise, in order to ensure the Constitutional guarantee of equality guaranteed under Article 14 of the Constitution of India. The Legal Services Authority's Act 1987 was enacted to give a uniform statutory framework to the legal aid schemes in India. The State Legal Services Authority[1] is set up under this Act, and one of its most important functions is to undertake Legal aid programs in association with law schools in order to create continuous awareness machinery on access to justice through free aid and alternate dispute resolution mechanisms. In the year 1998, this concept came to be initiated by the Bar Council of India, which mandated the establishment of legal aid cells in every law school. The law schools were advised to take up the role of facilitator and the students to be

---

[1] Section 6- Constitution of State Legal Services Authority of the Legal Services Act, 1987.

the value adders to the community. These clinics served as an effective tool for community education, and correspondingly, the law student developed a holistic experience.

Russian professor Alexander Lyublinski propounded the theory of legal aid committees in law schools in the year 1901. He explained that the students could get practical exposure by way of clinical education, and learning need not happen only through lectures. That law is a social profession, a way of living, and not just a livelihood, which has been emphasized time and again. (McGinley, 1955).

There are innumerable examples where communities and individuals have been empowered through access to legal aid as it contributes to reducing poverty and promotes the protection of human rights. Diverse legal aid approaches are used globally to ensure access to legal services for the needy, and University-based legal aid clinics are the strongest link in this endeavour (UNODC, 2016)

Law schools need to instil a consciousness of moral and social responsibilities in future lawyers and teach them to always be mindful of their powers and positions as Officers of the Court. The reality is explained as how the majority of lawyers are insensitive to their larger moral and social responsibilities, not because they don't recognise t such responsibilities exist but because their legal institutions did not foster attention to them in subsequent practice. (O'Connor, 1985).

The American Bar Association initiates many programmes to aid in the development of pro bono work in the form of mandatory pro bono services. Implied in all these activities is the notion that lawyers have moral and social responsibilities to be discharged by the bar, willingly or otherwise (ABA, 1982).

The researchers argue lest the sense of professional responsibility towards access to justice becomes a mere ceremonial exercise in law schools, the legal aid activity needs to be undertaken as a focused clinical legal education in law schools to effectively engage student participation for hands-on engagement in legal problems of the indigent clients. This would then be in line with the legal profession's ideals, benefiting the justice system and future lawyers. It is well evidenced that in a country like India, with a huge population and a significant population of social and economic poor, the civil and criminal justice system falls very short. Research on legal education revealed that the "latent curriculum "at law schools does very little to promote that sense of responsibility (Granfield, 1992; Rhode, 1995). Poor quality representation and a shortage of pro bono lawyers and legal services to address the requirements of the economically backward population are the major barriers to access to justice. In this regard, law schools can provide the strongest strategy by factoring concerns for professional ethics and responsibility for access to justice even in the core curriculum to increase students' culture for pro bono legal aid.

Drawing heavily from the perspective of a participant in a state-level Legal services clinic, the researchers offer practical recommendations and highlight the successful initiatives taken by Christ University that have the potential to step closer to the vision of access to justice for all and mutually benefit the law students. The legal aid service –scheme generally encapsulates the 'right to counsel movement', especially in rural areas, interviewing applicants for legal aid, prison visit, legal research and Legal advocacy, all of which are vital to the future law profession as it brings in an improved and practical legal education by developing proximity between the law students and real experiences of end users (Rickard, 2018). The researchers, through this chapter, aim to champion the cause of equal access to justice, making it central to their work as teachers and motivating students who are future generations of lawyers to join this cause.

2.3. Revolutions towards Free Legal Aid in India & U. K.

From a historical perspective, the concept of legal aid owes its origin to the pro-Bono support provided by lawyers. Reference is made to an Act in 1495 in England by which judges of the superior courts ordered advocates to hold briefs for poor litigants. However, during the 20th century onwards, there was a growth of voluntary free legal aid to people who were economically backward as a move towards access to justice campaigns which were the aftermath of welfare structures in Europe (Moore & Newbury, 2017). The Indian scenario is one in which a dominant portion of the people are socially and economically backward, and therefore, legal aid has a strong constitutional status. Its jurisprudential roots, social and legal character, and perspective attitude are evident from the Preamble of the Constitution, "We the people of India," which highlights social and economic justice as a rule of life and of law.

It is set out in Article 14 that every person should have equality before the law and equal protection of the laws, and in Article 22 that a person who is arrested should have the right to consult and be defended by an advocate of his choice. Article 14 enjoins the State to make effective provisions for securing the right of public assistance in cases of deserving need. Article 46 enjoins upon the State to promote with special care the economic interests of the weaker sections of the community and, in particular, scheduled caste and scheduled Tribes and protect them from social injustice and all forms of exploitation. All of this strikes a clear provision for the poor, weaker section and the minorities with distributive justice writ large. Article 42 provides for just and humane conditions of work, and Article 43 assures all workers, agricultural, industrial or otherwise.....A living wage and conditions of work ensure a decent standard of life. The 42nd Amendment Act introduced in 1976 brought article 39 (A) under the directive principles of state policy. Article 39(A) under the Indian Constitution provides for the concept of legal aid in India. As the Directive Principles of State Policy, it provides that the State shall secure the operation of the legal system to promote justice on the basis of equal opportunity and shall, in particular, provide free legal aid by suitable legislation or schemes or in any other way, to ensure that opportunities for securing justice are not denied to any citizen by reason of economic or other disability.

The Government of India addressed the question of legal aid for the poor from 1952 onwards. Towards 1960 some guidelines were framed for legal aid schemes in different states and were implemented through legal boards, societies and law departments. In 1962 the Third All India lawyers conference made important recommendations on legal aid, enjoining the Central and State governments to take up this obligation. The national conference on legal aid in the year 1970 recommended the enactment of legislation to make legal aid a statutory obligation of the State. It called upon the courts, bar councils, and law faculties to contribute to a nationwide programme to help the poor and indigent. It is important to note at this point the Bhagwati Committee, constituted in 1970, also known as the Gujarat Committee 1970, made a strong recommendation for free legal aid as a social and economic necessity in a country like India. The report of the legal aid committee, 1973, entitled 'Processual Justice to the People' by J Krishna Iyer, makes a specific observation of the halting and tentative fashion of the induction of legal aid provisions in the Advocate's Act due to the assumption that legal aid to the poor was aligned to the administration of justice falling within entry 3 of the State list making the scope of action by the Central government essentially advisory in this field. Examining the scope of legal aid, this report brought out a very pertinent aspect that legal aid had to be viewed as a part of economic and social planning and something that was related to the entire legal system making it an indispensable part of the justice delivery system. This brings us to the important point that the scheme of legal aid sought a bigger role for the legal profession itself to administer and give effect to the same. The aspect of legal aid was thus examined to have a wider domain than mere administration of justice through the courts as its actual purpose is the promotion of equality, social welfare and social justice and assistance in ascertainment, assertion and enforcement of fundamental as well as other legal rights. This is how a newly coined word, "Juridicare' came to be used to focus on the comprehensive coverage of legal aid.

In 1987 the Legal Services Authority Act (LSAA) was introduced to give structure and functions to the legal aid functionaries statutorily. While the National Legal Services Authority (NALSA) is the apex body under Section 3 of the Act, the Karnataka State Legal Services Authority was established under Section 6 of the Act to give legal service to people who come under the criteria laid down in the Act, to conduct Lok Adalat and to undertake preventive and strategic legal aid programmes. It is worth noting that there are defined criteria for entitlement to legal services as laid down under Section 12 of this Act. Section 12 provides that – a member of a scheduled caste or scheduled tribe, a victim of trafficking in human beings or a beggar as referred to in Article 3 of the Constitution, a woman or a child, a mentally ill or otherwise disabled person, victim of natural disaster, industrial workmen, person in custody (protective home, juvenile home or psychiatric hospital) or whose annual income is less than INR 9000 can seek free legal aid in civil and criminal matters.

Rule 1 Order 33 deals with suits by indigent persons. The Code does not deal with the subject of legal aid per se but provides for exemption of court fees in respect of persons who are indigent. The objective is to help persons who do not possess sufficient means other than property exempt from attachment to institute a suit without paying court fees.

2.4. Futuristic Legal Education through Legal Aid

The Association of American Law Schools [AALS] released a Report - Learning to Serve, which detailed what law schools should do to foster community service through legal aid. It outlines that the best justification for legal aid is the expansion of perspectives, practical training and professional contacts from which the students benefit. Further, such service is a professional responsibility, and universities should teach students to assume it (AALS, 1998; Power, 1994).

The students learn the necessity for keen observation, logical thinking, and lucid articulation through participation in legal aid services, which involves real lawyering by direct engagement with clients, interviewing and counselling them, negotiating, legal drafting etc. (McGinley, 1955). This enables the students to get a better understanding of their interests and strengths, as well as focus on further internship opportunities and placement efforts. The most valuable by-product is the goodwill with the Bench and Community, which leads to successful networks that can contribute to law school efforts in development, recruitment and community relations. It is noted from Cuny Law School experience exposure to pro bono legal activities -" reinforces the best instincts and highest aspirations of the law students" (Glen, 1998).

3. Methodology

This chapter has adopted a mixed method by adopting a triangulation of FGDs, in-depth interviews and doctrinal research. For the doctrinal research, the primary and secondary sources of data for this chapter were reviewed from Constitutional law; the legal services authorities act, 1987, the civil procedure code, 1908, the national legal services authority regulations, 2010 and the national legal services authority (legal aid clinics) regulations, 2011. Qualitative research was designed for this study by adopting in-depth interviews and Focus Group Discussions (FGDs) to evaluate the impact of legal aid on the development of Employability, entrepreneurship and foundation skills for law students. For this purpose, two questionnaires were used for alumni and existing students at the School of Law, Christ University, respectively. The questionnaire consisted of closed-ended and some open-ended questions. A total of 14 students participated in the interviews.

In-depth interviews and FGD with the district legal services Authority and State legal services authority were conducted to bring out the qualitative analysis of the study. Through the focus group discussion, in-depth data was collected on the benefits of participation for both students and institutions, as the law school provided legal aid. Phenomenology, as a method of qualitative research, proved specifically useful to this research, as the data was built on the description of experiences of students who had undertaken the legal aid activity, specific experience of Law Firm Partners in identifying skill sets gained from legal aid participation during the recruitment process and perception of High Court Judges on the value legal services participation renders in the long run of the profession. Two sitting High Court Judges were interviewed. The district judge, who is the member secretary of Karnataka State legal services authority, a member of Karnataka State District legal services authority, members, nonofficial members and Chairman State Bar Council and Partners of Law Firms, participated in the FGD.

During data analysis, certain significant statements from the interviews emerged, which formed specific themes in the data, which are analysed in the findings (Elangovan et al., 2021). This chapter is based on the primary data collected through a structured questionnaire from major stakeholders of the legal aid programmes taking the city of Bengaluru as the universe for the research. The research included respondents who are students – alumni, existing students and student coordinators and members of the legal aid committee of the School of Law, Christ University, District legal services authorities and Karnataka State legal services authorities (KLSA).

4. Results

Multiple techniques like' analysis of words' by employing - word repetitions and key-words-in contexts (KWIC) and Linguistic forms of transition approach to identify the transitions in the theme for coding the text are used. Sub-themes emerged from the in-depth interviews and FGDs. The same is presented in Table 1.

5. Discussion

This chapter sets the context for the nexus between institutional and legal aid services and the impact it has on future lawyers. The results show that institutional legal aid is effective in terms of developing core constitutional values in law students by instilling a strong pro bono culture which in turn is linked to the holistic development of law students.

Though the most relevant outcomes are the crucial professional competency and lawyering skills like - problem-solving skills, critical thinking and application capabilities that legal aid activities are able to provide due to lived experiences, clinical legal education uses a teaching method of the 20th century as an alternative to conventional teaching as it takes students to face to face with actual cases, shadowing the practising lawyers.

Table 1. Themes on the Role of Institutional Legal Aid Clinic for Law Students

Sl.No	Themes	Sub-themes	Descriptions	%
1	Career aspirations in joining the law school	Civil services, Litigation, Law academia, Corporate, Higher studies abroad	Students join law schools by choice, not by chance, with a clear focus on their goals. Their expectations are high regarding professional progression.	100
2	The expected outcome of the legal aid training	Community engagement, Networking, Problem-solving skills, Theory to Practice	Students are happy to participate in legal aid camps organised by the institution. They understand the concept of service to the downtrodden & expect to learn lawyering skills in real life setting	60
3	Sector on which legal aid was concentrated on	Rural sector	Students are willing to engage in legal literacy, sensitization and awareness in the rural areas relating to the Dowry Act, the prohibition of child marriage, and the Rights of women and children.	60
4	Participation in legal aid- Mandatory or optional	Optional in terms of choosing para-legal service as elective	All Students are involved in the legal services programme of the law school mandatorily.	65
		Mandatory legal service visits.	Para-legal service is an elective course which is taken by choice. It is observed this is a preferred choice by the majority of the students.	

Sl.No	Themes	Sub-themes	Descriptions	%
5	Services in legal aid	Client interviewing Client Counselling Legal Advocacy legal drafting Coordinating with State Legal Services Authority	**Para** services – a field study is an elective course for the final year students in the School of Law, Christ University. Legal aid service camps are mandatory for all students. A dedicated legal service clinic is established in the law school. The Legal Service Clinic was established under the mentorship of the High Court.	65
6	Skills gained through legal aid clinical education	Gives a strong ethical and professional base through the pro bono nature of work, Helps in understanding the social and economic issues, which later on can be a good base for practice, Develops writing and speaking Skills Develops networking which in turn helps in employability, Experience in pro bono work enhances scholarship opportunities for higher education abroad.	Students develop the said lawyering skills in this clinical setting.	100
7	Application of this learning in a career opportunity	Higher education abroad internship	Students use these skills to factor in the Statement of Purpose (SOP) for a master's in law when applying abroad. It is used for internship applications. However, no mention of this being used for placement opportunities.	100

Table 1. (Continued)

SlNo	Themes	Sub-themes	Descriptions	%
8	Helps in a placement opportunity	Law firms lawyers' office companies	It is observed very few students have made use of this for placement opportunities	10
9	Improvements suggested	Increasing the frequency of legal aid More activities in the legal services clinic. Introduction of mentorship with senior counsels during law school legal aid training. Focus not just on socio-legal issues but other issues like - gender mainstreaming, policy engagement, CSR etc. Students need better motivation.	The improvements will need to focus on a structure of law firm-student mentorship to help law students gain better networking with the professional community.	100

This provided the most important advantage of preparing the students for professional practice (Frank, 1933).

This chapter reveals a positive impact on global opportunities in terms of higher education. However, with respect to placement opportunities, one specific challenge observed was the students' perception of an absence of any direct impact. Nevertheless, the institutional visibility aspect and professional networking open a window of opportunity for students, which bears a direct impact on the potential for placement.

During the FGDs, one of the Panelists from the judiciary observed law schools are the most important part of the legal ecosystem, not only as producers of future lawyers but also as a stakeholder in the accreditation and training of lawyers. Law schools, therefore, need to make a major contribution to training them in legal ethics apart from just legal-technical education.

The FGDs reveal one of the most significant differentiators would be an institutional commitment to legal aid services. The panel advised legal aid programmes need to be structured as an outcome-based structure, with a provision for good faculty resources, motivated students, a dedicated legal aid committee and a formal legal aid clinic, preferably having collaboration with State Legal Services Authority. This formal structure to legal aid as clinical legal education would bring the strongest link in the development of lawyering skills and professional competence to law students, which produces both direct and indirect benefits. The direct effect would be translated into employability, entrepreneurship and foundation skills. And the indirect effect of university goodwill, productive professional networks and visibility for the students would have a tremendous impact on future career opportunities.

It was discussed in the FGD that one of the ways institutional legal aid services could be heavily utilized is to build a mentorship network through a triangulation strategy with universities, leading law firms and State Legal Services Authority. The Pro Bono Collaborative at Roger Williams University Law (RWU) is one successful model where the institution cemented the connection of lawyers with their law students through legal aid service. Further, the institutional infrastructure was leveraged to connect students to do real work under the supervision of lawyers. (Barron et al., 2010).

Another important point that was unravelled during the FGDs was to maximize the use of technology by law schools for legal services and access to justice for the community. Machine learning could be used to optimize searches, gather information and online triage. E- legal services can lead to transformative changes in the access to justice movement, and law schools are best equipped to perform this role through outreach programmes.

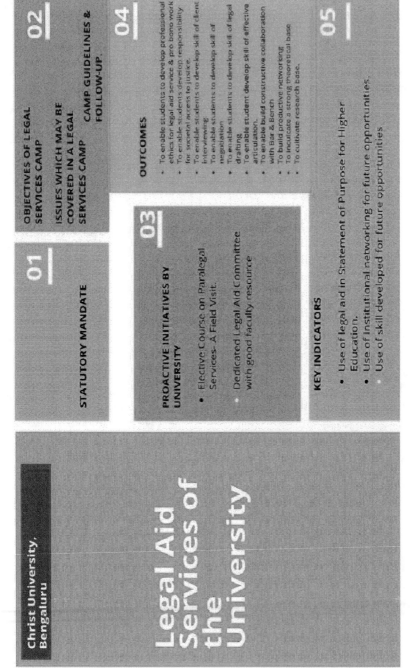

Figure 1. Legal Aid Services of the University.

Law schools should be like teaching hospitals to see a constructive nexus between experience-based practical legal education and empirical research on best practices, legal aid services and access to justice (Charn, 2003). This would enhance the productive partnership between the law school and the bar and increase law students' opportunities to work with lawyers and faculty on legal services policy debates.

This chapter contributes to a focused understanding of the institution's role in building a constructive collaboration between law students, Bar and Bench, and a professional triangulation which will take the students closer to their career aspirations through a professionally ethical path of social responsibility and legal service. The culture of student engagement in improving the lives of the downtrodden and the marginalized through the application of their law school teaching would contribute to University's the most important obligation.

An important outcome of this research is to create a model on the basis of the successful legal services initiatives undertaken by Christ University to help other law schools to take the lead to move a step closer to the vision of access to justice for all and to the mutual benefit of the law students.

The researchers argue this model can be replicated nationally in order to provide value to law students to impact employability, entrepreneurship and foundational skills to make them future-ready, as referred om Figure 1.

Conclusion

This chapter, which researched the role of Legal Aid Clinic in enhancing the employability, entrepreneurship and foundation skills of law students, noted that the institutional commitment and availability of resources is the differentiator. The Christ University model of a mixed approach between mandatory and optional-proactive legal aid services enhanced the intensity and quality of legal services provided to society. At the same time, instilling the constitutional values and culture of social responsibility has been its major triumph. Nevertheless, though it is a successful model, it could improve in terms of networking to produce mentorship-networking in a triangulation of Universities, Law Firms and the judiciary. Going further, law schools could partner with larger networks that may even transcend legal clinics, which could help in funding opportunities, transfer of expertise on best practices and advocacy in common issues.

Another concern noted was the negligible direct impact with respect to placements, although the indirect impact with respect to capacity building through participation in legal aid services as clinical legal education is immense. Lastly, as there is a paradigm shift from a traditional service model to a "commoditized" one, law schools should build initiatives built around specialized areas of need.

References

AALS (1998) *Learning To Serve : A Summary Of The Findings And Recommendations Of The Aals Commission On Pro Bono And Public Service Opportunities*. Commission On Pro Bono And Public Service Opportunities In Law Schools, Association Of American Law Schools (AALS).

ABA (1982). *A Guide And Explanation To Pro Bono Services*. **Standing Committee on Pro Bono & Public Service.** American Bar Association.

Barron, L., Harrington-Steppen, S., Tyler, E. T., & Vorenberg, E. (2010). Don't Do It Alone : A Community-Based Collaborative Approach to Pro Bono. *Georgetown Journal of Legal Ethics*, 23, 323.

Charn, J. (2003). Service and Learning : Reflections on Three Decades of the Lawyering Process at Harvard Law School. *Clinical Law Review*, 10, 75.

Dima, A. M., Vasilache, S., Ghinea, V., & Agoston, Si. (2013). A model of academic social responsibility. *Transylvanina Review of Administrative Sciences*, 38, 23–43. https://doi.org/10.14738/assrj.61.5256.

Elangovan, N., Yeon, G., Perumbilly, S., & Hormeila, S. (2021). Transitional Challenges In Technology Adoption Among Academic Communities Of Indian Higher Education. *Journal of International Technology and Information Management*, 30(2), 59-97.

Fernández, I. A., & Quintero, J. A. J. (2013). International experiences in University Social. *Visión de futuro*, 17(1), 17-29.

Frank, J. (1933). *Why not a clinical lawyer-school?*. University of Pennsylvania Law Review and American Law Register, 81(8), 907-923.

Giacalone, R., & Thompson, K. (2006). *Business ethics and social responsibility education: Shifting the worldview*. Academy of Management Learning and Education, 5, 266–277.

Glen, K. B. (1998). *Pro Bono and Public Interest Opportunities in Legal Education*. NY ST. BJ, 70, 20.

Granfield, R. (1992). *Making elite lawyers: Visions of law at Harvard and beyond*. Routledge.

Green, B. A. (2004). Deborah L. Rhode's Access to Justice : Foreword. *Fordham Law Review*, 73(3), 841.

McGinley, A. C. (1995). A Message from the President, *Fordham Law Review*, 24(9), 9-10.

Moore, S., & Newbury, A. (2017). *Legal Aid Reform in Historical and International Perspective*. In Legal Aid in Crisis : Assessing the impact of reform (pp.15-36). Bristol University Press. https://doi.org/10.2307/j.ctt1t8988q.6.

Naval, C., & Ruiz-Corbella, M. (2012). Aproximación a la responsabilidad social universitaria: La respuesta de la universidad a la sociedad. *Bordon*, 64(3), 103–115.

O'Connor, S. (1985). Legal education and social responsibility. *Fordham Law Review*, 53(4), 659-662.

Power, W. B. (1994). *Report On Law School Pro Bono Activities*. Commission on Pro Bono and Public Service Opportunities in Law Schools, Association of American Law Schools [AALS].

Rhode, D. L. (1995). Into the Valley of Ethics: Professional responsibility and educational reform. *Law and Contemporary Problems*, 58, 139.

Rickard, E. J. (2018). The Role of Law Schools in the 100% Access to Justice Movement. *Indiana Journal of Law and Social Equality*, 6(2), Article 3. https://www.repository.law.indiana.edu/ijlse/vol6/iss2/3.

Sandefur, R., & Selbin, J. (2009). The clinic effect. *Clinical Law Review*, 16(1), 57-108.

UNODC (2016). *Global Study on Legal Aid Global Report*. The United Nations Office on Drugs and Crime (UNODC). https://www.unodc.org/documents/justice-and-prison-reform/LegalAid/Global_Study_on_Legal_Aid_-_FINAL.pdf.

Vasilescu, R., Barna, C., Epure, M., & Baicu, C. (2010). Developing university social responsibility: A model for the challenges of the new civil society. *Procedia – Social and Behavioral Sciences*, 2, 4177–4182.

Chapter 12

Sensitization of University Students in Supporting Underprivileged Children

Budha Anuradha[*]
and Arumugam Senthil Kumar[†]

Department of Professional Studies, Christ University, Bengaluru, India

Abstract

Education is the fundamental right of every child and an essential element of human growth. Indian education is divided into two parts: private and government education. Underprivileged children, affected by socio-economic factors, predominantly choose government education. Government primary educational institutions have failed to cope with the requirements of the corporate world. On the other hand, the students studying in private higher educational institutions seldom think of the challenges that socio-economically underprivileged children face. Genesys is the forum that unites these socio-economically underprivileged children with students at Christ University. Teaching and training disadvantaged children are the social responsibilities of young people, especially those in higher education. Each student should teach at least one person to make it a win-win situation for both learner and trainer. It helps University students build social skills and provides them with the opportunity to become part of the nation-building process. The chapter employed the quantitative study method to analyze the students' perception of teaching underprivileged children and how demographic variables impact it. It also identified the factors influencing the student's academic performance and psychological well-being. The study found that the students gained different skills like interpersonal skills, adaptability, teaching skills, and happiness, and these skills

---

[*] Corresponding Author's E-mail: budha.anuradha@christuniversity.in
[†] Corresponding Author's E-mail: senthilkumar.a@christuniversity.in

In: Models for Social Responsibility Action by Higher Education Institutions
Editors: Joseph Chacko Chennattuserry, Elangovan N. et al.
ISBN: 979-8-89113-097-5
© 2024 Nova Science Publishers, Inc.

positively impacted their academic performance and psychological well-being. The expected outcome of the program supported by the university is to develop a win-win model for both University students and schoolchildren from low-income groups in society

Keywords: underprivileged children, higher education, perception, reverse mentoring, sensitization, teaching, training, volunteering

1. Introduction

Education has been commercialized and made competition-based among students globally. (Banu, 2017). With the fast technological development and globalization in the economy, education is essential for every human to survive. It is the fundamental right of every child in a nation. Equal opportunities for accessing quality education should be the primary objective of a sustainable society (Medina-García et al., 2020). After independence in India, various central and state governments have formulated many educational policies and introduced several welfare schemes for free access to education for socially and economically disadvantaged students (NCERT, n.d; Shannon, n.d). Indian education includes students with different cultural, religious, linguistic, social, and economic backgrounds. Hence, it is necessary to provide practical solutions to educational problems by focusing on economically and socially underprivileged children. Parent's inability to meet their children's learning needs in terms of material aspects like notebooks, study materials, stationaries, uniforms, and so on is a primary reason for the dropout of children from schools (Kapoor, 2008). Increasing students' enrolment by attractive policies cannot indicate their growth. Various measures are to be taken to improve their children's active participation in schooling. Few people are creating awareness of the importance of education, providing opportunities to help socially backward communities through financial support, taking care of their children with special teaching attention outside the school, and bringing better stability. Teachers should be aware of various teaching-learning aspects, and due care is essential while teaching socially backward children (NCERT, n.d). This chapter concentrates on the higher education students involved in specialized teaching for socially and economically underprivileged children in a selected location. This chapter studied the students' perception of teaching and training children from poor socio-economic backgrounds and outcomes through teaching-learning. The chapter results stimulate students' communities and educational institutions to participate in sustainable social development.

Socially disadvantaged students face educational problems, especially in adolescence, due to their parents' low-level occupations and ignorance (Mphale & Mhlauli, 2014). At present, the need of the hour is each student should teach at least one person (Berte, 2016; Janae & Philadelphia, 2020). Teaching and tutoring socially and economically backward students are the social responsibilities of young people, significantly higher education students, to stand up against illiteracy in a country. The National University of Educational Planning and Administration of India has specified various education service challenges in India. A few significant issues are as follows: i) the absence of quality in 'Early Childhood Care and Education (ECCE)' programs, ii) lower enrolment rates and higher dropout rates in school education, particularly among students belonging to socially and economically underprivileged people groups, iii) less number of children's presence in school in educationally underdeveloped states in India, iv) lower level of children participation in specific needs, v) lack of quality in teaching, vi) difficulty sustaining the contribution of the volunteer teachers/senior students in adolescent education programs, and vii) building sustainable literacy demand and need for funds for these education programs, etc. (National University of Educational Planning and Administration, 2014). The above issues can address in the following ways: a) ensuring quality access in the teaching-learning process, b) practical learning outcomes in children's education, c) reducing the gap in a social group, d) effective use of ICTs (information and communication technology) and e) creating a supportive continuing education system. Importantly, higher education students' voluntary involvement in children's special education and training programs with academic institutions is an effective remedial measure for the above issues. It provides mental satisfaction and peace of mind, changing the learner and senior students'/teachers'/tutors' lives. In this context, this chapter tries to examine the outcome and experiences of higher education students when teaching children. It is essential to know the perception of students teaching and tutoring economically and socially underprivileged children in 'each one to teach one campaign. In this chapter, the authors raise key research questions about students' perception of 'each one teaches one.' How effective is the teaching-learning process in improving children's performance? Whether teaching helps to improve their academic performance and psychological well-being? Is this helpful for acquiring additional skills in their academic career? What factors contribute to senior students' academic performance during each-one-teach-one system?

2. Review of Literature

"Each One Teach One" is an African American slogan that originated in the United States during the times of slavery (Laubach Literacy Ontario, n.d). This phrase was famous when the Africans were denied education. It is the responsibility of someone who learnt to teach someone else. Socially disadvantaged children are discriminated against in various modes: social, cultural, mental, physical, educational, and emotional (Bhatla, 2017). In most cases, socially and economically backward children belong to scheduled castes, scheduled tribes, backward class, low-income, and minority groups in India. Children from socially backward communities such as 'Dalits' and 'Adivasis' face continuous education hurdles (Desai & Kulkarni, 2008). There are other causes of the backwardness of children. It can be poor intellectual ability, physical defects and diseases, cynical intellectual, emotional atmosphere and disturbance, and neighborhood and environmental influence (Shivangi, n.d). Economically backward children of minority communities enter school with poorer academic, social, and emotional readiness competencies (Evans, 2004; Stipek, 1997). Backwardness in child education affects their entire personality, and it is also a significant hurdle for the nation's development.

Socially underprivileged children had significantly less access to effective teaching on an average from IV to school VIII standards (Isenberg et al., 2013). He also stated that the degree of variances in effective teaching for socially advantaged and disadvantaged children in a particular period was equal to a shift of two per cent points in the children's achievement gap. Elementary education offered is mixed up by several problems, such as inadequacy of teacher-student ratio and infrastructure, caste partialities, lack of quality in education, and minimal students achievements (Alexander et al., 1997; Finn, 1989; Entwisle & Alexander, 1988), lack of awareness of higher education (Tilak, 1997), lack of libraries in school (Busayo, 2011; Justina & Jacintha, 2015), etc. These problems cause to rise in the rate of school dropouts. Accessible meal facilities, free books, and uniforms offered to the children increase one-tenth of students' participation (Afridi, 2011). The problems of students' discontinuation in schools can be either grouped as economic, psychological, or societal. It isn't easy to apply uniform methods in India because of the vast socio-economic diversity (Chakraborty & Chaudhuri, 2019). The same problem continues in higher education. In his study, Berte (2016) stated several issues surrounding nurse practitioner students' precepting in clinical settings.

The learner's perception is central to the ultimate success of educational efforts. Faculty development efforts could take a more personalized approach, capitalizing on faculty members' existing strengths to improve procedural education effectiveness while maintaining individual style and personality traits (Janae & Philadelphia, 2020). A younger student learns from an older, knowledgeable student in a traditional mentoring education system. The older or senior student is not defined by age but can also be identified by experience. Younger students are more knowledgeable in digital technologies and tools than senior students. Two-way teaching and mentoring help the seniors get insight into the latest technologies and understand each other. Mixing up one-sided face-to-face mentoring resulting from multigenerational/cross-generational (Murphy, 2012), students' groups are sometimes called 'reciprocal mentoring' or 'reverse mentoring' (Keogh, 2018). Reverse mentoring also reduces gaps between generations and improves communication for future success in their career (Cotugna & Vickery, 1998). Three parties, viz. students, children, and institutions, benefit from reverse mentoring. The primary outcomes are talent management, social equity, understanding the latest teaching-learning trends, and reducing the technology gap (Murphy, 2012).

Teaching experience does not require a one-to-one basis of tutoring work. However, the person who teaches/trains schoolchildren must have complete patience and firm determination. The child should be respected and motivated. The teacher should understand the child's weaknesses. A socially and economically weak child needs praise, assistance, a sympathetic understanding of his problems, and continued concern for his teacher. Frank et al. (2020) supports the idea that students who perceive their teachers as caring, understanding, and listening are better able and more willing to engage in classroom activities. International comparative research has shown that students who experience the classroom climate as open also achieve higher citizenship competence scores (Schulz et al., 2018). Although all students gain a supportive and caring relationship with their teachers, it is more vital for highly educated parents than those with less-educated parents (Campbell, 2018; Frank et al., 2020). Contrary to our expectations, the results also showed that children from unemployed parents are more involved in society than children from families in which both parents are employed. In general, parental unemployment is negatively related to their children's social and academic outcomes (Levine, 2011; Powdthavee & Vernoit, 2013; Sleskova et al., 2006). Other students may value face-to-face interaction, pre- and post-class discussions, collaborative learning, and organic student-teacher bonding (Rovai & Jordan, 2004). 'Each one teaches one' based remedial teaching program helps each child improve their potential skills to their limits and attain distinct achievement for different children. Hence, the person/students who teach the children should be specialists in dealing with specific underprivileged. Most of the research (Banu, 2017; Bellamy, 1915; Hughes et al., 2005; Shivangi, n.d; Sundaresan, 2015) examined professional teachers' perceptions of backward students' teaching. A review of the research found a gap in the study to identify senior students' perception of teaching underprivileged children in each-one-teach-one mode. The research study of this chapter attempts to fill the above gap.

3. Methodology

The chapter is quantitative and action research, referring to examining actions in the Genesys forum, assessing their effectiveness in bringing about the desired outcome, and choosing a course of action based on our results. The study population is the student members of the "Genesys" forum, functioning on the campus of Christ University, Bengaluru, a private educational institution located in Urban Bengaluru, Karnataka State, India. The forum's main objective is to give training, teaching, mentoring, and financial support to economically and socially underprivileged children and wards of the university's housekeeping staff. Children studying primary to higher secondary education in Bengaluru city have participated in this specialized learning endeavour. One hundred six students voluntarily joined the forum during 2019-2020 and 2020-2021. The forum functions with the motto that each student should teach at least one child. The chapter focused on understanding higher education students' experiences, attitudes, behaviour, and interactions while teaching socially disadvantaged children on the 'each one teaches one' method.

Figure 1 describes the overall methodology of functioning of the social responsibility platform Genesys. The study's objective is to evaluate the impact of Genesys on the well-being of university students. It further identifies university students' perception of the social responsibility forum Genesys. It ascertains the effect of demographic variables on students' perception of each-one-teach-one moto of Genesys. This chapter further determines the impact of volunteering and social responsibility activities on the academic performance of university students.

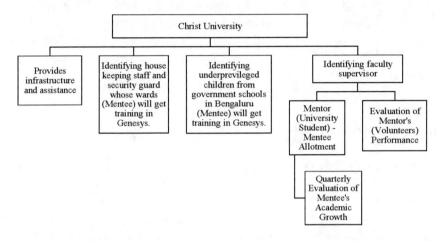

Figure 1. Genesys – Modus Operandi.

The census method was followed for collecting the primary data from all the 106 volunteers of Genesys. The questionnaire was administered to understand the views of volunteers about the forum "Genesys." Respondents are higher education students who joined the forum and voluntarily taught economically and socially backward children while studying at a Private Deemed to be University in Bengaluru, India, from 2019 to 2021. Hypotheses were tested by systematically collecting the data using questionnaires and analyzing data using appropriate statistical tools. Frequency distribution, factor analysis, Multivariate analysis, and multiple regression have been used. SPSS version 22 was used for data analysis. Kaiser-Meyer-Olkin's measure of sampling adequacy and Bartlett's sphericity test were made to measure the study variables for factor analysis. Factor analysis was made to reduce the number of variables used for students' perception of each-one-teach-one and determine students' primary underlying constructs. Using principal component analysis and varimax with Kaiser normalization, the rotated component matrix was employed for variable grouping. Normality and reliability tests were employed to test the normal distribution of data and the quality of the research. Dependent variables and independent demographic variables of the respondents, viz. gender, place of residence, number of teaching hours per month, and number of years active in the forum, were sourced from primary data collection to perform multivariate analysis. The study also determined the independent variables that predict the student's academic performance and psychological well-being using multiple regression analysis. The results in this chapter have a few shortcomings. The data collected were mainly the student's perceptions of each one teaches one. Respondents belong to a specific higher educational institution, and the population is meagre. The study results may differ from those conducted with a large population in other areas.

4. Analysis and Results

Every teacher should be updated regarding their knowledge of the latest digital technology in today's competitive world (Mangal, 2017). In the one-to-one teaching-learning method, mere teaching subject alone cannot provide ingredients to the children. The person who teaches underprivileged children suggests considering the following practices for an effective outcome. They are character training, more personal instruction, individual attention to health and social condition, motivation to participate in extra and co-curricular activities, keeping the desired outcome in mind, short and straightforward methods of instructions for the slow learners, remedial teaching for the advanced subject, audio-visual materials, habits of success and creating self-confidence, etc. In this study, the respondents were asked to answer 12 questions related to perception on each-one-teach-one in the questionnaire, and these were measured using a five-point Likert scale. Responders specified their level of perception of a statement typically in five points: Strongly disagree (1), Disagree (2), Neither agree nor disagree (3), Agree (4), and strongly agree (5).

4.1. Demographic Analysis

Table 1 demonstrates the demographic profiles of 106 respondents. The majority of the respondents were female (73%). The respondent's demographic variable, such as 'academic performance' considering their percentage of marks in all the semesters, was average and above. First and second-year students actively participated in the Genesys forum at a maximum (91%). To test the relevant hypotheses of the study, dependent and independent demographic variables of the respondents, viz. gender, place of residence, number of teaching hours per month, and number of years active, were sourced from primary data collection to perform univariate analysis.

Table 1. Details of demographic variables

Demographic Variables	Value Label	N	Percentage
Gender	Male	29	27%
	Female	77	73%
Place of residence	Day scholar	52	49%
	Hosteler	54	51%
Number of Teaching Hours	Less than 30	37	35%
	>=30 and < 60	43	41%
	Greater than equal to 60	26	24%
Academic Performance	Average	50	47%
	Outstanding	56	53%
Number of Years Active in Forum	One year	44	42%
	Two Years	52	49%
	Three years	10	9%

Source: Primary data

Table 2. Multivariate Test Analysis

Source	Dependent Variable	Type III Sum of Squares	df	Mean Square	F	Sig.
Place of Residence	Interpersonal skills	.260	1	.260	1.600	.209
	Adaptability	.363	1	.363	1.560	.215
	Teaching Skills	.192	1	.192	.234	.630
	Happiness	.257	1	.257	.472	.494
Gender	Interpersonal skills	.028	1	.028	.173	.679
	Adaptability	.125	1	.125	.539	.465
	Teaching Skills	.128	1	.128	.156	.694
	Happiness	.000	1	.000	.000	.985
Number of years active in the forum	Interpersonal skills	1.298	2	.649	3.989	.022*
	Adaptability	.399	2	.200	.859	.427
	Teaching Skills	3.403	2	1.701	2.076	.132
	Happiness	1.286	2	.643	1.180	.312
Number of Hours Teaching per Month	Interpersonal skills	.584	2	.292	1.795	.172
	Adaptability	.090	2	.045	.193	.824
	Teaching Skills	.175	2	.087	.107	.899
	Happiness	1.017	2	.509	.933	.397

Table 2. (Continued)

Source	Dependent Variable	Type III Sum of Squares	df	Mean Square	F	Sig.
Place of Residence * Number of Hours Teaching per month	Interpersonal skills	.300	2	.150	.921	.402
	Adaptability	.035	2	.017	.075	.928
	Teaching Skills	1.100	2	.550	.671	.514
	Happiness	2.324	2	1.162	2.133	.125
Place of Residence * Gender	Interpersonal skills	.010	1	.010	.059	.808
	Adaptability	.674	1	.674	2.898	.092
	Teaching Skills	.100	1	.100	.122	.727
	Happiness	3.090	1	3.090	5.671	.019*
Place of Residence * Number of years active in the forum	Interpersonal skills	.183	2	.092	.563	.572
	Adaptability	.405	2	.202	.871	.422
	Teaching Skills	1.310	2	.655	.800	.453
	Happiness	.186	2	.093	.170	.844
Gender * Number of Hours Teaching per month	Interpersonal skills	1.371	2	.686	4.215	.018*
	Adaptability	.642	2	.321	1.381	.257
	Teaching Skills	2.254	2	1.127	1.376	.258
	Happiness	1.475	2	.738	1.353	.264
Source	Dependent Variable	Type III Sum of Squares	df	Mean Square	F	Sig.
Number of years active in forum * Number of Hours Teaching per month	Interpersonal skills	1.482	3	.494	3.037	.033*
	Adaptability	.882	3	.294	1.264	.292
	Teaching Skills	4.265	3	1.422	1.735	.166
	Happiness	.394	3	.131	.241	.867
Gender * Number of years active in the forum	Interpersonal skills	2.028	2	1.014	6.235	.003*
	Adaptability	.319	2	.160	.686	.506
	Teaching Skills	3.235	2	1.618	1.974	.145
	Happiness	1.084	2	.542	.994	.374
Error	Interpersonal skills	14.153	87	.163		
	Adaptability	20.228	87	.233		
	Teaching Skills	71.291	87	.819		
	Happiness	47.412	87	.545		
Corrected Total	Interpersonal skills	22.196	105			
	Adaptability	25.388	105			
	Teaching Skills	88.899	105			

Source: SPSS Output.
* Significant at a 5% level of significance.

Table 2 shows the test results of any statistical difference between the independent and dependent variables. Test results say that there is no statistically significant difference between the independent variables such as place of residence, gender, the number of hours teaching per month, the combined effect of place of residence and the number of hours training per month, and the combined effect of place of residence and the number of years active in the forum and either of the dependent variables such as interpersonal skills, adaptability, teaching skills, and happiness. There is a significant difference in the mean level value between 'the number of years active in the forum' and the students' interpersonal skills ($p<.0005$). Similarly, the same significant difference in mean level ($p<.0005$) was found between the combined effect of 'place of residence and gender' and happiness; the combined effect of 'gender and number of hours teaching per month' and interpersonal skills; the combined effect of 'gender and number of years active in forum' and interpersonal skills; and the combined effect of 'the number of years active in the forum and number of hours teaching per month' and interpersonal skills.

4.2. Factor Analysis

Factor analysis was used to reduce the number of variables about the perception of each-one-teach-one factor. The respondents' answers for 12 statements were analyzed using Kaiser-Meyer-Olkin (KMO) Measure for sampling Adequacy, and the details are indicated in Table 3. The KMO test value is 0.740, more than 0.5, which can be considered acceptable and valid for the data reduction technique. In Table 3, Bartlett's test of sphericity helps a researcher decide whether factor analysis results are worth considering and whether we should continue analyzing the research work. Bartlett's Test of Sphericity was significant at <0.001, which shows a high correlation between variables, making it adequate to apply factory analysis.

The total variance contributed by the first component after rotation sums of squared loadings are 22.492, by the second component 14.982, by the third component 11.991, and by the fourth component 11.093. The eigenvalue for a given factor measures the variance in all the variables accounted for by that factor. It is also clear that four distinct parts have Eigenvalues greater than one from the given variables. The eigenvalue after rotation sums of squared loadings for factor 1 is 2.699, for factor 2 is 1.798, for factor 3 is 1.439 and for factor 4 is 1.331. The four-factor solution is responsible for the common variance constituting 60.55 per cent of the total variance. Since all these four factors have an eigenvalue greater than one and share maximum variance, they are essential in the present study.

Table 3. KMO and Bartlett's test

Kaiser-Meyer-Olkin Measure of Sampling Adequacy		.740
Bartlett's Test of Sphericity	Approx. Chi-Square	279.573
	Df	66
	Sig.	<0.001

Table 4. Factor analysis

Factors	Components	Item Description	Rotated Loading	% of variance	Eigen Value
1	Interpersonal Skill	It helped me develop relationship skills	.691	22.492	2.699
		Provided opportunity to develop social skills	.684		
		It was a new experience interacting with economically backward children	.630		
		It provided me with a sense of purpose	.629		
		It helped me in connecting with school-going children and to know the ground reality of primary education today in India	.619		
		Teaching children boosted my self-confidence	.579		
2	Adaptability	I learnt to adapt to a challenging situation	.841	14.982	1.798
		I realized empathy can be learnt by getting into ground realities	.667		
		I get a sense of fulfillment as a volunteer	.560		
3	Teaching Skill	I joined volunteering to enrich my profile	.835	11.991	1.439
		I developed teaching and convincing skills after interacting with children	.604		
4	Happiness	It brought happiness to my life	.892	11.093	1.331
		It was a new experience that brought a feel-good factor to my day-to-day routine.	.890		
		It became a pride factor.	.799		

Extraction Method: Principal Component Analysis.
Rotation Method: Varimax with Kaiser Normalization.
Rotation converged in 7 iterations.

The eigenvalue of factor 1 is 2.699 with 22.492 per cent of the variance. The variables are related to 'Interpersonal Skill.' Table 4 displays a very high significant loading for the six statements such as 'they have helped me developing relationship skills' (0.691), 'provided the opportunity to develop social skills' (0.684), 'it was a new experience interacting with economically backward children (0.630)', 'it provided me with a sense of purpose' (0.629), 'helped me in connecting with school-going children and to know the ground reality of primary education today in India' (0.619), and 'teaching children boosted my self-confidence' (0.579).

The eigenvalue of factor 2 is 1.798 with 14.982 per cent of the variance. The variables are related to "Adaptability." Factor 2 has significant high loading on 'I learnt to adapt in challenging situation (0.841)', 'I realized empathy could be learnt by getting into ground realities (0.667)', and 'I get a sense of fulfilment as a volunteer (0.560)', the eigenvalue of factor 3 is 1.439 with 11.991 per cent of the variance. The variables are related to teaching skills. The fourth-factor eigenvalue is 1.331, with an 11.093 per cent variation associated with the variable happiness. This factor significantly loads on 'brought happiness in my life (0.892)'. Happiness also brought a feel-good in the day-to-day routine, and respondents felt proud about the overall experience.

4.3. Factors Influencing the Academic Performance and Psychological Well-Being of the Students

> H_0: There is no significant impact of interpersonal skills, adaptability, teaching skills, and happiness on the academic performance of the Genesys volunteers.

The above hypothesis was tested by multiple regression analysis. It measures the degree of relationship between the academic performance of students (dependent variable) and the predicted value of interpersonal skills, adaptability, teaching skills, and happiness (independent variables). The respondents' academic performance was calculated by considering their average Cumulative Grade Points Average (CGPA), which start from 6.0, 7.0, 8.0, and 9.0 out of 10.0. Table 5 explains the R Square (Coefficient of Determination) value was .746. It means that 74.6 per cent of the variation in academic performance is defined by the variation in the independent variables such as interpersonal skills, adaptability, teaching skills, and happiness. The adjusted R-squared value was 0.736. It adjusts the statistic based on the number of independent variables in the model. That is the desired property of a goodness-of-fit statistic. Table 6 shows that all four independent variables statistically significantly predict students' academic performance, $F_{(4, 101)}$ = 74.014, p<.0005, which means that the regression model in Table 7 is a good fit for the data. The unstandardized coefficient values in Table 7 show how much academic performance varies with a predictor variable when all other predictor variables are constant.

Table 5. Model Summary – Factors Influencing Academic Performance

Model	R	R Square	Adjusted R Square	Std. Error of the Estimate
1	.863[a]	.746	.736	.5078

a. Predictors: (Constant), Happiness, Adaptability, Teaching Skills, Interpersonal skills

Table 6. ANOVA – Factors Influencing Academic Performance

Model		Sum of Squares	Df	Mean Square	F	Sig.
1	Regression	76.350	4	19.087	74.014	.000*
	Residual	26.047	101	.258		
	Total	102.396	105			

* Significant at a 5% level of significance.

Table 7. Relationship between a linear combination of the variables and academic performance (variables in Multiple Regression Analysis)

Model		Unstandardized Coefficients		Standardized Coefficients	t	Sig.
		B	Std. Error	Beta		
1	(Constant)	-1.103	.578		-1.908	.059
	Interpersonal skills	.866	.127	.403	6.839	.000*
	Adaptability	.395	.111	.197	3.558	.001*
	Teaching Skills	.503	.059	.469	8.597	.000*
	Happiness	.152	.067	.120	2.255	.026*

* Significant at a 5% level of significance.

Y (academic performance) = -1.103 + 0.866(X_1: interpersonal skills) + 0.395(X_2: adaptability) + 0.503 (X_3: teaching skills) + 0.152 (X_4: happiness)

The coefficient of X_1 in Table 7 Relationship between a linear combination of the variables and academic performance shows that one unit increase in the value of interpersonal skill would result in a .866 unit increase in academic performance, other variables being constant. This coefficient value is significant at the 5% level, and the t-statistic of interpersonal skills accounted for significant positive variation in academic performance. The coefficient of X2 tells that one unit increase in the value of adaptability would result in a .395 unit of growth in academic performance, with other variables being constant. This coefficient value is significant at the 5% level, and the t-statistic of adaptability also accounted for substantial positive variation in academic performance. The coefficient of X3 shows that one unit increase in the value of teaching skills would result in a .503 unit of positive change in academic performance, with other variables being constant. The coefficient of X4 indicates that a one-unit increase in happiness would result in a 152-unit increase in academic performance, with other variables being constant.

H_0: There is no significant impact on interpersonal skills, adaptability, teaching skills, and happiness developed in the Genesys forum on the psychological well-being of university volunteers.

Table 8. Model Summary – Factors Influencing Psychological Well-being

Model	R	R Square	Adjusted R Square	Std. Error of the Estimate
1	.880[a]	.774	.765	.377

Table 9. ANOVA – Factors Influencing Academic Performance

Model		Sum of Squares	df	Mean Square	F	Sig.
1	Regression	49.194	4	12.298	86.315	.000*
	Residual	14.391	101	.142		
	Total	63.585	105			

* Significant at a 1% level of significance.

Multiple regression was performed to predict students' psychological well-being from interpersonal skills, adaptability, teaching skills, and happiness. Tables 8, 9, and 10 show the results of this analysis. These variables significantly predicted psychological well-being, $F(4, 101) = 86.315$, $p<.0001$, $R^2=.774$. All four independent variables added statistically significant to the prediction, $p<.01$. The R Square (Coefficient of Determination) value in Table 8 was .774. It means that 77.4% of the variation in psychological well-being is explained by the variation in interpersonal skills, adaptability, teaching skills, and happiness. Table 9 shows the F value of 86.315, which confirms a good fit for the data, and the p-value was significant at the 1% level. The study results from Table 10 found that all four independent variables significantly influence the students' psychological well-being.

Table 10. Relationship between a linear combination of the variables and psychological well-being (variables in Multiple Regression Analysis) Co-efficient

Model		Unstandardized Coefficients		Standardized Coefficients	t	Sig.
		B	Std. Error	Beta		
1	(Constant)	-3.136	.430		-7.301	.000*
	Interpersonal skills	.835	.094	.493	8.870	.000*
	Adaptability	.409	.083	.258	4.958	.000*
	Teaching Skills	.260	.044	.308	5.982	.000*
	Happiness	.165	.050	.166	3.295	.001*

a. Dependent Variable: Psychological well-being. b. Predictors: Constant, Social enhancement skills, adaptability, teaching skills, happiness. * Significant at a 1% level of significance

Table 10 forms the following regression model for how far the independent variables (X_1, X_2, X_3, X_4) predict the dependent variable (Y).

Y (psychological well-being) = -3.136 + 0.835($X_{1:\ \text{interpersonal skills}}$) + 0.409($X_{2:\ \text{adaptability}}$) + 0.260 ($X_{3:\ \text{teaching skills}}$) + 0.165 ($X_{4:\ \text{happiness}}$)

The X_1 coefficient shows that one unit increase in the value of interpersonal skill would result in a .835 unit increase in the students' psychological well-being, other variables being constant. This coefficient value is significant at the 1% level, and the t-statistic of interpersonal skills accounted for significant positive variation in psychological well-being. Interpersonal skills impact a higher percentage of psychological well-being than the other three independent variables.

5. Discussion

Every child from an underprivileged background must have access to quality education and the required support from society as it develops the necessary skills to earn a living and contribute to the growth of society. Concentration on each child helps them to maximize their potential and attain financial independence. Teaching underprivileged children by students of higher education institutions as a part of their extension activities helps both of them to enhance their skills in various aspects. Most of the research studies (Banu, 2017; Hughes et al., 2005; Sundaresan, 2015) examined the professional teachers' perception of backward students' teaching. This chapter evaluates the university students' (trainer) perception of the social responsibility forum Genesys. The study on the effect of demographic variables on students' perception of each-one-teach-one moto of Genesys found that there is a significant difference in the mean level value between students' interpersonal skills and 'the number of years active in the forum', the combined effect of 'gender and number of hours teaching per month, the combined effect of 'gender and number of years active in forum' and the combined effect of 'the number of years active in the forum and number of hours teaching per month'. Teachers' effectiveness is measured by children's academic performance and social involvement (Afe, 2001). The study results from a linear combination of the variables show that the one unit increase in the value of interpersonal skills of university students would result in a .866 unit increase in their academic performance, other variables being constant. The study (Lander, 2016) found that learning from college students fosters a deep understanding of the material and a positive attitude toward the subject matter. It also said that the benefit is mutual in that simply preparing to teach others deepens one's own knowledge. The present study finds that Interpersonal skills impact a higher percentage of psychological well-being than the adaptability, teaching skills and happiness of the University Students (trainer).

Conclusion

The chapter explained university students' sensitization to voluntarily teach underprivileged children after regular academic study. The data was collected from all the university students who have been involved in this noble forum. Most of the respondents were female, and their percentage of academic performance was above average. Students from the first and second years were actively involved in the teaching services. Results found that the individualized tutorial/teaching program for underprivileged children facilitates respondents to improve their academic performances and psychological well-being. Also, the university students developed interpersonal skills, adaptability, teaching skills, and social skills that positively impacted their respective academic performance and psychological well-being. It was observed that the university students realized how privileged they were after interacting and spending time with underprivileged children. This forum and volunteering provided a sense of fulfilment that ultimately motivated them to work hard in their respective lives. The present study has many limitations. The respondents belong to one university. This chapter focused only on the outcome of respondents while performing teaching services to underprivileged school children. Hence, further research should compare the teaching input with the output of school children who participated in the each-one-teach-one method. Analysis and results encourage higher education students to perform social service activities that help them better prepare as citizens of this country.

References

Afe, J. O. (2001). *Reflection on becoming a teacher and the challenges of teacher education: Inaugural lecture series 64,* Benin City: University of Benin

Afridi, F. (2011). The impact of school meals on school participation: evidence from rural India. *Journal of Development Studies,* 47(11), 1636-1656.

Alexander, K. L., Entwisle, D. R., & Horsey, C. S. (1997). From first grade forward: Early foundations of high school dropout. *Sociology of Education,* 70, 87-107.

Banu, N. (2017). Remedial learning program for academically backward children. *International Journal of Educational Science and Research,* 7(2), 69-82.

Bellamy, R. (1915). Review of The Backward Child, A Study of the Psychology of Backwardness: A Practical Manual for Teachers and Students [Review of the book The backward child, a study of the Psychology of Backwardness: A practical manual for Teachers and Students, by B. S. Morgan]. *The Journal of Abnormal Psychology,* 10(1), 68-70. https://doi.org/10.1037/h0066516

Berte, C. M. (2016). Each One, Teach One. *The Journal for Nurse Practitioners,* 12(9), e397-e398, https://doi.org/10.1016/j.nurpra.2016.07.019.

Bhatla, S. (2017). Educational Status of Socially Disadvantaged Group in India, *Scholarly Research Journal for Interdisciplinary Studies,* 4(35), 6282-6293.

Busayo, I. O. (2011). The School Library as a Foundational Step to Children's Effective Reading Habits. *Library Philosophy and Practice* (e-journal), 665. https://digitalcommons.unl.edu/libphilprac/665

Campbell, D. E. (2008). Voice in the Classroom: How an Open Classroom Climate Fosters Political Engagement among Adolescents, *Political Behavior,* 30(4), 437–454. https://doi.org/10.1007/s11109-008-9063-z.

Chakraborty, S. & Chaudhuri, S. K. (2019). Inclusion of the economically backward students: Scope and tenet of Indian school libraries. Library *Philosophy and Practice* (e-journal). 2544. https://digitalcommons.unl.edu/libphilprac/2544

Cotugna, N., & Vickery, C. E. (1998). Reverse mentoring: A twist to teaching technology. American Dietetic Association. *Journal of the American Dietetic Association,* 98(10), 1166-8. https://lavasalibrary.remotexs.in/scholarly-journals/reverse-mentoring-twist-teaching-technology/docview/218389955/se-2?accountid=38885

Desai, S., & Kulkarni, V. (2008). Changing Educational Inequalities in India in the Context of Affirmative Action. *Demography,* 45(2), 245–270, https://doi.org/10.1353/dem.0.0001

Laubach Literacy Ontario (n.d.) *Each One Teach One.* http://www.laubach-on.ca/get involved/about us/eachone.

National University of Educational Planning and Administration (2015) *Education for All: Towards quality with equality.* https://unesdoc.unesco.org/ark:/48223/pf0000229873

Entwisle, D. R., & Alexander, K, L. (1988). Factors affecting achievement test scores and marks of black and white first graders, *Elementary School Journal,* 88, 449-471.

Evans, G. W. (2004). The environment of childhood poverty. *American Psychologist,* 59, 77-92.

Finn, J. D. (1989). Withdrawing from school, *Review of Educational Research,* 59, 117–142.

Frank H. K., Dijkstra, A. B. W., Maslowski, R., & Veen, I. V. D. (2020). The effect of teacher-student and student-student relationships on the societal involvement of students, *Research Papers in Education,* 35(3), 266-286, https://doi.org/10.1080/02671522.2019.1568529

Hughes, J. N., Gleason, K. A., & Zhang, D. (2005). Relationship influences teachers' perceptions of academic competence in academically at-risk minority and majority first grade students. *Journal of School Psychology,* 43(4), 303–320. https://doi.org/10.1016/j.jsp.2005.07.001

Isenberg, E., Max, J., Gleason, P., Potamites, L., Santillano, R., Hock, H., & Hansen, M. (2013 November), *Access to effective teaching for disadvantaged students.* National center for education evaluation and regional assistance, https://files.eric.ed.gov/fulltext/ED544345.pdf.

Janae K. H., & Philadelphia, M. D. (2020). See One, Do One, Teach One, Tell All. CHEST Journal, 158(5), 1820-1821, https://doi.org/10.1016/j.chest.2020.05.566

Justina, O., & Jacintha, U, E. (2015). Reviving the Reading Culture: School Library Programs in Promoting Voluntary Reading amongst Students: The Case of Imo State, Nigeria. *Library Philosophy and Practice (e-journal).* 1241. http://digitalcommons.unl.edu/libphilprac/1241

Kapoor, D. (2008). *Caste, Dalits and education in contemporary India.* In Education and Social Development. Leiden, Brill Sense. https://doi.org/10.1163/9789087904401_008

Keogh, O. (2018, December 14). Reverse mentoring: When younger workers lead the way: Reverse mentoring encourages different workplace generations to learn from each other. *Irish Times.* https://lavasalibrary.remotexs.in/newspapers/reverse-mentoring-when-younger-workers-lead-way/docview/2155495770/se-2?accountid=38885.

Lander, J. (2016, December 20). *Students as Teachers, Exploring the mutual benefits of peer-to-peer teaching — and strategies to encourage it.* https://www.gse.harvard.edu/uk/blog/students-teachers.

Levine, P. B. (2011). How Does Parental Unemployment Affect Children's Education Performance? In Duncan, G. J., & Murnane, R. (Eds.), Whither Opportunity? *Rising Inequality and the Uncertain Life Chances of Low-Income Children (*pp. 315–335). Russell Sage Foundation.

Mangal, S. K. (2017). Present *Education System and its Impact on the economically backward Students in Assam. International Journal of Research – Granthaalayah,* 5(6), 196-201 https://doi.org/10.5281/zenodo.81999

Medina-García, M., Doña-Toledo, L., & Higueras-Rodríguez, L. (2020). *Equal Opportunities in an Inclusive and Sustainable Education System: An Explanatory Model, Sustainability,* 12, 4626. https://doi.org/10.3390/su12114626

Mphale, L. M., & Mhlauli, M. B. (2014). An Investigation on Student's Academic Performance for Junior Secondary Schools in Botswana. *European Journal of Educational Research,* 3(3), 111-127.

Murphy, W. M. (2012). Reverse mentoring at work: Fostering cross-generational learning and developing millennial leaders. Human Resources Management, 51(4), 549–574.

NCERT (n.d). Policies, *Programs and Schemes for Educational Development of Children from Scheduled Castes,* Module 1, National Council of Educational Research and Training, Retrieved December 28, 2020, from https://ncert.nic.in/degsn/pdf/degsnmodule6.pdf

Powdthavee, N., & Vernoit, J., (2013). Parental Unemployment and Children's Happiness: A Longitudinal Study of Young People's Well-Being in Unemployed Households. *Labour Economics,* 24, 253–263. https://doi.org/10.1016/j.labeco.2013.09.008.

Rovai, A. P., & Jordan, H. (2004). Blended Learning and Sense of Community: A Comparative Analysis with Traditional and Fully Online Graduate Courses. *The International Review of Research in Open and Distributed Learning,* 5(2). https://doi.org/10.19173/irrodl.v5i2.192

Schulz, W., Ainley, J., Fraillon, J., Losito, B., Agrusti, G., & Friedman, T. (2018). *Becoming Citizens in a Changing World: IEA International Civic and Citizenship Education Study 2016.* International Report. Amsterdam: Netherlands IEA.

Shannon, O. (n.d). *Teaching Economically Disadvantaged Students,* Study.com. Retrieved December 5, 2021, from https://study.com/academy/lesson/teaching-economically-disadvantaged-students.html

Shivangi, Z. (n.d). How to educate a backward child? *Psychology.* Retrieved December 20, 2020, from https://www.psychologydiscussion.net/child-psychology/how-to-educate-a-backward-child-psychology/2621

Sleskova, M., Salonna, F., Geckova, A, M., Nagyova, I., Stewart, R. E., & Dijk, J. P. V. (2006). Does Parental Unemployment Affect Adolescents' Health? *Journal of Adolescent Health,* 38(5), 527–535. https://doi.org/10.1016/j.jadohealth.2005.03.021.

Stipek, D. (1997). Success in school for a head start in life. In Luthar, S., Burack, J., Cicchetti, D., & Weisz, J. (Eds.), *Developmental psychopathology: Perspectives on adjustment, risk, and disorder* (pp. 75–92). Cambridge.

Sundaresan, M. (2015). School Teacher's Perception Towards School Social Work. *International Journal of Social Science and Interdisciplinary Research,* 4(7), 10-14.

Tilak, J. B. (1997). The dilemma of reforms in financing higher education in India. *Higher education policy,* 10(1), 7-21.

Chapter 13

Student Engagement in Community Development: A Strategy for Whole-Person Development

Suparna Majumdar Kar[*]
Jince George[†]
and Jiby Jose E.[‡]
Christ University, Bengaluru, India

Abstract

Student engagement in community development has been closely linked to enhanced learning outcomes and whole-person development. The Centre for Social Action (CSA) at Christ University emerged as a student-led student-driven initiative to promote volunteerism and engagement in community development that enabled the student community to identify and work on development initiatives.

The objective of the chapter is to examine the factors that influence student engagement in community development initiatives and explore the factors that motivate them to volunteer. It also looks at their perception of the benefits for the two main stakeholders in the process, namely the students themselves and the community that they work with.

This chapter uses a qualitative framework, and the data is collected through in-depth interviews and focus group discussions with current and past volunteers with CSA. The participants in the study have been selected using purposive sampling techniques and represent students who

---

[*] Corresponding Author's Email: suparna.kar@christuniversity.in.
[†] Corresponding Author's Email: jince.george@res.christuniversity.in.
[‡] Corresponding Author's Email: jiby.jose@christuniversity.in.

In: Models for Social Responsibility Action by Higher Education Institutions
Editors: Joseph Chacko Chennattuserry, Elangovan N. et al.
ISBN: 979-8-89113-097-5
© 2024 Nova Science Publishers, Inc.

have worked on the major initiatives undertaken by CSA, namely the activity centre and the various social awareness and sensitization initiatives. The interviews and the focus group discussions have been conducted on virtual meeting platforms, and the data has been analyses thematically.

The research design lends itself to a rich exploration of student perception of their engagement in community development, their motivation, the benefits that they perceive of their engagement with the activities for both themselves and other stakeholders, and how it ties into the construct of whole-person development at the individual level and whole-person education at a broader level.

Keywords*:* student engagement, community development, volunteerism, whole-person development

1. Introduction

Higher education today is facing unprecedented challenges and debates with regard to its purpose and its relationship with the industry and other stakeholders. This is exacerbated by the volatility, uncertainty, complexity, and ambiguity (more commonly known by its acronym VUCA) of the contemporary context. VUCA has become an increasingly important framework for institutions of higher education to engage with as they work with the responsibility of ensuring that their students are well-equipped to deal with this rapidly changing world in terms of their knowledge, skills, and attitude. Encouraging the development of global citizens who can flourish in this scenario is an area that many institutions of higher education are working with. Whole Person Education emerges as a way to achieve these goals.

Christ University, India, has been working with the principles of Whole Person Education for the past 50 years. This focus is integrated into its Vision and Mission and is reinforced in the various activities that are taken up through the principles of holistic education. The university works towards whole-person development through its emphasis on four broad areas, namely academic excellence, personal skills, interpersonal skills, and societal skills, all of which have been integrated into the Graduate Attributes of the University.

Centre for Social Action (CSA) at the University emerged as a student-led student-driven initiative to promote volunteerism and engagement in community development in 1999, which paved the way for the student community to identify and work on development initiatives. It has, over time, transformed into an organization that works across five states in India.

This chapter focuses on how student engagement in community development can be seen as a strategy for whole-person development. It examines the factors that influence student engagement in community development initiatives and explores the aspects that motivate them to volunteer. It also looks at their perception of the benefits for the two main stakeholders in the process, namely the students themselves and the community that they work with. A qualitative framework is used, and the data is collected through focus group discussions and in-depth interviews with current and past volunteers with the CSA. This chapter explored the perceptions of how this volunteer activity in community engagement can contribute towards the development of crucial life skills and whole-person development for the students who are a part of this Center at the University.

2. Review of Literature

2.1. Whole Person Development

Whole person development is a progressive process through which the intellectual, physical, professional, psychological, social, and spiritual capacities of an individual can be holistically enhanced. According to the Cambridge English Dictionary, whole-person development refers to the development of different values and skills, such as civic responsibility, community care, cultural engagement, emotional health, intellectual capacity, and leadership quality. A whole-person approach to education nurtures an integrated development of the mind, heart, and ego of the learner. It fosters a holistic and equal growth of what the students understand, what they care about, and their daily actions and behaviours (Mustakova-Possardt, 1998).

Whole-person education refers to the initiatives taken up by educational institutions to scaffold whole-person development among their students. This marks a shift away from a focus only on academic development to encompass other domains such as emotional intelligence, physical, spiritual, social, psychological, and professional aspects, along with academic development. Whole person development focuses on these six components of life, which lead to holistic development and lifelong gains. This shifts the focus from an academically accomplished learner to one who has experienced holistic development in addition to their academic development within an institute of higher education that contributes towards the inculcation of necessary life skills.

Experiential learning closely aligns with whole-person education. Bandy (2011) writes that students achieve different skills through the experiential learning process. It has a greater impact on their academic performances and a positive impact on academic outcomes such as demonstrated complexity of understanding, problem analysis, problem-solving, critical thinking, and cognitive development, improved ability to understand complexity and ambiguity, having a greater sense of personal efficacy, awareness of personal identity, spiritual growth, and moral development which helps in greater interpersonal development, particularly the ability to work well with others, and building leadership and communication skills. It engenders improved social responsibility and citizenship skills.

Experiential learning also leads to the acquisition of life skills, which enables one to acquire holistic growth. Life skills refer to a large group of psycho-social and interpersonal skills that can help people to make informed decisions, communicate effectively, and develop coping and self-management skills that, in turn, help to lead a healthy and productive life. Learning of life skills occurs within and beyond a boundary wall of the classroom.

The United Nations Children's Fund emphasizes the concept of Life Skills and Citizenship Education (Hoskins & Liu, 2019, p. 5), which espouses the need to reimagine education in order to ensure that children and the youth have better life outcomes. It does so by focusing on four areas by working with a multidimensional approach to education encompassing cognitive, individual, social, and economic development. This vision also encourages adopting a humanistic and rights-based approach to learning, emphasizing nurturing lifelong learning and incorporating multiple ways to learn in formal and informal settings by engendering individual empowerment that thrives within an environment of social interconnectedness. These four dimensions of life skills range across the cognitive (learning to know through creativity, critical thinking, and problem-solving), instrumental (learning to do through cooperation, negotiation, and decision making), individual (learning to be through self-management, resilience, and communication), and the social dimensions (learning to live together through respect for diversity, empathy, and participation). The more significant focus is on helping the learner to evolve into an empowered, active citizen. These ideas tie in with the emphasis on community engagement in an institution of higher education, such as that expressed by the CSA at Christ University.

2.2. Student Engagement in Community Development

Community development: According to the United Nations, community development is a process where community members come together to take collective action and generate solutions to common problems.' It involves the active participation of civic leaders, activists, involved citizens, and professionals to build stronger and more resilient communities. It is observed that better and more sustainable social development outcomes are possible when the citizens are actively involved in the process of community development. Citizen participation is essential to a socially sustainable and healthy democratic society. Both the beneficiaries and the change agents gain different skills by engaging in the process of community development. Bender (2004) remarks that reciprocity is the central feature of service providing.

Student Volunteerism and Whole Person Development: Wilson (2000, pg. 215) has defined volunteerism as "any activity in which time is given freely to benefit another person, group, or organisation." He also draws attention to how the term is used to refer to a 'vast array of quite disparate activities' and raises the need for work on the consequences of volunteers, especially on its consequences for the subjective well-being of younger age groups. Hitlin (2003) says that the initiative in volunteering and social development activities helps in the development of the ability to read and respond to others' needs. College students who volunteer in different activities are found to develop more empathetic, benevolent, and universal values. Volunteering helps to remove social exclusion, and it benefits both volunteers and the communities involved. Students who get involved in community services develop skills that can be used in their careers later and help to make new contacts in the community through community services (Clary et al., 1998). Volunteering helps to challenge stereotypes and create acceptance of diversity. The interaction of the volunteers with different community members helps them to build more contacts which naturally creates inclusive and integrated communities.

Social interaction skills and technical skills help the volunteers to become more employable in the future. Learning from the community has been widely acknowledged to be an effective method for developing life skills. Numerous studies have shown that volunteers may derive physical, mental, and emotional health benefits from volunteering. Davis (2003) says that many volunteers find that volunteering helps them to feel as though they have a purpose in life, and they experience increased feelings of meaning, structure, and direction in their life. These improvements in physical, mental, and emotional well-being derived from volunteering may create a further positive impact on overall determinants of health for the individual.

Volunteerism is considered reciprocal in nature in which both the volunteer and the recipient exchange advantages. Volunteerism can help people to have healthy and meaningful connections to others in their community and foster a stronger sense of belongingness. Through volunteerism, people gain mastery as they develop skills, creativity, and talents that help them to participate in their communities and society more generally. Volunteerism leads to greater confidence and healthy self-esteem and encourages citizens to be leaders in their own communities. It has been established and is widely acknowledged that students who engage as volunteers during their education have high skills in problem-solving, collaboration, time management, communication, and leadership qualities compared to their peers.

It is also held that volunteerism gives people the opportunity to develop social skills as they are involved in community activities. Volunteering boosts one's self-confidence, self-esteem, and life satisfaction. Volunteering gives an opportunity to practice important skills used in the workplace, such as teamwork, communication, problem-solving, etc. Volunteers are empowered by serving the people around them and feeling the value of their contribution to society (Simpson, 2011).

These aspects of volunteerism tie in closely to the idea of whole-person education and holistic development in terms of how they allow the volunteer to develop across the cognitive, instrumental, individual, and social dimensions, which are considered to be integral life skills.

Community engagement: Service-learning and community engagement refer to pedagogy in higher education that combines 'learning goals and community service in ways that can enhance both student growth and the common good' (Bandy, 2021). It represents a form of experiential learning that encourages action and reflection from the students and, through this process, enhances the development of life skills and their whole person development. It enables the students to apply what they learn in their classrooms in real-life scenarios and, through this process, has a positive impact on the student's learning experience as well as on the community within which the student works.

The process of community engagement strengthens community relations. Working together in decision-making can change community dynamics and transform relationships between groups in a community. Fletcher (2006) identifies that meaningful student involvement can foster healthy and successful community engagement. It can be used by institutes of higher education to promote social engagement, responsibility, and democratic awareness among students. Boyer (1990) describes community engagement in an academic context. He says that it is the means by which universities are reshaped as they enter into collaborative arrangements with community partners to address pressing social, political, economic, and moral issues. It is through this process that student learning is reshaped and enhanced.

A significant benefit of community service learning is that it becomes beneficial equally to both the provider and the recipient of the service, and the process envisages the learning that takes place (Franco, 2000, pg. 12). During the community engagement process, different communities provide individuals with opportunities to interact with other community members. This process of interaction helps in developing the ability to critically think and be open-minded. A greater level of involvement with the community helps in the learning and in the growth process of the students. Students get a chance to experience local peoples' knowledge, civic involvement, decision-making, power, governance, and politics. The participation of students in community engagement activities has the potential to enhance community agency within the locality by revealing new perspectives and alternative approaches to developing and utilizing local resources (Shaw et al., 2014). Other studies have demonstrated how community engagement equips students to deal with their workspaces and develop a skill set that will be required there.

A study by Myer and Anderson concludes that through community engagement, students become more career-oriented and desire to grow and develop personally and socially. It also affects the students' attitudes towards different communities. Community Service-Learning, as part of curriculum-based community engagement, deliberately involves the students in activities in a community environment so that they will learn from the experiences. They also get an opportunity to gain first-hand information about community needs. Community Service-Learning enables students and teachers to grow personally and professionally (Franco, 2000; Myers & Bellner, 2000).

Franco (2000) points out that the process of Service-Learning helps to value civic democracy and civil diversity and to have the human touch learned and nurtured through service. This is reinforced by the study by Bhagwan (2017), who states that community engagement enables the transformation of students into social justice activists and agents of social transformation. It is observed that the majority of active participants in community development activities have a positive effect on their physical and psychological health, and a change is observed in self-confidence, self-esteem, sense of personal empowerment, and social relationships. Some studies have also shown that individuals face some adverse effects like exhaustion and stress (Attree et al., 2011).

Matarasso (1997) suggests that active engagement in community development activities has psycho-social benefits for participants. It boosts their self-confidence and self-esteem. In addition, community engagement may have a positive impact on individuals' perceptions of personal empowerment also. Some evidence suggests that active community engagement may benefit individuals' physical health, psychological health, and psycho-social well-being (Truman & Raine 2001). It is also believed that students who participate in community engagement develop a realistic self-concept that is to be implemented, stabilized, and consolidated in early adulthood.

For students, who engage in the process of community development as part of their curriculum, experiential learning equips students in critical thinking, problem-solving, and decision-making in contexts that are personally relevant to them. Integration of community services with learning experiences teaches civic responsibility and strengthens communities. Here, learning proceeds through a cycle of action and reflection as students seek to observe real issues and find deeper understanding and skills for themselves from the communities.

Students who are involved in experiential learning with different communities experience significant changes. These changes include exposure to and adoption of new or different attitudes, beliefs, and values (Lerner et al., 2005). Through the process of social interaction, human association is enhanced to build community capacity. Purposeful interaction and communication between people lead to the development of weak and strong ties, which allow information to be shared, resources to be identified, and action to be organized within the community (Kaufman, 1959).

Alinsky (1962) says that community engagement is grounded in the principles of community organisation, like fairness, justice, empowerment, participation, and self-determination. Community engagement and empowerment take place at three levels: the individual, the organisation or group, and the community. Empowerment at one level can influence empowerment at other levels. This process of empowerment is multidimensional in nature and takes place in social, psychological, economic, political, and other dimensions.

The literature review reveals that engaging with the community, either through volunteer work or service-learning initiatives, tends to positively impact student learning and the development of their life skills. It contributes to whole-person development by enhancing the holistic development of the student's intellectual, physical, professional, psychological, social, and spiritual capacities.

Given these findings, the researchers would like to propose a model to incorporate community engagement into the curriculum in institutions of higher education, which would contribute towards the development of the whole person with reference to the students. Student engagement in community development initiatives through voluntary initiatives would enable the students to grow holistically in conjunction with their academic development.

3. Methodology

This chapter examines how student volunteerism and community engagement in community development operate as a strategy for whole-person development. The study is based at Christ University, Bengaluru, India., India, and it examines volunteers with the CSA at the University.

A qualitative multimethod research framework was used with a sequential multimethod research design that uses two different qualitative methods. Multimethod studies, unlike mixed-method studies, use either only multiple qualitative methods or multiple quantitative methods (Schoonenboom & Johnson, 2017). The researchers selected this method as the use of multiple qualitative research methods would strengthen the study and add to the validity of the findings. The researchers chose qualitative methods that would allow them to explore the reasons underlying student volunteerism, their engagement in community development, and whether and how this contributes towards their whole person development. These methods also allowed the researchers to study the perceptions of the volunteers about the impact that their volunteerism has had on the area of their work and, through that, examine what motivates them.

4. Results

The researchers used focus group discussions followed by in-depth interviews to collect their data. Two focus group discussions were conducted on virtual platforms with 20 and 23 participants each. The participants were volunteers with CSA who gave their consent to be part of this study. These students were enrolled in Undergraduate and Postgraduate programmes in the different branches of Engineering, Psychology, Commerce and Management, and they had worked extensively with CSA as volunteers. They represented a diverse group in terms of their disciplines, regional backgrounds, and areas of interest and engagement with CSA. They have also worked with different wings in CSA, as a result of which they brought in diversity in terms of their experiences.

The researchers had identified themes to guide the focus group discussions, and these were followed in both rounds of the discussions. They focussed on the role taken up within CSA, their reasons for volunteering, their engagement with CSA, and details on their perceptions about their contributions and the impact of the same on the community that they were working with.

The findings from the focus group discussions were used to guide the framing of the interview schedule for the in-depth interviews which were conducted subsequently. Five current and ex-students were interviewed as part of the research process. These volunteers were randomly selected from a larger list of volunteers who had given their consent to be part of the research process. Of the five, one is part of the alumni, and the remaining four are current volunteers with the Centre.

The interviews and the focus group discussions have been conducted on virtual meeting platforms, as physical meetings were difficult during the research period as a result of the Pandemic related changes in 2020-2021. The discussions that took place were recorded and transcribed for analysis. The data has been analyzed thematically. The focus group discussions and interviews were complementary as the interviews allowed the researchers to explore further and elaborate upon the themes that emerged through the focus group discussions in the interviews. Analysis of the data from the first was integrated during the interview stage and again at the stage of analysis and interpretation.

Some of the themes that emerged during the focus group discussions were the extrinsic and intrinsic motivation behind volunteering with CSA, personal development, social impact, the impact of community engagement with the community as well as on the student, attitudinal shifts, academic engagement, and personal and professional development. These themes were explored further through the interviews with the respondents. These interviews were also transcribed and analyzed. The following section provides a discussion of the findings of this research.

5. Discussion

As elaborated upon earlier, the data for this study was collected through two focus group discussions followed by in-depth interviews with current and past volunteers with CSA. The participants in the study represent students who have worked on the major initiatives undertaken by the CSA, namely the activity centre and the various social awareness and sensitisation initiatives. The two focus group discussions were conducted with students who represent the wide diversity of programmes as well as identities within the university. The participants volunteered with the various wings of the CSA and dedicated between three and six hours per week to the Center. The in-depth interviews were conducted similarly with volunteers who are current students and alumni who have already graduated from the University. They have also worked with different units of CSA. The section on the discussion of the findings has been organised along the lines of community engagement, personal development, interpersonal development, and professional development.

5.1. Community Engagement

The desire to learn more about the community that they belong to, as well as to help those who were less privileged, was a driving factor that encouraged the participants to volunteer with CSA. Participants mentioned how important it was for them to be able to make a change, raise awareness about various issues and make a difference and 'empower society' and make a difference. On a personal note, they spoke of how important it was for them to help those who were 'less fortunate' than them. The desire to push their boundaries and to 'come out of their comfort zone' also encouraged the volunteers to participate. Another participant spoke about the need to 'give back' as one of the factors that drove her to become a part of CSA.

Participants spoke of how interactions with other volunteers and the orientations organized by CSA encouraged them to explore more about the initiatives taken up by the Center and ultimately volunteer there. The activities discussed by previous members were an inspiration to do more for society and provided opportunities to improve oneself. They spoke of both intrinsic and extrinsic motivators that encouraged them to participate. The rewards associated with working on areas that inspired them and their ability to see the impact of their contributions acted like powerful motivators. One of the participants spoke of how she 'felt energized' after working with CSA. Others spoke of a huge sense of satisfaction with her work.

5.2. Whole Person Development: Personal

Participants revealed positive perceptions about their contribution through CSA and expressed how they believe that it had contributed towards their holistic growth. In terms of personal growth, they reinforced how their volunteer work had taught them to be more aware and socially sensitive, which in turn has contributed to their sense of self. The implications of these findings have been discussed in numerous studies, such as those conducted by Matarasso (1997) and Truman and Raine (2001). They have discussed the benefits of community engagement for participants.

They have learnt to manage initiatives and execute projects that they have designed. In terms of management skills, one participant mentions the significance of 'coming up with ideas, generating a backup plan, coordinating with people, organizing events.' They have learnt to work together in groups, deal with diverse opinions, learn to exercise patience, and tolerance, learn from their mistakes, and how to manage their time and honour commitments that they have made. 'Being accountable' was reinforced as very important by a participant.

In terms of social sensitivity, participants reinforced how their volunteer work has proven to be an invaluable experience. A participant stated, 'Being more comfortable to share socially relevant topics (like awareness on menstruation) among my family members was a huge step for me.' Others mentioned how this has resulted in lifestyle changes in terms of choices that they now make. Being less wasteful and more considerate of others and their needs was considered to be very important.

In an interview, an alumnus mentioned how volunteering with CSA has shaped her future and broadened her horizons and ultimately changed the career path that she has taken now. She and other participants reinforced how their volunteer work with CSA has helped to shape their personalities and how they interact with others and emerge as mature, responsible adults. They have established valuable social networks and made 'friends for life.' They have also learnt how to balance different aspects of their life, their academic commitments and their work with CSA, for instance.

5.3. Whole Person Development: Interpersonal

One of the participants spoke of how they have 'grown together.' Another says, 'I feel that it has contributed to my ability to make decisions... I have learnt to be non-judgemental. This has contributed to my ability to make informed decisions... I have taken my work and learning at CSA to my workspace.' Another participant spoke of how this has contributed to 'personal transformation.'

Volunteering with CSA has also contributed towards spiritual development in terms of a deep sense of gratitude and appreciation. Participants mention how they have learnt to value things and the importance of giving back to the communities that they belong to. A participant noted how this experience has helped them with 'Discerning the divinity in all human beings and serving them as it is done to God.' Another state is that it has enabled them to 'grow as an individual on all spiritual, emotional, mental and intellectual levels.'

Participants were also asked to share their perceptions of the impact that their volunteerism has had on the communities that they have worked with. One of the participants of the focus group discussions states, 'The societal norms are rooted in traditional values. It is difficult to force people to change the perceptions they have learnt through childhood. But what the volunteers can do is educate children who are to be the future of the country. This can greatly impact the future of the country.'

While speaking about their work with children through the activity Centre and the annual Thanksgiving event, Gracias, another participant, states, 'The stakeholders, especially the children, got an exposure to learn skills that go beyond the general skills taught in schools and emphasize on creative expression.' Another participant spoke of her work with the community in Kolar. She had participated in a road-building exercise and spoke of how 'the results of the work taken up and engagement with the community are immediately apparent. Local leaders spoke about community development during the feedback sessions with the community. I feel that this participation has been very rewarding. Some of these activities have had a long-term impact. The road in Kolar has had a long-lasting impact.'

As seen in the work done by scholars like Boyer (1990), Fletcher (2006), and Franco (2000), student engagement in community development is beneficial for both the students as well as the community. The students learn by doing and growing holistically which contributes towards their development into effective global citizens.

5.4. Whole Person Development: Professional

Personal and interpersonal development has shaped professional growth for the students. They have inculcated numerous skills and learnt to work in diverse groups with multiple needs and emerge as leaders who have learned to be both members of large teams and, at times, lead them. Some of the skills that participants mentioned have been technical skills, content writing, managing large groups, mentoring other volunteers, and 'inspiring others to work for the cause.' One of the participants mentioned that she has learnt to be a 'cultural ambassador' through exposure to interns from various countries and educational backgrounds, student exchange programmes, and volunteers from across the world. One of the areas of professional growth discussed was learning to work with a large organisation and its structure. The development of interpersonal skills and improved communication were treated as invaluable.

This is reinforced in the study conducted by Hironimus-Wendt & Lovell-Troy (1999), where they focus on how this kind of experiential learning can prepare students for the challenges that they will face in the workplace. Their work throws light on how learning from experience gives students the opportunity to put theory into practice and also gain insight into the expected tasks and community issues they may face in the workplace. The findings from this study reinforce this as the participants reveal how their volunteerism and engagement with CSA have helped them to grow.

5.5. Community Engagement and Whole Person Development: A Model

The researchers would like to propose the adoption of the following initiatives in institutions of higher education. It is essential to incorporate community engagement into the curriculum in institutions of higher education. This is necessary not just for the students in terms of how this would contribute towards the development of the whole person but also for the larger community, which is the ecosystem within which a University and other such institutions of higher education thrive. This engagement with the wider community is essential for institutions of higher education, and it offers them an opportunity to connect and contribute in a positive fashion.

Student engagement in community development initiatives through voluntary initiatives would enable the students to grow holistically in terms of their personal and professional growth as well as the development of interpersonal skills. It is important that this be incorporated into the curriculum. Some institutions have taken up this agenda through initiatives such as Service Learning.

A model that has worked for Christ University is the establishment of an independent Center, namely CSA, that has to a large extent, been shaped by the students who are a part of it. This Center, as we have discussed, has worked on a number of community development initiatives. Even as CSA engages with community development, it aligns extremely well with the larger focus of the University on whole-person development. In addition to the focus on academic and physical development that is built into the curriculum of the various programmes offered by the University, engagement with CSA has helped the students to focus on civic responsibility as well as develop skills that have contributed towards personal growth, enhanced interpersonal engagement, and professional development.

Their volunteer work has defined the way in which they have engaged with the wider community and the other initiatives that they have taken up. These initiatives, in turn, have helped them to grow, as the research reveals. Their engagement with the larger community has resulted in lifelong learning for them and the development of skills that have proven to be invaluable. This is a model for volunteer-driven community engagement that contributes towards Whole Person Development for the volunteers that can be replicated in other institutions of higher learning.

Conclusion

This chapter establishes the need for further exploration into how community engagement through organisations like CSA, which operate within institutions of higher education, can be integrated into the curriculum for students of higher education. The linkage between student engagement in community development and their whole-person development in terms of academic excellence, personal skills, interpersonal skills, and societal skills is an area that needs to be further studied extensively. This chapter has established that there is a relationship between the two and that students who have engaged in community development at the University through CSA and its initiatives strongly feel that their contributions have had an impact on the community as well as their own personal growth and contributed towards their whole person development.

Whole-person education is an essential need for institutions to prepare students to thrive in an increasingly uncertain world. It aligns well with the inculcation of essential life skills. Christ University has adopted this approach through its emphasis on the development of personal, interpersonal, and social skills, in addition to academic excellence. Engagement in community development is either done through service-learning initiatives which are built into the curriculum, or through volunteerism with organisations such as CSA, which facilitates whole-person development through engagement with the cognitive, instrumental, individual, and social dimensions of growth.

This chapter reveals that volunteering for community engagement programmes such as the initiatives taken up in urban slums, activity centers for children, child sponsorship and continuing education programmes, and community development projects helps the student volunteers to evolve holistically. Participants of the study revealed how their engagement with CSA has contributed to their personal development in terms of their ability to take responsibility, manage their time, honour commitments, work effectively, and balance all their different aspects of life. They reflected on how their ability to interact with others, work with different people from diverse backgrounds, take up leadership roles, and work with teams have been enhanced. Participants also shared how they have enhanced their social sensitivity and feel motivated to continue working with the wider community. Some revealed how rewarding it is to see the impact of their community engagement.

The chapter reinforces how volunteerism contributes to personal growth and the development of interpersonal and societal skills. Students firmly believed that their engagement in community development through CSA has contributed towards the growth in their intellectual, physical, professional, psychological, social, and spiritual capacities. They reinforced how this engagement has resulted in lifelong changes in their lives, the nature of which has been described by many scholars as a shift that encourages active citizenship and engagement with society and allows them to thrive in a VUCA world.

References

Alinsky, S. D. (1962). Citizen participation and community organisation in planning and urban renewal. *Industrial Areas Foundation.*

Attree, P., French, B., Milton, B., Povall, S., Whitehead, M., & Popay, J. (2011). The experience of community engagement for individuals: a rapid review of evidence. *Health & social care in the community,* 19(3), 250-260.

Bandy, J. (2021, July 15). What is Service Learning or Community Engagement ? Retrieved from *Vanderbilt University Center for Teaching:* https://cft.vanderbilt.edu/guides-sub-pages/teaching-through-community-engagemen/.

Bender, C. J. G. (2004). Community service and service-learning at the University of Pretoria: An institutional review. [*Unpublished institutional report*]. Pretoria, South Africa: University of Pretoria.

Bhagwan, R. (2017). Towards a conceptual understanding of community engagement in higher education in South Africa. *Perspectives in Education,* 35(1), 171–185.

Boyer, E. L. 1990. Scholarship reconsidered: Priorities of the professoriate. Princeton, N. J: *Carnegie Foundation for the Advancement of Teaching.* [Online] Available: http://www.csusm.edu/community/facultyengagement/scholarshipreconsidered.pdf.

Clary, E. G., Snyder, M., Ridge, R. D., Copeland, J., Stukas, A. A., Haugen, J., & Miene, P. (1998). Understanding and assessing the motivations of volunteers: A functional approach. *Journal of Personality and Social Psychology,* 74(6), 1516-1530.

Davis, M. H., Hall, J. A., & Meyer, M. (2003). The first year: Influences on the satisfaction, involvement, and persistence of new community volunteers. *Personality and Social Psychology Bulletin,* 29(2), 248-260.

Fletcher, A. (2006). Sound Out: Serving the school as community. *ServiceLine Journal,* 16 (1). 3. Washington State Office of Superintendent of Public Instruction.

Franco, R. (2000). The community college conscience : Service-learning and training tomorrow's teachers. *Service Learning, General.* 117.

Hironimus-Wendt, R. J., & Lovell-Troy, L. (1999). Grounding service learning in social theory. *Teaching Sociology,* 27 (4), 360-372.

Hitlin, S. (2003). Values as the core of personal identity: Drawing links between two theories of self. *Social Psychology Quarterly,* 66(2), 118-137.

Hoskins, B., & Liu, L. (2019). Measuring life skills: In the context of life skills and citizenship education in the Middle East and North Africa. *UNICEF.* https://www.unicef.org/mena/media/7011/file/Measuring%20life%20skills_web.pdf.pdf.

Kaufman, H. F. 1959. Toward an interactional conception of community. *Social Forces.* 38(1) :8–17.

Lerner, R. M., Lerner, J. V., Almerigi, J. B., Theokas, C., Phelps, E., Gestsdottir, S., Naudeau, S., Jelicic, H., Alberts, A., Ma, L., Smith, L. M., Bobek, D. L., Richman-Raphael, D., Simpson, I., Christiansen, E. D., & von Eye, A. (2005). Positive Youth Development, Participation in Community Youth Development Programs, and Community Contributions of Fifth-Grade Adolescents : Findings From the First Wave Of the 4-H Study of Positive Youth Development. *The Journal of Early Adolescence,* 25(1), 17–71. https://doi.org/10.1177/0272431604272461.

Matarasso, F. (1997). *Use or ornament?: The social impact of participation in the Arts.* Comedia.

Mustakova-Possardt, E. (1998). Critical consciousness: An alternative pathway for positive personal and social development. *Journal of Adult Development,* 5(1), 13-30.

Myers, C., & Bellner, M. (Eds.). *Embedding Service-learning Into Teacher Education (ESTE) : Issue Briefs.* Indiana State Department of Education, 2000.

Schoonenboom, J., & Johnson, R. B. (2017). How to Construct a Mixed Methods Research Design. *Kolner Zeitschrift fur Soziologie und Sozialpsychologie,* 69(2), 107-131. https://doi.org/10.1007/s11577-017-0454-1.

Shaw, A., Brady, B., McGrath, B., Brennan, M. A., & Dolan, P. (2014). Understanding youth civic engagement : debates, discourses, and lessons from practice. *Community Development,* 45(4), 300-316.

Simpson, J. A., & Beckes, L. (2010). Evolutionary perspectives on prosocial behavior. In M. Mikulincer & P. R. Shaver (Eds*.), Prosocial motives, emotions, and behavior: The better angels of our nature* (pp. 35-53). American Psychological Association.

Truman, C., & Raine, P. (2001). Involving users in evaluation: the social relations of user participation in health research. *Critical Public Health,* 11(3), 215-229.

Wilson, J. (2000). Volunteering. *Annual review of sociology,* 26(1), 215-240.

Chapter 14

Volunteering-Based Student Engagement: A Model for Student Well-Being in Higher Education Institutions

Joseph Chacko Chennattuserry[1],*
Shinto Thomas[2]
and Phinu Mary Jose[2]
[1]Vice Chancellor, Christ University, Bengaluru, India
[2]Assistant Professor, Christ University, Bengaluru, India

Abstract

Student well-being issues are rising alarmingly, and addressing these well-being concerns takes the predominant focus of higher education institutions, together with competency building. Understanding the importance of student engagement in student well-being, Christ University, Bengaluru, India, adopted a student engagement model based on volunteering. The current paper tries to understand the dynamics between volunteering and student well-being. It explores the relationship between volunteering and personal responsibility, social responsibility, meaning in life, and a helping attitude. It also tries to check whether the relationship between a helping attitude and student well-being is mediated by personal responsibility and social responsibility. Further, it explores whether volunteers and non-volunteers differ in their social responsibility, personal responsibility, and student well-being. A group of 350 students, of which 175 volunteers and 175 non-volunteers, were approached to participate in the study. Post data cleaning procedure, 327

---

* Corresponding Author's Email: josecc@christuniversity.in.

In: Models for Social Responsibility Action by Higher Education Institutions
Editors: Joseph Chacko Chennattuserry, Elangovan N. et al.
ISBN: 979-8-89113-097-5
© 2024 Nova Science Publishers, Inc.

data points qualified for analysis, and it was found that there exists a relationship between volunteering and personal responsibility, social responsibility and helping attitude, and personal responsibility and social responsibility mediated the relationship between helping attitude and student well-being. Results also revealed that volunteers and non-volunteers differed in their helping attitude, personal responsibility, and student well-being. These findings point towards the fact that the student engagement model based on volunteering has a positive impact on student well-being. A detailed discussion of the application of these findings is provided in the full paper.

Keywords: student well-being, student engagement, volunteering, higher education institution, social responsibility, personal responsibility, helping attitude

1. Introduction

The ancient Indian system of education, the *Gurukul* system, focused on the overall development of the student. It focused on imparting knowledge, skills, ethics and values like humility, truthfulness, discipline, self-reliance and respecting all creations. And the place of learning was associated with temples and religious places. Thus, it brought the notion of sacredness to the learning process (Ghonge et al., 2020). The colonization by different foreign powers brought different traditions of learning to India. The western system of education, which emphasized scientific temper and academic concepts of education, side-lined the Indian traditional system. A few decades after independence, it is noted that the focus of the higher education institution shifted from the academic concept of education to creating manpower for national development (Ross, 1973). Here competency takes the pivotal role rather than the overall development of the student.

Subjective well-being is generally understood as one's own overall satisfaction with life and self-perception of positive inner events that are defined as personally or socially desirable patterns of thinking (cognition) and feeling (emotion) (Zhang & Renshaw, 2020). The subjective well-being of college students is a growing concern for many higher education institutions (Beiter et al. 2015; Twenge et al. 2018). Poor subjective well-being leads to severe mental health and behavioural issues such as depression, anxiety, self-harm behaviours, risk behaviours, and college dropout (Keyes et al., 2010, 2012; Renshaw, 2018; Deb et al., 2016). Recently, Student anxiety in higher education institutions in the UK has jumped from 17% to 31%. About 70% of the university authorities admit that their pressing issue is addressing students' mental health needs. It is also noted that 31% of the students want more mental health and well-being support from the educational institution (Marsh, Tue, May 23, 2017). Covid-19 and related disruptions have led to an increase in mental health concerns. Student dropouts due to mental health issues have trebled in recent years. All these pinpoints the crisis in student well-being. The scenario in India is not different. Mental health concerns are alarming. There has been an increase in depression and emotional problems among students (Chaudhary et al., 2021). The psychological well-being of the students significantly dropped (Satpathy & Ali, 2020; Philip et al., 2021). Many of them were experiencing loneliness and isolation (Anilkumar, June 20, 2021). Addressing these well-being crises without compromising the competency required for nation-building became a need of the hour for Higher Education Institutions.

Christ University, with its focus on learning and overall student development, tried to bring a balance between the two notions; the academic concept of education and the competency model of education with due emphasis on the socio-emotional development and well-being of the student. Various student engagement models in higher education settings emphasize the overall development of the students (Payne, 2019; Abdelsamea & Bart, 2016). Students' emotional and cognitive engagement in the learning space also significantly contribute to their well-being and achievements in student life (Pietarinen et al., 2014). Christ University considers student engagement as a key component of student well-being, which is aptly reflected in the graduate attributes (Christ University, n.d.). The University creates an environment where learners can actively engage in the learning process through various curricular, co-curricular and extracurricular activities. The University considers volunteering as a tool for better student engagement on campus and has different initiatives through the Centre for Social Action (CSA) where students voluntarily take part.

1.1. CSA Volunteering: Process, Procedure and Opportunities

The Centre for Social Action is a student-volunteering body of the University and has been the face of social responsibility for the academic fraternity as well. The broader aim of CSA is to build a humane and just society where student communities are sensitized on various issues affecting the poor and the marginalized sections of our society. Thereby contributing to nation-building through (https://christuniversity.in/center/C/Centre-for-Social-Action) strengthening the student community with a view to enabling positive changes in society. This is one of the driving forces for the establishment of CSA in 1999 and remains the motivating factor for undertaking various developmental projects and social sensitization programs. CSA intends to create a community of empathetic students who can work proactively for society.

It tries to accomplish its vision of "Every student is aware, sensitive, empathetic and contributes to sustainable changes in the society" by encouraging volunteering among students to make them socially responsible citizens.

1.2. Recruitment Process

The recruitment process of Volunteers begins with announcements on campus and on social media platforms. Applications are invited from exuberant and committed students who are passionate about dedicating their efforts towards the growth of society, thereby improving themselves too. Registrations are facilitated in the first few weeks of joining the institution. Like all other Clubs and Associations at Christ University, Senior Volunteers make presentations to the new batch of students and set up Registration Desks across the campus. Interested students enroll as Volunteers. Following their registrations, formal Inauguration and Orientation Sessions are arranged. Leaders are introduced, and the scope of activities is detailed in order for the new volunteers to choose their area of service. Typically, Volunteers have options to serve through Activity Centre, Media and Communications, Drishti and Prayatna. These four groups have evolved over the years through Volunteer deliberations and stakeholder support (https://christuniversity.in/view-pdf/cu-students-handbook-2021).

1.3. Volunteering Opportunities

At CSA, the Volunteers are invited to choose their commitment to serve in any of the following areas.

Child Sponsorship Program

Also called 'Educate a Child Sponsorship Program', this is the flagship program of CSA, where children belonging to poor and marginalized families from 3 slums in Bengaluru, India are sponsored every year exclusively by the students at the University. The sponsorship is for their education and life skills development. Volunteers of CSA assist them in their studies throughout the year. Nutrition, health care and life skills development opportunities are provided in addition to various enhancement programs.

Children's Activity Centre (CAC)

CAC is an intricate system of providing value education to underprivileged children and consequently sensitizing student volunteers about the ground realities of those from the economically weaker sections of society. Student Volunteers conduct sessions and take tutoring classes for the sponsored children to improve the learning levels and cognitive skills of children. Classes are conducted on life skills, soft skills, personality development, etc. Major events like Talent's Day and Sports day are also conducted by the students for the sponsored children. Students from various departments of the University take part in such activities.

Exposure Program for Social Sensitization

CSA volunteers are taken to slum communities, NGOs and institutions. They are given exposure to the poor and marginalized sections of society like children and women in distress, children and persons with disabilities, HIV/AIDS infected and affected children. The rural visits make students aware of the rural realities. It gives an opportunity to witness and interact with different stakeholders regarding rural issues, urban developmental issues, educational support program, life and conditions of slums, Self Help Groups, Child Nutrition and Health Care, land development activities, waste management, etc. Students are given exposure to social realities and encouraged to realize their roles as "agents of change" in society.

Drishti

"Drishti" means 'The Vision', and this theatre team of the Centre for Social Action, was born with the mission of spreading awareness about various social issues in the University and in a larger framework, the society, regarding burning social issues, through different forms of theatre. The team reaches out to the students and the public by performing street plays on social issues in institutions, college campuses, villages, slums, NGOs, shopping malls and so on. Child Rights, Women Empowerment, Environment, Road Safety, De-addiction, and Mental Health are some of the themes on which street plays are performed.

Media and Communication Team

The Media and Communication (M&C) wing of the Centre for Social Action is mainly involved with the documentation of all events in CSA. It is the link that connects all Christites, CSA volunteers and Social Work facilitators. M&C holds discussions on contemporary issues and ventures out on a photo walk around the city, documenting the lives of people, which is also displayed in photo exhibitions. The wing comprises a cohesive team of volunteers who work together in the background for all activities of CSA. The team publishes an annual magazine, 'We Care', which contains articles, poems, cartoons, posters, essays, etc. pertaining to various social and development issues to create awareness among the student community. The team also updates the CSA blog, produces short documentaries, facilitates photo walks and anchors interactive group sessions on contemporary social issues through a forum called "Chat over Coffee" (COC).

Prayatna

Prayatna is the wing of CSA that aims at addressing environmental issues as a strong platform. With the focus on sensitizing Christites and other citizens, CSA volunteers and students at Christ University, with the support of academic and non-academic departments, create awareness about environment and climate change issues among the student community. Paper recycling, handmade recycled paper products, organic and food composting, biogas and wastewater treatment and recycling units have been set up to promote zero waste and a sustainable environment on the campus.

All these platforms, together with other curricular, co-curricular and extracurricular activities, ensure students' active participation and engagement in the University. The explorations of Gable and Haidt (2005) on the conditions and processes that optimize human functioning and potentials mainly centered around subjective well-being. When it comes to students' subjective well-being, the educational environment is the key determinant. Educational environments include both classroom climate and institutional climate. The classroom climate refers to aspects of teaching, how involved the students are, peer relationships, and peer-teacher relationships in rather small groups of students (i.e., a specific class). The institutional climate, on the other hand, consists of more global dimensions that focus on the institution in general. In an extensive literature review, Wang and Degol (2016) distinguished between four institution climate domains: Academic (quality of the academic atmosphere), community (quality of interpersonal relationships), safety (emotional security, e.g., disciplinary practices), and institutional environment (organizational features of the institutional environment).

2. Conceptuel Framework

There are different theoretical approaches linking institutional climate and student subjective well-being. Ecological system theories assume an impact of family, school, and other layers of the environment on children's and adolescents' positive development (e.g., Bronfenbrenner, 1979). In this context, schools might have an important influence as an environment that contributes to a healthy and positive adjustment and hence, to the well-being of children and adolescents (Baker et al., 2003). Baker et al. (2003) refers to different aspects of school climate as distal environmental aspects that influence well-being.

The stage-environment fit approach by Eccles et al. (1993) is grounded in the person-environment fit paradigm and is consistent with this theory. According to this approach, children's healthy development is possible only if the environment fulfils the prerequisites for healthy development. On the basis of these theoretical approaches, one might assume that Student well-being, as one sign that a student is developing in a healthy way, is impacted by a positive school climate because schools constitute a very important environment for children and adolescents given the amount of time they spend in school (Steinmayr et al., 2018).

Research in exposure describes that exposure creates a favourable attitude towards the activity (Zajonc, 1968). Active participation in volunteering provides a sense of direction, purpose and responsibility to individuals (Miller, 2011; Boccalandro, 2018; Wood et al., 2019), a responsibility towards self and society. Fishbein and Ajzen (1975) in theory of reasoned action and planned behaviour (1980) stated that behaviour is the function of an intention to carry out a particular act. The behavioural intention is determined by the beliefs system, the subjective norms and the individual's evaluation of the capacity to perform the act. The favourable attitude towards act, high social acceptance and personal evaluation that the person has enough resources to perform the act, would lead to the actual performance of act. Participation in volunteering and such activities improves one's well-being (Pilkington et al., 2012; Stuart et al., 2020). Based on these theoretical assumptions the current study developed the following conceptual models.

2.1. Conceptual Model

Students enjoy different immediate and long-term benefits from their active participation in volunteering activities. Volunteering provides an opportunity to master some new skills or upgrade some of the already acquired skills. It helps them in developing new networks, which aids them at personal and professional levels and ignites their concern for others and society. It provides them with a sense of direction, reduces their exposure to the vulnerable environment, and acts as a coping mechanism. It also provides them with an opportunity to apply theoretical knowledge in practical settings while ensuring the active participation of students in the learning process. Volunteering is indirectly associated with student fulfilment and success (Healey et al., 2016). More significantly, it controls the student's frustration and feeling of alienation (Fredricks et al., 2004).

Active participation in volunteering activities has a larger impact on student life (Figure 1). Through participation in volunteering activities, the students become sensitive to the needs of others and channelize their potential to create the necessary social capital required to ensure safe, sustainable and vibrant communities (Holdsworth, & Brewis, 2014; Evers & von Essen, 2019; Bird et al., 2016). Participation in these activities familiarizes them with democratic values and helps them to build a generalized trust – that extends beyond the boundaries of kinship and friendship and, finally, the well–being of the person (Elias et al., 2016). The use of volunteering provides double benefits in nation-building and ensuring student well-being. So, the current research aims at exploring the dynamics between helping attitude and student well-being. It also looked at the relationship between volunteering and attitude towards helping behaviour and personal and moral responsibility. Further, it aims to explore if volunteers and non-volunteers differ in their subjective well-being (Figure 2).

2.2. Objectives

- To explore the association between a helping attitude and personal and moral responsibility and volunteering.

- To understand whether there is any relationship between a helping attitude, personal and social responsibility and student well-being

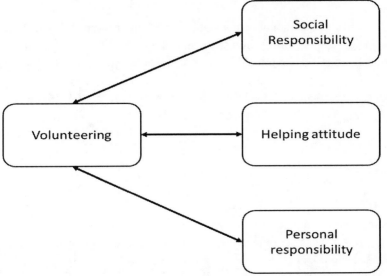

Figure 1. The relationship between volunteering behaviour, helping attitude, social responsibility and personal responsibility.

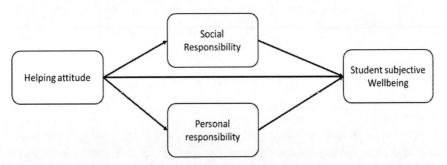

Figure 2. Dynamics between helping attitude, social responsibility, personal responsibility and student subjective well-being.

- To study whether personal and social responsibility mediates the relationship between helping attitude and student well-being
- To investigate whether volunteers and non-volunteers differ in their helping attitude, personal and social responsibility and student subjective well-being.

2.3. Hypothesis

H1: Volunteering, personal responsibility and social responsibility are related
H2: Social responsibility and personal responsibility will mediate the relationship between helping attitude and student subjective well-being.
H3: There will be differences in student subjective well-being, personal responsibility, social responsibility and helping attitude among volunteers and non-volunteers.

3. Methods

The current study aimed to find the relationship between the variables and explore whether volunteers and non-volunteers differ in their subjective well-being. To test these set objectives, the current research adopted a post-facto research design.

Around 164 student volunteers who are part of the Centre for social action (CSA) and 163 non-volunteers from the CHRIST Deemed to be University took part in the study. The participants were selected using a purposive sampling technique. Both groups had similar socio-demographic and economic backgrounds.

3.1. Variables and Operational Definitions

Volunteering
Volunteering is time willingly given for the common good and without financial gain. Here those students who participate in the various volunteering activities of CSA are considered volunteers.

Student Subjective Well-being
Student subjective well-being generally consists of a student's overall life satisfaction, general tendency to experience positive affect, and a global sense of happiness (Diener et al. 2009).

Social Responsibility
Social responsibility is understood as an individual's obligation to act for the benefit of society at large.

Personal Responsibility
Personal responsibility means an individual enjoys the freedom to choose their activities and holds oneself morally and legally responsible for the action and its outcomes.

Helping Attitude
It is a willingness and concern for the welfare of others. And it is considered as the predisposition for helping behaviour.

3.2. Tools for Data Collection

1. **A semi-structured questionnaire** for collecting Socio-demographic data
2. Helping **attitude scale (Nickell, 1998).** A 20-item measure of respondents' beliefs, feelings, and behaviours associated with helping. Each item is answered on a 5-point Likert scale, ranging from 1 (strongly disagree) to 5 (strongly agree). The test-retest reliability of the scale is r = .847. The internal consistency for the scale is .869. The scale is also used in the same culture and geographical region (Fernandes, Sanyal, & Fatima, 2015).
3. **Individual and Social responsibility scale (Watson et al. 2003).** The original Personal and Social Responsibility Questionnaire (PSRQ) developed by Watson et al. (2003) and modified afterwards by Li et al. (2008) is used to measure individual and social responsibility. The questionnaire included fourteen items distributed by two dimensions. Self-direction and respect and caring for others. All items were measured using a 6-point Likert-type scale that ranged from 1 (strongly disagree) to 6 (strongly agree).
4. Meaning **in life (Steger et al., 2006).** A 10-item questionnaire designed to measure two dimensions of meaning in life: (1) Presence of Meaning (how much respondents feel their lives have meaning), and (2) Search for Meaning (how much respondents strive to find meaning and understanding in their lives). Respondents answer each item on a 7-point Likert-type scale ranging from 1 (Absolutely True)

to 7 (Absolutely Untrue). In the normative sample, both subscales had Cronbach's alpha values between 0.82 and 0.88 and one-month test-retest stability of 0.70 (MLQ-P) and 0.73 (MLQS).
5. **The Student Subjective Well-being Questionnaire (SSWQ) (Renshaw, 2019)** is a 16-item self-report behaviour rating scale for measuring youths' school-specific well-being. It comprises four subscales: (1) Joy of Learning, (2) School Connectedness, (3) Educational Purpose, and (4) Academic Efficacy. Subscale scores can be used as standalone well-being indicators or summed to create an Overall Student Well-being composite scale. All the dimensions have adequate reliability and validity. The Cronbach alpha for the dimensions ranged from .72 -.86 (school connectedness = .72, joy of learning .74, educational purpose. 72, academic efficacy .78)

The study followed the ethical guidelines proposed by the APA. After getting approval from the institutional review board, the participants were approached online. The details of the volunteers were collected from the CSA office, and they were approached to get consent for the study. Those volunteers who consented to the study were sent the data collection tool. After the data collection on volunteers, a basic analysis was performed to see the demographic details of the volunteers. The non-volunteers from the same socio-demographic and educational background were approached to be part of the study. Based on their consent, the data collection tools were shared with them. Participation in the study was purely voluntary, and the participants did not receive any monetary benefits or rewards. There were no psychological or physical harms associated with the study.

Data screening, coding, and cleaning were carried out soon after the data collection, and validity checks of the measures and descriptive analysis of the socio-demographic variable were carried out in the initial stage. All the scales got adequate reliability. Since the data failed to fulfil the assumption of normality, Mann Whitney U Test and Spearman Correlation were carried out to test the hypothesis. The mediation analysis with the help of the SPSS Process Macro was also carried out.

The final proposal, informed assent of adolescents and consent of the adult population were sent for ethical approval at Institute Review Board, Christ University. All the study participants were thoroughly explained about the study and procedures, and written informed assents and consents were sought from the participants before their participation.

4. Results

In the current study, 327 participants took part, while 164 were volunteers and 163 were non-volunteers. Table 1 presents the demographic profile of the participants. The sample is spread across different academic streams. Among the participants, 110 were males, 213 were females, and 4 of them did not prefer to reveal their gender.

The current study first explored the association between volunteering, a helping attitude, and social and personal responsibility. The correlation between the variables is presented in Table 2.

A bi-serial correlation was run to determine the relationship between a helping attitude, social and personal responsibility, meaning in life and volunteering. The results are presented in Table 3. There is a positive correlation between helping attitude (r_{pb} = .175, n = 327, p = 001), social (r_{pb} = .109, n = 327, p = 048), and personal responsibility (r_{pb} = .136, n = 327, p = 014), and volunteering, while meaning in life (r_{pb} = -.057, n = 327, p = 303), did not show any statistically significant relationship.

Table 1. Demographic details of the participants

	Variable	Frequency (%)
Participants	Volunteers	164
	Non- volunteers	163
Gender	Male	110
	Female	213
	Prefer not to say	4

Table 2. Relationship between helping attitude, social and personal responsibility, meaning in life and volunteering

	Volunteering	HeL	ScoR	PeR	MeL
Volunteering	1				
HeL	.175*	1			
ScoR	.109*	.473**	1		
PeR	.136*	.447**	.658**	1	
MeL	-.057	.374**	.467**	.488**	1

**. Correlation is significant at the 0.01 level (2-tailed).
*. Correlation is significant at the 0.05 level (2-tailed).

Table 3. The relationship between helping attitude social and personal responsibility and student subjective well-being

	HeL	ScoR	PeR	SSW	Joy	Connected	Purpose	Efficacy
HeL	1							
ScoR	.473**	1						
PeR	.447**	.658**	1					
SSW	.301**	.435**	.489**	1				
Joy	.292**	.370**	.460**	.875**	1			
Connected	.205**	.311**	.349**	.861**	.693**	1		
Purpose	.261**	.343**	.377**	.812**	.676**	.564**	1	
efficacy	.255**	.436**	.454**	.798**	.554**	.581**	.533**	1

**. Correlation is significant at the 0.01 level (2-tailed).
*. Correlation is significant at the 0.05 level (2-tailed).

The analysis revealed that student subjective well-being is positively associated with a helping attitude (r = .301, p = .001, social (r = .435, p = .001 and personal (r = .489, p = .001) responsibility. The relationship was found to be statistically significant. The strength of the relationship varied from .301 to .489, which is moderate. All dimensions of student subjective well-being, the joy of learning, school connectedness, educational purpose and academic efficacy were also positively associated with a helping attitude and social and personal responsibility.

4.1. Mediation

This section explains the mediating role of Personal responsibility and social responsibility on the relationship between helping attitude and student subjective well-being. Personal (M1) and social (M2) responsibility are taken as the mediator variable. This model is tested to determine the indirect effect of these mediators on the relationship between helping attitude and student subjective well-being.

As recommended by Preacher and Hayes (2008), a bootstrapping method is used as it is considered the most powerful, most effective method to use with small samples and the least vulnerable to Type I errors. The data is re-sampled 5000 times as recommended by Hayes. For the single analysis, SPSS macro-PROCESS (model 4) was used, applying three significant mediators for every single analysis. As recommended by Hayes (2013), the regression/path coefficients are all in unstandardised form, as standardised coefficients generally have no useful substantive interpretation. As recommended by Baron and Kenny (1986), mediators have to be significantly correlated with both the predictors and outcome variables. All the variables were correlated.

Table 4. Direct and indirect effect of helping attitude on student subjective well-being through personal responsibility and social responsibility

Variables	Path coefficients				Indirect effects		
	HeL	PeR	ScoR	SSW	Estimate	\multicolumn{2}{c}{Bias corrected bootstrap 95% confidence interval}
						Lower	Upper
Helping attitude (HeL)	-	.28(.03)	.36(.04)	.04 (.08)			
Personal Responsibility (PeR)	-	-	-	.85 (.16)			
Social Responsibility (ScoR)	-	-	-	.33 (.13)			
Student Well-being (SSW)	-	-	-	-			
Total					.40 (.08)	.25	.56
HeL→Per→SSW					.24(.07)	.12	.36
HeL→Sco→SSW					.12(.06)	.01	.25
Total indirect effect					.36 (.08)	.22	.53

Table 4 provides the parallel mediation with Personal Responsibility (PeR) and Social Responsibility (ScoR), as the mediators yielded a significant indirect path in the present analysis. The first indirect path (helping attitude to personal responsibility to student subjective well-being) coefficient (.24) was found with bias-corrected confidence intervals of .12 in the lower region and .36 in the upper. Since the confidence intervals do not include a zero in between, it was found significant. The total effect path coefficient (.40) with a confidence interval of .25, .56 was also found significant. However, the direct path (helping attitude to student subjective well-being) with a coefficient (.04) with bias-corrected confidence intervals -.12 on the lower side and .21 on the upper side wasn't significant since there was a zero between the upper limit and the lower lime. It shows a total mediation effect of the proposed mediator, namely personal responsibility.

The second indirect path (helping attitude to social responsibility to student subjective well-being) coefficient (.12) was found with bias-corrected confidence intervals of .01 in the lower region and .25 in the upper. The path seemed to be significant since the confidence intervals did not include a zero in between. However, the direct path was not significant, and the effect of the independent variable on the dependent variable was entirely through the mediator variable, which indicates complete mediation. In total, this parallel mediation model with related personal responsibility and social responsibility explained 10% of the variance in the relationship between helping attitude and student subjective well-being.

Table 5 indicates that a helping attitude is higher among CSA volunteers (mean rank = 183.41) compared to non-volunteers (144.48). From the analysis, it can be concluded that the helping attitude among the CSA volunteers was statistically significantly higher than the non-volunteers ($U = 10183.5, p = .000$). The effect size r = 0.21 is small. According to Cohen (1988), 0.10 – < 0.30 is small, 0.30 – < 0.50 is medium and ≥ 0.50 is a large effect. Personal responsibility is higher among CSA volunteers (mean rank=176.88) compared to the non-volunteers (mean rank = 151.04). The analysis also revealed that the difference noticed is statistically significant ($U = 11253.0, p = .013$). The effect size r = 0.14 is also small. Students' subjective well-being is also found to be higher (176.39) among volunteers than among non-volunteers (151.53); the difference noticed was statistically significant ($U = 11334.000, p = .017$). The other variable, social responsibility ($U = 11893.5, p = .084$), did not show any statistically significant differences between volunteers and non-volunteers.

Table 5. Comparing the social sensitization variables among volunteers and non-volunteers

Variables	Grouping variable	Mean Rank	Sum of Ranks	Mann-Whitney U	Wilcoxon W	Z	Asymp. Sig. (2-tailed)
HeL	Volunteers	183.41	30078.50	10183.500	23549.500	-3.731	.000**
	Non-Volunteers	144.48	23549.50				
ScoR	Volunteers	172.98	28368.50	11893.500	25259.500	-1.730	.084
	Non-Volunteers	154.97	25259.50				
PeR	Volunteers	176.88	29009.00	11253.000	24619.000	-2.485	.013*
	Non-Volunteers	151.04	24619.00				
SWTTT	Volunteers	176.39	28928.00	11334.000	24700.000	-2.380	.017*
	Non-Volunteers	151.53	24700.00				

**. Correlation is significant at the 0.01 level (2-tailed).
*. Correlation is significant at the 0.05 level (2-tailed).

5. Discussion

The current research first explored the hypothesis that volunteering and meaning in life, personal responsibility, and social responsibility are related. The data analysis provided evidence for the assumed positive relationship between volunteering and helping attitude, personal responsibility and social responsibility and supported previous findings (Schwartz, 1970; Cheung et al., 2015). Intrinsic motivation is a driving force that helps students to participate in volunteering activities. Participation in volunteering activities benefits the student in multiple ways. It creates social consciousness and initiates altruistic behaviours in the students. Continuous exposure to volunteering activity brings an attitudinal change in the participant towards volunteering or altruistic behaviours. It also noted that volunteering shapes individuals' personalities and helps them to become more responsible.

The various functions that volunteering serves, such as a coping mechanism, a tool to upgrade skills, an opportunity to gain self-confidence and so on, help the volunteer maintain their health and Subjective well-being (Steinmayr et al., 2018). On the contrary, there are instances where volunteers end up in trouble because of their volunteering behaviours as well. The second hypothesis explored these observations. The analysis revealed that the effect volunteering has on well-being is only through personal responsibility and social responsibility. Volunteering did not have any direct impact on student well-being. Volunteers who express the characteristics of responsibility, mainly personal responsibility and social responsibility, would be the ones who show better well-being (Heffner & Antaramian, 2016). If the volunteers lack these qualities, they won't benefit in terms of well-being from their engagement in volunteering activities (Plagnol & Huppert, 2010; Stuart et al., 2020). In a nutshell, participation in volunteering creates attitudinal and behavioural change in volunteers and volunteers with social responsibility and personal responsibility enjoy better well-being than those who are poor in personal and social responsibility.

The findings that volunteer have better well-being, helping attitude and personal responsibility compared to non-volunteers clearly indicate the significance of volunteering and the model. It also supports the previous findings that a favourable attitude towards the action is a prerequisite to actively engaging in that activity.

6. Recommandations and Limitations

The current findings throw light into certain areas where educational institutions could improve student mental health on campus. One, volunteering can be used as a tool for better student engagement and student well-being. Two, the institutions should have a special focus on the nature of volunteering and should include those activities that will help the students to become more responsible citizens and strengthen their commitment to society. Three, the institutions should adopt measures that will create a favourable attitude towards volunteering among students.

Higher Education Institutions around the world build in the learner a special interest in seeking knowledge and applying the same to societal contexts. Irrespective of their discipline of study, each student graduates to become a citizen of the world, responsible and responsive to the needs of society. Student Well-being during their study is imperative for their experiencing holistic development and the joy of learning. It is in this direction that most clubs and associations at HEIs create platforms for youngsters to engage with others and explore themselves deeply through the activities and programs organized. Social action and engagement are intricately entwined with student growth and development. Hence it is considered worthwhile to invest in enriching their societal experiences fruitfully on and off campus.

Students would also benefit in multiple ways from their participation in volunteering. It provides them with social support, acceptance and recognition. The volunteers also experience a sense of worth and find meaning and purpose in their life. So, participation in volunteering provides focus and orientation to students in their campus life. Though the current study established the link between volunteering, personal and social responsibility and student well-being, the overall effect is low. Detailed research with a large sample size would provide more clarity and more directions for generalizations.

7. Conclusion

The current research found that volunteering is positively related to a helping attitude and personal and social responsibility. Social responsibility and personal responsibility mediate the relationship between a helping attitude and students' subjective well-being. It is also noted that volunteering students enjoyed better well-being than those who did not participate in any of the volunteering activities.

This research endeavour was a reinforcement of the University's charism of education that caters to the holistic development of the learner. In addition to disciplinary learning experienced through academics, HEIs must focus their efforts on building a conducive ecosystem for the student community to involve in some volunteering activities which help them to go through real-life problems and challenges in society and be well-equipped to overcome them and resolve issues in one's own personal life as well.

References

Abdelsamea, M. A., and Bart, W. M. (2016). *A Proposed Model for Student Engagement and Standards-based Education.*, 26(90), 261-20.
Ajzen, I., and Fishbein, M. (1975). A Bayesian analysis of attribution processes. *Psychological bulletin*, 82(2), 261.
Anilkumar, B. S. (June 20, 2021, 08 :27 IST), 60% of college students in Kerala suffer depression: Study, The Times of India, City News, Thiruvanthapuram News. https://timesofindia.indiatimes.com/city/thiruvananthapuram/60-of-college-students-suffer-depression-study/articleshow/83674534.cms.
Baker, J. A., Dilly, L. J., AupperJohal, J. L., and Patil, S. A. (2003). The developmental context of school satisfaction : Schools as psychologically healthy environments. *School Psychology Quarterly*, 18(2), 206.
Baron, R. M., and Kenny, D. A. (1986). The moderator–mediator variable distinction in social psychological research: Conceptual, strategic, and statistical considerations. *Journal of personality and social psychology*, 51(6), 1173.
Beiter, R., Nash, R., McCrady, M., Rhoades, D., Linscomb, M., Clarahan, M., and Sammut, S. (2015). The prevalence and correlates of depression, anxiety, and stress in a sample of college students. *Journal of affective disorders*, 173, 90-96.
Bird, Y., Islam, A., and Moraros, J. (2016). Community-based clinic volunteering: an evaluation of the direct and indirect effects on the experience of health science college students. *BMC Medical Education*, 16, 1-10.
Boccalandro, B. (2018). Increasing employee engagement through corporate volunteering. Retrieved from https://www.beaboccalandro.com/wp-content/uploads/2019/01/Engagement-Report-Voluntare_eng_04122018-2.pdf.
Bronfenbrenner, U. (1979). *The ecology of human development: Experiments by nature and design*. Harvard university press.
Chaudhary, A. P., Sonar, N. S., Jamuna, T. R., Banerjee, M., and Yadav, S. (2021). Impact of the COVID-19 pandemic on the mental health of college students in India: cross-sectional web-based study. *JMIRx med*, 2(3), e28158.

Cheung, C. K., Lo, T. W., and Liu, S. C. (2015). Relationship between volunteerism and social responsibility in young volunteers. *VOLUNTAS : international journal of voluntary and nonprofit organisations*, 26(3), 872-889.

Christ University. (n.d.). Retrieved January 22, 2023, from https://christuniversity.in/graduate-attributes.

Deb, S., Banu, P. R., Thomas, S., Vardhan, R. V., Rao, P. T., and Khawaja, N. (2016). Depression among Indian university students and its association with perceived university academic environment, living arrangements and personal issues. *Asian journal of psychiatry*, 23, 108-117.

Diener, E., Scollon, C. N., and Lucas, R. E. (2009). The evolving concept of subjective well-being: The multifaceted nature of happiness. In *Assessing well-being* (pp. 67–100). Dordrecht: Springer.

Eccles, J. S., Midgley, C., Wigfield, A., Buchanan, C. M., Reuman, D., Flanagan, C., and Mac Iver, D. (1997). Development during adolescence : The impact of stage–environment fit on young adolescents' experiences in schools and in families (1993).

Elias, J. K., Sudhir, P., and Mehrotra, S. (2016). Long-term engagement in formal volunteering and well-being: An exploratory Indian study. *Behavioral Sciences*, 6(4), 20.

Evers, A., and von Essen, J. (2019). Volunteering and civic action : Boundaries blurring, boundaries redrawn. *VOLUNTAS : International Journal of Voluntary and Nonprofit Organizations*, 30, 1-14.

Fernandes, T., Sanyal, N., and Fatima, A. (2015). Helping attitude and psychological well-being in older widowed women. *The International Journal of Indian Psychology*, 2(3), 4-17.

Fredricks, J. A., Blumenfeld, P., and Paris, A. (2004). School engagement : potential of the concept, state of the evidence. *Rev. Educ. Res.*, 74, 59–109. DOI : 10.3102/00346543074001059.

Ghonge, M. M., Bag, R., and Singh, A. (2020). Indian Education : Ancient, Medieval and Modern. In *Education at the Intersection of Globalization and Technology*. IntechOpen.

Healey, M., Flint, A., and Harrington, K. (2016). Students as partners: reflections on a conceptual model. *Teach. Learn. Inq.*, 4, 1–13. DOI : 10.20343/teachlearninqu.4.2.3.

Heffner, A. L., and Antaramian, S. P. (2016). The role of life satisfaction in predicting student engagement and achievement. *Journal of Happiness Studies*, 17(4), 1681-1701.

Holdsworth, C., and Brewis, G. (2014). Volunteering, choice and control : a case study of higher education student volunteering. *Journal of Youth Studies*, 17(2), 204-219.

Keyes, C. L., Dhingra, S. S., and Simoes, E. J. (2010). Change in level of positive mental health as a predictor of future risk of mental illness. *American journal of public health*, 100(12), 2366-2371.

Keyes, C. L., Eisenberg, D., Perry, G. S., Dube, S. R., Kroenke, K., and Dhingra, S. S. (2012). The relationship of level of positive mental health with current mental disorders in predicting suicidal behavior and academic impairment in college students. *Journal of American college health*, 60(2), 126-133.

Li, W., Wright, P. M., Rukavina, P. B., and Pickering, M. (2008). Measuring students' perceptions of personal and social responsibility and the relationship to intrinsic motivation in urban physical education. *Journal of Teaching in Physical Education*, (27), 167-178.

Marsh, S. (Tue May 23 2017, 12.06 BST). Number of university dropouts due to mental health problems trebles, The Guardian. Retrieved from https://www.theguardian.com/society/2017/may/23/number-university-dropouts-due-to-mental-health-problems-trebles.

Miller, E. T. (2011). Benefits of volunteering. *Rehabilitation Nursing Journal*, 36(3), 90.

Nickell, G. (1998). The Helping Attitudes Scale. Paper presented at 106th Annual Convention of the American Psychological Association at San Francisco, August, 1998.

Payne, L. (2019) Student engagement : three models for its investigation, *Journal of Further and Higher Education*, 43 :5, 641-657, DOI : 10.1080/0309877X.2017.1391186.

Philip, S., Molodynski, A., Barklie, L., Bhugra, D., and Chaturvedi, S. K. (2021). Psychological well-being and burnout amongst medical students in India: A report from a nationally accessible survey. *Middle East Current Psychiatry*, 28(1), 1-6.

Pietarinen, J., Soini, T., and Pyhältö, K. (2014). Students' emotional and cognitive engagement as the determinants of well-being and achievement in school. *International Journal of Educational Research*, 67, 40-51.

Pilkington, P. D., Windsor, T. D., and Crisp, D. A. (2012). Volunteering and subjective well-being in midlife and older adults: The role of supportive social networks. *Journals of Gerontology Series B : Psychological Sciences and Social Sciences*, 67(2), 249-260.

Plagnol, A. C., and Huppert, F. A. (2010). Happy to help ? Exploring the factors associated with variations in rates of volunteering across Europe. *Social Indicators Research*, 97(2), 157-176.

Preacher, K. J., and Hayes, A. F. (2008). Asymptotic and resampling strategies for assessing and comparing indirect effects in multiple mediator models. *Behavior research methods*, 40(3), 879-891.

Renshaw, T. L. (2018). Psychometrics of the revised college student subjective well-being questionnaire. *Canadian Journal of School Psychology*, 33(2), 136-149.

Renshaw, T. L. (2019, May 14). Development and Validation of the Student Subjective Well-being Questionnaire (SSWQ). Retrieved from osf.io/d54zs.

Ross, A. M. (1973). The role of higher education institutions in national development. *Higher Education*, 2(1), 103-108.

Satpathy, B., and Ali, E. (2020). A study on psychological well-being of final year management students during COVID-19 pandemic lockdown in India. *International Journal of Indian Psychology*, 8(2), 1-25.

Schwartz, S. H. (1970). Elicitation of moral obligation and self-sacrificing behavior: an experimental study of volunteering to be a bone marrow donor. *Journal of personality and social psychology*, 15(4), 283.

Steger, M. F., Frazier, P., Oishi, S., and Kaler, M. (2006). The meaning in life questionnaire : assessing the presence of and search for meaning in life. *Journal of counseling psychology*, 53(1), 80.

Steinmayr, R., Heyder, A., Naumburg, C., Michels, J., and Wirthwein, L. (2018). School-related and individual predictors of subjective well-being and academic achievement. *Frontiers in Psychology*, 9, 2631.

Stuart, J., Kamerāde, D., Connolly, S., Paine, A. E., Nichols, G., and Grotz, J. (2020). The Impacts of Volunteering on the Subjective Well-being of Volunteers: A Rapid Evidence Assessment.

Twenge, J. M., Joiner, T. E., Rogers, M. L., and Martin, G. N. (2018). Increases in depressive symptoms, suicide-related outcomes, and suicide rates among US adolescents after 2010 and links to increased new media screen time. *Clinical Psychological Science*, 6(1), 3-17.

Watson, D. L., Newton, M., and Kim, M. (2003). Recognition of values-based constructs in a summer physical activity program. *Urban Review*, 35, 217-232.

Wood, N., Charlwood, G., Zecchin, C., Hansen, V., Douglas, M., and Pit, S. W. (2019). Qualitative exploration of the impact of employment and volunteering upon the health and well-being of African refugees settled in regional Australia: a refugee perspective. *BMC Public Health*, 19(1), 1-15.

Zajonc, R. B. (1968). Attitudinal effects of mere exposure. *Journal of Personality and Social Psychology*, 9 (2 : 1-27.

Zhang, D. C., and Renshaw, T. L. (2020). Personality and college student subjective well-being: A domain-specific approach. *Journal of Happiness Studies*, 21(3), 997-1014.

Chapter 15

Developing Authentic Thought Leaders Through the DREAMS Model of Social Action

Lijo Thomas[1,*]
Anuradha Sathiyaseelan[2,†]
and B. Sathiyaseelan[3,‡]

[1]Department of Psychology, Christ University, Bengaluru, India
[2]Department of Psychology, Christ University Bengaluru, India
[3]School of Business and Management, Christ University, Bengaluru, India

Abstract

DREAMS is a three-year curriculum-based after-school intervention program for enhancing leadership qualities among the underprivileged and college/university youngsters. It is an innovative model providing a platform for the mentors and the mentees to share their thoughts and knowledge and create a future generation with a growth mindset. The current world is expecting authentic thought leadership among its workforces. This leadership would help the constantly changing world to guide and lead the followers effectively for a better outcome. This study explores the impact of the DREAMS intervention program by Christ University in entrenching authentic thought leadership among its undergraduates. The study employs a qualitative approach to explore the perceptions among Christ University undergraduates about the contributions the DREAMS has made to their leadership development. The study finds evidence that DREAMS initiatives at Christ University have transformed undergraduates into authentic thought leaders.

---

[*] Corresponding Author's E-mail: lijo.thomas@christuniversity.in.
[†] Corresponding Author's E-mail: anuradha.sathiyaseelan@christuniversity.in.
[‡] Corresponding Author's E-mail: sathiyaseelan.b@christuniversity.in.

In: Models for Social Responsibility Action by Higher Education Institutions
Editors: Joseph Chacko Chennattuserry, Elangovan N. et al.
ISBN: 979-8-89113-097-5
© 2024 Nova Science Publishers, Inc.

Keywords: authentic thought leadership, Intervention, DREAMS

1. Introduction

> "Dream is not that which you see while sleeping. It is something that does not let you sleep."
> *Abdul Kalam*

DREAMS (Desire, Readiness, Empowerment, Action, and Mastery for Success) is a three-year curriculum-based, an after-school program for underserved teenagers towards academic success, professional nourishment, and ultimately toward holistic success, implemented by college student mentors and community volunteers. The DREAMS intervention program aims to enhance the leadership qualities of youth with the following motto "*Success* belongs to those *who work hard* to reach their dreams" (Thomas, 2014). This intervention program focuses on developing leadership qualities of youngsters for their future through positive psychology approaches based on the concept "positive nature of humans" of Carl Rogers. Duckworth et al. (2005) explain that positive psychology brings clarity to positive outcomes. Seligman et al. (2009), the famous positive psychologist, confirm that service learning brings affirmative community systems and holistic growth among youngsters.

The current world is looking for a workforce with the following qualities, namely effective communication skills, honesty, integrity, interpersonal skills, motivation, initiative, and work ethics. This clarifies the need of the hour, which is for an authentic thought leader to lead the world. These leaders focus less on their own image and more on adding value to their audience by providing clear messages and directions and leading them by example. Since the world is constantly changing and time and again going into VUCA circumstances, there is a demand for this leadership style for leading and directing the followers. Hence the expectations fall on the universities and colleges to promote this leadership style among youngsters. DREAMS is such an initiative to promote an authentic leadership style among the youth at Christ University. It is a three-year community collaborative intervention that was developed to complement the holistic educational efforts of our schools by involving college/university students as peer mentors and community members as adult mentors. This curriculum-based intervention model utilizes different forms of pedagogy, along with traditional sessions transforming underserved middle school children, who are the primary stakeholders.

The second set of stakeholders of the DREAMS intervention program consists of youth, namely college youth mentors from colleges and universities. They act as big sisters and big brothers to the mentees from middle schools, posting their training on mentoring and service learning (Thomas, 2014). Buddy systems and peer mentoring promote leadership qualities among the youth (Kern et al., 2015). As mentioned by Kielsmier (2010), service learning is a bridge between the community and the campus and is influential in the learning process (Turner 1998) and enhances self-esteem (Prosser & Levesque, 1997) increases critical thinking and social responsibility (Lemieux & Allen (2007) and brings in positive changes in personal and professional growth. Above all, it gives students a space to develop into capable young leaders (Marais et al., 2000).

The system of education is evolving from the traditional teaching style to the contemporary one involving mentoring and modelling (DeAva, 1999). The study by Segrott et al. (2013) on school-based intervention programs explains how it brings in interpersonal challenges for the formation of a healthy forum to engage and gain meaning in life for students and mentors. In line with that, DeMoulin, (2002) clarifies that the youth achieve mastery in these circumstances through effective interactions, which helps in personal maturity, leading to holistic development.

Mastery-oriented students place soaring intrinsic value on their learning process (Butler, 1987), on self-regulation (Covington, 1999) and adapt to failures (Dweck, 1986; Dweck & Leggett, 1988). They pursue high-risk tasks comparatively (Archer, 1994; Church et al., 2001). On the other hand, students who are performance-oriented tend to outperform others and don't have long-term goals. Studies by (Ames, 1992; Nicholls, 1984; Chow et al., 2002) suggest that schools need to make it part of their curriculum to enhance flourishing among the youth.

Interventions through summer camps modify interpersonal skills, hopeful thinking, positive strategies related to goal setting and fulfilment of realistic goals (Kirshchman et al., 2010). The DREAMS intervention program is a service-learning program initiated and time-tested in various countries. Integrating such service learning into the educational curriculum is an important and essential step towards grooming service leaders. The components of learning, such as selfless service to the needy in the community, enrich the learning experience. Once people understand that they can learn by helping others, they begin to grow personally as leaders (Levesque & Prosser, 1996). The effectiveness of service learning is seen in studies by Herbst (2003) and Lambert et al. (2005), in which they found that students who had service learning in their curriculum showed greater achievements in life than their counterparts who did not have them. Enhancing service learning ensures that students' moral development and awareness of issues related to society encourages them to have a social consciousness and develop open-mindedness for diversity, enhancing relational abilities (Boss, 1994; Eyler & Giles, 1999).

The DREAMS intervention program is structured and implemented in such a way that more than 40 college youth mentors at each chapter get active leadership roles and responsibilities for three years consecutively. The identified underserved middle school students will be divided into six subgroups, and each of these groups will be assigned to college mentors to mentor and lead the team. There are other organizational and leadership roles such as overall coordination, coordinators for activities, games, music, theatre, operations, documentation, media, marketing, etc. There is also a systematic accountability and reporting system in place.

The underperforming students will be identified with the help of school counsellors and class teachers. College youth mentors and senior community mentors are identified for mentoring, modelling, motivating and training the participants. The college youth mentors and volunteers are the key personnel of the project.

The college youth mentors will be trained to be sensitive to the psychosocial and leadership needs of the teenage students in schools and help them develop those skills through diverse interventions such as training, mentoring, games, music, theatre, activities, etc., with a set curriculum. The groups are introduced to the DREAMS model and trained on the value of mentoring, project design how to initiate and implement an action plan to make the program sustainable and make a positive difference in the lives of those underperforming teenagers through a program called Young Community Leadership Program (YCLP) They are trained to develop leadership, mentoring, organizational, and entrepreneurial skills through community-based initiatives in this program through periodic evaluation.

The program helps to influence and foster young aspiring college youth mentors as organizers, leaders, entrepreneurs, and mentors with the skills and experience needed to generate transformative social change. The interdisciplinary program emphasizes highly applied coursework, relationship building, and hands-on practical experiences, which are essential components for developing strong leadership, mentoring and coaching skills.

The DREAMS project is a college/university-community intervention for school students. The host college/university plays a pivotal role in organizing it through its undergraduate students and faculty supervisors. The host college/university supervises the project, and the faculty in charge is the connecting link between the school faculty and community volunteers. This also provides an opportunity for the college/university to be connected to the local community and other community organizations.

As there is pressure on academicians and educational institutions to enhance and develop effective leadership in their students (Pless et al., 2017), programs like DREAMS are definitely needed for social upliftment. Preparing youngsters for leadership challenges and ethical dilemmas is the need of society and the hour (Mintzberg & Gosling, (2002). Providing opportunities such as the DREAMS intervention program for college youth mentors to know about societal needs and to make them understand their responsibilities is imperative.

DREAMS is an innovative model providing a platform for mentors and mentees to share their thoughts and knowledge and create a future generation with a growth mindset. The purpose of this study is to investigate whether the DREAMS intervention programme has helped the undergraduate students at Christ University, namely youth college mentors, in developing their authentic thought leadership skills or not. This study explores the impact of the DREAMS intervention program in entrenching holistic development among mentors. The study employs a qualitative approach to explore perceptions among mentors about contributions the intervention program has made to their holistic development through social innovation, with the following question:

- How has the DREAMS intervention program helped its mentors to become authentic thought leaders?

2. Review of Literature

The researchers have reviewed the literature extensively from the past 20 years until the first quarter of 2021. They have used the following search engines, namely google scholar, Ebsco, ProQuest, Publon, and Jstor, for the literature of the said period.

The review reveals that there is a growing need for developing authentic thought leaders as we witness numerous unethical decisions from the most prominent leaders of society to the school classroom leaders.

This growing trend of leaders acting unethically for their own personal gain is calling for urgent attention and response to address these challenges. To mitigate these challenges, authentic thought leadership has emerged as a response to this situation to promote more ethical and socially responsible leadership. In the past couple of decades, scholars and practitioners have been attracted to this positive form of leadership.

The term authentic leadership was proposed by Luthans and Avolio (2003) as a basic construct for a positive style of leadership that provides confidence and trust to the followers. From this basic construct emerged other positive leadership styles like charismatic, transformational and ethical leadership (Avolio & Gardner, 2005; Gardner et al., 2004).

Studies show that positivity, centred on the well-being, self-awareness and regulations of both the leader and followers, is critical for successful leadership (Luthans & Avolio, 2003). Few other studies, such as a study by Gardner et al. (2005), posit that authentic thought leadership focuses on the development of the followers by modelling positive values and behaviours. Authentic thought leaders share their personal values with their followers and encourage their relationships with the followers inked through those values (Avolio et al., 2004). There is an emotional contagion in this leadership style where both leaders and followers are mutually influenced (Ilies et al., 2005).

If we look into the authentic thought leadership construct, then we can see it has got three different perspectives such as intrapersonal, interpersonal and developmental. Intrapersonal focuses on the leader's personal beliefs, values, behaviours and unique values (Shamir & Eilam, 2005). Leaders are authentic when they are aware of themselves and act based on their values and beliefs (Steffens et al., 2021; Walumbwa et al., 2008).

The interpersonal perspective focuses on the relationship between leader and followers Sparrowe (2005) explains that authentic thought leaders practice self-consistency, which helps the followers to easily understand the model portrayed by the leader and helps them to enhance their skills. Harris et al. (2018), in their discussion, point out that the authentic thought leadership style promotes adaptability, which makes the leaders cooperative and easily adjust to the situations. This helps them to have a good relationship with their followers (Zehir & Narcikara, 2016). Empathy helps leaders to strengthen the bond with their followers, and this elicits a positive feeling in the organization. (Goldstein et al. 2014). These studies identify that authentic thought leaders practice empathy.

The developmental perspective regarded it as something to be designed and developed (Avolio & Gardner, 2005; Walumbwa et al., 2008). Authentic thought leadership is a blend of many positive psychological aspects, and one of the most crucial aspects is the self-awareness and self-regulated behaviours nurturing positive self-development (Gatling et al., 2013; Walumbwa et al., 2008; Ilies et al., 2005). The concept of authenticity is centred on self-inquiry and the journey toward one's self-actualization.

Further, we could see many studies explain the key characteristics of an authentic thought leader. Specifically, the innovator's ability plays a very important role in authentic leadership, and it strengthens responsiveness for the benefit of the leader's authenticity. Authentic leaders' strengths are innovation and innovative resilience (Todt et al., 2019).

Innovation and creativity are very decisive in successful leadership (Arena et al., 2017). Authentic leaders' natural behaviour prompts the team members to have higher emotional safety, and they will have increased confidence in proposing unconventional ideas. Studies have shown that authentic leadership promotes more creativity and innovation among its followers (Avolio et al., 2004; Cerne et al., 2013). The DREAMS intervention provides college student mentors with an opportunity to try innovative ideas and learn from their implementation.

Authentic leadership focuses on the strengths and achievements of the person rather than the flaws of the person (Jensen & Luthans, 2006; Peterson & Luthans, 2003). The focus on the strengths would create more trust and emotional safety in the leader. This organizational situation would provide them with the confidence to try out new things and take more risks (Cerne et al., 2013). The term authentic itself means to be natural and original. Only having this emotional safety and trust would make someone natural and original (Shamir & Eilam, 2005).

There are many studies on the significance and the need for ethical and authentic thought leadership. However, there is a scarcity of studies on the program designs established to generate authentic thought leaders. Providing opportunities for college students' personal appraisals and self-knowledge is very important in developing them into more authentic thought leaders. These alternative opportunities would build their self-awareness and self-acceptance. The DREAMS intervention program is one of these to bring in the positive and necessary changes among young adults to prepare them as authentic thought leaders.

This particular study stems from a genuine aim to create some solutions by evaluating such an initiative called the DREAMS intervention program with the following Objective: – *understanding the experiences of college youth mentors in the DREAMS intervention program in their growth as authentic thought leaders.*

3. Methodology

This qualitative study focuses on a phenomenological approach in which lived experiences of the participants are explored. It involves the descriptive examination of the participants' experiences and thoughts on the topic, and hence it is phenomenological. With an idiographic focus, this approach aims to bring insight into how the mentors learn and makes sense of the authentic thought leadership style during the DREAMS intervention program. This is the best approach for finding the innermost deliberation of the participant on the given phenomenon.

The study employed the following operational definitions.

- ***DREAMS intervention program.*** It is an acronym for Desire, Readiness, Empowerment, Action, and Mastery for Success.
- **Thought leadership:** An individual who possesses mastery in a specialized field.
- **Authentic thought leaders:** These individuals focus less on their own image and more on adding value to their audience.
- **College Youth Mentors:** The college/university students who mentor middle school children in the DREAMS intervention program.

In this study, purposive sampling was used, as the research study focused on non-probability sampling. This sampling method was found to be appropriate for the study because it required the researcher to reach a target sample that would fulfil the criteria and also keep the prevalence of the sample in mind. Since the study comprises a qualitative framework, sampling proportionality is not a main concern, and hence the method of purposive sampling was found to be pertinent.

Participants were 120 undergraduate students - both male and female, namely youth mentors from the DREAMS intervention program at Christ University. With informed consent, 84 participated in the semi-structured interviews, and 36 participated in the focus group discussions. Those who participated in the interviews were not included in the FGDs.

With the help of an extensive review of the literature, a semi-structured interview schedule and a set of questions for the FGD were prepared. The formulated schedules were validated by an expert panel consisting of five experts in qualitative research and in education, specifically mentoring. The participants were the youth mentors of the DREAMS intervention program. Informed consent was obtained from the participants, post which they were briefed on about the study. After the briefing, the data was collected in two phases. The details are as follows.

Phase 1. In this phase, the data was collected from 84 youth mentors using a semi-structured interview guide. Both in-depth and qualitative survey methods were employed to understand their perceptions of holistic growth and development. Due to the current pandemic scenario, the data was collected online using Google Meet and Google Forms. Each interview was transcribed, and memo questions were prepared for further clarity. The answers to these memo questions were included verbatim. The final transcript was shared with the participants to check the member check process, which is important for data validation.

Phase2. In this phase three, FGDs were conducted with the mentors to understand their experience in leadership development online, using Google Meet with 36 youth mentors. Both the written informed consent and the oral informed consent were obtained from the participants during the focus group discussions. The entire focus group discussion was prepared as a transcript and was validated with the participants through a member check process.

The interpretive phenomenological approach and the thematic analysis bring in the lived-in experiences of the participants, in which the traditional manual method, as well as NVivo, integrates rich themes. The analysis was done by two independent coders, and the results were drawn, keeping common themes from both. The inter-rater reliability was found to be 0.70, indicating good reliability. Initial themes were prepared by identifying the recurring themes from the transcripts and given codes. Then the initial themes were grouped based on similarity, which formulated the basic themes. Similarly, basic themes were grouped into organizing themes under the umbrella of global themes.

All ethical considerations were kept in mind during the data collection as well as during the analysis. Both written and oral informed consent was taken from participants. Personal details such as the names of the participants and other significant details were kept hidden. If the participants were not willing to be part of the study, they were not forced to contribute. If the participants wanted to withdraw during the data collection process, they were allowed to do so. There was no risk in participating.

4. Results and Discussion

This study focused on understanding the experience of the youth mentors in the DREAMS intervention program in their growth as authentic thought leaders. The participants were the college/university youth mentors currently pursuing an undergraduate degree, both boys and girls in the age group of 18-21 years from all over India and studying at Christ University. Through personal interviews and focus group discussions, the participants were interviewed, and the data was collected as audio recordings. These were later prepared verbatim which was used for the data analysis. Data trustworthiness was maintained using validation processes.

The study's results indicate that the innovative social initiative, DREAMS, which Christ University students undergo, increases their awareness and understanding of their growth as authentic thought leaders. The themes that emerged from data analysis are represented in Table 1. An authentic thought leader is a person who influences others using their innovative ideas and showing the followers their way of life.

Table 1. Objective – understanding the experiences of college youth mentors in the DREAMS intervention program in their growth as authentic thought leaders

Global Themes	Organizing Theme	Basic Themes
1. Complemented growth as an authentic thought leader	1.1 Emerging traits	1.1.1 Self-awareness
1.1.2 Innovative
1.1.2 Risk-taking behaviour
1.1.3 Strong belief
1.1.4 Consistency
1.1.5 Adaptable
1.1.6 Empathetic

1. Complemented Growth as an Authentic Thought Leader. The role of any educational institution is to complement the growth of its pupils using several strategies. These strategies need not be academically oriented; rather, they can be based on Howard Gardener's multiple intelligence (Gardner,

2000). Research clearly states that when students are given opportunities to engage in various activities, their learning increases multifold, and they do learn better (Darling-Hammond, 2010). Gardner also clarifies that when a student is looking into different perspectives, his/her knowledge deepens (Gardner, 2011). We can sum up by saying that individuation and pluralization posit that each individual differs from others by way of their learning and growth. Hence, the role of the higher education institution is very important, as value-based training and nurturing are being imparted to the younger generation. Value-based nurturing helps an individual to grow holistically with morals and values in his actions and behaviours (Herbst, 2003; Lambert et al., 2005). Value-based nurturing includes service learning also, as per the authors (Lester et al., 2005). Service-learning increases leadership qualities and propels the pupil to succeed in life. DREAMS has complemented the mentor's growth and propelled their holistic development at Christ University.

1.1. Emerging Traits. Mentors emerge as empowered thinkers with compassion to sow the seed for social change in the DREAMS intervention program. The process of helping, guiding and mentoring others empowers them to be socially conscious individuals with leadership qualities that can foresee the future. As seen from the above point on developing competencies, it is clear that youngsters involved in this program as mentors are developing leadership skills directly associated with competencies

1.1.1. Self-Awareness. A leader, who identifies his own competencies along with weaknesses, emerges as an effective leader and shows authenticity. An authentic thought leader is a person who shows his genuine, real self and guides and mentors those around him with his actions and behaviour. In this program, the mentors, too, show authentic thought leadership.

The following verbatims from individual interviews and the focus group discussions reveal how youngsters have developed self-awareness and become authentic thought leaders.

P 25 & P 60 Personal communications, 2020	"Helped me in developing key factors of an effective team leader."
P 21, P 36 & P 50 Personal communications, 2020	"Helped me to be a better leader with problem-solving skills in complex situations."
P 6 & P 76 Personal communications, 2020	"Contributed to my public speaking skills to be a leader."

Table. (Continued)

P 17 Focus group discussions, 2021	"Learned to plan ahead about each and every proceeding, and I pay a lot of attention to details, and the interaction makes me an authentic leader,
P 2, Focus group discussions, 2021	"Leaders usually lead, but I perceive myself as one who brings everyone together, where we can have an equal amount of discussion before coming to a solution together.
P 27, focus group discussions, 2021	"leading on my way of being in a group affects the way I am influencing the people, and so once I define and refine my thought process in the way I speak, I do not need to tell them I have to do things very explicitly as they will fall into the success automatically they might not be perfect, but I've tried to make them perfect so that I do not influence them in any wrong way I feel that observing and learning is one of the greatest things in which I contributed to developing leadership.

The main focus of authentic thought leadership is self-inquiry. This concept leads one from the inquiry level to the self-actualization level (Steffens et al., 2021) and to the final self-development (Gatling, Castelli, & Cole, 2013; Ilies et al., 2005; Walumbwa et al., 2008). The entire institution needs to focus on developing students' moral and ethical character, keeping in mind the diverse environment they are coming from (Minow et al., 2008). Several studies have mentioned that these programs are at times called character education, focusing on ethical knowledge and actions (Berkowitz & Bier, 2006; and preparing them for future leadership roles (Shek 2013); DREAMS is such an intervention program that brings in this among mentors and makes them aware of themselves to be an authentic thought leader. This awareness helps them to be aware of their strengths and weaknesses and, at the same time, helps them to capture the need of their mentees, which brings the compassion needed to provide help to them.

1.1.2 Innovative. A leader who shows a growth mindset with innovative ideas and creativity always thinks about how he/she can make things better for society/world. Always focus on the improvements in the tasks. They show openness and focus on the tasks, which brings positive results. The following are a few verbatims from the participants showing how they have learned to become innovative and also enhanced it in their journey with DREAMS.

P 4 Personal communications, 2020	I have gained the confidence to innovate strategies and activities relevant to the mentees.
P 22 Personal communications, 2020	I became curious to optimize the activities, which helped me to be innovative.
P 36 Personal communications, 2020	I have grown open-minded in the process, which led me towards more innovative ideas.
P 8, Focus group discussions, 2021	"In society, through people who take action to people who want to create an impact or change the way that things exist. You know, creating an impact that's beyond their daily life and is beyond just college or school or their normal day-to-day functioning is something that is created or is made for the good of other people. This is the best learning I have got."
P 3 Focus group discussions, 2021	"Instead of discussing the negatives that are present, and the things that you know, and that you need a lot of time to change, what we can do is start finding solutions, start finding innovative ways to solve problems that have existed for a long time. So I feel a leader plays a very important role in initiating this social change and bringing about social innovation. But once it's brought about, and once people start accepting it, it can really create an impact in the society and among people."

The above verbatims of the participants describe how DREAMS helped them to be open-minded and innovative. They also speak about the new possibilities that happened because of this innovative mindset (Todt et al., 2021). Several findings prove the correlation between innovation and authentic thought leadership (Avolio et al., 2004; Cerne et al., 2013). The competency to innovate is an important strength of an authentic thought leader because it helps him in his resilience and responsiveness. The DREAMS intervention provides college youth mentors with an opportunity to try innovative ideas and learn from their implementation. This is the same philosophy the model consistently establishes in their relationship with their mentees as well. Even during the pandemic, these college youth mentors were seen bringing in out-of-the-box strategies to connect with the mentees and helped them to continue the sessions without any hiccups. This connectivity and continuity were much needed during the pandemic to bring the mentees to focus on their overall development. Along with that, this helped them to cope with the uncertainty.

1.1.3 Risk-taking behaviour. A leader taking out-of-the-box ideas needs to be bold, confident and risk-taking. In this program, the mentors have brought in out-of-the-box ideas to roll out the program even during the pandemic without any glitches showing their risk-taking nature of them and also showing the characteristic of an authentic thought leader like many, namely Steve Jobs. The following are a few verbatims from the participants showing how they have learned the art of taking risks for a positive outcome and also enhanced it in their journey with DREAMS.

P 17 Personal communications, 2020	I didn't stop even during the pandemic – I motivated my peers and brought in new ideas, and implemented it.
P 28 Focus group discussions, 2021	Especially during the pandemic, it was like we were about to close it, but the program itself motivated us to bring in changes super-fast, and we did it.
P 54 Personal communications, 2020	We never bothered about the consequences. We just proceeded to implement the new ideas we know will bring in good for the mentees. This level of taking the risk came to me only from this program.

The above-mentioned verbatims clearly show the risk-taking behaviours of these leaders. Even in adversities, they stood firm and brought quick changes in the program, which benefited the mentees. Emotional safety and trust in others help the authentic thought leader to take the risk to innovate for a better future (Cerne et al., 2013). As mentioned in the study by Cerne et al. 2013, college youth mentors have shown this behaviour tremendously during the pandemic lockdown. Since the mentees are from an underprivileged background with not much financial and social support, through the DREAMS intervention program, they were supported to face the lockdown blues and dilemmas. The college youth mentors have taken all possible steps to reach out to these mentees and their families and continued to conduct the session online, which required a lot of strategic support. But because of these mentors' authentic thought leadership style, it became a possibility, and the mentees benefited from it.

1.1.4. Strong belief. Leaders who possess strong beliefs about what they think and do are highly valued in society. This absolute faith increases the confidence of the followers and brings in a positive outcome. The following are a few verbatims from the participants showing how they have learned to believe in themselves and also enhanced it in their journey with DREAMS.

P 1 Personal communications, 2020	I believed in myself – which helped me to bring in changes faster and quicker as this program promotes the concept of believing in self.
P 48 Personal communications, 2020	My strong belief in the program and the need for it for the mentees helped me to run it without any doubts – this brought the necessary impact on them.
P 14 Focus group discussions, 2021	I always believed in positivity and confidence – these are my traits – most of the time, these characteristics help me to move ahead – as this is the core of this program.

The above verbatims of the participants declare their strong confidence level and their belief in doing good. It is obvious these are the characteristics people admire and tend to follow too. These findings prove that focusing on the strength of a person is core to the authentic leadership style (Jensen & Luthans, 2006; Peterson & Luthans, 2003;). The term 'authentic' itself brings in the clarity of being natural and original and stems from 'trust' (Shamir & Eilam, 2005). In the DREAMS intervention program, the college youth mentors show this skill as big brother and big sister and role modelling to the mentees, which provided the mentees with a lot of learning. There are several success stories from the mentees on how they developed confidence and self-esteem and started to believe in themselves are testimonials for college youth mentors who believe in themselves.

1.1.5. Consistency. Authentic thought leaders show consistency in their ideas, are consistent in implementing their ideas and keep promoting innovative ideas wherever it is possible to their followers. The following are a few verbatims from the participants showing how they have learned consistency and also enhanced it in their journey with DREAMS.

P 9 Personal communications, 2020	We were consistent in our thoughts (ideas) and in our implementation of the program because consistency is highly recommended in the mentoring process – you cannot take the risk of losing your mentor's progress.

Table. (Continued)

P 58 Personal communications, 2020	Whether pandemic or not, we were consistent in our implementation of the program, which is our USP.
P 33 Focus group discussion, 2021	"We had many problems, and the program ended abruptly, and we had to restart it, but then we managed it somehow, so I feel all my leadership skills came into play. We tried to manage it, but I guess we managed it properly."
P 28, Focus group discussions, 2021	"In order to incorporate different views and maintain the calm in a situation like in your team would be, would be something that I think I've learned to kind of strike the middle ground and actually successfully implement that."

It is very critical for leaders to be consistent with their values, beliefs and actions (Walumbwa et al., 2008). Therefore, according to Sparrow (2005), self-consistency is one of the key predictors of authentic leadership. The followers are looking for consistency between what the leaders are communicating and their behaviours. This perceived degree of self-consistency makes the followers define a leader as authentic, and they follow. In the DREAMS intervention program, the college youth mentors show this skill outwardly and without any lagging, even during the pandemic period. Their consistency was a major helping factor in running the intervention session online without any difficulty. From wherever they were, they connected to the mentees via online platforms and continued their mentoring, which was a need of the hour during the pandemic. Most of the mentees were clueless and confused due to their families' financial conditions and lack of awareness about the pandemic. But with the handholding and consistent mentoring of the college youth mentors, the mentees have crossed this crucial period without many hiccups. This is the testimonial for the self-consistency of these authentic thought leaders.

1.1.6. Adaptable. Adapting themselves and helping their followers to adapt to the situation is one major trait of an authentic thought leader. The following are a few verbatims from the participants showing how they have learned adaptability and also enhanced it in their journey with DREAMS.

P 14, Personal communications, 2020	"Always adapting to the situations, this is what I have learned …during the pandemic, as many organizations, which were offline, suddenly switch to online communication, so it is very difficult to hold their attention. It is very important that other people stay motivated and take the initiatives to meet, discuss and work towards the goal we set in the pre-corona times."
P 1 Focus group discussions, 2021	"Being a leader is not just leading people to success but guiding and supporting them throughout the journey, Obstacles are faced in different ways as we all have varied perspectives, so the ability to understand the situation and an individual is something essential for a leader."
P 36 Focus group discussions, 2021	Approachable and accommodating, and adjusting is what is my mantra (P36 focus group discussions, 2021)

Thoughtful leaders are more adaptable at a higher level of their authenticity (Harris et al., 2018). Harris et al. (2018) state that when leaders are high in authenticity, they seem more adaptive in their approaches. Authentic leaders seem more adaptable to change and more cooperative with their followers and forming new relationships (Zahir & Narcikara, 2016). As Mahatma Gandhi said, be the change you want to see in the world. College youth mentors have role modelled their adaptable nature as big brothers and big sisters to their mentees. This helped the mentees from underprivileged backgrounds to learn the art and science of adaptability and the fruit of adaptability. Especially during the pandemic, this was very clearly evident that the college youth mentors have stood sternly on their belief in supporting the mentees through intervention sessions adapting quickly to the need of the hour and converting their sessions to online mode. Not only that but through their network, they have procured the facilities needed for the online sessions.

1.1.7 Empathy. It is not enough to just have an idea. Successful thought leaders can convey their ideas to an audience in a way that's relatable. Empathy plays an important role in reaching out and communicating with followers effectively. The following are a few verbatims from the participants showing how they have learned empathy and also enhanced it in their journey with DREAMS.

P1 Focus group discussions, 2021	"Being a leader is not just leading people to success but guiding and supporting them throughout the journey, Obstacles are faced in different ways as we all have varied perspectives, so the ability to understand the situation and an individual is something essential for a leader."
P 24, Personal communications, 2020	"I learned from DREAMS to be empathetic and to be understanding with my followers."

The above verbatim shows how these participants have learned the empathetic approach and enhanced it during the DREAMS intervention program, which contributed to their authentic thought leadership style. This finding gets support from the following study by Goldstein et al. (2014). When they show empathy to their followers, in this case with the mentees, it strengthens the amount of support and relationship with them and elicits a lot of positive feelings. The handholding nature of mentoring as big brother and big sister provided them with the needed learning on empathy and enhancing it as well.

To summarize, in this chapter, the DREAMS intervention program, the participants have clearly shown the characteristics of authentic thought leaders by projecting the following themes, namely self-awareness, innovation, risk-taking behaviour, self-belief, consistency, adaptability and empathy. These characteristics are evident from the verbatims listed above. As mentioned in the studies, the contributions of an individual who is aware of this to society are highly effective compared to others (Campbell et al., 1999). These authentic thought leaders would be highly conscious of what is happening around them (Markus et al., 1993; Rhoads, 1997) and will quickly adapt to the need. The role of higher educational institutions (HEIs) is to provide training for these skill sets. One of the methods for training is through social service/social innovative activities through community service (Tucker et al., 1998). Through this, they can help an individual in their professional growth and also become global leaders (Pless et al., 2017). This is evident from the experiences of the college youth mentors of the DREAMS intervention programme.

5. Limitations

A mixed research method with a quantitative questionnaire for measuring leadership would give additional information to understand these variables. Due to the lockdown and pandemic, the qualitative part of the study was conducted through an online platform. A face-to-face interaction, both individually and in FGD, would have been better for the exploration of the concepts and constructs.

Conclusion

This study is a preliminary attempt to understand how the DREAMS intervention programme is helping college youth mentors to gain authentic thought leadership, which is imperative for their success and for the world. This study brings clarity to how the college youth mentors have developed these characteristics and their vision of how it will benefit them in the outside world. These kinds of programmes are in great need because the world has been undergoing tremendous change in recent years due to several unexpected happenings. We need to prepare the next generation to equip themselves to face uncertainties. However, some limitations are listed here for exploration. As the famous quote by Ruth Badar Ginsberg, "Who will take responsibility for the next generation?" – the major responsibility is with us, the academics and academic institutions. Intervention programs like DREAMS can be promoted and inculcated in the curriculum to start the training as early as possible to kindle the young mind.

Conflict of Interest

The primary investigator and the co-investigators declared no conflict of interest.

Acknowledgements

The investigators would like to acknowledge Ms Namrata V Warrier and Ms Ananya R Shankar for their help in the FGD and the transcript preparation.

References

Ames, C. (1992). Classrooms: Goals, structures, and student motivation. *Journal of Educational Psychology, 84*, 261-271.

Archer, J. (1994). Achievement goals as a measure of motivation in university students. *Contemporary Educational Psychology, 19*, 430-446.

Arena, M., Cross, R., Sims, J., & Uhl-Bien, M. (2017). How to catalyze innovation in your organization. *MIT Sloan Management Review, 58*(4), 39–47.

Avolio, B. J., & Gardner, W. L. (2005). Authentic leadership development: Getting to the root of positive forms of leadership. *Leadership Quarterly, 16*, 315-338.

Avolio, B. J., Gardner, W. L., Walumbwa, F. O., Luthans, F., & May, D. R. (2004). Unlocking the mask: A look at the process by which authentic leaders impact follower attitudes and behaviours. *Leadership Quarterly, 15*, 801-823.

Berkowitz, M. & Bier, M. (2006). *What works in character education: A research-driven guide for educators*. Center for Character and Citizenship.

Boss, J. A. (1994) The effect of community service work on the moral development of college ethics students. *Journal of Moral Education, 23*, 183-198.

Butler, R. (1987). Task-involving and ego-involving properties of evaluation: Effects of different feedback conditions on motivational perceptions, interest, and performance. *Journal of Educational Psychology, 79*, 474-482.

Campbell, L., Gulas, C. S., &Gruca, T. S. (1999). *Corporate Giving Behavior and Decision-Maker Social Consciousness*. Springer, 375-383.

Černe, M., Jaklič, M., & Škerlavaj, M. (2013). Authentic leadership, creativity, and innovation: A multilevel perspective. *Leadership, 9*(1), 63–85. https://doi.org/10.1177/1742715012455130

Chow, P., Thompson, I. S., Wood, W., Beauchamp, M., & Lebrun, R. (2002). Comparing The Personal Development of College Students, High School Students, With Prison Inmates. *Education, 123*(1).

Church, M. A., Elliot, A. J., & Gable, S. L. (2001). Perceptions of classroom environment, achievement goals, and achievement outcomes. *Journal of Educational Psychology, 93*, 43-54.

Covington, M. V. (1999). Caring about learning: The nature and nurturing of subject matter appreciation. *Educational Psychologist, 34*, 127-136.

Darling-Hammond, L. (2010). Performance Counts: Assessment Systems That Support High-Quality Learning. *Council of Chief State School Officers*.

DeAva, M. L. (1999). Education: A liberating tool. *Diabetes Spectrum, 12*(3), 116-132.

Demoulin, D. F. (2002). A student's creditability and personal development are essential elements for college success. *College Student Journal, 36*(3), 373-380.

Duckworth, A. L., Steen, T. A., & Seligman, M. E. P. (2005). Positive psychology in clinical practice. *Annual Review of Clinical Psychology, 1*(1), 629–651.

Dweck, C. S. (1986). Motivational processes affect learning. *American Psychologist, 41*, 1040-1048.

Dweck, C. S., & Leggett, E. L. (1988). A social-cognitive approach to motivation and personality. *Psychological Review, 95*, 256-273.

Eyler, J., & Giles Jr, D. E. (1999). *Where's the Learning in Service-Learning?* Jossey-Bass Higher and Adult Education Series.

Gardner, H. E. (2000). *Intelligence reframed: Multiple intelligences for the 21st century.* Hachette.

Gardner, H.E. (2011). *Frames of mind: The theory of multiple intelligences.* Hachette.

Gardner, W. L., Avolio, B. J., Luthans, F., May, D. R., & Walumbwa, F. (2005). "Can you see the real me?" A selfbased model of authentic leader and follower development. *Leadership Quarterly,* 16, 343-372.

Gatling, A. R., Castelli, P. A., & Cole, M. L. (2013). Authentic Leadership: The Role of Self-Awareness in Promoting Coaching Effectiveness. *Asia-Pacific Journal of Management Research and Innovation,* 9(4), 337–347. https://doi.org/10.1177/2319510X14523097

Goldstein N.J., Vezich I.S. & Shapiro J.R. (2014) Perceived perspective taking: when others walk in our shoes. *Journal of Personality and Social Psychology* 106 (6), 941–960.

Harris, B., Cardador, T., Cole, M., Mistry, S., & Kirkman, B. (2018). Are followers satisfied with conscientious leaders? The moderating influence of leader role authenticity. *Journal of Organizational Behavior.* 40(4), 456-471.

Herbst J.D. (2003). *Organizational Servant Leadership and its Relationship to Secondary School Effectiveness.* PhD Thesis, Florida Atlantic University.

Ilies, R., Morgeson, F. P., Nahrgang, J. D. (2005). Authentic leadership and eudaemonic well-being: Understanding leader-follower outcomes. *The Leadership Quarterly,* 16(3), 373–394.

Jensen, S. M., & Luthans, F. (2006). Relationship between Entrepreneurs' Psychological Capital and Their Authentic Leadership. *Journal of Managerial Issues,* 18(2), 254–273.

Kern, M. L., Waters, L. E., Adler, A., & White, M. A. (2015). A multidimensional approach to measuring well-being in students: Application of the PERMA framework. *The Journal of Positive Psychology, 10*(3), 262-271.

Kielsmeier, J. C. (2010). Build a Bridge between Service and Learning. *The Phi Delta Kappan, 91(5),* 8-15.

Kirschman, K. J. B., Roberts, M. C., Shadlow, J. O., & Pelley, T. J. (2010). An evaluation of hope following a summer camp for inner-city youth. In *Child & Youth Care Forum* (Vol. 39, No. 6, pp. 385-396). Springer.

Lambert, W. E., Miears, L. D., Anderson, K. P., Irving, J. A., Iken, S. L., Krebs, K. D., &Arfsten, D. J. (2005). Servant leadership qualities of principals, organizational climate, and student achievement: A correlational study, *Dissertation abstracts International,* 66(2).

Lemieux, C.M, & Allen, P.D. (2007) Service Learning in Social Work Education: The State of Knowledge, Pedagogical Practicalities, and Practice Conundrums, *Journal of Social Work Education,* 43(2), 309-326

Lester, S. W., Tomkovick, C., Wells, T., Flunker, L., & Kickul, J. (2005). Does service-learning add value? Examining the perspectives of multiple stakeholders. *Academy of Management Learning & Education,* 4(3), 278-294.

Levesque, J., & Prosser, T. (1996). Service-learning connections. *Journal of Teacher Education, 47*(5), 325-334.

Luthans, F., & Avolio, B. J. (2003). Authentic leadership development. In R. E. Quinn (Ed.), *Positive organizational scholarship* (pp. 241-261). Barrett-Koehler.

Marais, J. D., Yang, Y., & Farzanehkia, F. (2000). Service-Learning Leadership Development for Youths. *The Phi Delta Kappan,* 678-680.

Markus, G. B., Howard, J., & King, D. 1993. Integrating community service and classroom instruction enhances learning: Results from an experiment. *Educational Evaluation and Policy Analysis. 15*(4), 410-419.

Minow, M., Shweder, R., & Markus, H. (Eds.). (2008). *Just schools: Pursuing equality in societies of difference.* Russell Sage Foundation.

Mintzberg, H., & Gosling, J. (2002). *Educating managers beyond borders.* Academy of Management Learning & Education, 1(1), 64-76.

Nicholls, J. G. (1984). Achievement motivation: Conceptions of ability, subjective experience, task choice, and performance. *Psychological Review, 91*(3), 328-346.

Peterson, S.J. and Luthans, F. (2003) The Positive Impact and Development of Hopeful Leaders. *Leadership & Organization Development Journal,* 24, 26-31. http://dx.doi.org/10.1108/01437730310457302

Pless, N. M., Maak, T.& Stahl, G. K. (2017). *Developing Responsible Global Leaders Through International Service-Learning Programs: The Ulysses Experience.* Academy of Management.

Prosser, T. M., & Levesque, J. A. (1997). Supporting literacy through service learning. *The Reading Teacher, 51*(1), 32-38.

Rhoads, R. A. 1997. *Community service and higher learning: Explorations of the caring self.* SUNY.

Segrott, J., Rothwell, H., & Thomas, M. (2013). Creating safe places: an exploratory evaluation of a school-based emotional support service. *Pastoral care in education, 31*(3), 211-228.

Seligman, M. E., Ernst, R. M., Gillham, J., Reivich, K., & Linkins, M. (2009). Positive education: Positive psychology and classroom interventions. *Oxford Review of Education, 35*(3), 293-311.

Shamir B and Eilam G (2005) 'What's your story?' A life-stories approach to authentic leadership development. *The Leadership Quarterly* 16(3): 395–417.

Shek, D. T. (2013). Promotion of holistic development in university students. *Best Practices in Mental Health,* 9(1), 47-61.

Sparrowe, R. T. (2005). Authentic leadership and the narrative self. *Leadership Quarterly, 16*(3), 419–439.

Steffens, N. K., Wolyniec, N., Okimoto, T. G., Mols, F., Haslam, S. A., & Kay, A. A. (2021). *Knowing me, knowing us: Personal and collective self-awareness enhances authentic leadership and leader endorsement. The Leadership Quarterly,32(6), 101498.* https://doi.org/10.1016/j.leaqua.2021.101498

Thomas, L. (2014). *Evaluation of the DREAMS Program: An Intervention Model* for *The Success of Low Performing Middle School Students. PhD Thesis,* University of Louisiana. Monroe.

Todt, G., Weiss, M., Hoegl, M., (2019). Leading Through Innovation Project Setbacks: How Authentic Leaders Keep Their Innovators Resilient. *Project Management Journal, 50(4), 409–417.* https://doi.org/10.1177/8756972819853124

Tucker, M. L., McCarthy, A. M., Hoxmeier, J. A., & Lenk, M. M. (1998). Community service-learning increases communication skills across the business curriculum. *Business Communication Quarterly, 61*(2), 88-99.

Turner, J. H. (1998). *The Structure of sociological theory* (6th ed.). Wadsworth Publishing Company.

Walumbwa, F.O., Avolio, B.J., Gardner, W.L., Wernsing, T.S., Peterson, S.J. (2008). Authentic leadership: Development and Validation of a Theory-based measure. *Journal of Management,* 34(1),89-126. https://doi.org/10.1177/0149206307308913

Zehir, C., Narcıkara, E., (2016). Effects of Resilience on Productivity under Authentic Leadership. *Procedia - Social and Behavioral Sciences,* 235, 250–258. https://doi.org/10.1016/j.sbspro.2016.11.021

Chapter 16

Service-Learning: A Pathway to Social Responsibility

Rory L. Bedford[1,*]
Ellen D. Smiley[2,†]
and Prentiss C. Smiley[3,‡]

[1]Continuing Education and Service-Learning, Grambling State University, Louisiana, USA
[2]Earl Lester Cole Honors College, Grambling State University, Louisiana, USA
[3]Grambling State University, Louisiana, USA

Abstract

Studies show that when service is a component of classroom learning, students are more likely to stay in school, graduate, and become engaged in their communities throughout their lives. Thus, the world becomes stronger because of a better-educated, well-rounded workforce with practical experience that is realized through an application.

In order to gain this experience, many educators are beginning to use an innovative academic interactive learning tool defined as service-learning or experiential learning. In addition to contributing to the quality of human capital, service learning is credited with increasing retention, persistence, and graduation rates at universities. Students who participate in meaningful service identify with groups and develop pillars of support to enhance their university experience. This chapter will provide examples of service-learning engagement activities that support

---
[*] Corresponding Author's Email: bedfordr@gram.edu.
[†] Corresponding Author's Email: smileye@gram.edu.
[‡] Corresponding Author's Email: smileyp@gram.edu.

In: Models for Social Responsibility Action by Higher Education Institutions
Editors: Joseph Chacko Chennattuserry, Elangovan N. et al.
ISBN: 979-8-89113-097-5
© 2024 Nova Science Publishers, Inc.

sustaining social, ecological, environmental, technical, and economic development toward promoting social responsibility. It will also chronicle the establishment of a successful service-learning program and show its impact on retention at a select University based on information acquired from the University's fact book. To remain anonymous, the University will be referred to as University X.

1. Introduction

Service-Learning/Experiential Learning has a significant effect on student retention, grade point average, and graduation rates (Mungo, 2017). In fact, as evidenced in a study by Reed et al., (2015), experiential learning pedagogy is a major contributor to undergraduate persistence. Students who participate in meaningful service identify with groups and develop pillars of support to enhance their university experience. As more students persist and graduate, the world becomes stronger because of a better-educated, well-rounded workforce with practical experience that is realized through an application. The overarching effect contributes to the quality of human capital in the workplace. Regardless of the academic discipline, service learning can help students better understand the value of their major.

This chapter looks at University X, a university where students are at risk of dropping out and never returning to school or stopping out and returning years later, and the perceived impact that implementing service-learning across the curriculum from the freshman to senior level has had on retention. The consistent level of relevant engagement provides opportunities for students and faculty to develop and implement sustainable social, ecological, environmental, technical, and economic development projects.

2. Background

2.1. Defining Service-Learning

Since the beginning of the service-learning movement, Campus Compact has been recognized as the authority as it relates to experiential learning and student engagement. While there are numerous definitions of service learning, practitioners normally rely on Campus Compact for a universal definition. Campus Compact defines service-learning as "incorporating "community work into the curriculum, giving students real-world learning experiences that enhance their academic learning while providing a tangible benefit for the community." Service-Learning is hyphenated to demonstrate equality of service and learning. In other words, the service component of the project is just as important as the learning component.

University X has two forms of service learning. Academic service-learning and community service service-learning. The University defines academic service-learning as projects assigned by the professor, linked to the objectives of the class, and count towards the final grade. On the other hand, community service service-learning is volunteer service that builds on one's educational foundation but is not necessarily directed through a classroom setting.

2.2. Developing the Service-Learning Program

University X is a member of an educational system that envisioned that students at member institutions would be extended an opportunity to have meaningful service-learning experiences prior to graduation. In order to ready the campus for service-learning activities, University X established the Office of Service-Learning in the fall semester of 2008 as the hub for service-learning faculty training, coordinating the engagement and recording service-learning activities.

Students are required to complete at least 160 hours of service-learning in preparation for "citizenship in a democratic society." Eighty hours of academic service-learning and eighty hours of community service service-learning hours should be achieved. It is important to note that the hours are not clock hours; they are project hours that are determined by the director and associates within the project approval process.

The design of the program designates certain courses as service-learning courses at each level of matriculation to ensure continuous engagement. For example, sections in the following courses are designated as service-learning courses: Freshman English; College Survival (First Year Experience); Freshman Mathematics; and others. In addition, upper-level courses are selected to provide opportunities for the students. Community partners have been identified, and the program has expanded over the years.

In order to ensure a quality program with meaningful outcomes, a mechanism is in place to train faculty regarding implementing service learning into the classroom and the course project approval process. In addition, as it relates to community service service-learning, forms and a prior approval process are in place for students and organizations. Finally, an electronic record-keeping process and database track service-learning engagement. Prior to graduation, the Office of Service-Learning certifies that students have completed the necessary requirements.

At University X, engaging students in service-learning/experiential learning has proven to impact retention and persistence rates. The increase in retention parallels the implementation of the service-learning program. While University X has incorporated several other programs and processes to increase retention, they are ever-changing, and some lack the longevity of leadership and consistency. After the development and implementation of the program, opportunities for meaningful engagement have increased, and so has the retention rate.

As stated earlier, of all the factors that impact persistence and retention, it appears that the only identifiable, common, consistent thread for all undergraduate students enrolled at University X is service learning/experiential learning. Evidence is provided below in Table 1 University X Retention Rates that reflects retention rates for a 5-year period after the institutionalization of the service-learning program. Data prior to the 5-year period show a similar trend.

Table 1. University X Retention Rates

Semester Fall to Fall	2015 - 2016	2016 - 2017	2017- 2018	2018 - 2019	2019 - 2020
Cohort (Starting Year)	618	846	906	896	855
Students Returning First Year	372	575	656	667	659
Percentage	60.19%	68.70%	72.41%	74.44%	77.07%
Students Returning Second Year	273	451	501	495	---
Percentage	73.38%	78.43%	76.37%	74.21%	---
Student Returning to the Third Year	221	381	416	---	
Percentage	80.95%	84.47%	83.03%	---	
Students Returning to the Fourth Year	159	248	---		
Percentage	25%	29%			

Source: (University X, Factbook and the Office of Institutional Effectiveness).

3. Discussion

University X has developed many sustainable projects that promote social responsibility. Each project has found its success in the leadership and commitment of not only the faculty but also the students. Student-led projects that possess a passion for a worthy cause tend to be sustainable and are continued by others with similar goals and objectives. Some successful sustainable projects will be discussed in the remainder of the chapter.

3.1. Social

While all service-learning projects that involve teamwork and group activities, in general, promote social development, some projects are strategically developed to sustain social development. Such is the case with the project "Using Movies to Develop Leadership Skills." The project paired University students with middle school students to identify and develop leadership skills. The University students selected the movies to be shown and developed a worksheet to define the various leadership styles and techniques. While developing the project, the University students enhanced their leadership skills by becoming responsible for the curriculum and workshop delivery. The workshop covered the span of 5 days. On the fifth day, middle schoolers were awarded a certificate from their university mentors and the Office of Continuing Education and Service-Learning.

Over the course of the workshop, movies were used to demonstrate leadership skills. The middle schoolers began to express what type of leadership qualities they wanted to possess. They also began to identify with various leaders observed in the movie and, ironically, leaders among the University students. To enhance the experience, higher education leaders from the campus were selected for the students to shadow for a day. This presented an environment of leadership observed among the movie figures, leadership observed among the University student leaders, leadership observed among their peers (the middle schoolers), and leadership observed among higher education leaders. In each instance, social skills were enhanced.

The University students worked together to develop social skills among the middle schoolers. However, by working on the project, the University students enhanced their social development and became more aware of the necessity to strengthen social development. This project has continued over the years and was only interrupted recently because of COVID-19 restrictions.

3.2. Ecological and Environmental

Recognizing that water pollution is a serious problem, a biology professor engaged her students in a service-learning project that helped to eliminate waste that could ultimately land in streams and other waterways. Students cleared drainage ditches and other areas that led to rivers and streams and identified the type of waste that was being discarded. In addition, the professor taught in-service teachers how to test water for its quality. In turn, the in-service teachers (K-12) taught their students how to test water quality. This project helped young students become aware of the impact of waste on the environment and water quality. Early awareness of the disadvantages of unclean water instils in the students the necessity to eliminate litter.

In another project geared to address ecological and environmental issues, students and faculty partnered with their state affiliate of Keep America Beautiful. The students and faculty representatives hosted awareness sessions about sustainability and the need to recycle to reduce litter. The students manned an information booth in front of the student union at times when foot traffic was heaviest. Students educated others about the problems associated with not recycling and the benefits of recycling. They then asked other students if they would support a self-assessed fee to promote recycling.

The campaign continued for several days. At the appropriate time, student leaders, in conjunction with the Office of Service-Learning, drafted a bill for the ballot to be voted on by the student body. The fee passed. Students continue to engage in recycling projects at the University, and the fee continues to be collected.

3.3. Economic Development

Service-Learning allows students to serve beyond their immediate community. In partnership with Canduit, students are able to conduct virtual service learning with international economic impact. Canduit is "a cloud-based Software-as-a-Service platform that enables universities to host company-sponsored projects for their students while creating a collaborative environment where users can engage in project-based learning with companies and gain real-world experience."

One successful project paired an English major with "Abriendo Mentes." Abriendo Mentes is "a nonprofit organization operating in two rural villages in Guanacaste, Costa Rica." The nonprofit's purpose since 2009 has been to provide education and community development resources geared towards enhancing the lives of the residents and "breaking the cycle of poverty."

The focus of the project was to boost economic development in the country through tourism. Tourism is one of the driving forces behind the economy in Costa Rica. For jobs in tourism, being able to speak English is a requirement. Unfortunately, a minimal number of adults in the area meet this requirement. Therefore, there was a need for someone to teach online English classes to residents in Costa Rica.

The project promoted adults learning to speak English so that they could gain employment that would enhance the tourism industry towards increasing economic development. The student created lesson plans and taught on an online platform for 1 hour two times per week. The student also administered tests to those she taught during the service experience. Projects such as these are easily sustainable because of the minimal resources needed to ensure the continuation of the engagement.

3.4. Technical

We live in a world where technology is the guiding tenant for most processes. This became even more evident when COVID-19 began a worldwide pandemic. This phenomenon caused people across the world to depend on technology more in order to conduct business and even address medical issues. Thus, telehealth became the norm. Purchasing items and paying bills online became a way of life. One of the groups that had to adjust to this phenomenon most was the elderly. Unfortunately, many of them lack the skills to use technology and find it frustrating to manoeuvre.

As a sophomore at the University, a student had developed a service-learning project and invited some of his peers to assist by helping to teach people over 50 how to use technology. The project paired people over 50 with college students who taught them how to use the internet; how to set up email accounts; how to safely shop online; and other everyday uses for the computer, cell phone, and other technologies. The students and participants became very close during the project. At the end of the program, the student project leader gave his telephone number to the group and said, "Remember to call me if you have any questions in the future."

Over the course of the next few years, the project leader would hear from the participants every now and then. On occasions, he would see one of them out shopping or at a gathering. As the years passed, the student graduated from undergraduate and graduate school. As time went on, the calls became less frequent, and the sightings were minimal. The young man lost touch with his former students, aged 50 and above. And then, one day, believe it or not, some of the participants and their friends began contacting the young man during the pandemic for guidance with technology.

While they continued to use technology, there were new ways to engage that they needed help with, such as Zoom, Facebook, Teams, Canvas, Moodle, Blackboard, and other modes of delivery. Their church services, meetings, and visits with children and grandchildren had been transformed. They needed to understand how to operate in this new environment.

Although he was no longer a student, the young man engaged with those who called and their friends to assist them virtually so that they could continue to function despite the limitations imposed by the new normal, one may ask why the young man felt compelled to assist with no financial gain for his service. The answer is simple; Service-Learning and the value added promote social responsibility. After engaging in numerous projects, and in the case of this young man, over 160 hours of service-learning projects, he had a moral and ethical obligation to help.

Conclusion

In our opinion, social responsibility is a learned behaviour. While there may be other methods to help students learn social responsibility, by far, participating in service projects is one of the best. When properly implemented, the cycle of service-learning forms the foundation for social responsibility. The cycle, according to The Educators Consortium for Service-Learning, includes 1. The investigation, 2. Preparation and Planning, 3. Action, 4. Reflection, and 5. Demonstration. Collectively the components of the cycle provide levels of understanding that increase the knowledge base and sensitivity towards the need being addressed, thus, forming the foundation for social responsibility and building on that foundation each time engagement occurs. The feeling of adding value to the lives of others and giving back to society becomes an embedded social responsibility. Those who practice social responsibility can impact future generations by encouraging them to participate in socially responsible acts and mentoring them through the process.

References

Mungo, M. H. (2017). Closing the Gap : Can Service-Learning Enhance Retention, Graduation, and GPAs of Students of Color? *Michigan Journal of Community Service Learning, 23*(2), 42-52.

Reed, S. C., Rosing, H., Rosenberg, H., & Statham, A. (2015). Let us pick the organization: understanding adult student perceptions of service-learning Practice. *Journal of Community Engagement and Scholarship, 8*(2), 74.

Chapter 17

Self-Reflective Learning: A Didactic Model for the Development of the Professional Identity of Social Work Students During the Practical Phase in the Context of the COVID Pandemic

Grit Höppner[*]
Sabine Ader[†]
and Swantje Notzon[‡]

Department of Social Work, Catholic University of Applied Sciences, Münster, Germany

Abstract

The development of a professional identity is one of the primary goals of social work studies. For the professional qualification of students, the practical phase is a critical period. Especially in times of crisis like the one resulting from the Covid pandemic, professors are responsible for developing didactic models that support students in the development of their professional identity during this phase.

This chapter presents a didactic model for a self-reflective learning process, which we, the authors, have developed and tested to help students to develop a professional identity. The model is based on sequence analyses of so-called micro-stories conducted in seminar groups. First, we elaborate on the importance for students of self-

---

[*] Corresponding Author's Email: g.hoeppner@katho-nrw.de.
[†] Corresponding Author's Email: s.ader@katho-nrw.de.
[‡] Corresponding Author's Email: s.notzon@katho-nrw.de.

In: Models for Social Responsibility Action by Higher Education Institutions
Editors: Joseph Chacko Chennattuserry, Elangovan N. et al.
ISBN: 979-8-89113-097-5
© 2024 Nova Science Publishers, Inc.

reflective and case-based approaches to practice for this developmental task. Next, we present a rigorously developed didactic model for self-reflective learning during the Covid pandemic, as well as the findings generated through its testing in different student groups. Finally, we discuss both the added value and the limitations of this didactic model in the context of the social responsibility of the protagonists engaged in the process of supporting the development of students' professional identities.

Keywords: self-reflective learning, professional identity as a social worker, case-based learning, sequence analysis, social responsibility, Corona pandemic

1. Introduction

The Covid pandemic has had many effects on social work. The fields of action are challenged in different ways due to their various structures, conceptual-methodological orientations, and offerings, as well as the needs of the addressees. Particularly at the beginning of the pandemic, there was hope that the systemic relevance of social professions would lead to an upgrading of these activities (Becka et al., 2020). In fact, rapid development in the field of digitalization of social work resulted in the increased availability of online services (Bergougnan & Fondeville, 2021). The failure of many services was a cause for concern because it was feared that the situation of clients would deteriorate (Lorenz, 2021, p. 14). The situation of students, for whom learning processes were suddenly taking place almost exclusively online, was also discussed and researched (Misamer et al., 2021). Less attention was paid to the question of how the pandemic might affect practical study phases in social work. When practical-training institutions change or reduce their offerings, this influences students who complete their practical phase there. These students may have fewer opportunities to try things out but may also have different responsibilities from the ones they had before the pandemic. They also experience the pandemic's burden on their clients and the exacerbated psychosocial problems (Butterwegge, 2021; Wagner, 2020).

As professors in a university social work program, the questions of what social work students understand by the term professional identity and how they experience the development of their own professional identity in practice against the background of the current pandemic are particularly urgent for us, because the associated changes and restrictions could get in the way of an essential goal of the program: to support students in the formation of a professional identity.

2. Review of Literature

There is a broad professional discourse on the concept of professional identity (e.g., Becker-Lenz et al., 2013; 2012). There are different understandings of what the defining factors of professional identity are and how they relate to each other. A common definition in the German-speaking area is that of von Spiegel (2018), for whom one's professional identity is the sum of the following areas of competence:

- Knowledge and understanding (descriptive knowledge, explanatory knowledge, understanding values, understanding change),
- A professional attitude (professional motivation, professional ethics, values-based standards),
- Methodological skills (capacity for communicative action, etc.).

There are some studies that examined the development of professional identity in social work students in the period before the Covid pandemic: Wiles (2013, 2017) interviewed seven social work students who were concluding their studies. She found that students sometimes associated professional identity as a social worker with certain desired characteristics, sometimes constructed a shared identity with other social workers, and sometimes described the development of professional identity as a very individual process. Wiles sees the development of professional identity as a "key aim of social work education" (Wiles, 2017, p. 2) and concludes that it is important to provide spaces for reflection in the curriculum to support this development. Bruno and Dell'Aversana (2018) analyzed 21 journals of master's degree students in social work in which the students reflected on their experiences during a seminar that used the "work-integrated learning" approach. According to the authors, the seminar helped students develop professional expertise; the reflection journal and feedback on that journal fostered professional self-awareness, and the social relationships with the learning group facilitated a sense of belonging.

Shlomo et al. (2012) surveyed 160 students who had just completed their bachelor's degree in social work using questionnaires. They found that the development of professional identity is supported by one's satisfaction with supervision and by personal values. In another study, 1245 first-year students in social and health-related disciplines were surveyed about their professional identity. Cognitive flexibility, prior professional experience in social or health professions, a better understanding of teamwork, and self-reported greater knowledge of their discipline correlated with a more pronounced professional identity (Adams et al., 2006).

Wheeler (2017) interviewed nine social work students in practice and five supervisors of students in practice on professional identity development. She concluded that professional identity develops in interactions between students and supervisors, but also among students and between students and addresses.

The empirical studies cited provide clear indications that didactic models that support the development of professional identity are particularly useful in the study of social work. It is true that the formation of a professional identity is to be understood as an individual process to which various factors contribute. However, self-reflection plays an important role in this process. Our goal was, therefore, to make conscious use of the irritant of the Covid pandemic in a didactic model aimed at promoting self-reflection.

In this chapter, we first elaborate on the importance for students of self-reflective and case-based approaches to practice in this developmental task. We then present our rigorously developed didactic model for self-reflective learning during the Covid pandemic, as well as the findings generated in the testing of that model in student groups. Finally, we discuss the added value as well as the limitations of the didactic model in social work in the context of the social responsibility of the protagonists who support the development of professional identity.

3. Self-Reflective and Case-Based Approaches to Practice: Reflective Learning from Observations and Narratives

The goal of practice-based courses is for students to analyze and reflect on their own practical experiences. This involves both subject- and field-specific content as well as reflection on individual experiences in the conflict area between person, role, and institution. Students often remain unaware of the importance of institutional, economic, sociopolitical, and legal framework conditions for professional action until they reach the supervised practice phase of their social work studies. Through the theory-practice relationship and (self-)reflective processing in the corresponding courses, professional identity can thus develop gradually (cf. Becker-Lenz et al., 2012).

In the developed didactic model, case-based work is considered extremely beneficial for the development of professional identity during the study, which opens up students' possibilities for learning through the reflective and self-reflective consideration of social work practice as it is experienced (cf. Ader, 2021). Reflection and self-reflection are counted among the constitutive components of comprehensive professional competence, as are theoretical knowledge and understanding, a professional attitude, and methodological skills. The central concern of case-based work is to understand a case more precisely and to learn about these insights. The concept of a case is a broad one. The focus of a real-life observation can be on addressees and their lives as well as on one's own professional action or specific structural and action-governing conditions of social work. In these contexts, it is always a matter of a professional quest that broadens the individual professional perspective of the student bringing the case and unfolds the complexity of a social situation more broadly so that the object of analysis and understanding initially becomes even more complex than it usually already is. It is about becoming aware of and displacing practiced patterns of perception and interpretation - which means it is also always about self-reflection. For the framing of this "work of understanding," Hörster (2018) names three central structural features:

- A thorough *case report* (written description or narrative of an action situation, oral narrative, audio/video recording).
- A *learning and educational space*, i.e., a place for reflection independent of any action.
- *Displacement*, i.e., a temporal and spatial decoupling from the actual situation, interrupts the ordinariness of understanding and makes it possible to recognize new horizons of meaning within it.

The specific opportunity of such a structured place of reflection lies in the fact that fields of tension in professional practice can be mirrored and taken up here. Case-based learning essentially means learning from a real situation, and this is by creating a tense (learning) space between the poles of *distance and proximity*, between *cognitive-analytical thoughtfulness* and *perceptible affectivity*. If real situations from professional practice are brought into university courses, a distancing from the real experienced event inevitably occurs. With the benefit of time, students can adopt a bird's-eye view and engage in thoughtful consideration of what they have experienced. At the same time, the cases brought to seminars always remain linked to the experiences, emotions, and internal images of those who bring them along. Without having one's own practical experience, it is far more theoretical, less emotional, and easier to talk about closeness and distance than when, for example, a furious child in a residential group has spat in a student's face, for it is only with this experience that the child's anger, perhaps also despair or fear, can be felt, or indeed fright, degradation, or disgust on the part of the student herself. The power of the case-based space lies precisely in this *tension of cognitive-analytical distancing (from the real situation) and emotional participation* because - unlike before the accompanying practice phase - there are now views, effects, and an inner experience of the practical situations. Students often find this way of appropriating information easily; it generates personal interest through the emotional content of the case description and enables the dialectic of cognition and emotion.

At the same time, the relationship between *understanding a case and general understanding* can be understood and practiced in case-based work. In practice, social work professionals are confronted daily with the complexity and unpredictability of life, often with challenging life situations and the sometimes-idiosyncratic coping strategies of addresses. Their actions take place within the structural uncertainty of social situations (cf. Thiersch, 2002; Klatetzki, 1993), which are unique and must always be understood anew. In social work, the relevant know-how consists of a canon of various bodies of knowledge that must be used in a comprehensible and well-founded way to understand, interpret and intervene. Only in this way can professionals do justice to the uniqueness of each situation, which at the same time does not release them from explaining their own actions based on theory and classifying the individual case under the aspect of the "general" (cf. Müller, 2012). The dialectical relationship between the general and the requires both knowledge about a particular topic and the hermeneutic ability to reconstruct and understand the individuality of the case.

The precise way in which the individual case reveals itself in such a learning setting always remains (initially) bound to the person who perceives this case as a case. The recording of complex situations and case descriptions always take place in a selection process; perception and exploration are never 'purely objective' but also always the product of the author: case descriptions are always an individual construct. While constructing a professional identity, casework requires the development of both analytical and classifying competence as well as the capacity to communicate and understand (cf. Heiner, 2004).

Against this background, our goal was to develop and test a didactic model that facilitates case-based learning in the practice phase of social work studies. We wanted to consider and reflect on the challenges posed by the Corona pandemic, especially regarding the potentially changed possibilities of professional identity development.

4. Methodology

In this section, we first present our didactic model for self-reflective learning (cf. Höppner et al., 2022), then the results generated in the testing of the model in three different seminar groups.

4.1. Description of the Didactic Model

So that students could experience the importance of self-reflective learning and reveal what for them would be new, untraveled paths toward knowledge, we developed a specific didactic model and tested it with students in the fifth semester of the bachelor's Program in Social Work at the Catholic University of Applied Sciences, Münster, Germany. This semester, the students complete a six-month practical phase in institutions covering various fields of social work. The students are guided by lecturers in a weekly seminar. Each seminar consists of a fixed group of 11 to 14 students who work together over the entire period.

The didactic model developed comprises the following steps:

Step One: Contextualization of the project as preparation for the students for the self-reflective learning process.

With the help of a professional stimulus, the importance of self-reflective learning for the acquisition of professional identity in social work is explained to the students. It is made clear that self-reflective processes can be triggered, for example, by understanding so-called micro-stories (Wilke, 2004, pp. 89 ff.). A micro-story is a situation or a key experience that the students have faced during the practical phase. The student writes down the experience on one or two pages, describing it as vividly as possible. It is important that this description is spontaneous and also includes how the students experienced the situation and what concerned them about it. Finally, the students are asked to write down a spontaneous thought that came to mind while reading through their own texts.

We have twenty such micro-stories from students who completed the practical phase between August 2020 and February 2021. Every one of them relates to the Corona pandemic.

Step Two: Methodical preparation of the students for the self-reflective learning process.

It is then made clear to the students that these micro-stories can be used to analyze, among other things, constructions of the professional identity. To do this, it is important to understand micro-stories from a scholarly perspective. For this purpose, the structures of a written narrative are analyzed, and in this way, insights into the individual cases are generated, which in a further step, can be condensed into objective structures of the meaning of social actions (Oevermann et al., 1987). In order to be able to reconstruct structural logic in a micro-narrative, this second step introduces sequence analysis (cf. Kruse, 2014) as a methodological approach that follows five rules:

- *Contextuality*: The text is approached with an "artificial naiveté."
- *Literalness*: The "textuality of social reality" represents a guiding principle. This means that the text at hand forms the basis of interpretation, however contradictory it may be.
- *Sequentially*: Text analysis begins with the first utterance of an interaction segment (initially word by word, later sentence by sentence), generating as many potential readings as possible. This is followed by the analysis of the subsequent interaction segment. Here, readings are generated which tend to confirm one or more readings established in the first step and which may lead to new interpretive hypotheses.
- *Extensiveness*: Only small amounts of text are evaluated, but these are evaluated in as much detail as possible.
- *Parsimony*: Only those possibilities for interpretation are considered which are "forced" by the text.

The students are told that a sequence analysis is to be carried out in a group. Rules are established (e.g., order of speaking, no evaluation of contributions). These two phases of student preparation should take no longer than 45 minutes.

Step Three: Conducting a sequence analysis with the students.

The lecturer selects the micro-story to be analyzed from the micro-stories written by students in the previous year, ensuring anonymity.

In this third step, the seminar group conducts a sequence analysis of a micro-story under the guidance of the lecturer. Depending on the length of the text, a sequence analysis takes between 1 and 1.5 hours. Due to the rather unusual sequential procedure for students, the beginning of the analysis usually takes more guidance and activation by the lecturer, and the students initially tend to focus on the content. As the analysis progresses, the students' associations and interpretations increase, and language issues are also addressed.

This third step is concluded with the generation of superordinate theses on the structure of a micro-story and the construction of professional identity, with a professional classification of the analyzed content and with concluding impressions.

Step Four: Reflection on the sequence analysis.

After completing the sequence analysis, students are asked for feedback on the insights generated and the methodological approach. Since lively discussions often arise during the feedback phase, and students report "aha experiences" with regard to their own professional actions, sufficient time should be allowed for this fourth step (20-30 minutes).

4.2. Outline of the Selected Micro-Stories

For the sequence analyses, we selected three micro-stories. The first untitled micro-story had been written by a student who had completed her practical semester at a mother-child facility. She described how she had accompanied a resident of the mother-child facility during an abortion. She had accompanied this resident first to a counselling center for pregnant women in conflict situations and sometime later to the actual abortion at a doctor's office.

The second micro-story, entitled "(Social) Participation – Goodbye!" was written by a student who had completed her practical phase at a counselling center and shelter for women affected by violence. In the micro-story, the student described how she had tried to organize a place in a dance class for a client during the pandemic in order to promote the social integration of the client, who was undergoing asylum proceedings.

The author of the third text had completed her practical phase in a residential group for girls. The text was entitled "The Corona pandemic has resulted in resource impoverishment." It was about two girls who were both dealing with coping with their traumatic history. After repeated arguments with staff, they left the residential group and did not return for a night.

5. Results and Discussion

In the following paragraphs, we present the results of the three sequence analyses, taking into account the competence areas that, for von Spiegel (2018), in sum, constitute professional identity: knowledge and understanding ("head"), professional attitude ("heart"), and methodological skills ("hand"). Nevertheless, the testing of the didactic model in the seminar groups showed that in these practical learning settings, not all three competence dimensions contributed equally to stimulating self-reflective discussions. For this reason, we present the concepts of professional attitude and methodological skills in more detail with real-life examples while we outline the area of knowledge more thoroughly in relation to the central findings.

5.1. Knowledge

Professional identity is expressed through professional knowledge, which von Spiegel (2018), following Staub-Bernasconi (2007), differentiates into descriptive and explanatory knowledge, a knowledge of values, and the capacity to handle change.

Descriptive knowledge helps to present and assess a current situation or problem as appropriately as possible (cf. von Spiegel, 2018, p. 48). It is usually found at the beginning of the micro-stories. It serves primarily to contextualize the narrative that follows, as well as to describe formal processes and collaboration with other social work institutions (e.g., counselling centers) or professions (e.g., physicians). The descriptions of the situation or problem presented are not always detailed and exact, which sometimes leads to irritation in the seminar groups. By problematizing and explaining the facts presented in the micro-stories, the students were able to gain new insights into the help system (e.g., admission conditions in mother-child facilities) and formal processes (e.g., the asylum procedure).

Explanatory knowledge helps in the effort to make causes and connections for a problem understandable (von Spiegel, 2018, pp. 52-53). This form of knowledge tends to be used by the authors in the concluding section, where students were asked to write down an associative thought flash about the text. Here, the authors take a meta-perspective on the described situation and partly underpin it with vocabulary ("[social] integration," "participation," "psychological stress") from social work, sociology, and psychology. The students in the seminar interpreted this – i.e., having specialized vocabulary – as an aspect of professional identity. However, it also became apparent in a micro-story that the author used a few phrases using specialized vocabulary. What she did employ was a series of pre-taken positions and justifications in order to classify the situation. The students interpreted this as her attempt to compensate for her immature professionalism and her uncertainty by presenting herself as a knower.

Understanding Values is referred to as "the capacity to make assessments" (von Spiegel, 2018, p. 61). It helps social workers to align professional practice with religious, ethical, and political value orientations as well as notions of human needs. In particular, ethical aspects were explored by the students in the micro-story on abortion. These considerations referred to the request that had been made to the student in the practical phase to accompany the resident to the doctor's office, where she had her abortion. Here, one student raised the concern that such a request could result in someone experiencing an ethical dilemma, e.g., if she herself was against abortions. This objection contributed to the student's awareness of the ambivalence of any institutional mandate for action against personal positioning.

Understanding of change consists of a "repertoire of proposed actions of different scope for defined purposes in a defined context" (von Spiegel, 2018, p. 66). For example, in the micro-story "(Social) Participation – Goodbye!" The author reports on the long search for a suitable dance class for the client, which remained unsuccessful. During the sequence analysis, the students addressed the author's role as the bearer of bad news, into which the author placed herself through her methodical actions and which was accompanied by feelings of frustration and powerlessness. The students problematized the applied method of searching for a dance course and made suggestions for alternative methodological action.

In the story "Resource Impoverishment," *understanding of change* and *understanding of values* play together: The author describes the institutional mandate for the staff to control the homeschooling of the residents during the pandemic in their rooms, and at the same time, claims not to approve of this institutional mandate herself. The tension between help and control, as well as the dilemma between institutional mandate and one's own professional behavior, was discussed in the seminar.

In summary, the sequence analyses contributed to a reactivation of the awareness of different bodies of knowledge that the students had already acquired in the course of their studies. Likewise, the strong significance of professional knowledge and understanding as proof of one's own professionalism became clear.

5.2. Professional Attitude

According to Von Spiegel, a professional attitude encompasses the ethical and values-based standards that underlie professional behavior. This refers to an attitude that "values people as independent subjects who shape their own paths, not as objects" (von Spiegel, 2018, p. 30). The goal is to support and accompany people in their self-education processes and not to patronize them through pedagogical interventions. Such an attitude can only be realized if a working alliance is entered that is based on the principle of co-productivity (Galuske & Rosenbaum, 2004, p. 320). This means that interventions must enable clients' participation in the assistance process and must respect their life practices.

The working principle of co-productivity and participation was also addressed several times in the sequence analyses. In the micro-story "(Social) Participation – Goodbye," the students worked out that the professional claim of a co-productive working alliance can be made only to a limited extent. The author writes that she "was tasked with finding a recreational activity in the form of a dance class for a client and tying her in with the people in charge." Aside from the institution's framing of the student's role in the practice phase (a passive formulation that leaves no room for independent decision-making), students first discussed that the dance class was sought "for" rather than jointly "with" the client and was interpreted as less than participatory. Next, students engaged with the phrase "to tie someone in with." It was noted that this formulation is familiar to social work practice and that students use this formulation themselves when speaking. However, in writing, this phrase evoked new associations. For a while, some students associated the term "tie in with" with enabling social participation, while others equated the term with being or becoming involuntarily tied to a table leg or torture stake because "tie in with" implied to them that the writer did not trust the resident to integrate on her own. They felt that the author was trying to limit as much as possible the president's ability to escape the dance class. The students were not able to come to an understanding concerning the term "to tie in with" until they came up with the more neutral term, "to enroll," which all agreed would have been more appropriate in this passage. In the seminar, there was an exchange on the meaning of language and consciously or unconsciously used idioms in the practice of professionals. The interpretation of the expression "to tie in with" as a form of binding was verified during the sequence analysis because the author used this word three times in the micro-story and wrote elsewhere that the resident was difficult to motivate for leisure activities. The students worked out that a participative working alliance based on dialogue and reciprocity was not realized in this case presentation, and thus an important working principle of social work was not realized.

In the micro-story on abortion, too, no co-productive working alliance is described at first. The author writes: "A few days later, an appointment was arranged at a pregnancy conflict counselling center." Here, the students were particularly struck by the fact that the sentence was phrased passively. They concluded that it was probably not the resident herself but someone from the facility who had called the pregnancy conflict counselling center. There was discussion about when it would be appropriate to leave such a call to the resident and when such a call should be undertaken by social workers. In the course of the micro-story, it became apparent that the working alliance was developing because the resident herself made an appointment for an abortion at the doctor's office. This was seen by the students as a sign of a consolidated decision and as an indication that she was assuming more responsibility.

The situation is somewhat different in the "Resource Impoverishment" micro-story. The students found it interesting that the author neither clearly assigns herself to the staff nor to the target group, i.e., the girls of the residential group. The author explicitly classifies herself as a member of the professional staff only in a text passage in which it is stated that during the homeschooling period, the staff must check whether the girls are carrying out the tasks they are supposed to perform. Furthermore, from the way the story is told, it becomes clear that the author takes the perspective of the two girls and describes the events from their point of view. This presumably has the consequence that the girls' absence overnight is hardly problematized by her. She interprets the quarrel between the girls and the staff because of the lack of retreat possibilities for the residents; the girls' running away and staying away overnight she sees as the logical consequence. With regard to the question of attitude, it is remarkable that the author does not develop an individual and subject-oriented view of the target group: The girls are consistently described as one person with the same voice, the same experience, and the same behavior ("both girls," "they stated," "they clash with the staff").

Professional attitudes also include one's own involvement with and awareness of ethical standards. These were discussed in the abortion micro-story. Regarding counselling, the author writes: "When I was on the phone with the counselling center, I was told that I would have to wait outside (…). The resident said several times that she did not want to enter the counselling center alone (…). Accordingly, I asked again on-site. An exception was then made, and I was allowed into the conversation to support her." In contrast, the author writes about the Corona regulations in the doctor's office: "Arrived at the practice, we were told that under no circumstances could I stay in practice and that I had to wait for her outside." Here, the author describes two ways professionals deal with Corona regulations. While the social worker at the counselling center agrees, when asked, to allow the author of the micro-story to accompany the woman during counselling, this request is clearly denied at the doctor's office. Here, the students suspected that sanitation played a greater role in a doctor's office and that the risk of infection was greater. Professional characteristics with regard to flexibility in dealing with concepts of sanitation also became clear. Whereas in social work, the individual and his/her needs for crisis accompaniment are placed above the applicable Corona protective measures, and the regulations are therefore negotiable, in the medical context, the regulations are enforced with rigour. That the Corona regulations are non-negotiable in the medical context results in a certain powerlessness on the part of the woman involved and the author of the micro-story, the following sentence shows that the psychosocial needs of the client were given little space in the doctor's office: "On the way back, she [the resident] told me that she had sat undressed in the treatment room for 30 minutes, waiting for the doctor." This situation was characterized by one student as "degrading" and illustrated to students the different ethical standards that can underlie working with people.

The sequence analysis illustrates the various dimensions that characterize a professional attitude:

- Regarding the clients, the relevance of a co-productive working alliance, the maintenance of a balance between the assumption of responsibility and independence, and the adoption of an individual-subject-oriented view of the clients were explored.
- Regarding the team and the social work professionals, the necessity of identifying with one's own profession was emphasized.
- Regarding interdisciplinary collaboration, profession-specific settings and different ways of dealing with clients and patients were pointed out.

In addition, this section illustrates the discursive processes of negotiation that are necessary to raise awareness of one's own views, communicate them, hear new perspectives, and develop one's own professional positions.

5.3. Skills

According to von Spiegel (2018, p. 74), proficiency comprises a professional competence to communicate and act methodologically, in contrast to everyday competence.

The author of the abortion micro-story was considered to have high competencies during the sequence analysis. The students maintained that this was demonstrated by the fact that she was able to accompany the resident in the counselling session despite the pandemic, even though this request had initially been rejected. The students discussed the general benefit of accompanying clients to such talks. One student stated that it was simply important to have "someone there." Another student said that one would also be able to better reflect on the conversation with the client if one had been present. It became clear in the analysis that both the ability to successfully represent the interests of clients vis-à-vis institutions and empathic conversation and support are important competencies of social workers.

Looking at intra-organizational collaboration, it was interesting to note that none of the three authors specifically included their colleagues in the micro-stories. Team structures are named only implicitly through work plans, house rules, and through passive formulations that convey a hierarchy ("I was asked").

The sequence analyses addressed the idea that self-perception and self-reflection are expressed in the language used. Individual terms discussed that irritated in the written language (e.g., "to tie in with"), technical phrases were discussed ("structure-promoting measure"), double terminology was discussed as an assurance that everything had been considered ("integration and participation"), and filler words were examined for comfortable certainties and presuppositions ("namely," "of course"). The use of personal pronouns, as in the phrase "my client," was interpreted as possessive, and the importance of having "one's own client" in the practice phase was pointed out, which was seen as an expression of a professional role. Also, the form of language (use of technical language or colloquial language) was addressed, and the conclusion was that professionalism is expressed through technical language. This was particularly evident in the "Resource Impoverishment" micro-story, in which the author's identification with the residents of the girls' group was inferred through the predominant use of everyday language. Overall, this story is permeated by a clear indecisiveness, sometimes also ambivalence, which, according to the students, reflects the author's quest with regard to her own professional identity. In some passages, technical terms and phrases are used, but the description of a several-week experience on the practice site sounds, for the most part, familiar, with little technical contextualization, tending toward the associative.

The degree of self-awareness and self-reflection was also evident in the weighting of content in the micro-stories. This is particularly evident in the "(Social) Participation – Goodbye" micro-story, which includes an exhaustive description of the unsuccessful search for a dance class and the obstructive general conditions due to the Corona pandemic. The nature of the narrative gave students the impression that the author was very concerned with her own professional role, which she may have felt was in jeopardy due to her failure to find a dance class. Here the question arose to what extent the author implicitly addressed her own lack of integration in or affiliation with her colleagues with the headline "(Social) Participation – Goodbye," which would mean that this was the central motive of this micro-story and not the resident's lack of (social) integration.

In summary, the sequence analyses address competencies in relation to students' practical actions in their interactions with clients and, less often, with social work professionals. Interestingly, "skills" are expressed not only in the act of doing but also in the act of talking about the doing.

Conclusion

We conceived the didactic model presented in this chapter in order to focus on the issue of the development of professional identity during the practical phase of social work studies, especially in the current situation in which the Covid pandemic is changing social work practice. It was our intention to support students during this six-month practical phase in the development of a professional identity through a self-reflective learning process. The current pandemic has created pressure for change in social work at both the institutional and conceptual levels, which has led, among other things, to a one-sided dissolution of constitutive areas of tension in social work (e.g., help and control, participation and heteronomy) and to a greater emphasis on "thinking safety." Practices have tended to become more paternalistic, limiting, and controlling (cf. Meyer & Alsago, 2021). Given this situation, the learning setting we presented here was able to provide a counterweight by very consciously bringing questions of professional identity and practice into view, thus encouraging students to reflect on central standards of social work, especially against the background of the pandemic.

In the following paragraphs, we discuss both the added value and the limitations of this didactic model.

The students themselves stressed the attraction of the methodological procedure of sequence analysis, as it enables the adoption of a meta-perspective and a multi-perspective view of professional practice in a joint discussion. The students recognized that even small and seemingly banal everyday situations are significant because they can clarify specific patterns in more complex casework. The engagement in reflection at every step focuses the trained eye on experienced practice and one's own actions. By becoming more aware of these situations and talking about them, students can gain more confidence in their actions while at the same time recognizing that there are usually different options for action that are tied to a given reading of the situation and also to their own person. They recognized that the necessary justification of professional actions taken and the working out of criteria for deciding between alternative courses of action are important professional competencies. Such a learning setting opens the opportunity for reflective thinking and acting to become part of the professional identity of students. In discussion with the students, it became clear that different people can develop different perspectives on a situation and that this is not directly a matter of right and wrong.

This methodological approach trained the students to engage patiently with the micro-stories and to let themselves be guided by them until some readings could be confirmed and others discarded. The immanent constructivist understanding of the sequence analysis made it clear to the students that there is not one definition or expression of professional identity in social work but that it always has to be seen in the context of the relevant social framework, legal foundations, institutional requirements, case-specific characteristics, and the professional and biographical modes of socialization of the protagonists involved. Nevertheless, there are overriding working principles and ethical principles that are constitutive of professional activities in social work. Thus, the students were sensitized to the importance of a co-productive working alliance and, along with it, to the facilitation of participation. They were encouraged to rethink their own professional understanding of their role and to develop it both dialogically and independently, and to do so in a way that allows social workers to be a part of a society that works for and not for people. This kind of professional attitude ensures that clients are not objectified but seen as independent subjects. In turn, respect for human dignity is ensured, and the right to participate should be taken for granted as the fundamental guiding principle in professional practice.

When analyzing the micro-stories, the students experienced social work as something important and positive and discussed which aspects are particularly significant in this regard. From our point of view, such discussions can strengthen the students in their self-confidence as social workers, especially in relation to other professions.

Taking a critical attitude, the students asked whether the procedure of sequence analysis could be applied in professional practice due to the time involved. This discussion should be conducted alongside the practice; in our opinion, however, institutionally guaranteed places are also needed in everyday professional life, which interrupt and consciously reflect practiced routines. This is especially true in times of crisis when places for reflection in everyday professional life become even rarer than they usually are because proactive action has priority. For social work students, we see the university and its lecturers as having a responsibility to ensure a sound education. A case-based approach makes it possible to work out "blind spots" in a case description and to better recognize the complexity of social work with all its unconscious elements. In addition to the interpretation of the content of the case descriptions, this can succeed through sensitization to the use of language: Professionalism expresses itself in a professionally sound language culture.

Sequence analysis is about shared interpretation processes. If, before engaging in sequence analysis, rules for the joint analysis are discussed, one-sided or even derogatory interpretations and conclusions can be avoided. The entire working method is designed to make students aware of their social responsibility. Lecturers serve as role models for social responsibility by taking what happens in practice seriously, making it the central object of learning processes, showing empathy for all involved, and refraining from rash and one-sided interpretations. This attitude is of great importance for future social work professionals. For in practice, it will be their task to work with addressees in challenging life situations and with idiosyncratic coping strategies, which can succeed if the social worker engages in an unprejudiced working alliance on equal terms.

Case-based learning also has limitations. The practical learning processes of the students are less easy to guide than when using other learning methods. What associations a case description arouses, what aspects are brought up during a dialogue, and which direction a discussion takes – all these depend strongly on the students involved and the group process. Reflection on one's own actions and attitude is more important in case-based learning than in the more pre-structured transfer of knowledge. In addition, the small-step approach to sequence analysis requires a high degree of concentration, and students may perceive it as tedious and a long way from practice. Therefore, sequence analysis should not be placed at the end of a learning unit, and the analyzed text should not be too long. After an initial word-by-word analysis, it is possible to move on to somewhat longer texts. If students are concentrating somewhat too heavily on content in their analysis, they can be encouraged through follow-up questions to address language issues or institutional and structural issues implicit in the narrative.

In summary, the didactic model we have developed can, in the spirit of *learning by understanding*, enable students to practice close perception and observation through a self-reflective approach before they develop explanations and plan interventions. The didactic model makes it possible for future social workers to generate new insights into a case presentation ("head"), to reflect on their professional attitude ("heart"), and to review their methodological skills ("hand"), to initiate ideas for further development in their professional work and their professional identity.

References

Adams, K., Hean, S., Sturgis, P., & Clark, J. M. (2006). Investigating the factors influencing professional identity of first-year health and social care students. *Learning in health and social care*, 5(2), 55-68.

Ader, S. (2021). "Es könnte so sein, aber auch ganz anders …!" – Kasuistische Zugänge in praxisbegleitenden Lehrveranstaltungen. In Kriener, M., Roth, A., Burkard, S. & Gabler, H. (Eds.). *Praxisphasen im Studium der Sozialen Arbeit*. Beltz Juventa, 160-177.

Becka, D., Bräutigam, C., Evans, M., Herrmann, J., Ludwig, C., Öz, F., Schmidt, C., Schröer, L. & Völz. S. (2020). Soziale Dienstleistungsarbeit und Corona-Pandemie: Rückkehr in eine aufgewertete Normalität, *IAT Discussion Paper*, 20/03, Institut Arbeit und Technik (IAT).

Becker-Lenz, R., Busse, S., Ehlert, G., & Müller-Hermann, S. (2013). *Professionalität in der Sozialen Arbeit. Standpunkte, Kontroversen, Perspektiven* (3rd ed.). Springer.

Becker-Lenz, R., Busse, S., Ehlert, G. & Müller-Hermann, S. (2012). *Professionalität Sozialer Arbeit und Hochschule. Wissen, Kompetenz, Habitus und Identität im Studium Sozialer Arbeit*. Springer.

Bergougnan, R. & Fondeville, F. (2021). Social Work Education and Training in France: A Long History of Being Energised by an Academic Discipline and International Social Work. In Laging M. & Žganec, N. (Eds.), *Social Work Education in Europe. European Social Work Education and Practice*. Springer, 65-88. https://doi.org/10.1007/978-3-030-69701-3_4.

Bruno, A., & Dell'Aversana, G. (2018). 'What shall I pack in my suitcase?': the role of work-integrated learning in sustaining social work students' professional identity. *Social Work Education*, 37(1), 34-48. https://doi.org/10.1080/02615479.2017.1363883.

Butterwegge, C. (2021). Das neuartige Virus trifft auf die alten Verteilungsmechanismen: Warum die COVID-19-Pandemie zu mehr sozialer Ungleichheit führt. *Wirtschaftsdienst*, 101(1), 11-14.

Galuske, M. & Rosenbaum, N. (2004). Der Sozialpädagogische Blick - und wie man ihn ausbildet. In Hörster, R., Küster, E. & Wolff, S. (Eds.), *Orte der Verständigung*. Lambertus, 315-335.

Heiner, M. (2004). *Fallverstehen, Typen der Falldarstellung* und *kasuistische Kompetenz*. In Hörster, R., Küster, E. & Wolff, S. (Eds.), *Orte der Verständigung*. Lambertus, 315-335, 91–108.

Höppner, G., Ader, S., & Notzon, S. (2022). Selbst- und praxisreflexives Lernen: Ein didaktisches Konzept zur Herausbildung professioneller Identität von Studierenden der Sozialen Arbeit in der Praxisphase. *Neue Praxis - Zeitschrift für Sozialarbeit, Sozialpädagogik und Sozialpolitik*, 4, 357-376.

Hörster, R. (2018). Sozialpädagogische Kasuistik. In Otto, H.-U., Thiersch, H., Treptow, R. & Ziegler, H. (Eds.), *Handbuch Soziale Arbeit. Grundlagen der Sozialarbeit und Sozialpädagogik* (6th ed.). Reinhardt, 1563–1571.

Klatetzki, T. (1993). *Wissen, was man tut. Professionalität als organisationskulturelles Handeln. Eine ethnographische Interpretation*. KT-Verlag.

Kruse, J. (2014). *Qualitative Interviewforschung. Ein integrativer Ansatz*. Beltz Juventa.
Lorenz W. (2021). Introduction: Current Developments and Challenges Facing Social Work Education in Europe. In Laging M. & Žganec N. (Eds.), *Social Work Education in Europe. European Social Work Education and Practice*. Springer: Cham. https://doi.org/10.1007/978-3-030-69701-3_1.
Meyer, N. & Alsago, E. (2021). Soziale Arbeit am Limit ? Professionsbezogene Folgen veränderter Arbeitsbedingungen in der Corona-Pandemie. *Sozial Extra*, 3, 210-218.
Misamer, M., Signerski-Krieger, J., Bartels, C., & Belz, M. (2021). Internal locus of control and sense of coherence decrease during the COVID-19 pandemic: A survey of students and professionals in social work. *Frontiers in Sociology,* 6. https://doi.org/10.3389/fsoc.2021.705809.
Müller, B. (2012). *Sozialpädagogisches Können. Ein Lehrbuch zur multiperspektivischen Fallarbeit* (7th ed.). Lambertus.
Oevermann, U., Allert, W. T., Konau, E. & Krambeck, J. (1987). 21. Structures of Meaning and Objective Hermeneutics. In Meja, V., Misgeld, D. & Stehr, N. (Eds.), *Modern German Sociology*. Columbia University Press, 436-448. https://doi.org/10.7312/meja92024-024.
Shlomo, S. B., Levy, D., & Itzhaky, H. (2012). Development of professional identity among social work students: Contributing factors. *The Clinical Supervisor*, 31 (2), 240-255.
Staub-Bernasconi, S. (2007). *Soziale Arbeit als Handlungswissenschaft*. Haupt.
Thiersch, H. (2002). Sozialpädagogik – Handeln in Widersprüchen. In Otto, H.-U., Rauschenbach, T. & Vogel, P. (Eds.), *Erziehungswissenschaft: Professionalität und Kompetenz*. Leske und Budrich, 209–222.
Von Spiegel, H. (2018). *Methodisches Handeln in der Sozialen Arbeit. Grundlagen und Arbeitshilfen für die Praxis* (6th ed.). Ernst Reinhardt.
Wagner, L. (2020). Soziale Arbeit und "Corona." *Sozial Extra*, 44, 236–238. https://doi.org/10.1007/s12054-020-00291-6.
Wheeler, J. (2017). Shaping identity? The professional socialisation of social work students. In Webb, S. A. (Eds.), *Professional Identity and Social Work.* Routledge. https://doi.org/10.4324/9781315306957-13.
Wiles, F. (2013). 'Not easily put into a box': constructing professional identity. Social Work Education, 32 (7), 854-866. https://doi.org/10.1080/02615479.2012.705273.
Wiles, F. (2017). Developing social work students' professional identity: the role of England's Professional Capabilities Framework. *European Journal of Social Work*, 20 (3), 349-360.
Willke, H. (2004). *Einführung in das systemische Wissensmanagement*. Carl-Auer.

Chapter 18

Institutional Forces of the Social Responsibility Programs of an Indonesian University Beyond Complying with the Law: A Case Study of the Unpad Model

Ersa Tri Wahyuni[*]

Faculty of Economics and Business, Universitas Padjadjaran, Bandung, West Java, Indonesia

Abstract

All Indonesian Universities, by law, are bounded to perform three activities: Research, Teaching and Social Responsibility or community service activities. Thus, by law, lecturers and students should participate in social responsibility activities. So much so, the remunerations and the promotion of the lecturers to become tenured professors are also determined by their achievements in social responsibility activities, not only their research publications. However, only a few universities can confidently express that their universities have embedded social responsibility in their daily virtue and not only performing activities to comply with the government's regulations. One of the government's Universities in Indonesia which has a very strong social responsibility embedded in their university's culture, is Universitas Padjadjaran (Unpad). This chapter showcases the institutional forces of Unpad to achieve such a strong culture of social responsibility. The author will discuss 3 R (Rules, Rhetoric and Resources) in Unpad to institutionalize the social responsibility virtues among their lecturers and students, as well as explain some of the social responsibility programs for lecturers and students. This chapter contributes to the literature and also

---

[*] Corresponding Author's Email: ersa@unpad.ac.id.

In: Models for Social Responsibility Action by Higher Education Institutions
Editors: Joseph Chacko Chennattuserry, Elangovan N. et al.
ISBN: 979-8-89113-097-5
© 2024 Nova Science Publishers, Inc.

management practices for higher education institutions in developing their social responsibility programs.

Keywords: Social responsibility Activities, Indonesia, Universitas Padjadjaran

1. Introduction

Universities, traditionally, have been perceived as expert institutions in society, and academia has the privilege of elite intellectual groups. However, the role of universities as an expert model has evolved over the last decades to also as a public service institution and engage more with the industry and the society at large, (Moeliodihardjo et al., 2012; Roper & Hirth, 2005; Weerts & Sandmann, 2008). The recent development in the role of the university emphasizes a shift away from an expert model of delivering university knowledge and innovation to the public, as well as toward a more collaborative model with society (Weerts & Sandmann, 2008).

Teaching has been long prioritized by Indonesian higher education institutions (HEIs), and only recently, over the last decade, some Indonesian universities are moving forward into more research activities. Besides teaching and research, universities in Indonesia are also expected to excel in another mission: social responsibility. In Indonesia, these three functions (teaching, research and social responsibility) are called "Tri Dharma". Many use the term community service programs to explain the social responsibility function of the university (Aragón & Kismadi, 2015; Mastuti et al., 2014). However, few Indonesian universities make this social responsibility an embedded value of the university and not only satisfy the mandatory requirement stipulated by the government. Such embedded values need to be instilled in the university's culture by key actors for a considerable long period of time.

The purpose of this chapter is to showcase how social responsibility virtue is embedded in university culture in Indonesian Universities. Universitas Padjadjaran (Unpad), the case of this chapter, is one of the public universities in Indonesia with a very strong social responsibility value in its activities. The data presented in this chapter derives from university documents and government reports as well as the authors' observations over the last 13 years of her working period at the university as a lecturer.

2. Background

Historically, the higher education system in Indonesia was highly influenced by the Dutch (Cummings & Kasenda, 1989; Logli, 2016). The oldest University in Indonesia (Universitas Indonesia) was inherited from a medical school established by the Dutch in the 1850s. Over time the higher education system in Indonesia has grown into a highly complex system (Moeliodihardjo et al., 2012). The system has around 8.4 million students, with 2 million new students entering the system every year. There are 122 public institutions, more than 3,000 private institutions, and more than 1200 institutions under the Ministry of Religious Affairs (Dikti, 2020), as detailed below in Table 1 Higher Education Institutions in Indonesia year 2020.

Table 1. Higher education institutions in Indonesia year 2020

Type Higher Education Institutions	Number of Higher Education Institutions
Public higher education institutions (PTN)	122
Private higher education institutions (PTS)	3044
Government higher education institutions (PTK/L)	187
Religious higher education institutions	1240
Total	4593

Source: Higher Education Statistics 2020 (Diktri, 2020).

Despite more than 4000 HEIs operating in Indonesia, most of them are on Java Island. More than half of that number is in Java Island. The size and the quality of HEI are also varied from an institution with more than 60,000 students and a specialized institute with only about 3000-4000 students. Universitas Padjadjaran (Unpad) is the biggest public university in West Java province in terms of total assets. The distribution of HEIs in Indonesia is detailed in Figure 1.

Source: Higher Education Statistics 2020 (Dikti, 200).

Figure 1. Provincial Distribution of HEIs.

In the past, the main role of universities in Indonesia was to provide education and training to satisfy the demand of the industry. However, the rapid economic growth combined with structural change in the industry called for a greater emphasis on the relevance of education and a new demand for research-based collaborations (Moeliodihardjo et al., 2012). While a vast majority of universities in Indonesia remain focused on teaching, some universities are moving toward research-oriented institutions, especially large government Universities, which gained the privilege of a certain autonomy. Since the 2000s, several government universities have transformed from rigid government institutions to more independent ones with some degree of self-regulated authority. This legal status is called PTNBH (Perguruan Tinggi Negeri Berbadan Hukum) or a Separate Legal Entity of a Government Higher Education Institution. Universitas Padjadjaran (Unpad), the university of this chapter, was granted this status in 2014 by the Ministry of Education.

2.1. Social Responsibility in the Indonesian HEI: Rules and Practices

The sustainability of universities has been a major concern for the higher education ecosystem in Indonesia. Universities were expected to thrive not only in Tri Darma (education, research and community service) but also contribute to the sustainable environment in fulfilling their role. There has been an increasing interest as well for the universities in Indonesia to report their sustainability activities. The Green Metric World University Rank published by the University of Indonesia in 2018 surveyed 66 institutions, and as many as 48 universities presented reports on sustainability. A study by Sari et al., (2020) indicates that from those 48 universities, there are no significant differences between private and public universities in reporting their sustainability performance.

To encourage better interaction with industry and promote greater research orientation, DGHE (Directorate Government of Higher Education/ Dirjen Dikti) has consistently launched a number of initiatives to support university research and community service. Since the early 1990s, DGHE has provided more than 20 different grant schemes, ranging from grants for fundamental research to applied and collaborative research (Moeliodihardjo et al., 2012). These grants are always competitive where lecturers applied for the grants and were selected based on certain selection criteria.

Considering PTNBH is a government-supported institution, its sustainability is much better compared to private universities. PTNBH Universities, much larger and more independent than other government universities, enjoy more freedom in allocating funds for research and also for community service activities. For PTNBH universities, DGHE provided them with more authority in selecting the research proposal of their own lecturers. Apart from the government fund, PTNBH Universities such as Unpad also provide their own competitive research grants for lecturers to conduct smaller-scale research or community service activities.

2.2. Universitas Padjadjaran (Unpad) and its Social Responsibility Programs

Unpad is a government university in West Java Province, established in 1957 and currently has 16 faculties and one school of graduate studies. The faculties range from medicine to communication, including a strong faculty in economics and business as well as social science and medicine. As of November 2021, there are 33,000 students enrolled at Unpad in 190 study programs, ranging from vocational, undergraduate, to postgraduate programs, the last of which include the specialist, professional, master's, and doctoral programs. This number also represents approximately 200 international students. Unpad has gained a good reputation nationally, which makes it a very popular choice for high school graduates from all provinces.

West Java province, where Unpad operates, is the largest province in term of population, where about 20% of the country's population live. West Java was inhibited by almost 50 million people in 2020 (BPS, 2022) than twice the population of Australia with much less land. Being the largest and oldest government university in West Java, Unpad gained a stellar reputation nationally, but in particular among people in West Java who mostly belong to Sundanese ethnicity. Historically, Unpad was established by prominent noble leaders among Sundanese people and also the provincial government. The strong root of Sundanese culture has been cultivated and preserved until now. For example, during the formal convocation of Unpad, including the graduation ceremony, mars of the University (Karatagan Padjadjaran) are always sung. The lyric of Karatagan Padjadjaran uses the traditional Sundanese language, and the iconic music is also produced using traditional Sundanese musical instruments[1].

The strong root of West Java and Sundanese culture has encouraged Unpad to focus its social responsibility activities in the West Java province. In 2013, The University launched social responsibility program called *"Unpad Nyaah Ka Jabar"* or "Unpad Loves West Java", focusing on developing human resources of the province in 27 cities/municipalities. This initiative was then followed by the establishment of the Centre of Strategic Alliance of Unpad-West Java (ASUP Jabar), which is supported by the provincial government and local city governments of some cities in the province. One of the important programs of ASUP Jabar is the community program called "One Professor One Village," in which one professor of Unpad is required to develop a community in one village. Each professor receives funding from the university to develop and execute their own particular community program plan. The program is varied among villages, for example, improving people's health, empowering village economic activities, improving their agricultural techniques, and many more. Each community program is led by a professor who also brings students to be involved in the program (Arisanti et al., 2018; Djuyandi et al., 2020; Judistiani et al., 2018). Research and community program on water sustainability was also one of the main focus of Unpad to be part of the agent of change in the development of people of West Java. Unpad, for example, has been heavily involved in the Citarum Revitalization project by the government. Citarum River, one of the most polluted rivers in the world, received the government's attention after Washington Post and other international media wrote about it in 2017. Citarum River runs over 270 km supply 80% of raw water to people in the capital city of Jakarta. This largest river on Java Island supports 26 million residents who rely on the water for their agricultural and domestic use. Sadly, this river also has become the main waste disposal sewage for many textiles industry, and the water has become very toxic (Shara et al., 2021).

Unpad, in particular, is also focused on building an "Eco Campus" by developing efficient, sustainable water management on their campuses. The Eco Campus masterplan tries to develop integrated goals such as developing Eco Behaviour and not only building infrastructure for water management. For example, students and lecturers are encouraged to bring their own drinking bottles, and a drinking water fountain is available on campus. The roadmap for the Eco Campus master plan is available in Figure 2.

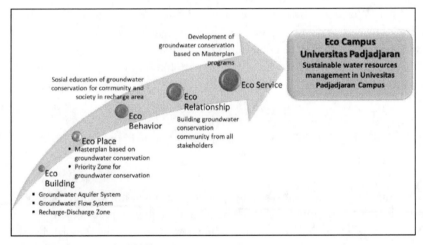

Source: (Endyana et al., 2018).

Figure 2. Unpad Eco Campus Masterplan.

Unpad also became the first university in Indonesia which establish a Centre for Sustainable Development Goals Studies or SDG Centre2. Since its establishment in 2016, Unpad SDG Centre has been organising conferences, conducting and publishing research in relation to SDGs, and it plays an important role in the SDGs policies in Indonesia. Other Universities in Indonesia followed the Unpad role and established similar SDGs Centre, a few of them were research unit in one of the faculty, while the Unpad SDG centre was the research centre at the university level, which attract multidiscipline researchers. Unpad is seriously involved in instilling the SDGs in their students and making Sustainable Development Goals the discussion topics for all new students during their induction, as well as essay topics in some class assignments. Moreover, all lecturers in Unpad, when they apply for a research grant or submit their publication as their performance evidence in the compensation report, are required to answer which goal in SDGs has been addressed by their research publication.

Due to the strong commitment to the environment, water sustainability a well as SDGs in general, Unpad received several awards in relation to social responsibility, such as:

- The Indonesia Green Award 2013,
- Indonesia Green Campus Award 2014,

Green World Award 2017, an award from Green Organization which offers Unpad as the Ambassador for Green Organization in Education and Best Practice Sector for the environment worldwide.

Unpad also received Excellent award International Fair of Youth Research and Education (IFYRE) 2021 for research on eco-friendly detergent

3. The Mechanism of Institutionalising Social Responsibility Value in Unpad

Based on the author's observations, social responsibility value has been institutionalised in Unpad using three institutionalising mechanisms: Rule, Rhetoric and Resources. This section will discuss the rule, the rhetoric and the resource being used by actors in Unpad to institutionalise social responsibility values among Unpad lecturers and students.

3.1. The Rule

The rule is one of the important pillars of an organisation (DiMaggio & Powell, 1983; Scott, 2013; Wang et al., 2014). Government regulation for Indonesian Universities to engage with community service is widely understood among academia and university management. Within the Tri Darma pillars of universities, the government include community service as one of the roles of higher education institutions.

In the past, community service activities as part of Tri Darma have been loosely enforced in Unpad. The lecturers are encouraged to be involved in community service activity, but it was never directly related to their remuneration. In 2014 Unpad legal status became PTNBH (still a government institution but with a wider authority), and many new rules were introduced. From early 20183, all lecturers will be assessed semi-annually to determine monthly performance remuneration on top of their basic salary. Twice a year, every February and August, all lecturers are required to submit their performance outputs from their last semester, which include teaching, research publications and community service activities. Each activity attracts points. For example, publishing research in a top journal has a higher point than publishing an article in a local newspaper.

A lecturer had to submit at least one community service activity for their performance evaluation to be approved. Community service activity does not attract any point, unlike teaching and research, but if a lecturer does not have any community service activity at all, their performance evaluation report cannot be approved by the head of the department. Community service activity becomes the necessary, sufficient condition for the performance evaluation to be approved. This new rule was a game changer as that was the first-time community service activity became mandatory and not only needed to be performed once a year but twice a year.

When the new rule was first applied, some lecturers who were more focused on teaching and research started to see community service activity as an important duty. Not only did the rector decree impose this hard rule, but Unpad also provided guidelines and a handbook for lecturers on how to conduct and evaluate their community service activity. Some training for lecturers on how to conduct community service activities was also organised. Unpad also launched thematic community projects where students and lecturers were involved in four themes of projects: entrepreneurial, community health, agriculture, and humanity projects.

Unpad also integrated the community project by students and the community project by a lecturer in which students are granted credits to be involved in the lecturer community project. Before 2017, all students needed to take the "community service" project as a compulsory course, which is organised centrally by the university. Students in large groups from different disciplines and faculties would stay in one rural village for several weeks to be engaged with local communities and develop some community projects together. One or two lecturers would be assigned as their mentors during the project period. However, this tradition was changed in that a smaller group of students were assigned to one lecturer project in a thematic community project. With this change, more lecturers were involved in the community project activity. For example, in the early year of 2020, 1,742 Unpad students were deployed to 88 villages in West Java, where they stayed for 35 days in the village to develop entrepreneurial community projects with local village people. This project involved 102 lecturers who supervised the projects in each village.

3.2. The Rhetoric

Rhetoric or strategic use of language in an institutional life is important to the operation and maintenance of an organisation (Alvesson, 1993; Green Jr & Li, 2011). Actors of the organisation deploy rhetoric to strengthen the organisation's values and practices. In order to produce certain claims or myths of the organisation, the organisation and its key actors engaged actively in rhetoric as a way of providing convincing accounts (Alvesson, 1993).

In Unpad, the rhetoric was also used by top management to strengthen the culture of social responsibility among lecturers, staff and students. For example, on many occasions, the rector and other top management of the university stressed the Sundanese roots of Unpad and the importance of collaboration with the community and other stakeholders, especially in West Java province. The focus on the development of West Java province was apparent during Prof Tri Hanggono as the Rector during 2015-2019. In many of his addresses at formal convocations, he emphasised the strong root of the university to the West Java culture and people. Also, he mentioned that the university has a moral obligation to support the development of the West Java province. Many of his programs were innovative and brought a stronger awareness of provincial challenges. For example, he pointed out the large inequality and lack number of practising medical doctors (MD) in many rural areas in West Java. This has encouraged him to offer a special scholarship program for students in the medical faculty.

The rhetoric for research in the university also sent a strong message of integrating research with community projects. Integrated Research Design Collaboration (IRDC) is a model that is encouraged by the university's top management to be pursued by their lecturers. Research by lecturers should be carried out together with students, and during the research process, collaboration with various stakeholders, including the government and community, is encouraged. The IRDC model, as illustrated in Figure 3, has also become the framework for the project of sustainable water resources at the Citarum River (see Endyana et al., 2018).

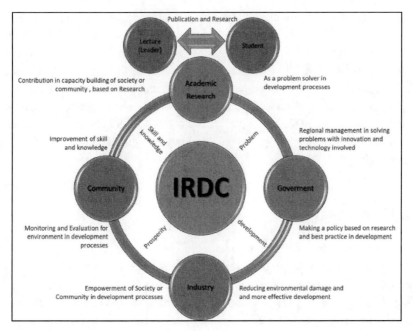

Source: (Endyana et al., 2018).

Figure 3. IRDC model

Besides the West Java-centric rhetoric, the university also uses SDGs as the rhetoric on many occasions to build social responsibility awareness among lecturers and students. Many seminars, academic discussions and conferences were held focusing on SDGs as global issues. While West Java rhetoric encouraged Unpad's academics to solve domestic challenges, SDGs issues persuaded them to be part of the global movement. Any community service program developed by lecturers and students should have a clear argument to answer which SDGs would be addressed by their activity.

Different rhetoric was deployed by the new rector in 2020, Prof. Rina Indiastuti. Although the West Java-centric remained relevant, the new rector emphasises the international reputation and positive impact of the university on society. In the University's Development Masterplan 2021-2045, the university's highlighted the development of technology, including artificial intelligence and blockchain and economic disruption (Unpad, 2021). The new rhetoric, heavily on the international focus, has also started to influence research and community service activities.

In terms of setting up a high standard for social responsibility, Prof Rina Indiastuti planned to increase the number of community service activities from 453 activities in 2020 to 1000 activities by the year 2024. Not only the increasing quantity of activities but also the quality of the community service projects. The new KPI of the university's top management also includes the number of community service activities which answer major development issues. It is expected by 2024, Unpad will be involved in 90 community service activities providing solutions to answering strategic development issues (Unpad, 2022).

3.3. The Resources

Rules and Rhetoric are important factors in building an institution's culture, but without resources being disposed of by actors, the value may remain to be the myth of the institutions instead of becoming a practice (Battilana et al., 2009; Garud et al., 2007). Resources allocated to a certain goal may also indicate the seriousness of the key actors in achieving it. Funding may be the most important resource allocated to achieve one goal, but besides that, an institution may also offer other intangible resources, such as network capital. Funding and network capital are the two examples of resources being deployed by key actors in the Unpad case.

Funding as the main resource for community service activities was provided in terms of annual activity grants. A lecturer may apply for such a grant by submitting an activity proposal. If a lecturer applies for a research grant, he also needs to embed a community service activity. For example, if one applies the research on the impact of microfinance institutions on the macro economy, a community service activity could be to host a series of workshops to improve the financial literacy of household wives in a certain village. The grant for community service activity ranges from around IDR 10 million – IDR 25 million (approximately USD 750 – USD 1700) for each activity. Campus transportation facilities, like campus buses and minibuses, can also be utilized by the lecturer and students in carrying out community service activities, subject to schedule availability.

In terms of network capital resources, Unpad also offers a wide network in the government sectors. The community service activity in some rural areas is often in cooperation with the local governments who are in favour of Unpad intellectual contribution to develop their villages. Unpad has very strong collaborations and synergies with some regency and village leaders, especially in West Java (see, for example, Djuyandi et al., 2020). As a very respectable government university in the province, many regents are in favour of, even persuade, Unpad to come to their regency with its community service activities. In one of the author's own experiences, a village leader came to the research centre of Unpad and asked if an academic could come to his village to give advice on what activities can be developed in his coastal village to improve the villager's prosperity and health. The university's research centre then assigned the author to develop a community project activity in the village with some funding from Unpad.

Many social responsibility activities organised by lecturers and students are on the theme of recycling waste management and improving awareness for a cleaner environment. Unpad responsibility to the community and environment is not only applied to the external but also to their internal campus. Internally, Unpad always tries to promote a green campus. In 2018, for example, Unpad organised a campaign to conserve water and reduce plastic waste by building several drinking fountains on the campus and banning all plastics cup and bottles in the meetings. Unpad also gave away the university's tumblers to lecturers and staff and encouraged them to bring their own water tumblers to the formal meetings.

One of the biggest surprising social responsibility acts of Unpad, which became headlines in major news outlets, happened in 2016 when Unpad waived all tuition fees for students in the faculty of medicine. All students who wanted to become a doctor, both to become an MD or a specialist, could study for free for the duration of the entire program. This became the big news in Indonesia as the tuition fee of medical school, in general across all universities in the country, is the most expensive compared to other majors. The high fee for medical schools arguably made it less accessible to bright students from less fortunate backgrounds, and only rich families can send their children to medical school. The free medical school had never been offered by any university in Indonesia before, and until the program was terminated in 2019, Unpad was the only University in Indonesia which offered such a bold move.

The "free medical school" was actually designed as a scholarship, and the fund came from the city and regency governments in West Java. Thus, the graduates from the scholarship program should be willing to work as medical doctors in the rural areas of West Java province. The pros and contras for the program were much talked about both internally and externally. For example, the execution of the programs was not as smooth as expected because many of the local governments were not ready to commit such funding for 4-5 years. Unpad faced challenges in collecting committed funding from the local governments. Also, this program was started in 2016, two years after PTNBH status, and which government expected PTNBH University to become more "entrepreneurial" by finding alternative income to the government funding.

This scholarship program for more than 250 students had made Unpad's financial statement bleed out. Government Audit Board recommended Unpad terminate the program as it reduced the possibility for government revenue. Unpad is still a government institution, after all, and medical school used to be the most prosperous faculty in Unpad with the highest revenue. After considering many recommendations, Unpad terminated the scholarship program in 2019. When the program was terminated in 2019, it recruited more than 900 students in the specialist medical programs and more than 800 students in the undergraduate medical program.

Nevertheless, the decision to make medical school free had been marked as the most selfless act of a university trying to solve a common problem of a developing country, the deficient number of MDs and the inequality of them serving more in big cities than rural areas. In 2016 when this shocking news came out, many Unpad lecturers and students felt very proud to be part of this university which had the courage to make a significant difference for society at large.

Conclusion

Universities, as a beacon of civilisation, have shifted their role from the ivory tower of science to true agents of change in society through their social responsibility activities and leadership. Universities are expected to play a more active role in society with collaboration, joint research and also community service activities. Universities in Indonesia are also expected to perform three activities or "Tri Darma", which are Research, Teaching and Social Responsibility (or Community Services). These three pillars of universities are imposed by the government through various regulations and also funding of grants. Until recently, teaching has been the major focus of most Indonesian universities, but research has also become a new focus for several government universities that are expected to become research universities. Community service is often perceived as something voluntary and not a priority for the survival of a university. After all, community service activities require resources such as funding and human and expertise resources.

The case of Universitas Padjadjaran (Unpad) is quite unique in terms of the embedded social responsibility culture in their academia. The key actors of the university (the top management) are important institutional factors for such culture, but Unpad as an institution also has been deploying rules, rhetoric and resources to reinforce social responsibility as a culture. The rule for university involvement in social responsibility activities is loud and clear in Indonesia, way up from the top government. The rule is also enforced by the internal regulations of the university, coercing the lecturers and the students to be involved in such activities. The rule may coerce lecturers and students to comply with regulations set up by the university. However, the powerful rhetoric by the key actors of the university has strengthened the practice. The rhetoric of West Java root and SDGs have made actors believe that their actions are not merely to comply with government regulations but genuinely to achieve something good for society at large. Lastly, any rule and rhetoric would be useless unless the university is willing to provide resources for social responsibility activities. Funding is always an important resource, but as this case study revealed, network capital is also important in supporting community service activities.

References

Alvesson, M. (1993). Organisations as rhetoric: Knowledge-intensive firms and the struggle with ambiguity. *Journal of Management Studies*, *30*(6), 997–1015.

Aragón, A. O., & Kismadi, B. (2015). *Capacity Building for University-Community Engagement in Indonesia*. Packard Foundation Capacity Development Study, Root Change

Arisanti, N., Arya, I. F., Amelia, I., Mutyara, K., & Setiawati, E. P. (2018). Evaluation on the implementation of rural-based program for undergraduate medical student. *Global Med Health Commun*, *6*(2), 148–154.

Battilana, J., Leca, B., & Boxenbaum, E. (2009). 2 how actors change institutions : towards a theory of institutional entrepreneurship. *Academy of Management Annals*, *3*(1), 65–107.

BPS. (2022). *Jumlah Penduduk Hasil Proyeksi Menurut Provinsi dan Jenis Kelamin*. https://www.bps.go.id/indicator/12/1886/1/jumlah-penduduk-hasil-proyeksi-menurut-provinsi-dan-jenis-kelamin.html

Cummings, W. K., & Kasenda, S. (1989). The origin of modern Indonesian higher education. P. G. Altbach & V. Selvaratnam (Eds) *From dependence to autonomy* (pp. 143–166). Springer.

Dikti. (2020). *Higher Education Statistics 2020*. Ministry of Education and Culture of Indonesia.

DiMaggio, P. J., & Powell, W. W. (1983). The iron cage revisited: Institutional isomorphism and collective rationality in organisational fields. *American Sociological Review*, 147–160.

Djuyandi, Y., Pradana, A., & Luqman, F. (2020). Synergity Between The Village Government And Padjadjaran University In Encouraging The Development Of Community Entrepreneurs In Jatimukti Village. *International Journal of Management, Innovation and Entrepreneurial Research*, 6(1), 51–57.

Endyana, C., Husodo, T., & Achmad, T. H. (2018). Universitas Padjadjaran concern for sustainable water resource from West Java to national and to the world. *E3S Web of Conferences*, 48, 05004. https://doi.org/10.1051/e3sconf/20184805004.

Garud, R., Hardy, C., & Maguire, S. (2007). Institutional entrepreneurship as embedded agency: An introduction to the special issue. Organisation studies, 28(7), 957-969.

Green Jr, S. E., & Li, Y. (2011). Rhetorical institutionalism: Language, agency, and structure in institutional theory since Alvesson 1993. *Journal of Management Studies*, 48(7), 1662–1697.

Judistiani, T. D., Wijaya, M., Susanti, A. I., Elba, F., Sundari, R. P., Wardhani, Y. S., & Fitriani, B. (2018). How Students Perceived "Community Internship": An Innovation for Vocational Studies in Midwifery Education at the Faculty of Medicine Universitas Padjadjaran. *Advanced Science Letters*, 24(12), 9845–9848.

Logli, C. (2016). Higher education in Indonesia: Contemporary challenges in governance, access, and quality. In C.S. Collins, N.N. L Molly, J. N. Hawkins & D.E. Neubauer (Eds) *The Palgrave Handbook of Asia Pacific higher education* (pp. 561–581). Springer.

Mastuti, S., Masse, A., & Tasruddin, R. (2014). University and community partnerships in South Sulawesi, Indonesia: Enhancing community capacity and promoting democratic governance. *Gateways: International Journal of Community Research and Engagement*, 7(1), 164–173.

Moeliodihardjo, B. Y., Soemardi, B. W., Brodjonegoro, S. S., & Hatakenaka, S. (2012). University, industry, and government partnership : Its present and future challenges in Indonesia. *Procedia-Social and Behavioral Sciences*, 52, 307–316.

Roper, C. D., & Hirth, M. A. (2005). A history of change in the third mission of higher education: The evolution of one-way service to interactive engagement. *Journal of Higher Education Outreach and Engagement*, 10(3), 3–21.

Sari, M. P., Hajawiyah, A., Raharja, S., & Pamungkas, I. D. (2020). The report of university sustainability in Indonesia. *International Journal of Innovation, Creativity and Change*, 11(8), 110–124.

Scott, W. R. (2013). *Institutions and organisations : Ideas, interests, and identities*. Sage publication.

Shara, S., Moersidik, S. S., & Soesilo, T. E. B. (2021). Potential health risks of heavy metals pollution in the downstream of Citarum River. *IOP Conference Series: Earth and Environmental Science*, 623(1), 012061. https://doi.org/10.1088/1755-1315/623/1/012061

Unpad. (2021). *Development Master Plan Universitas Padjadjaran 2021-2045*.

Unpad. (2022). *Rencana Kerja dan Anggaran Tahunan (RKAT) 2022 Universitas Padjadjaran*.

Wang, H.-K., Tseng, J.-F., & Yen, Y.-F. (2014). How do institutional norms and trust influence knowledge sharing ? An institutional theory. *Innovation*, *16*(3), 374–391.

Weerts, D. J., & Sandmann, L. R. (2008). Building a two-way street: Challenges and opportunities for community engagement at research universities. *The Review of Higher Education*, *32*(1), 73–106.

Index

A

academic performance, 34, 38, 46, 167, 181, 182, 184, 225, 227, 231, 232, 237, 238, 239, 241, 250

authentic thought leadership, 289, 290, 293, 294, 295, 296, 299, 300, 301, 302, 306, 307

B

behavioral, 40, 115, 167, 168, 169, 170, 172, 174, 175, 176, 178, 179, 180, 200, 201, 202, 203, 223, 286, 311, 360

behavioural problems, 166, 178

business students, 181, 182

C

case-based learning, 324, 327, 329, 341

child development program, 21, 22

child sponsorship, 22, 25, 27, 29, 31, 32, 34, 48, 111, 262

child-centered development, 72

children, 15, 16, 21, 22, 24, 25, 26, 28, 29, 30, 31, 32, 33, 34, 35, 36, 37, 38, 40, 41, 42, 43, 44, 45, 47, 57, 60, 62, 63, 64, 65, 67, 72, 75, 76, 77, 79, 80, 85, 88, 91, 93, 96, 111, 117, 119, 120, 121, 122, 123, 127, 128, 129, 130, 131, 132, 133, 134, 137, 138, 141, 142, 143, 146, 147, 148, 152, 159, 160, 162, 165, 166, 167, 168, 169, 170, 176, 177, 178, 179, 180, 185, 216, 225, 226, 227, 228, 229, 230, 231, 232, 236, 237, 241, 242, 244, 250, 259, 262, 269, 271, 290, 296, 320, 357

clinic(s), 205, 206, 207, 209, 210, 211, 214, 216, 217, 218, 219, 221, 223, 285

community development, 21, 22, 23, 24, 25, 26, 27, 28, 29, 35, 36, 37, 38, 43, 45, 46, 47, 56, 71, 72, 74, 75, 76, 79, 81, 82, 83, 84, 85, 91, 99, 101, 102, 110, 111, 112, 119, 147, 247, 248, 249, 251, 253, 254, 255, 259, 260, 261, 262, 319

community participation, 21, 22, 35, 71, 98

constructive outcome evaluation, 72

corona pandemic, 324, 329, 330, 332, 338

D

dimensions of empowerment, 50, 56

DREAMS, 43, 149, 151, 289, 290, 291, 292, 293, 295, 296, 297, 298, 299, 300, 301, 302, 303, 304, 305, 306, 307, 310

E

economic empowerment, 36, 95, 97, 117, 118, 120, 126, 151, 152, 155

economic status, 41, 142, 148, 150, 156, 158

educational intervention, 165, 166, 168, 169, 175

emotion regulation, 166, 167, 168, 169, 171, 174, 175, 176, 178, 179

employability, 111, 205, 206, 207, 208, 214, 217, 219, 221

empowerment, 4, 8, 9, 14, 15, 18, 21, 25, 26, 27, 28, 36, 45, 49, 50, 51, 52, 53, 54, 55, 56, 60, 62, 63, 65, 66, 67, 68, 69, 70, 75, 80, 81, 87, 88, 89, 90, 91, 93, 95, 96, 97, 98, 110, 118, 124, 125, 148, 149,

150, 151, 152, 153, 154, 155, 156, 161, 162, 163, 164, 184, 188, 250, 254, 270, 290, 296
entrepreneurship, 112, 126, 152, 155, 187, 189, 205, 206, 207, 208, 214, 219, 221, 359, 360
environment(s), 1, 2, 3, 4, 5, 7, 8, 9, 12, 13, 14, 15, 16, 17, 18, 19, 22, 24, 63, 70, 85, 93, 97, 100, 103, 105, 109, 110, 111, 119, 122, 124, 127, 130, 146, 153, 155, 161, 162, 168, 183, 186, 188, 190, 208, 243, 250, 253, 267, 270, 271, 272, 285, 286, 300, 308, 317, 318, 319, 320, 348, 352, 357
exchange student(s), 118, 122, 137, 138, 139, 146

F

familial status, 150, 156, 159

H

health, 2, 5, 16, 18, 23, 35, 42, 46, 51, 69, 72, 76, 77, 80, 85, 88, 110, 111, 112, 113, 117, 118, 119, 123, 124, 126, 127, 128, 129, 130, 131, 133, 134, 137, 138, 139, 141, 142, 144, 146, 147, 148, 150, 152, 153, 166, 171, 177, 179, 209, 232, 244, 249, 251, 253, 254, 263, 264, 266, 269, 270, 283, 284, 285, 286, 287, 288, 310, 326, 342, 350, 353, 357, 359, 360
helping attitude, 265, 266, 272, 273, 274, 275, 277, 278, 279, 280, 281, 283, 284, 286
higher education institution(s), xiii, 1, 6, 7, 48, 83, 118, 119, 124, 127, 165, 166, 168, 169, 198, 199, 208, 241, 265, 266, 287, 299, 346, 347, 352
higher educational institutions, 1, 2, 24, 122, 124, 165, 166, 168, 182, 183, 199, 225, 306
holistic development, 21, 22, 27, 28, 31, 32, 35, 79, 112, 168, 195, 205, 215, 249, 252, 255, 284, 285, 291, 293, 299, 310

I

Indonesia, 34, 345, 346, 347, 348, 351, 352, 357, 358, 359, 360
institutional, 77, 94, 102, 154, 162, 166, 181, 182, 184, 189, 190, 191, 192, 205, 215, 216, 219, 221, 263, 270, 271, 276, 316, 326, 333, 334, 339, 340, 341, 345, 354, 359, 360, 361
institutional support, 181, 182, 184, 190, 191, 192
intervention(s), 25, 27, 28, 36, 45, 48, 49, 53, 54, 56, 59, 61, 72, 74, 79, 81, 83, 87, 90, 91, 94, 95, 96, 97, 111, 117, 119, 120, 122, 127, 128, 132, 134, 135, 136, 137, 138, 139, 141, 142, 143, 144, 146, 150, 155, 165, 167, 168, 169, 170, 177, 178, 179, 182, 183, 184, 186, 187, 289, 290, 291, 292, 293, 295, 296, 297, 298, 299, 300, 301, 302, 303, 304, 305, 306, 307, 310, 334, 341

L

legal aid service, 206, 208, 211, 214, 215, 217, 219, 221, 222
livelihood, 2, 21, 26, 36, 46, 49, 50, 51, 52, 54, 55, 56, 57, 58, 59, 60, 64, 67, 77, 78, 82, 87, 88, 110, 111, 127, 128, 129, 130, 131, 132, 139, 141, 142, 143, 146, 166, 171, 210
livelihood intervention, 50, 64, 139

M

model for legal services clinic, 206
moderation, 100, 107, 109, 181

P

perception, 36, 42, 44, 45, 56, 66, 99, 101, 107, 108, 109, 113, 171, 181, 184, 188, 194, 196, 214, 219, 225, 226, 227, 229, 230, 231, 232, 235, 241, 245, 247, 248, 249, 266, 327, 328, 337, 341

Index

U

underprivileged children, 24, 165, 168, 171, 225, 226, 227, 228, 230, 232, 241, 269
Universitas Padjadjaran, 345, 346, 347, 348, 349, 359, 360
university social responsibility, 100, 115, 116, 180, 182, 200, 203, 223
urban slums, 117, 118, 120, 123, 128, 130, 133, 145, 147, 169, 262
USR model, 100, 110, 113

V

volunteering, 103, 105, 107, 108, 109, 112, 114, 226, 231, 236, 242, 251, 252, 256, 258, 259, 262, 264, 265, 266, 267, 268,

269, 270, 286, 331, 332
volunteerism, 99, 247, 248, 251, 252, 255, 259, 260, 262, 286

W

waste management, 1, 2, 3, 4, 5, 6, 7, 8, 9, 10, 11, 12, 13, 17, 18, 19, 20, 46, 105, 110, 112, 123, 269, 357
whole-person development, 35, 40, 247, 248, 249, 255, 261, 262
women, xii, 4, 7, 9, 12, 13, 14, 15, 16, 18, 19, 41, 49, 50, 51, 52, 53, 54, 55, 56, 57, 59, 60, 61, 62, 63, 64, 65, 66, 67, 68, 69, 70, 77, 79, 80, 81, 87, 88, 90, 91, 92, 93, 94, 95, 96, 97, 98, 110, 111, 112, 117, 125, 126, 127, 132, 135, 147, 148, 149, 150, 151, 152, 153, 154, 155, 156, 158, 160, 161, 162, 163, 164, 166, 169, 171, 216, 269, 270, 286, 331, 332
women empowerment, 4, 50, 70, 96, 97, 111, 125, 149, 150, 161, 164, 166

179, 183, 184, 188, 199, 205, 206, 207, 213, 216, 218, 219, 225, 226, 227, 230, 232, 235, 244, 263, 291, 292, 299, 306, 307, 315, 324, 342, 348, 353

271, 272, 273, 274, 277, 283, 284, 285, 286, 287, 288

Index 365

R

regulation(s), 5, 163, 165, 167, 168, 169, 171, 173, 174, 175, 176, 178, 179, 189, 214, 291, 294, 336, 345, 352, 358, 359
reverse mentoring, 226, 229, 243, 244
rural, 4, 5, 10, 12, 47, 50, 51, 85, 87, 88, 89, 90, 91, 92, 93, 110, 112, 123, 149, 150, 151, 152, 153, 154, 155, 161, 163, 164, 165, 166, 168, 169, 187, 207, 208, 211, 216, 242, 269, 319, 353, 354, 356, 357, 358, 359
rural women, 5, 50, 87, 89, 90, 149, 151, 152, 155, 164

S

scheduled tribes, 72, 82, 92, 228
SDG-1, 72
self-esteem, 34, 40, 48, 63, 93, 103, 126, 134, 144, 153, 154, 165, 166, 167, 168, 169, 171, 174, 175, 176, 177, 178, 179, 180, 189, 252, 253, 254, 291, 303
self-help approach, 50, 71, 72, 74, 79, 81
self-help group, 70, 78, 79, 88, 126, 132, 135, 145, 154, 164
self-reflective learning, 323, 324, 326, 329, 330, 339
sensitization, 8, 9, 43, 183, 186, 216, 225, 226, 241, 248, 268, 269, 282, 340
sequence analysis, 324, 330, 331, 333, 335, 336, 337, 339, 340, 341
SHG, 53, 55, 58, 59, 60, 61, 62, 64, 65, 67, 80, 95, 96, 149, 150, 151, 153, 154, 155, 156, 158, 159, 160, 162, 164
social behavior, 172, 174, 175, 176, 182
social responsibility activities, 101, 109, 197, 231, 345, 346, 350, 357, 358, 359
social responsibility model, 71, 72
social status, 55, 59, 150, 153, 156, 158, 159, 161
status, 47, 50, 55, 59, 60, 69, 75, 87, 88, 89, 92, 94, 115, 123, 128, 131, 134, 142, 148, 149, 150, 151, 153, 154, 155, 156, 157, 158, 159, 160, 161, 162, 166, 182, 201, 211, 242, 348, 353, 358
structural equation model, 99, 100, 107, 114, 193
student engagement, 122, 221, 247, 248, 249, 255, 260, 261, 265, 266, 267, 284, 286, 287, 314
student satisfaction, 99, 100, 101, 107, 109, 114
student volunteer(s), 1, 2, 6, 8, 9, 17, 18, 19, 24, 32, 33, 34, 103, 255, 262, 269, 274, 286
student well-being, 265, 266, 267, 271, 272, 273, 283, 284
sustainable environment protection, 1, 2, 6,

T

teaching, xi, 102, 103, 105, 109, 111, 129, 132, 133, 134, 137, 138, 146, 181, 183, 185, 186, 199, 209, 215, 221, 225, 226, 227, 228, 229, 230, 231, 232, 233, 234, 235, 236, 237, 238, 239, 240, 241, 243, 244, 263, 270, 287, 291, 345, 346, 348, 353, 358
training, 44, 53, 56, 57, 58, 60, 61, 63, 75, 78, 80, 96, 102, 105, 111, 112, 125, 126, 135, 139, 141, 145, 163, 170, 172, 175,

personal responsibility, 186, 188, 265, 266, 273, 274, 275, 277, 278, 279, 280, 281, 283, 284
professional identity as a social worker, 324, 325
professional(s), 35, 36, 45, 48, 119, 140, 145, 147, 166, 170, 188, 189, 196, 205, 207, 208, 210, 213, 215, 216, 217, 218, 219, 221, 223, 225, 230, 241, 249, 251, 255, 256, 257, 260, 261, 262, 272, 290, 291, 306, 323, 324, 325, 326, 327, 328, 329, 330, 331, 332, 333, 334, 335, 336, 337, 338, 339, 340, 341, 342, 343, 349
protection, 1, 4, 6, 7, 8, 9, 13, 14, 18, 25, 66, 81, 103, 105, 161, 162, 172, 210, 211